Teach Yourself Microsoft® Visual C++
the Quick and Easy Way

Learn Visual C++ Now

Mark Andrews

Microsoft Press

PUBLISHED BY
Microsoft Press
A Division of Microsoft Corporation
One Microsoft Way
Redmond, Washington 98052-6399

Library of Congress Cataloging-in-Publication Data
Andrews, Mark.
    Learn Visual C++ now : the complete learning solution for Visual
  C++ / Mark Andrews.
        p.   cm.
    Includes index.
    ISBN 1-55615-845-9
    1. C++ (Computer program language)   2. Microsoft Visual C++.
  I. Title.
  QA76.73.C153A487   1996
  005.26'2--dc20   95-26475
                                                                CIP

Printed and bound in the United States of America.

  2 3 4 5 6 7 8 9   QMQM   1 0 9 8 7 6

Distributed to the book trade in Canada by Macmillan of Canada, a division of Canada Publishing Corporation.

A CIP catalogue record for this book is available from the British Library.

Microsoft Press books are available through booksellers and distributors worldwide. For further information about international editions, contact your local Microsoft Corporation office. Or contact Microsoft Press International directly at fax (206) 936-7329.

Thanks to Tareh Kryger for letting us use the Beyond Ti picture.

Adobe Illustrator is a registered trademark and PostScript is a trademark of Adobe Systems Inc. Macintosh is a registered trademark of Apple Computer, Inc. CorelDRAW is a registered trademark of Corel Systems Corporation. DEC is a trademark of Digital Equipment Corporation. Intel and Pentium are registered trademarks of Intel Corporation. Macromedia Freehand is a trademark of Macromedia, Inc. MS-DOS, Visual C++, Win32, Windows, and Windows NT are registered trademarks of Microsoft Corporation. MIPS is a registered trademark of MIPS Technologies, Inc.

Companies, names, and/or data used in screens and sample output are fictitious unless otherwise noted.

Acquisitions Editor: David Clark
Manuscript Editor: Jennifer Harris
Technical Editor: Christina Anagnost
Project Editor: John Pierce

For Lakshmi

Acknowledgments

The author wishes to thank his agent, Carole McClendon, and the many individuals at Microsoft Press who helped to complete this book.

Table of Contents

Introduction

The world is full of books about Visual C++. Why is *Learn Visual C++ Now* different?

One reason is that this book comes with a complete copy of the Microsoft Visual C++ version 1.0 compiler—the same Professional Edition Visual C++ compiler that sold for hundreds of dollars when Visual C++ was introduced. Another special feature is that this book teaches you the C++ language using Microsoft Visual C++—the de facto standard for writing Windows-based programs and the most widely used compiler for creating and developing Windows-based programs in C++.

Learn Visual C++ Now is intended for programmers with a basic knowledge of the C language who would like to learn to write Windows-based programs in C++. And in addition to teaching you the ins and outs of Visual C++, this book provides an introduction to the basics of programming in Windows and a two-chapter overview of the C++ language and the principles of object-oriented programming.

This book also provides you with the personal assistance of the best Visual C++ teachers on the planet—the wizards that come with Visual C++. The Visual C++ wizards include AppWizard, which can generate a working Visual C++ application at the touch of a menu command, and ClassWizard, which can create and manage classes in Visual C++ programs. For a personal tutoring session from either of these wizards, all you have to do is ask. You can learn C++, Visual C++, and good programming practices simply by examining the code that the Visual C++ wizards produce. The wizards never write bad code, so you can rest assured that you'll get well-behaved code that adheres to Microsoft standards.

As you become more familiar with programming in Visual C++, you can add to your understanding of the basic principles by observing how the wizards do the spadework needed to make your applications work. And that's probably the most painless method yet discovered for learning both Visual C++ and Windows programming!

What You'll Need to Use This Book

The version of Visual C++ that comes with this book runs under Microsoft Windows 95 and Microsoft Windows NT, as well as under earlier versions of Windows. It generates 16-bit applications that can be executed immediately, without any editing or tweaking.

To follow the examples in this book, you'll need an Intel 386, 486, or Pentium processor and Microsoft Windows 95, Microsoft Windows NT, or Microsoft Windows version 3.0 or 3.1. (Windows version 3.1 is preferred.) You'll also need a hard disk with enough disk space to install the options that you want, and you'll need at least 4 (and preferably 16) MB of RAM (depending on your operating system). And, of course, to install the Visual C++ compiler included on the companion CD-ROM, you'll need a CD-ROM drive.

NOTE If after finishing this book you decide to upgrade to a later version of Visual C++, you can use your new compiler to recompile any of the sample programs presented in this book and any programs that you built using Visual C++ version 1.0. You can even recompile the programs presented in this book and your own Visual C++ version 1.0 programs using Borland C++ version 5.0 or later (which supports the MFC library and source code written using Visual C++).

What You Get with This Book

The companion CD-ROM provides the Microsoft Visual C++ version 1.0 compiler, the Visual C++ linker, and the complete Visual C++ development environment—including the Visual C++ editor, the Source Browser, a source code and assembly language debugger, a complete set of online help files, and a collection of tools for creating and maintaining resources and C++ classes.

The companion CD-ROM also provides a collection of notes (located in the /MSVC/HELP directory) in Microsoft Word/Windows 95 Notepad format that contains miscellaneous information about Visual C++ and the Visual C++ version 1.0 compiler.

> **NOTE** No product support is provided for the Visual C++ software that comes with this book.

Getting Online Help

You can get help at any time by consulting the online help files that come with Visual C++ version 1.0. To access online help, all you have to do is choose the topic for the kind of help you need from the Visual C++ editor's Help menu. Help topics include the C/C++ language, the Windows Software Development Kit (SDK), and the Microsoft Foundation Class (MFC) Library version 2.0. The Visual C++ online help files can also provide you with information about the tools that come with the Visual C++ software development environment.

What's in This Book

Here is a description of the topics we'll cover in *Learn Visual C++ Now*.

Chapter 1, "Introducing Visual C++," acquaints you with the Visual Workbench, AppWizard, and other important tools and programming principles you'll use when developing applications in Visual C++.

Chapter 2, "Introduction to Windows Programming," provides an overview of the construction of Windows-based programs. What you learn in this chapter will come in handy in later chapters, when we explore how AppWizard constructs frameworks for Visual C++ programs.

Chapter 3, "C++ Basics," looks at some of the most important features of generic C++ and object-oriented programming. This chapter explains some of the differences between C and C++ and shows you how to create and implement C++ classes, member variables, and member functions.

Chapter 4, "Objects and Member Functions," like Chapter 3, is dedicated to the study of generic C++ and the fundamental principles of object-oriented programming. In this chapter, we take a look at how objects and member functions are used in C++ programs and also at other important principles of C++ programming, including inheritance, polymorphism, virtual functions, function overloading, and friend functions.

Chapter 5, "Visual C++ Tools," describes in detail how to use the programming tools in Visual C++ and shows—with the help of a straightforward example program—how programming in Visual C++ differs from traditional Windows API–style programming.

Chapter 6, "The MFC Library," shows how the MFC library has enhanced generic C++ and the Windows API by adding new classes and member functions specifically designed for use by Windows programmers. Topics covered in this chapter include the *CObject* class, the *CWnd* class, and other important classes in the MFC library.

Chapter 7, "Of Mice and Messages," introduces the concept of mouse events and shows how you can use mouse events to interact with the user in Visual C++ programs. More information is provided about menus, messages, message handlers, and message maps.

Chapter 8, "Dialog Boxes," shows you how to use App Studio to design dialog boxes and equip them with controls. This chapter explains and demonstrates both ordinary dialog box controls and user-drawn controls. An example program shows how you can use message boxes, modeless dialog boxes, and modal dialog boxes with many different kinds of controls in your own Visual C++ programs.

Chapter 9, "Managing Data," continues our examination of dialog boxes. This chapter shows you how to create member variables for dialog box classes using ClassWizard and how to use those member variables as connection points between dialog box controls and member functions in Visual C++ applications. The key to this magic is the Visual C++ DDX (dialog data exchange) and DDV (dialog data verification) mechanisms, which you can use to pass information back and forth between your application and dialog box controls.

Chapter 10, "Visual C++ Graphics," introduces you to Windows graphics and animation and shows you how to incorporate exciting graphics routines into your Visual C++ applications. In this chapter, you'll learn to use device-dependent bitmaps (DDBs), device-independent bitmaps (DIBs), sprite graphics, step graphics, and transparent bitmap copying. This chapter presents two example programs: one demonstrates the use of sprite graphics using standard DDBs, and one performs similar magic using DIBs.

Also included is a list of additional references about Visual C++ and object-oriented programming.

Installing the Companion CD-ROM

To install the source code, sample programs, and Visual C++ software that is included on the companion CD-ROM, follow the procedures outlined below.

Installing the *Learn Visual C++ Now*
Files Under Windows 95

To install the *Learn Visual C++ Now* files under Windows 95, follow these steps:

1. From the Windows 95 desktop, click the Start button.

2. Choose the Run menu item.

3. In the Run dialog box, click the Browse button.

4. In the Browse dialog box, navigate to the root directory of the companion CD-ROM.

5. Click the SETUP.EXE icon.

6. Click the Open button.

7. When the Run dialog box reappears, click OK, and follow the on-screen instructions.

Installing the *Learn Visual C++ Now* Files in Other Environments

If you are running Windows 3.*x* or Windows NT version 3.5 or earlier, you can install the *Learn Visual C++ Now* files by opening File Manager, navigating to the root directory of the companion CD-ROM, and double-clicking the SETUP.EXE icon. Alternatively, you can follow these steps:

1. From Program Manager, choose the Run item from the File menu.

2. In the Run dialog box, navigate to the root directory of the companion CD-ROM.

3. Click the SETUP.EXE icon.

4. Click the Open button.

5. When the Run dialog box reappears, click OK, and follow the on-screen instructions.

Installing Visual C++

The Visual C++ compiler on the companion CD-ROM generates 16-bit Windows-based applications that will run under Windows 95, Windows NT, or Windows 3.*x*.

Under Windows 95

To install Visual C++ under Windows 95, follow these steps:

1. From the Windows 95 desktop, click the Start button.

2. Choose the Run menu item.

3. In the Run dialog box, click the Browse button.

4. In the Browse dialog box, navigate to the /MSVC folder on the companion CD-ROM.

5. Click the SETUP.EXE icon.

6. Click the Open button.

7. When the Run dialog box reappears, run the Installer by clicking the OK button.

In other environments

If you are running Windows 3.x or Windows NT version 3.5 or earlier, you can install Visual C++ by opening File Manager, navigating to the /MSVC folder on the companion CD-ROM, and double-clicking the SETUP.EXE icon. Alternatively, you can follow these steps:

1. From Program Manager, choose the Run item from the File menu.

2. In the Run dialog box, navigate to the /MSVC folder on the companion CD-ROM.

3. Click the SETUP.EXE icon.

4. Click the Open button.

5. When the Run dialog box reappears, run the Installer by clicking the OK button.

Customizing Your Installation Options

If you prefer, you can customize your installation using the Installation Options dialog box, which opens when you start the Installer.

To customize your installation, follow these steps:

1. To determine whether you have enough disk space to install the complete Visual C++ package, check the Disk Space Information panel at the bottom of the Installation Options dialog box. In the Disk Space Information panel, the Installer displays the name of the disk drive on which Visual C++ is about to be installed.

2. If you want, you can click the Directories button to specify a different disk for your Visual C++ installation. The Installer then opens the Directory Options dialog box.

3. By specifying multiple drives in the Directory Options dialog box, you can install different parts of the Visual C++ package on different drives. If you have enough hard disk space, it is recommended that you install all the items listed in the Installation Options dialog box. If you can't find enough hard disk space to install every item, you can uncheck the Sample Source Code check box. The Installer will then skip the sample programs provided with Visual C++ version 1.0.

Later you can load any sample project you want directly from the companion CD-ROM.

4. After you have specified a directory setup for your Visual C++ installation, close the Directory Options dialog box by clicking the OK button. Once again, the Installation Options dialog box becomes the active window.

Now that you're all set up, let's start learning about Visual C++.

Introducing Visual C++

Learning to program with Microsoft Visual C++ is different from learning to develop software in other computer languages. When you design a program in an older, conventional computer language, such as C, Basic, or Pascal, you generally have to do everything yourself; every time you want the computer to do something, you have to write a line or a block of code.

When you write a program using Visual C++, a lot of the work is done for you. In many cases, Visual C++ provides the general code the computer needs to perform many of the tasks you want it to perform. You then add to and tailor the code that Visual C++ provides to create more specific applications.

That shortcut frees you from having to write every line of code that's needed to perform repetitive tasks such as handling keyboard and mouse operations and drawing windows to the screen. With Visual C++, you can focus your attention on more creative work—such as writing the code that implements what's really new and different about the application you are developing.

This chapter introduces Visual C++ and familiarizes you with the tools that make up the Visual C++ programming environment. It also introduces the Microsoft Foundation Class (MFC) Library version 2.0, a large library of C++ classes and member functions that are designed especially for developing Windows-based programs in Visual C++. At the end of this chapter, you'll see how one Visual C++ tool, a utility named AppWizard, uses the MFC library to generate a fully functioning Windows-based application at the click of a menu item. In later chapters, you'll learn how to write the code necessary to expand the application frameworks generated by AppWizard into more sophisticated Visual C++ applications.

These are the main topics covered in this chapter:

- The Visual Workbench programming environment, which introduces the Visual C++ editor and the Visual C++ wizards

- How the Visual C++ wizards help you learn Visual C++

- How to compile and link a Visual C++ program

- How the MFC library—the "new Windows API"—can help you write powerful Visual C++ programs

- A step-by-step guide to writing a framework MFC program using Visual C++

The Visual C++ Programming Environment

When you develop applications in Visual C++, you use the Visual Workbench, sometimes abbreviated VWB. The Visual Workbench is the primary editing and debugging tool provided with Visual C++; it serves as the command center for Visual C++ programming and provides a host of programming utilities, including the following:

- The AppWizard application generator

- The App Studio resource manager

- The ClassWizard class manager

- The Visual C++ Source Browser

- The Visual C++ debugger

- The Visual C++ editor

■ The Visual C++ compiler

■ The Visual C++ linker

Figure 1-1 shows what the Visual Workbench window looks like when it first opens. From the main Visual Workbench window, you have access to a number of the editing and programming components. Most of the main components of the Visual Workbench environment are described in the sections that follow. You'll learn more about the others as you move through this book.

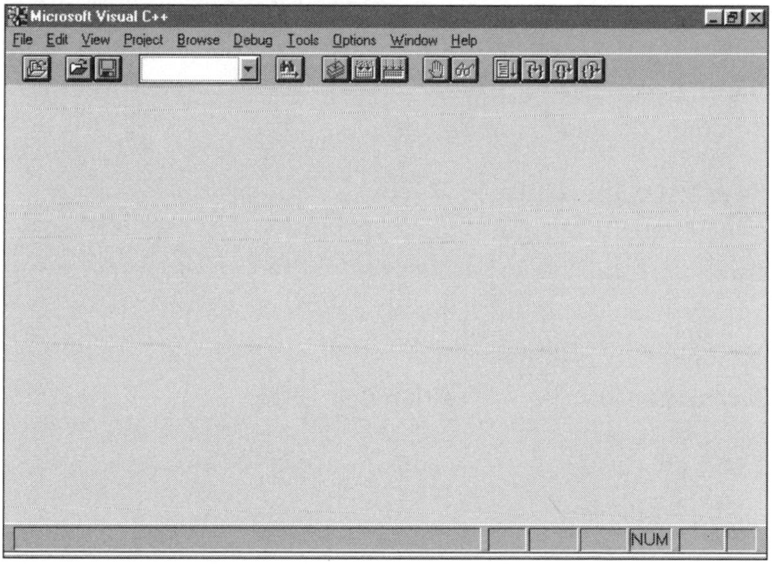

Figure 1-1. *The main Visual Workbench window.*

The Visual C++ Editor

When you start Visual C++, you see the Visual C++ editor window. The Visual C++ editor is a standard Windows-based text editor equipped with a number of special features for writing Visual C++ programs.

One of these features is a built-in Source Browser, used to track down definitions and references to variables and C++ classes. Another is color-coded highlighting of different keywords used in Visual C++.

The color-coded syntax feature makes it easy to spot occurrences of special kinds of words or phrases in Visual C++ programs. For example, C-language keywords appear in blue, C++ keywords are displayed in red, and comments appear in green. Debugger breakpoints show up in reverse video inside a red band. (These are default settings; if you prefer some other convention, you can modify the Visual C++ editor's default color settings by choosing the Color item from the Options menu.)

Other special features of the Visual C++ editor include automatic indentation of lines in functions, a search-and-replace utility, bookmarks that can provide instant access to a selected line of text, and a built-in source code debugger. You can access any of these tools—and many more—from the menu bar or from the toolbar, which provides point-and-click access to 14 common menu commands.

Keystroke Shortcuts

When you write source code with the Visual C++ editor, you can use a number of special keystrokes to edit text and to move around in your source files. Table 1-1 lists some of the common keystroke combinations recognized by the Visual C++ editor.

Keystroke Shortcut	Editing Operation
Ctrl-Left arrow	Move one word to the left
Ctrl-Right arrow	Move one word to the right
Home	Move to the first indentation of the current line
Home, Home	Move to the beginning of the current line
Ctrl-Enter	Move to the first indentation of the current line
End	Move to the end of the current line
Ctrl-Home	Move to the beginning of the file
Ctrl-End	Move to the end of the file
Ctrl-Z or Alt-Backspace	Undo the last edit

Table 1-1. *Keystroke shortcuts for editing operations.*

Keystroke Shortcut	Editing Operation
Ctrl-A	Redo the last edit
Ctrl-T	Delete to the end of the word
Ctrl-C or Ctrl-Ins	Copy selected text to the Clipboard
Ctrl-X or Shift-Del	Cut selected text to the Clipboard
Ctrl-V or Shift-Ins	Paste text from the Clipboard
Ctrl-]	Move to the matching brace
Tab	Insert a tab
Ctrl-Alt-T	Toggle the display of tab symbols

To learn more about the Visual C++ editor and its many features and capabilities, choose the Visual Workbench item from the Visual Workbench Help menu, and then click the button labeled Using The Editor.

The Visual C++ Wizards and App Studio

The Visual Workbench comes with a set of programming tools called *wizards*. In the Visual C++ development environment, wizards perform complex sequences of tasks for you, so you don't have to remember all the details yourself. For example, the tool named AppWizard can set up an application at the click of a menu item. ClassWizard, another Visual C++ wizard, lets you use dialog box controls to connect resources such as menus and dialog boxes to the code in your Visual C++ programs. Let's look at these wizards and a related tool, named App Studio, in a little more detail.

AppWizard

An application generated by AppWizard is sometimes referred to as an *application framework*. An application framework is a minimal Visual C++ program that you can customize by adding whatever special-purpose code your application requires.

Figure 1-2 on the following page shows you what AppWizard looks like when it first starts up.

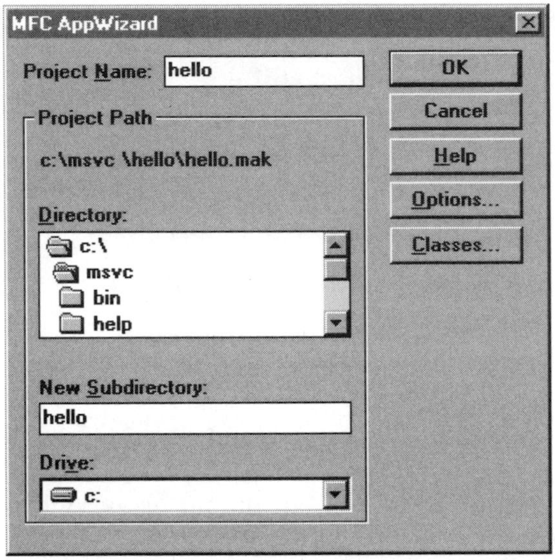

Figure 1-2. *The MFC AppWizard dialog box.*

To start AppWizard, you simply choose the AppWizard item from the Visual C++ Project menu. AppWizard then displays various dialog boxes that you can use to specify attributes of the application you want to create When you have finished, AppWizard generates a functioning Visual C++ application that meets your specifications and contains all the essential ingredients of a Windows-based application, including the following:

■ A main frame window and any other windows required by the kind of application being created

■ A menu bar equipped with the standard Windows menus, such as File, Edit, and Help

■ All the menu items and dialog boxes needed to open files, save files, print files, and implement print-preview functionality

■ A toolbar and a status bar

- OLE support for container and server objects
- All the source files and resource files needed to create an application built around the Visual C++ classes provided in the MFC library

When AppWizard has generated an application framework, it's up to you to turn that framework into the kind of Windows-based application that you want to design.

At the end of this chapter, you'll get a chance to create an application framework using AppWizard. In later chapters, you'll learn how to add code to an application framework that can give the program its own set of interesting functionality. By the time you finish this book, you'll know how to expand AppWizard frameworks in many different ways to create many different kinds of applications.

You will learn much more about AppWizard and the MFC AppWizard dialog box in Chapter 5, "Visual C++ Tools."

App Studio

After you have generated a bare-bones application with AppWizard, you can use other tools provided with Visual C++ to expand your AppWizard framework into a more useful application. One of the Visual C++ tools you'll use often is App Studio—a graphically based, mouse-driven resource editor. With App Studio, you can create and design dialog boxes, menus, bitmaps, and other kinds of resources for your Visual C++ programs.

When you create or modify a resource using App Studio, App Studio automatically modifies your project's resource (.RC) file to reflect your changes. To use App Studio, you select the App Studio item from the Visual Workbench Tools menu. Then you can choose from several different kinds of resource editors that are built into App Studio, such as the dialog box editor shown in Figure 1-3 on the following page.

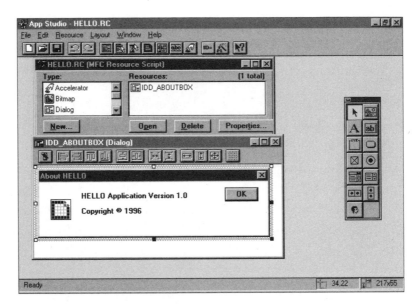

Figure 1-3. *The App Studio dialog box editor.*

You'll learn more about App Studio in Chapter 7, "Of Mice and Messages," and Chapter 8, "Dialog Boxes."

ClassWizard

Another important Visual C++ utility is ClassWizard, a tool that connects resources such as menus and dialog boxes to the code that implements your Windows-based programs. In later chapters, when you start learning how to write object-oriented programs using C++, ClassWizard can also help you create and manage C++ classes.

To create a new C++ class using ClassWizard, you select the ClassWizard item from the Browse menu. Figure 1-4 on the following page shows the ClassWizard dialog box.

ClassWizard, like AppWizard, is an expert at writing C++ code. But while AppWizard creates a general application framework, ClassWizard is a specialist that, at your request, can write C++ routines that process user-generated events such as mouse clicks and mouse movements. ClassWizard even inserts the code it has written at the appropriate spot in your program. You can then add whatever code you need to make your application respond to user events in whatever way you want.

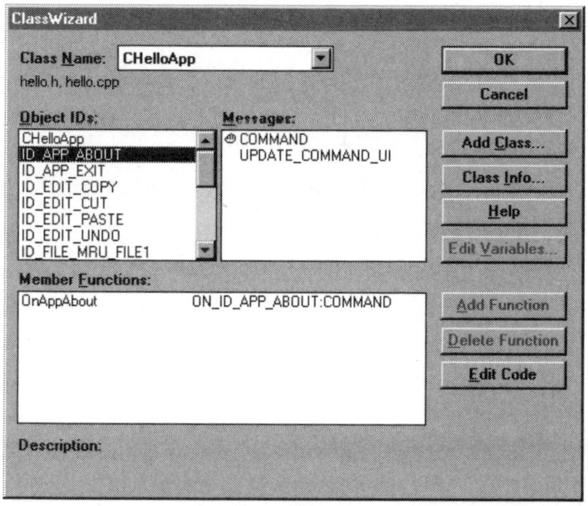

Figure 1-4. *Managing Visual C++ classes with ClassWizard.*

You'll get a close-up look at ClassWizard in Chapter 7, "Of Mice and Messages," and Chapter 8, "Dialog Boxes."

Programming with Visual C++

By freeing software developers from the ridiculous so that they can work on the more sublime, Visual C++ is not only bringing about an enormous change in the way people write Windows-based programs, it's also beginning to change the way people study computer programming.

When you learn Visual C++, you don't have to master every detail in every routine before you move on to the next level. Instead, you can learn at whatever pace you want, letting the Visual C++ wizards take care of the programming details that you haven't explored yet. Later on, in order to get a better idea of exactly how Visual C++ works, you can go back and take a closer look at some of the subtleties you've skimmed over.

But you don't ever have to do that unless you want to—and there are many highly specialized areas and murky corners of Visual C++ that you may never get around to exploring. The point is that with Visual C++, you can learn what you need to know at the moment, and you can leave the rest for later if you want. That's the approach we'll take as you learn to use Visual C++.

As you study Visual C++ programming using this book, your real teachers will be the Visual C++ wizards. They will write most of your source code for you—and they'll always write it perfectly, which is more than most flesh-and-blood teachers of programming can do. This book will serve mainly as a guidebook; it will show you the code the wizards have written for you and explain how that code works. Meanwhile, you'll have opportunities to experiment with the code that the wizards create. You'll also be able to modify that code and incorporate it in your own Visual C++ programs.

The Visual C++ Build Process

As you know if you are an experienced programmer, the code that you write when you create an application is called *source code*. When you compile your source code with a compiler, the compiler generates files that contain *object code*—that is, binary code that your computer understands. When your compiler has converted your source code to object code, you can use a *linker* to link your object code files with other object code files named *libraries*. Linking with libraries is an important operation in the Visual C++ build process because most Visual C++ applications rely on external libraries that are supplied as part of the Visual C++ development package. You can also create libraries yourself and use them in your Visual C++ applications.

The process of compiling and linking a Visual C++ program is known as *building* the application. During the linking phase of the build process, several kinds of library files can be linked to your application. Some library files have an .LIB filename extension and are known, logically enough, as *library files.* Another variety of library file is the *dynamic-link library, or DLL,* which often has the filename extension .DLL.

Library files and DLLs have important differences that you'll learn about in later chapters. For now, the most important thing to know is that both .DLL and .LIB files are object code files that can contain implementations of C and C++ procedures, or *functions,* that you can use in your applications.

When the Visual C++ linker links your application with all the library files it needs to run properly, the result is an *executable file* that you can run on your computer. You'll write and run many executable applications as you study the material in this book.

In most situations, you don't have to know much about the Visual C++ build process to compile and link your Visual C++ programs. AppWizard generates an application at the click of a menu command, so you can compile and link your program without worrying much about the internal operations of the Visual C++ linker and compiler.

As you advance to more complex Visual C++ projects, however, it might be helpful for you to understand how the Visual C++ compiler and linker work together to generate executable Windows-based applications. More detailed information about the compiler, the linker, and the build process will be presented in later chapters.

The MFC Library

Perhaps the most important feature of Visual C++ is that it works together with the MFC library, the C++ successor to the C-language Windows application programming interface (API). The Windows API—a large collection of functions implemented in a set of dynamic-link libraries—was released with Windows and has been the foundation of all Windows programming. The MFC library version 2.0, which made its debut with Visual C++ version 1.0, is a C++ library that encapsulates almost all the functions implemented in the Windows API.

MFC: The "New Windows API"

The MFC library is now the most widely used C++ library for writing Windows-based programs. In fact, it has become what some Microsoft executives call the "new Windows API."

There are good reasons for the popularity of the MFC library. The Windows API contains many kinds of functions that are implemented in many ways. The MFC library has rounded up almost all these functions and organized them into class hierarchies that make them more manageable. Also, because the MFC library is written in C++, it equips the functions in the Windows API with object-oriented features such as inheritance, data abstraction, data encapsulation, and virtual functions.

You will learn more about these and other features of C++ in Chapter 3, "C++ Basics," and Chapter 4, "Objects and Member Functions," which are designed as a crash course in generic C++ and object-oriented programming. You'll learn more about the MFC library in Chapter 6, "The MFC Library."

MFC and Visual C++

Visual C++ is designed as a programming environment for writing MFC-based Windows applications. When you use AppWizard to create a Visual C++ program, AppWizard generates an application framework by using classes and member functions implemented in the MFC library.

Every Visual C++ program that AppWizard generates is an object of an MFC library class named *CWinApp*. When you examine the structure of an AppWizard application, you find that it has a number of other MFC library classes built into its framework. For example, every application generated by AppWizard contains an MFC library class named *CView*, which manages the drawing and display of the program's windows, and an MFC library class named *CDocument*, which manages the program's data.

The *CWinApp*, *CView*, and *CDocument* classes are examined in more detail in Chapter 6, "The MFC Library."

Writing a Visual C++ Program

The tools provided with Visual C++ are specially designed to work with software development efforts that are organized into *projects*. In Visual C++, a project is a collection of the files that are needed to build an application. Projects simplify the creation of Visual C++ applications because they provide an easy way to work with all the files as a group. When you construct a Visual C++ application by creating a project, you can automatically create a framework for your application by using the AppWizard tool. You can then manage your application's C++ classes using ClassWizard, and you can create and manage your application's resources using App Studio.

Understanding Visual C++ Projects

There are two ways to create a project: you can let AppWizard generate your project for you, or you can create the project manually.

When AppWizard creates a Visual C++ project, several different kinds of files are generated automatically. When you build a Visual C++ project, several more files are created.

Table 1-2 lists and describes the kinds of files that are generated when you create and build a Visual C++ application.

Kind of File	Filename Extension	Description
Header (include) file	.H	A text file that contains function declarations and class definitions.
Source file	.C, .CPP, .CXX	A text file that contains function definitions and (in C++) implementations of classes.
Object file	.OBJ	A nonexecutable object code file; it can be linked to applications by the Visual C++ linker.
Library file	.LIB	An object code file that is linked to an executable or to another library.*
Resource file	.RC	A text file that creates and manages Windows resources. In Visual C++, resource files are created and managed by App-Studio.

* Library files, which have the filename extension .LIB, are precompiled object files containing functions that can be called from user-written programs. Visual C++ comes with a large collection of .LIB files, and you can also create your own.

Table 1-2. *Kinds of files used in Visual C++ projects.*   *(continued)*

Table 1-2. *continued*

Kind of File	Filename Extension	Description
Module-definition file	.DEF	A text file that describes the name, attributes, exports, imports, system requirements, and other characteristics of an application or a DLL. In Visual C++ version 1.0, .DEF files are required for DLLs and some kinds of MS-DOS programs. (See the online help for details.) They are optional but recommended for other kinds of segmented executable files, such as Windows-based applications.
Browser database file	.BSC	A database file used by the Visual C++ Source Browser. (You'll learn more about the Source Browser in Chapter 5, "Visual C++ Tools.")
Makefile	.MAK	A text file that the compiler uses to build your application. (See Chapter 5.)
Executable file	.EXE	An executable application.

Writing a Visual C++ Program Step by Step

Now that you're familiar with the Visual C++ programming environment and Visual C++ projects, you're ready to create your first Visual C++ program. To do that, follow these steps:

1. Start Visual C++ if it isn't started already.

2. Choose AppWizard from the Project menu. AppWizard starts and displays a dialog box labeled MFC AppWizard, as shown on the following page.

3. Using the Directory list box—and the Drive list box, if you need to—navigate to a folder in which you want to store your application, and then select that folder.

4. In the Project Name text box, type your project's name. For this exercise, type *framewrk.* As you type, notice that the filename you give your project also appears in the New Subdirectory text box. By default, AppWizard creates a folder inside the main folder you have selected and gives that folder the same name you've given to your project. Your project's files are then stored in the folder AppWizard has created.

5. By clicking buttons along the right side of the MFC AppWizard dialog box, you can set a number of options that AppWizard then uses to create your program. The buttons labeled Options and Classes open dialog boxes that you can use to set various attributes of the program you are creating.

   When you click the Options button, AppWizard opens a dialog box similar to the one on the following page.

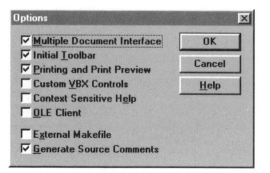

You can then choose the options you need. Here are descriptions of some of the options you'll use most often:

■ The Multiple Document Interface option creates a multiple-document interface (MDI) application—that is, an application that supports multiple child windows. If you don't check this option, AppWizard creates a single-document interface (SDI) program. For this exercise, leave the MDI option turned on.

■ The Initial Toolbar option creates a standard toolbar with several buttons already installed. Toolbars are useful in Windows-based programs and are easily created by AppWizard, so leave this option selected too.

■ The Printing And Print Preview option provides your application with support for printing and preview operations. The program you create in this exercise won't make use of AppWizard's printing option, but most applications do, so you might as well leave this selected.

■ The Generate Source Comments option places comments in your source code. If you deselect this option, AppWizard generates uncommented code, which nobody—including you—is likely to understand. It's best to leave this button in its default (selected) state so that AppWizard will generate commented code.

6. To close the Options dialog box and leave all its options at their default settings, click the Cancel button.

7. When the MFC AppWizard dialog box again has the focus, click the Classes button. AppWizard opens the Classes dialog box, shown below. The Classes dialog box gives you a chance to review the names of certain files that AppWizard will create for your project.

By default, AppWizard creates a set of project files based on the name you have given your project. If you've given your project a short name, that's usually fine. For example, when you compile this chapter's sample project, named FRAMEWRK, AppWizard creates a pair of files named FRAMEDOC.CPP and FRAMEVW.CPP. In other cases, however, AppWizard comes up with default filenames that look odd. For example, if you created a project named HELOPROJ, AppWizard's default names would be HELOPDOC.CPP and HELO-PVW.CPP. To change names like those into names that look more attractive—such as HELLODOC.CPP and HELLOVW.CPP—you can type new filenames in the Classes dialog box's edit boxes.

8. When you've finished examining the Classes dialog box, you can close it by clicking OK or Cancel.

9. When the MFC AppWizard dialog box again has the focus, you're ready to generate your application. To do that, simply click OK. In response, AppWizard opens a New Application Information dialog box containing important information about the application you are about to create, as shown on the following page.

10. Read over the specifications listed in the New Application Information dialog box to verify that they're OK, and then click the Create button. AppWizard generates the source code and resource files for your application.

11. After AppWizard has generated your application, you can build it by choosing the Build item from the Project menu. The result is an executable file named FRAMEWRK.EXE, which you can run from the Windows desktop or directly from Visual Workbench. To run your program from Visual Workbench, choose Execute from the Project menu.

When your application starts, you should see a main frame window and a child window like those shown here:

Congratulations! Without writing a line of code, you have just created your first Visual C++ program.

Take some time to experiment with your application to see how it works. Notice that you can display and hide the program's toolbar and status bar by opening the View menu and selecting and deselecting the Toolbar and Status Bar items. You can also open and close files and windows, cascade and tile windows, and display a simple, default-style About box. Also notice that there are a few operations you can perform by clicking toolbar buttons. Quite a bit of functionality for performing a few simple steps.

What's Next?

This chapter introduced Visual C++ and the Visual Workbench—a sophisticated set of tools used to build Visual C++ programs. This chapter also gave you a chance to use AppWizard to create a fully functional Visual C++ application at the click of a menu command.

In later chapters, you'll learn how to add different kinds of functionalities to the application frameworks you create. Before we do that, however, we need to gain a little perspective. Chapter 2, "Introduction to Windows Programming," introduces you to the Windows API, the bedrock on which all Windows-based programs are built. Chapter 3, "C++ Basics," and Chapter 4, "Objects and Member Functions," introduce the fundamentals of generic C++ and the basic principles of object-oriented programming. After that we'll return to the specifics of creating Windows-based applications in Visual C++.

Introduction to Windows Programming

This chapter is a blast from the past. It will show you something about the structure of a Windows-based program and how people used to write Windows-based programs—using the Windows application programming interface (API)—before there was any such thing as Microsoft Visual C++. This knowledge is valuable to a Visual C++ programmer for several reasons. First, knowing something about basic Windows programming is important because, behind the scenes, applications created with Visual C++ that use classes and member functions provided by the Microsoft Foundation Class (MFC) Library do their work by calling raw C-language functions that are implemented in—you guessed it—the Windows API. So if you know a little about how to write a Windows-based program without using Visual C++, you'll start your journey toward learning Visual C++ with a valuable understanding of the organization and architecture of a Visual C++ program.

Second, knowing how to write Windows-based programs without Visual C++ will give you a head start toward learning how to use the Visual C++ debugger. When your debugger encounters a problem in a Visual C++ program, it often stops in an MFC source file that was not written by you. If you have no idea what's going on in that file, things can be confusing. Having some idea of how Windows-based programs work can ease your confusion considerably.

And third, although the tools built into Visual C++ are useful and are becoming more and more widely used, Visual C++ is not the only development environment for Windows on the market; you might encounter C++ programs for Windows that are not written in Visual C++. Because C++ code is designed to be reused, you might find opportunities to incorporate code that wasn't written in Visual C++ into your Visual C++ programs. When that need arises, it's helpful to understand the non–Visual C++ code that you're confronted with.

The main topics covered in this chapter are:

- The differences between MS-DOS–based programs and Windows-based applications

- How a peculiar function known as a window procedure interprets user events such as mouse clicks and keypresses in Windows-based programs

- How the Windows operating system builds and displays windows

- A step-by-step tutorial that shows you how to build and execute this chapter's sample program

The World's First C-Language Program

In his classic book *The C Programming Language* (Prentice-Hall, 1978), Brian Kernighan introduced the world to C by presenting the following program for printing a line of text on the screen:

```
#include <stdio.h>

main()
{
    printf("Hello, world!\n");
}
```

"Hello, world!" is so short and straightforward that it's easy to understand, but it's also so simple that it doesn't do very much. If you rushed home after your first computer science class and demonstrated the "Hello, world!" program, your mother might be impressed, but your friends probably wouldn't be.

Nevertheless, the "Hello, world!" program is a complete C-language application. And because C is an almost perfect subset of C++, you can also compile "Hello, world!" as a Visual C++ program, so you could say that "Hello, world!" is a fully functional C++ program too.

"Hello, world!" is not a Windows-based program, however. It lacks many of the special routines that an application must have in order to take full advantage of the Windows operating environment. It doesn't contain functions to detect mouse movements, manipulate windows, respond to menu commands, or interact with other applications running in the Windows environment. To expand the "Hello, world!" program into a full-fledged Windows-based program, you'd have to add much more functionality.

Architecture of the "Hello, world!" Program

Understanding the simple architecture of the "Hello, world!" program will help you to learn what's required to create a comparable program for Windows and will also help you understand what happens in programs you create with Visual C++.

You might recall that every text-based C application has one (and only one) function named *main*. Text-based C++ programs also follow this rule. In a text-based C or C++ program, the *main* function is always the first function that executes when the program starts. The primary job of the *main* function is to call—either directly or indirectly—all other functions in the program. In the "Hello, world!" program, the *main* function contains a single statement that calls the *printf* function, as shown here:

```
printf("Hello, world!\n");
```

The *printf* function then works some magic that prints the line *Hello, world!* on the screen. When the *main* function in a program terminates, the program ends.

Interestingly, non–Visual C++ programs written for Windows (sometimes called Windows API–style programs) always break one fundamental rule of C. A Windows API–style program never has a *main* function. Instead, the entry function is always a function named *WinMain*.

In a Windows API–style program, the *WinMain* function performs the same job as a traditional *main* function, with some Windows-specific functionalities added. Every function in a Windows API–style program is executed, either directly or indirectly, from the *WinMain* function. When the *WinMain* function terminates, the program ends.

Windows Events and Messages: An Overview

Windows is sometimes referred to as an *event-based, message-driven* operating system. During the execution of a Windows-based program, every time the user takes an action that affects a window—such as resizing a window or moving or clicking the mouse—the user's action triggers what is known as an *event*. Each time an event is detected, the operating system sends a *message* to the program so that the program can handle the event.

The idea of a message sometimes confuses novice Windows programmers. In Windows terminology, a message is simply a block of data that Windows generates each time it detects a user-generated event. This block of data contains information that specifies what kind of event has been generated and identifies the window that the event affects.

Every Windows-based program is based on events and messages and contains a main event loop that constantly and repeatedly checks to see whether any user events have taken place. Each time a user event is detected, the program responds to the event. For example, if a user resizes a window during the execution of an application, the application's event loop detects the user's action and starts a series of events that causes the window to be redrawn to the screen. As soon as the window is resized, the application checks to see whether another user event has occurred. If one has, the application handles the event and then checks for the next event. The application repeats this process until the user terminates the program.

Message Queues and Message Pumps

When the Windows operating system detects a user-generated event and generates a message in response, it places that message in a *message queue* that belongs to the application being executed. When an application needs to determine whether any events have been generated by the user and what kinds of events they are, it gets the information it needs by retrieving each message that the operating system has placed in the message queue.

To retrieve event messages, a Windows API–style application repeatedly checks on the status of its message queue by executing a series of statements that reside in its *WinMain* function. These statements execute in a loop called a *message pump*.

The first statement in a message pump is usually a call to a Windows API function named *GetMessage*. Each time an application's message pump calls *GetMessage*, the *GetMessage* function returns information about any message that might be waiting in the application's message queue. After an application's message pump calls *GetMessage*, it generally calls a couple of other functions that manage dialog boxes and keyboard input and output. Then the message pump calls a Windows API function named *DispatchMessage*.

The Window Procedure

The *DispatchMessage* function is an important part of the Windows event-handling mechanism. The main job of the *DispatchMessage* function is to call a function known as a window procedure, often named *WndProc*.

Figure 2-1 on the following page shows how the *GetMessage* function, the *DispatchMessage* function, and a windows procedure work together during the execution of a Windows-based program.

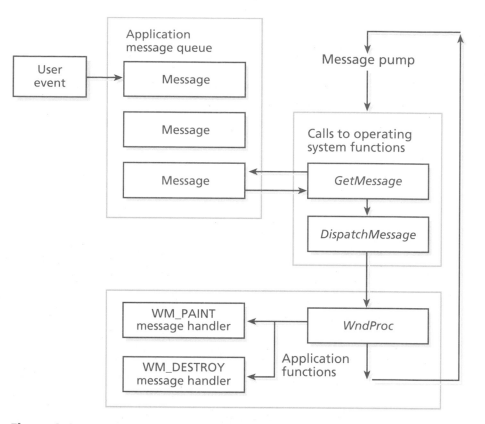

Figure 2-1. *How the window procedure works in a Windows-based program.*

WndProc is not, however, a Windows API procedure—it's a procedure that your Windows-based application must provide. The procedure does not have to be named *WndProc*; you can give a window procedure any name. An application can have more than one window procedure, and if an application has multiple windows, each window can have its own window procedure.

When *DispatchMessage* calls an application's *WndProc* function, it tells *WndProc* what kind of event has taken place. *WndProc* then responds to the event by calling still another kind of function provided by the program being executed. This function is called a *message handler*.

Message Handlers

Each time an application receives a message from the Windows operating system, the application's window procedure determines how the message should be handled. The application then passes the message to a message handler. Typically, Windows-based applications are equipped with various kinds of message handlers that are specially designed to handle particular kinds of messages. An application that you create might handle a mouse double click differently from the way it is handled in someone else's application. The way your application handles a double click is determined by your application's double-click message handler.

When you write a Windows API–style application, you are responsible for writing most of the code that detects user events and dispatches the appropriate messages to appropriate windows. You also have to write the message handlers that implement the responses that are appropriate to each event. The system for handling messages and events is illustrated in Figure 2-2.

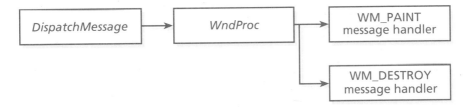

Figure 2-2. *How Windows processes messages and events.*

As you'll see in Chapter 5, "Visual C++ Tools," creating message-handling mechanisms for a Visual C++ program doesn't take as much work as writing message-handling routines for a Windows API–style program. In a Visual C++ program, you can create most kinds of message handlers simply by opening a ClassWizard dialog box and selecting the kind of message handler you want to create from a list box. ClassWizard then generates your message handler automatically.

Example: The HELLO Program

This chapter's sample program, named HELLO, shows how the *WinMain* function and a *WndProc* function work in a simple Windows API–style program. When you execute the HELLO program, it opens a blue-bordered window that contains the familiar "Hello, world!" greeting neatly centered in the window's client area, as shown in Figure 2-3.

Figure 2-3. *The HELLO program's window.*

Methods of Building the HELLO Program

You can execute the HELLO program in two ways and compare how each works. One way is simply to load the program from the companion CD-ROM and execute it. The other way—creating a project for the program and then building your project—is more challenging and will teach you more.

The second method is recommended because it shows you how to create and build a Visual C++ program without using AppWizard—a useful thing to know if you ever need to use Visual Workbench to load and build a program that wasn't created using Visual C++.

Building the HELLO Program Step by Step

To build the HELLO program using Visual Workbench, follow these steps:

1. Choose the New item from the Visual Workbench Project menu.

2. In the New Project dialog box, browse to the directory in which you want to create the new project (or type in the path to where you want to locate the project), as shown here:

3. For the project name, type *Hello*, and then click OK.

4. When the Edit dialog box appears, close it by clicking Close.

5. Open a new text-file window by choosing New from the File menu.

6. When your new window opens, type in the source code from Listing 2-1 beginning on page 31, or use the Visual C++ editor to copy the listing from this chapter's folder on the companion CD-ROM and paste it into the text window.

7. Save the source file you have just created as HELLO.CPP. Be sure that you save the file in the project directory you selected in step 2.

8. Choose the Edit item from the Visual Workbench Project menu.

9. Add your new HELLO.CPP file to the project you are creating by selecting the file's name in the File Name list box and clicking the Add button, as shown on the following page.

10. Close the Edit dialog box by clicking the Close button.

11. Choose Build from the Project menu.

12. Visual Workbench will now display a message box asking you whether you want to create a *module-definition file*. A module-definition file is a text file that the Visual C++ linker uses to link an application's source code to any external libraries that are required to build the application. (For details, see Table 1-2 beginning on page 13 in Chapter 1.) Visual C++ version 1.0 programs require module-definition files, so click the Yes button.

13. Visual Workbench creates a module-definition file and opens it in the Visual C++ editor window. Choose Build from the Project menu again.

14. Visual Workbench displays a message asking whether you want to build your new files. Click the Yes button.

15. When your program is built, execute it from Visual Workbench by choosing Execute from the Project menu.

Listing 2-1 shows the source code for the HELLO program.

HELLO.CPP

```cpp
#include <windows.h>

long FAR PASCAL _export WndProc(HWND hwnd, UINT message,
    UINT wParam,LONG lParam)
{
    HDC          hdc;
    HPEN         hpen, hpenOld;
    PAINTSTRUCT  ps;
    RECT         rect;

    switch (message) {
        case WM_PAINT:
            hdc = BeginPaint(hwnd, &ps);
            GetClientRect(hwnd, &rect);
            hpen = CreatePen(PS_SOLID, 6, RGB(0, 0, 255));
            hpenOld = SelectObject(hdc, hpen);
            Rectangle(hdc, rect.left + 10,
                rect.top + 10,
                rect.right - 10,
                rect.bottom - 10);

            DrawText(hdc, "Hello, world!", -1, &rect,
                DT_SINGLELINE | DT_CENTER | DT_VCENTER);

            SelectObject(hdc, hpenOld);
            DeleteObject(hpen);
            EndPaint(hwnd, &ps);
            return 0;
        case WM_DESTROY:
            PostQuitMessage(0);
            return 0;
    }
    return DefWindowProc(hwnd, message, wParam, lParam);
}

int PASCAL WinMain(HANDLE hInstance, HANDLE hPrevInstance,
    LPSTR lpszCmdParam, int nCmdShow)
{
    static char szAppName[] = "Hello";
    HWND         hwnd;
    MSG          msg;
    WNDCLASS     wndclass;
```

Listing 2-1. *The HELLO program.* *(continued)*

Listing 2-1. *continued*

```
    if (!hPrevInstance) {
        wndclass.style          = CS_HREDRAW | CS_VREDRAW;
        wndclass.lpfnWndProc    = WndProc;
        wndclass.cbClsExtra     = 0;
        wndclass.cbWndExtra     = 0;
        wndclass.hInstance      = hInstance;
        wndclass.hIcon          = LoadIcon(NULL, IDI_APPLICATION);
        wndclass.hCursor        = LoadCursor(NULL, IDC_ARROW);
        wndclass.hbrBackground  = GetStockObject(WHITE_BRUSH);
        wndclass.lpszMenuName   = NULL;
        wndclass.lpszClassName  = szAppName;

        RegisterClass(&wndclass);
    }

    hwnd = CreateWindow(szAppName,      // window class name
        "HELLO Program",                // window caption
        WS_OVERLAPPEDWINDOW,            // window style
        CW_USEDEFAULT,                  // initial x position
        CW_USEDEFAULT,                  // initial y position
        CW_USEDEFAULT,                  // initial x size
        CW_USEDEFAULT,                  // initial y size
        NULL,                           // parent window handle
        NULL,                           // window menu handle
        hInstance,                      // program instance handle
        NULL);                          // creation parameters

    ShowWindow(hwnd, nCmdShow);
    UpdateWindow(hwnd);

    while (GetMessage(&msg, NULL, 0, 0)) {
        TranslateMessage(&msg);
        DispatchMessage(&msg);
    }
    return msg.wParam;
}
```

How the HELLO Program Works

The HELLO program contains two functions: a window function named *WndProc* and a *WinMain* function. The *WinProc* function paints the window when necessary and destroys it when it's no longer needed. The *WinMain* function creates the window and also contains a main message loop that detects and handles two kinds of messages, WM_PAINT and WM_DESTROY. This is the *WinMain* function in the HELLO program:

```
int PASCAL WinMain(HANDLE hInstance, HANDLE hPrevInstance,
    LPSTR lpszCmdParam, int nCmdShow)
```

The *WinMain* function takes four parameters:

- *hInstance*—Handle to the current instance of the executing application.

- *hPrevInstance*—Handle to the previous instance of the executing application.

- *lpszCmdParam*—Pointer to a command line that can be called to start the application.

- *nCmdShow*—Constant or set of constants—separated by bitwise OR operators (¦)—that can be used to specify the window's size, its coordinates, and other attributes that specify how the window is displayed. To obtain a list of all the constants that can be used in this parameter, look up the *WinMain* function in the Visual Workbench online help.

If a *WinMain* call is successful, it returns the value returned by the Windows API *PostQuitMessage* function. If the function does not succeed, it terminates before it enters the message loop and returns *NULL*.

Using Handles in Windows-Based Programs

The *WinMain* function takes two handles as parameters: a handle to the current instance of the executing application, and a handle to any previous instance of the application that might exist. In Windows, a *handle* is a pointer to a pointer; it points to an address stored in a table or in a list. The address that a handle points to can be used to access the object associated with the handle.

In Windows, this kind of indirect access is necessary because the Windows Memory Manager often moves objects around in memory—

(continued)

Using Handles in Windows-Based Programs. *continued*

to compact memory, for example—without notifying your application that the address of the object has changed. If your applications relied on a pointer to keep track of objects created and managed by Windows, the result would be a lot of dangling pointers. That is why handles were created. When Windows moves an object from one memory location to another, the Windows Memory Manager ensures that the object's handle is still valid.

In the Windows operating system, many different kinds of objects are designed to be accessed through handles. There are so many such objects, in fact, that they have a special name, *Windows objects*. (Windows objects are not the same thing as C++ objects; they have nothing to do with C++ or object-oriented programming. In Windows terminology, Windows objects are merely objects that can be accessed via handles; they can be—and are—used in C-language Windows-based programs as well as in Windows-based programs written in C++.)

Handles are used so often in Windows-based programs that you'll quickly become accustomed to using them. Many Windows API functions return handles, and many others take handles as parameters. In your Windows-based applications, you use handles in the same way that you use any other data type. Because Windows dereferences handles automatically whenever it needs to, you shouldn't run into any problems.

How the *WinMain* Function Works

When a Windows-based program starts, its *WinMain* function always checks to see whether a previous instance of the application is running. (In Windows, multiple instances of the same application can be executed simultaneously.) If no previous instance of the program is running, *WinMain* registers a new window class—an operation described later in this chapter. Then *WinMain* executes the program's message pump, described earlier in this chapter in the section "Message Queues and Message Pumps" on page 25, as shown here:

```
while (GetMessage(&msg, NULL, 0, 0)) {
    TranslateMessage(&msg);
    DispatchMessage(&msg);
}
```

In the HELLO program, this message pump manages the operation of the application by repeatedly calling the *GetMessage*, *TranslateMessage*, and *DispatchMessage* functions. The loop ends when the *WinMain* function receives a WM_QUIT message sent by the *PostQuitMessage* function. Then the *WinMain* function ends, and the current instance of the application terminates.

The *GetMessage* function

The *GetMessage* function retrieves messages dispatched by the Windows operating system. In the HELLO program, the *GetMessage* function is called with four parameters, as shown here:

```
GetMessage(&msg, NULL, 0, 0);
```

The first parameter passed to *GetMessage*—*&msg*—is the address of a C-language *struct* called a MSG structure. The MSG structure is defined as follows in the WINDOWS.H file (the *#include* file that defines Windows API functions and data structures):

```
typedef struct tagMSG {
    HWND    hwnd;
    UINT    message;
    WPARAM  wParam;
    LPARAM  lParam;
    DWORD   time;
    POINT   pt;
} MSG;
```

As you can see, a MSG *struct* is a short structure that the *GetMessage* function uses to pass along information about Windows messages. In its *hwnd* and *message* fields, a MSG *struct* identifies the message being referred to and the window that the message affects. In its *wParam* and *lParam* fields, the MSG *struct* stores information about the kind of event the message refers to and the source of the event—for example, if the event is caused by a keyboard input, the MSG *struct*'s *wParam* and *lParam* fields identify the key being pressed and also reveal whether a command key was being pressed at the same time.

When you call *GetMessage* and pass it the address of a MSG *struct*, the *GetMessage* function responds by placing essential information about the event it is retrieving in the MSG *struct* that you have provided. Your application can then use that information to carry out an appropriate response to the event.

In the call to *GetMessage,* the *msg* parameter is significant because it is later accessed by *TranslateMessage* and *DispatchMessage.* It might also be accessed by other functions in a message pump that handle the operation of modal dialog boxes (when the message being retrieved deals with dialog boxes) or keyboard shortcuts for menu commands.

Switch statements in window procedures

Typically, a Windows API–style *WndProc* function contains a long switch statement that analyzes each message received from *GetMessage* and routes the message to an appropriate message handler. (The window procedures used in Visual C++ programs usually look quite different—and you generally don't have to write them because AppWizard does that for you. You'll learn how Visual C++ window procedures work in Chapter 5, "Visual C++ Tools.")

Listing 2-2 shows a portion of the switch statement used in the HELLO program (shown in its entirety in Lising 2-1 on page 31).

```
switch (message) {
    case WM_PAINT:
        hdc = BeginPaint(hwnd, &ps);
        GetClientRect(hwnd, &rect);
        ⋮
        DrawText(hdc, "Hello, world!", -1, &rect,
            DT_SINGLELINE ¦ DT_CENTER ¦ DT_VCENTER);
        ⋮
        EndPaint(hwnd, &ps);
        return 0;

    case WM_DESTROY:
        PostQuitMessage(0);
        return 0;
}
```

Listing 2-2. *A switch statement in a window procedure.*

In the code fragment shown in Listing 2-2, the *message* parameter used by the switch statement identifies the message that the *DispatchMessage* function has passed to the *WinProc* function containing the switch statement. The switch statement tests the message ID that has been passed to it and then uses its case prefixes to implement—or call—the appropriate message handlers.

This switch statement has only two clauses: a WM_PAINT clause, which is executed each time the window associated with the window procedure needs to be redrawn, and a WM_DESTROY clause, which is executed whenever the window needs to be destroyed.

The WM_PAINT clause executes a message handler that displays the words "Hello, world!" in the application's main window and decorates the window with a blue border. You'll learn how the program's WM_PAINT message handler works in the section "Drawing Text in a Window" on page 42.

The WM_DESTROY clause calls a Windows API function named *PostQuit-Message*, which informs Windows that the application is ready to terminate. When an application posts a message to Windows by calling *PostQuit-Message*, the Windows operating system performs all the housekeeping that is necessary to let the application exit from its main message loop.

Registering a Window Class

When you execute the HELLO program, the first thing it does is perform a procedure call to register a window class. When you create a Windows-based application, every window you use in the application belongs to a particular window class.

It's important to understand that in a Windows-based program, a window class is not the same thing as a C++ class. In Windows terminology, a window class is simply a particular kind of window that is registered for use in a given application. Windows classes, like Windows objects, can be (and are) used in C-language programs as well as in C++ programs.

Calling the *RegisterClass* function

You can use as many different window classes as you want in a Windows-based application. Before you can create a window that belongs to a particular class, however, you must register the window's class. In the HELLO

program, the following statement (which appears in the *WinMain* function)
registers a window class named *szAppName*:

```
WNDCLASS    wndclass;
if (!hPrevInstance) {
    wndclass.style         = CS_HREDRAW | CS_VREDRAW;
    wndclass.lpfnWndProc   = WndProc;
    wndclass.cbClsExtra    = 0;
    wndclass.cbWndExtra    = 0;
    wndclass.hInstance     = hInstance;
    wndclass.hIcon         = LoadIcon(NULL, IDI_APPLICATION);
    wndclass.hCursor       = LoadCursor(NULL, IDC_ARROW);
    wndclass.hbrBackground = GetStockObject(WHITE_BRUSH);
    wndclass.lpszMenuName  = NULL;
    wndclass.lpszClassName = szAppName;
    RegisterClass(&wndclass);
}
```

NOTE Notice that the *RegisterClass* function is called from inside an *if* statement. In C++, *if* statements work the same way they work in C. In this case, if
a previous instance of the HELLO program is running, no new window class
is created. That precaution conserves system resources because it prevents
the *RegisterClass* function from performing multiple registrations of the
same window class.

The WNDCLASS structure

In the preceding code fragment, the HELLO program declares a data structure named *wndclass*, which is a particular type of data structure called a
WNDCLASS structure, and then fills in the structure's fields with data
that can be used to set up various properties of a window.

The WNDCLASS structure is defined this way in the WINDOWS.H file:

```
typedef struct tagWNDCLASS {    /* wc */
    UINT       style;
    WNDPROC    lpfnWndProc;
    int        cbClsExtra;
    int        cbWndExtra;
    HINSTANCE  hInstance;
    HICON      hIcon;
    HCURSOR    hCursor;
    HBRUSH     hbrBackground;
    LPCSTR     lpszMenuName;
    LPCSTR     lpszClassName;
} WNDCLASS;
```

When the window's properties have been specified, the application registers a window class that has those properties by calling a Windows API function named *RegisterClass* and passing to it the address of the data structure in which the attributes of the window class being created are stored.

RegisterClass registers a window class that has the attributes you requested and gives this new class the name you have specified—in this case, *szAppName*. The WNDCLASS structure must also contain in the *lpfnWndProc* field a pointer to the procedure or function that will be associated with your window class. You must also define the window's style in the WNDCLASS structure's *style* field, using predefined style constants that are defined by the Windows API.

Setting window styles

In the *RegisterClass* function shown in the preceding example, two predefined constants—separated by the bitwise OR operator (¦)—are used to set the style of the window used in the HELLO program, as shown here:

```
wndclass.style = CS_HREDRAW ¦ CS_VREDRAW;
```

When you use predefined constants such as these in a Windows-based program, you don't have to worry about what their exact values are. All you have to know is what their effects are.

In this case, when you set the *CS_HREDRAW* constant, windows that belong to the class you are creating are redrawn whenever their horizontal size changes. Similarly, the *CS_VREDRAW* constant causes a window to be redrawn whenever its vertical size changes. In the HELLO program, setting these two constants ensures that the application's window is redrawn each time its size changes. That action automatically centers the "Hello, world!" greeting that is displayed inside the window.

The *CS_HREDRAW* and *CS_VREDRAW* constants are not the only style constants available in Windows; there are many other style attributes that you can use when you register window classes. (See the online help for a complete list.)

Loading application resources

You can call Windows API functions to set window-class attributes in a *RegisterClass* statement. For example, the *RegisterClass* statement used in the HELLO program calls the Windows API functions *LoadIcon* and *Load-Cursor* to fill in the *hIcon* and *hCursor* fields of the window class that is being registered, as shown here:

```
wndclass.hIcon = LoadIcon(NULL, IDI_APPLICATION);
wndclass.hCursor = LoadCursor (NULL, IDC_ARROW);
```

The *hIcon* field identifies the class icon. This member must be a handle to an icon resource. If this member is NULL, the application must draw an icon whenever the user minimizes the application's window.

The *hCursor* field identifies the class cursor. This member must be a handle to a cursor resource. If this member is NULL, the application must explicitly set the cursor shape whenever the mouse moves into the application's window.

Creating and Displaying a Window

After you have created a window class in a Windows-based application, you can call the Windows API functions *CreateWindow* and *ShowWindow* to create a window of the class you have specified and to display the window on the screen. Then you can call the *UpdateWindow* function whenever your window needs to be redrawn.

The *CreateWindow* function can create an overlapped window, a popup window, or a child window, depending on the parameters you pass to it. (For descriptions of these and other kinds of windows, see Chapter 5, "Visual C++ Tools.") When you call *CreateWindow*, you can specify the class, the title, the style, and (optionally) the initial position and size of the window you are creating. You can also specify the new window's parent (if there is one) and the new window's menu.

The *CreateWindow* function

Here is the *CreateWindow* function:

```
HWND CreateWindow(LPCSTR lpszClassName, LPCSTR lpszWindowName,
    DWORD dwStyle, int x, int y, int nWidth, int nHeight,
    HWND hwndParent, HMENU hmenu, HINSTANCE hinst,
    void FAR* lpvParam)
```

The parameters expected by the *CreateWindow* function are as follows:

- *lpszClassName*—Address of the name of a registered window class.

- *lpszWindowName*—Pointer to a string that specifies the name of the window being created.

- *dwStyle*—Constant or set of constants—separated by the bitwise OR operator (¦)—that can be used to specify various attributes of a window. You can obtain a list of all the constants that can be used in this parameter by looking up the *CreateWindow* function in the online help.

- *x* and *y*—Horizontal and vertical positions of the window being created.

- *nWidth* and *nHeight*—Width and height of the window being created.

- *hwndParent*—Handle of the parent window of the window being created (if there is one).

- *hmenu*—Parameter whose meaning depends on the style of the window being created. For overlapped or popup windows, the *hmenu* parameter identifies the menu to be used with the window. If the default menu for the window's class is to be used, this value can be NULL. For child windows, the *hmenu* parameter is an integer value that identifies the child window. For more details, look up the *CreateWindow* function in the online help.

- *hinst*—Handle of the current application instance.

- *lpvParam*—Pointer to a value that is passed to the window through the CREATESTRUCT structure referenced by the *lParam* parameter of the WM_CREATE message. If an application is calling *CreateWindow* to create a multiple-document interface (MDI) client window, *lpvParam* must point to a CLIENTCREATESTRUCT structure.

Calling *CreateWindow*, *ShowWindow*, and *UpdateWindow*

In the *WinMain* function of the HELLO program, the block of code shown on the following page calls *CreateWindow*, *ShowWindow*, and *UpdateWindow*.

```
hwnd = CreateWindow(szAppName,    // window class name
    "HELLO Program",              // window caption
    WS_OVERLAPPEDWINDOW,          // window style
    CW_USEDEFAULT,                // initial x position
    CW_USEDEFAULT,                // initial y position
    CW_USEDEFAULT,                // initial x size
    CW_USEDEFAULT,                // initial y size
    NULL,                         // parent window handle
    NULL,                         // window menu handle
    hInstance,                    // program instance handle
    NULL);                        // creation parameters

ShowWindow(hwnd, nCmdShow);
UpdateWindow(hwnd);
```

The *ShowWindow* function displays the window specified in its *hwnd* parameter, using the style specified in the *nCmdShow* parameter. (See the online help for a list of styles that can be passed to the *ShowWindow* function.)

The *UpdateWindow* procedure draws the window specified in its *hwnd* parameter. It is used after the call to *ShowWindow* to draw the window used in the HELLO program.

Drawing Text in a Window

One of the first hurdles you come to in the study of Windows programming is the problem of how to draw an image in a window—or, when the time comes to print an image on paper, the problem of transferring the image to the printed page. A Windows-based program has to be capable of drawing many different kinds of images to many different kinds of output devices. There are many varieties of video cards and Windows accelerators that display different sets of colors in different ways, and there are different sizes of monitors with different color capabilities, different screen sizes, and different resolutions. And, of course, there are many different kinds of printers—color and black-and-white, PostScript and non-PostScript—to say nothing of pen-equipped and ink jet plotters.

Because there are so many kinds of output devices—and because there are no standards that mandate any particular rules about drawing to output devices—Windows provides a mechanism called a *device context*, or *DC*, that can be used as a gateway between Windows-based applications and the low-level APIs (called *device drivers*) that control output devices. A device context is a Windows object that accepts drawing commands from Windows-based applications and translates those commands into lower-level instructions that are issued directly to device drivers.

When a Windows-based application draws an image by issuing a set of commands to a device context, it does not have to be concerned with what kind of output device is being used to display or print the image or with the specific kind of device driver that is being used to control the output device. Instead the application simply obtains a handle to a device context and draws to that device context. The device context that is associated with the drawing operation then performs whatever magic is necessary to convert the application's drawing commands to lower-level device driver commands and dispatches them to a device driver. The device driver then sends the device context's commands to the appropriate output device, which does the final job of displaying the object in a window or printing it on a page.

Along with device contexts, Windows uses another kind of object—called a *GDI object*, or *graphics device interface object*—to draw images in windows and on the printed page.

In Windows, a device context is an object on which images can be drawn (a kind of electronic canvas), and GDI objects serve as drawing implements, such as brushes, pens, bitmaps, and fonts. Figure 2-4 on the following page is a fanciful illustration that shows how Windows uses device contexts and GDI objects to draw images in windows and on printed pages.

Figure 2-4. *Drawing an image in a Windows-based program.*

Because Windows requires the use of device contexts and GDI objects in drawing operations, you must use both kinds of objects whenever you want to draw an image in a Windows-based application. The specific steps that are used to draw an image can vary from application to application, depending on the requirements of the particular program being executed. The drawing operation used in the HELLO program is fairly typical. Here are the steps that are used to print the greeting "Hello, world!" in a window

1. Call the Windows API function *BeginPaint*, which prepares a specified window for painting and fills a data structure called a PAINTSTRUCT with information about the painting. The *Begin-Paint* function takes two parameters: the handle of the window in which the painting is to take place and the address of the PAINT-STRUCT. (The HELLO program doesn't use the information stored in the PAINTSTRUCT that is passed to *BeginPaint*; see the online help for details about the PAINTSTRUCT structure.)

2. Obtain a handle to a device context. There are a number of Windows functions that you can call to obtain a DC handle. The HELLO program obtains a DC handle when it issues the following *BeginPaint* call:

```
hdc = BeginPaint(hwnd, &ps);
```

3. Call the Windows API procedure *GetClientRect* to retrieve the coordinates of the client area of the window that is to be painted. The client area of a window is the area inside the window's frame and below the window's menu bar.

4. Obtain a handle to the specific kind of GDI object you plan to draw with. The GDI object used by the HELLO program is a pen, which is created in this statement:

```
hpen = CreatePen(PS_SOLID, 6, RGB(0, 0, 255));
```

The *CreatePen* function takes three parameters: a pen-style parameter, a width parameter, and a color parameter. In the HELLO program, the parameters passed to the *CreatePen* function are *PS_SOLID*, which creates a solid pen; the integer *6*, which creates a pen that is 6 pixels wide; and the macro *RGB(0, 0, 255)*, which creates a blue pen. The RGB macro itself takes three parameters: the intensity of the color red, the intensity of the color green, and the intensity of the color blue. Intensities range from 0 through 255, and they can be mixed and matched. The HELLO program passes the parameters *0, 0*, and *255* to the RGB macro, so the result is a pure blue color.

5. Call a Windows function that associates the device context you have obtained with the GDI object you are going to use. In Windows jargon, this step is often referred to as *selecting* a GDI object *into* a device context. In the HELLO program, the following statement selects a pen object into the variable *hdc*, the handle of the DC object that was obtained in step 2:

```
hpenOld = SelectObject(hdc, hpen);
```

The *SelectObject* function returns a handle to a GDI object. This handle can then be stowed away for safekeeping during the drawing operation that is about to occur. The handle returned by *SelectObject* is kept because it might already be in use by a previously selected GDI object. If that is the case, the handle can be restored with another call to *SelectObject* as soon as it is no longer needed by the drawing operation that is about to take place. The handle is then freed once again for use by the object that originally owned it. (In step 7, you'll see how *SelectObject* can be used to restore a handle to its original owner.)

6. Perform your drawing operation. In the HELLO program, the *Rectangle* function is called to draw a blue border around the application's window, as shown here:

```
Rectangle(hdc, rect.left + 10, rect.top + 10,
    rect.right - 10, rect.bottom - 10);
```

After the HELLO program calls the *Rectangle* function, it makes a call to the *DrawText* function to print the greeting "Hello, world!" inside the window, as shown below. The *DrawText* function does not require the specific use of a GDI object, but it does require five other parameters: the handle of the window into which text is to be printed, the address of the string to be printed, the length of the string (or the number –1, which allows the string to be computed automatically), a pointer to the structure containing dimensions of the window's client rectangle, and a set of text-drawing flags.

```
DrawText(hdc, "Hello, world!", -1, &rect,
    DT_SINGLELINE | DT_CENTER | DT_VCENTER);
```

7. Restore the handle used by the *Rectangle* function to its original owner by making another call to *SelectObject*, as shown here:

```
SelectObject(hdc, hpenOld);
```

8. Free the DC object that was obtained in step 2 by calling *BeginPaint*, as shown here:

```
DeleteObject(hpen);
```

9. Call the API function *EndPaint* to terminate your painting operation, as shown here:

```
EndPaint(hwnd, &ps);
```

The preceding steps—with program-specific variations—are used in all drawing operations in Windows API–style programs. In Visual C++ programs that use the Microsoft Foundation Class (MFC) Library version 2.0, the steps vary slightly.

What's Next?

In Chapter 1, "Introducing Visual C++," you learned how to create an application framework by using AppWizard. In this chapter, you learned how Windows-based programs are created using functions provided by the Windows API.

In the next two chapters, we'll take a step back and examine some of the basic features of generic C++ and some of the fundamentals of object-oriented programming. Then, in Chapter 5, "Visual C++ Tools," we'll focus our attention once again on Visual C++ and take a detailed look inside the AppWizard application generator.

C++ Basics

In Chapter 1, "Introducing Visual C++," you saw how AppWizard can create a fully functioning Visual C++ application at the click of a menu item. In Chapter 2, "Introduction to Windows Programming," you saw the basics of how a Windows-based program works. In later chapters, you'll learn how you can use Visual C++ wizards and the other tools that come with Visual C++ to expand the simple kinds of programs presented in Chapters 1 and 2 into powerful, customized Visual C++ applications.

Before we move on to more complex Visual C++ programs, however, it will be helpful to look at some of the features of generic C++—the object-oriented programming language that lies at the root of Visual C++. In this chapter, we'll focus on C++ data structures and C++ classes, the building blocks of all Visual C++ programs. In Chapter 4, "Objects and Member Functions," you'll see how objects are created from classes and how C++ member functions are used in programs.

This chapter contains a number of sample programs that show how structures and classes work in C++ programs. These sample programs are compiled using the QuickWin utility, a Visual C++ tool that makes it easy to write and execute text-based procedures and programs in Windows. Quick-Win is handy for quickly testing and fine-tuning routines before you incorporate them into full-fledged Windows-based programs.

To create a QuickWin application, follow the steps that were outlined in the section "Example: The HELLO Program" in Chapter 2 on page 28—with one exception. When the New Project dialog box opens, select Quick-Win as your project type. Then be sure to choose Edit from the Project menu and add the appropriate source code files to your project. You can find all the sample programs in appropriately named folders in the Chap04 folder on the companion CD-ROM.

Together, this chapter and Chapter 4 are a crash course in C++. The topics they introduce are vital to the study of Visual C++, and many books on C++ are devoted almost entirely to the material these chapters cover. If you are a C programmer, I guarantee that you will also be a C++ programmer by the time you finish Chapters 3 and 4. I'm not promising that you'll be on intimate terms with every arcane construct that is available in C++, but you will understand how C++ works, and—even more remarkably—you will be writing your own C++ programs.

This chapter covers a host of topics, including the following:

- Object-oriented programming: a brief explanation of the uses and features of object-oriented programming languages.

- An overview of some C++ keywords and data types that aren't available in C or that are used differently in C++ from how they are used in C.

- Creating and using classes: how the C-language *struct* has evolved into the C++ class, the keystone of object-oriented programming in the C++ language.

- Other C++ programming techniques, including access specifiers, operators for accessing member functions and member variables of classes, constructors and destructors, copy constructors, and the *this* pointer.

What's Object-Oriented Programming?

Throughout this book, you'll notice that the word "object" is used many times. That shouldn't surprise you in a book about C++, an object-oriented programming language. But exactly what is an object-oriented language?

Some people assume, logically enough, that object-oriented programming languages are used to create and manage menus, icons, and the other elements of the user interface that you encounter in Windows-based programs. Windows programmers, however, have created and managed on-screen objects for years using the Windows API (application programming interface), and the Windows API is not an object-oriented tool.

Many people also define an object-oriented language as a language that makes it possible to reuse code. This definition is a little closer to the truth, but it still isn't accurate. A good C programmer, for example, can write C functions that are reusable from one application to the next, and a poor C++ programmer can just as easily write code that isn't reusable at all. As an object-oriented language, C++ does offer a number of programming mechanisms that make it easier to write reusable code, but those mechanisms are not its defining features.

The most useful way to understand C++ as an object-oriented language is to understand how C++ takes advantage of the following features:

■ **Inheritance**—In a non-object-oriented language such as C, you can't create a data structure that inherits characteristics from another data structure. Every time you want to create a data structure, you have to start from scratch. In C++, you can create a data structure that inherits characteristics from another data structure and then supplements those characteristics with unique characteristics of its own. Furthermore, you can create functions (known as *member functions*) that "belong" to C++ data structures, and you can then create other data structures that inherit those functions and use other functions of their own. In C++, structures that inherit data and functions from other structures are arranged in inheritance *hierarchies*. By making use of these hierarchies, you can not only write code that is reusable, you can also write data structures (called *classes*) that contain variables and functions that are also reusable, either in full or in part.

■ **Data encapsulation**—In C++, member functions can access all member variables of the same class. However, an object can safeguard its member functions and member variables from being accessed or modified by other classes. The ability that an object has to conceal its data from other parts of a program is called *data encapsulation*. If you've ever tried to track down a function that has modified a global variable in a C program, you'll appreciate the benefits of C++ data encapsulation.

■ **Data abstraction**—When you design a C++ class, you can conceal the details of how its data is represented and handled—that is, you can hide this information from other classes and other functions in your C++ program. By making use of data abstraction, C++ functions can ignore the details of how an operation is implemented and can concentrate instead on the jobs they want to perform.

You'll learn more about all these features of object-oriented programming later in this chapter and in Chapter 4, "Objects and Member Functions."

Old Friends, New Faces

C++ is sometimes called a superset of C, which means that C++ contains all the features of C along with some new features of its own. (In fact, that's how C++ got its name. Bjarne Stroustrup, the inventor of C++, says he named it C++ because it's an "incrementation" of C.) Also, some of the techniques and elements that C programmers are familiar with have changed in C++. In this section, we'll take a look at some of those changes.

Type Specifiers

To specify exactly how various kinds of data are stored in memory, the designers of C and C++ established a number of data types. In both C and C++, a keyword that specifies the data type of a particular piece of data is called a *type specifier*. For example, the keyword *int* is a type specifier for integers. Similarly, the keyword *char* is a type specifier for characters. Many other type specifiers—such as *float*, *double*, and *long*—are used in C++.

The C++ language is equipped with several data types that are not available in C. These additions to C++ correct some deficiencies that have always existed in C and provide C++ with some extra programming power. The following four data types available in C++ require some specific discussion:

- The *enum* data type, which is also available in C and has been promoted to a full data type in C++

- The *struct* data type, which existed in C but was not a full-fledged data type

- The reference data type, which behaves like a pointer but can be treated like a variable, eliminating the overhead that is ordinarily required to dereference a pointer

- The class data type, a powerful new data type that is the keystone of object-oriented programming in C++

We'll cover the first three of these data types in the sections that follow. Classes are covered in detail in the section "C++ Classes," on page 65.

The *enum* data type

In C++, an *enumeration* is an integral data type that defines a list of named constants. Enumerations, like *struct*s and *const*s, are available in C but are more flexible and more powerful in C++. In C++, the *enum* keyword is a real type specifier, so it is more flexible than it is in C.

The *struct* data type

As a C programmer, you're familiar with *struct*s; they have been used extensively in C programs ever since the language was invented. But there's a difference between the way *struct*s are implemented in C and the way they are implemented in C++.

In C, a *struct* is not a full-fledged data type; it is merely a data structure made up of data items, each of which has its own data type. In C++, a *struct* is a full-fledged data type. For example, the following code defines a new data type named *Person*:

```
struct Person {
    char* name;
    int height;
    int weight;
    int age;
};
```

You'll notice that when declaring a C++ pointer variable, the unary operator (*) is placed immediately after the variable type rather than immediately in front of the variable name. You can still use C-style pointer declarations if you prefer—C++ understands both forms of pointer declarations—but Visual C++ generates code using the C++ style of pointer declarations.

Variables of type *Person* are declared in the same way that other variables are declared. For example, the following line declares a variable named *Charlie* of type *Person*:

```
Person Charlie;
```

As with C-style *struct*s, individual data members of a C++ *struct* are accessed using the dot operator (.). Likewise, pointers to C++ *struct*s are accessed using the arrow operator (–>).

The biggest difference between a C-style *struct* and a C++ *struct* is that a C++ *struct* can contain functions as well as data. Variables that are declared inside a *struct* definition are called *member variables*. Functions that are declared inside a *struct* definition are called *member functions*. Member functions are more closely associated with classes, however, so they'll be covered in the section "C++ Classes," on page 65.

A C++ *struct* has all the power and versatility of any other data type. In fact, the C++ class—the basic building block of C++ object-oriented programming—is based on the kind of *struct* used in C++.

References

A *reference* is a new data type that C++ provides. References are not available in C. This is what a reference looks like in a C++ program:

```
&aReference
```

In C++, a reference is a hybrid data type that combines the behavior of an ordinary variable with the behavior of a pointer. You can use a reference in the same way that you might use any other kind of variable in C, but with a reference, a function can change the value of a variable that is outside the function's scope without having to bother with the overhead of dereferencing a pointer.

To understand how references work, it helps to view a reference as an alias for a variable. But a reference is not just a copy of the variable it refers to. Instead, it is the same variable made available under a different name.

How references are used in C++   In C++, references are most often used
to pass arguments to functions and to return values from functions. To
initialize a reference, you associate it with a variable that has already been
declared. Once you have initialized a reference, it is permanently associated with its corresponding variable. You cannot reinitialize it to be an
alias for a different variable; Visual C++ returns an error if you try.

To declare a reference, you use the symbol & (the unary AND operator), as
illustrated in the following example:

```
int anIntVar;
int& aReference = anIntVar;   // reference declaration
```

The first statement in this example declares an integer variable named
anIntVar. The second statement creates a reference named *aReference* that
is an alias for *anIntVar*.

Once these two operations are complete, you can use the name *aReference*
in exactly the same way that you would use *anIntVar*. When you perform
an operation on the reference named *aReference*, the operation has the
same result as if you had performed it on the variable named *anIntVar*.
Listing 3-1 shows how a variable and a reference associated with it can
be used interchangeably.

VAR_REF.CPP

```
#include <iostream.h>

void main()
{
    int anIntVar = 100;
    int& aReference = anIntVar;

    cout << '\n' << anIntVar;
    cout << '\n' << aReference;
    aReference++;
    cout << '\n' << anIntVar;
    cout << '\n' << aReference;
    anIntVar++;
    cout << '\n' << anIntVar;
    cout << '\n' << aReference;
}
```

Listing 3-1. *Variables and references.*

The program in Listing 3-1 produces the output shown in Figure 3-1. As you can see, the operations performed on *anIntVar* and on *aReference* in the preceding example yield the same results.

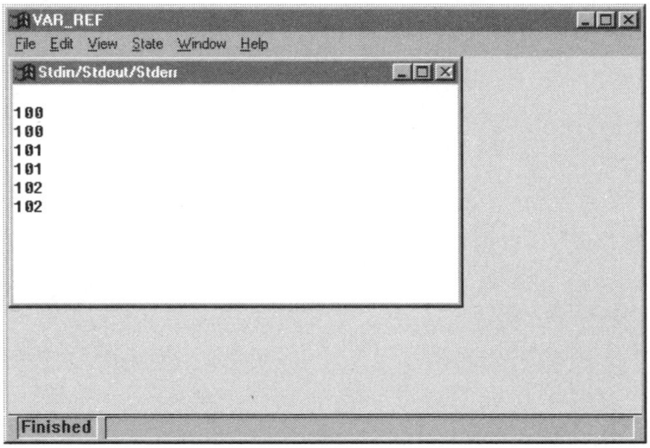

Figure 3-1. *Using a variable and a reference interchangeably.*

Printing Text with *cout* <<

In C++, the construct *cout* << is often used to output text, in much the same way that the *printf* family of functions is used to print text in C. In C++, text and numeric information is sent to the *cout* object by means of the << symbol. The << symbol is defined using a mechanism known as *operator overloading*. As you will see in Chapter 4, "Objects and Member Functions," operator overloading is a C++ feature that is often used to customize operator symbols such as +, –, =, and ++. With operator overloading, you can make an operator symbol behave differently when it is used with objects of different classes. In the construct *cout* <<, the << operator is overloaded to work like a command that writes the contents of a *cout* object to standard or diagnostic output, which can be either a printed page or the screen.

Listing 3-2 provides another example of the use of a reference; it shows that a variable and a reference to that variable have the same memory address.

```
REF_ADDR.CPP

#include <iostream.h>

void main()
{
    int anIntVar = 123;
    int& aReference = anIntVar;

    cout << "The variable address is: "
         << &anIntVar << '\n';
    cout << "The reference address is: "
         << &aReference << '\n';
}
```

Listing 3-2. *Obtaining the address of a reference.*

Using the & operator with variables and references   The unary operator
(&) is used in two different ways in C++. When you declare a reference, as
in the following statement:

```
int& aReference = anIntVar;
```

the & operator is part of the reference's type. In contrast, when you define
an ordinary pointer, as in this example:

```
int anInt;
int *pAnInt = &anInt;
```

the & symbol stands for a memory address—in this case, the address of the
pAnInt variable.

In Listing 3-2, the & operator is used both ways. In the statement

```
int& aReference = anIntVar;
```

the name *aReference* is declared to be a reference to an *int* or a variable of
type *int&*—a usage that is unique to C++.

In the following statements, however, the & operator precedes the address
of the variable it is applied to. This usage is common to both C and C++.

```
cout << "The variable address is: "
     << &anIntVar << '\n';
cout << "The reference address is: "
     << &aReference << '\n';
```

When you run the program shown in Listing 3-2, it prints the same address for both *anIntVar* and *aReference*, as shown in Figure 3-2. (The address that is printed depends, of course, on the configuration of your system.)

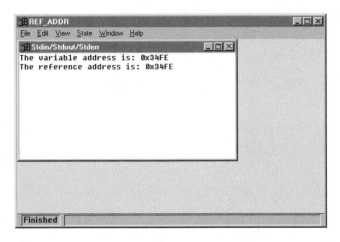

Figure 3-2. *A reference and its corresponding variable have the same address.*

How references work   Now that you know how references are used, it's time to reveal how they work. What makes a reference really special is that from the viewpoint of your Visual C++ compiler, a reference is associated with a variable's address. So although you can use a reference in exactly the same way that you use a variable, Visual C++ treats the reference as if it were a pointer.

Because references behave in this way, you can use them to get around some of the limitations of using nonpointer variables in C. In C, when you want to change the value of a local variable of a function from within a different function, you must use a pointer and follow all the manipulations that are necessary to dereference the pointer. In C++, you can change the value of the variable simply by associating it with a reference. Then, by changing the value of your reference, you also change the value of its associated variable.

Listing 3-3, a program named USINGREF, shows how a function can use a reference to change the value of a local variable declared in a different function. Notice that in C++, references allow you to perform this kind of operation without the overhead that is required to perform a similar operation using a pointer in C.

```
USINGREF.CPP

#include <iostream.h>

// function prototype
void ChangeValue(int& aRef);

void main()
{
    int anIntVar = 123;
    int& aReference = anIntVar;

    cout << "The value of anIntVar is "
        << anIntVar << '\n';

    ChangeValue(aReference);

    cout << "The value of anIntVar is now "
        << anIntVar << '\n';
}

void ChangeValue(int& aRef)
{
    aRef = 456;
}
```

Listing 3-3. *Using a reference.*

In the *main* function of the USINGREF program, a local integer variable named *anIntVar* is declared and assigned a value of 123. A reference named *aReference* is then declared to be an alias of *anIntVar*.

When *anIntVar* has been initialized and *aReference* has been defined, the *main* function calls another function, named *ChangeValue*, that changes the value of the reference named *aReference*.

Because both *aReference* and *aRef* are aliases of *anIntVar*, changing the value of *aRef* also changes the value of *anIntVar*—even though *anIntVar* is a local variable that is declared and defined inside another function!

To perform this kind of operation in C, you would have to declare a pointer to *anIntVar*, pass the pointer to *aRef*, and then dereference the pointer to obtain its new value. In C++, you can use a reference for this task instead of a pointer. This technique eliminates the overhead of dereferencing a pointer.

Advantages of using references   In a program as short and simple as the one shown in Listing 3-3, the time and effort you save by using a reference instead of a pointer is minimal. But if you need to use a pointer to access a long sequence of memory locations—for example, the contents of a very large array—you might find that you can speed up processing significantly by using an array and eliminating the extra time and effort that dereferencing a pointer would require.

Dangers in using references   All this power and flexibility can be dangerous if you don't know exactly what you're doing. In C, you can always tell when you're working with a pointer because you have to use the dereference operator (*) to obtain the value of a variable being accessed through a pointer. In contrast, a reference does not have to be identified using any special kind of symbol. That means that in your source code, a reference can look the same as a variable even though it packs a lot of extra power.

So you should not go around indiscriminately declaring and using references. You should use them with caution, and you should always be sure that you identify them in comments. That makes it much safer for other developers who might be assigned to work with your source code after you have made your millions and retired to Monaco.

Qualifiers

In C and C++, a *qualifier* is a keyword that either modifies a type specifier or defines the behavior of a function. When a qualifier is used to modify a type specifier, it is called a *type qualifier*. For example, the keyword *const* is used in the following statement as a type qualifier that declares a constant named *aConst*:

```
const int aConst;
```

The following statement shows how a qualifier can be used to define the behavior of a function. In this case, the keyword *inline* is a qualifier that declares *AFunction* to be an inline function. (Inline functions are described in more detail in the section "Inline Member Functions" on page 67.

```
inline void AFunction(int paramA);
```

> **NOTE**   A function qualifier can also be referred to as a *function modifier*.

As these examples illustrate, you can use both a qualifier and a type specifier in the definition of a variable or a function. When you do that, the type qualifier modifies the type specifier or the function, in much the same way that an adjective modifies a noun.

For example, when you precede the name of a variable with the *const* keyword, the variable becomes a constant. To create a *const* in a C++ program, you use a statement like this:

```
const int aConstVar = 100;
```

or a statement like this:

```
const float aConstVar2 = 129.95;
```

In C++, both of the preceding statements are called *initialization statements.* In the first of these statements, *aConstVar* is declared to be a constant integer and is initialized to a value of 100. In the second statement, *aConstVar2* is declared to be a constant of the *float* type and is initialized to a value of 129.95.

Assignment and Initialization in C++

In C programming, "assignment" and "initialization" are two words that mean essentially the same thing. Both describe the assignment of a value to a constant or to a variable. The only difference in C++ is that an initialization operation declares a variable and assigns a value to it in a single step. Here's an example of an initialization statement:

```
int x = 5;
```

You cannot use an assignment operator to assign a value to a *const* data type. As you saw earlier in this chapter, you can create a *const* and assign a value to it using an initialization operation, as follows:

```
const int aConstVar = 100;
```

(continued)

Assignment and Initialization in C++. *continued*

> But you cannot create a *const* and then use an assignment operation
> to assign a value to it. The following assignment operation is not legal
> in C++:
>
> ```
> const int y;     // illegal; generates
> y = 5;           // a compiler error!
> ```
>
> It is also important to understand the difference between initializa-
> tion operations and assignment operations when you create member
> variables of C++ classes. When you declare a member variable of a
> class inside the class's declaration, you cannot assign a value to the
> member variable using an initialization operation. Instead, you must
> first instantiate an object of a class and then use an assignment opera-
> tion to assign a value to a member variable of the class. You'll learn
> how to create classes and member variables of classes in the section
> "C++ Classes" on page 65.

If the keyword *const* were not used in the preceding statements, *aConstVar*
and *aConstVar2* would be ordinary variables. But because they are declared
using the *const* keyword, they are constants and their values cannot be
changed once they have been initialized.

Other type qualifiers that did not exist in C or have been given increased
power and versatility in C++ include the following:

■ The *inline* qualifier, which makes it possible to embed short functions inside other functions instead of calling them indirectly. This
  qualifier can speed up processing at the cost of a little extra code.
  (For more details on inline functions, see the section "Inline Member Functions" on page 67.)

■ The *virtual* qualifier, which makes it possible for derived classes to
  override inherited member functions in special ways. (We'll cover
  derived classes, member functions, and the *virtual* qualifier in
  Chapter 4, "Objects and Member Functions.")

■ The *friend* qualifier, which provides classes with special kinds of
  access to member variables and member functions of other classes.
  (The *friend* qualifier is also covered in Chapter 4.)

The *const* type qualifier

In C++, the *const* qualifier lets you create type-safe constants. The *const* qualifier is also available in C, but *const*s are much more powerful in C++ than they are in C. In C, about all you can do with a *const* is initialize it and then use it in place of its value in your program. In C++, you can use *const*s in many different ways with pointers, references, and functions. You can write functions that take *const*s as arguments, write functions that return *const* values, and even declare entire C++ objects to be *const*s.

The *const* qualifier and the *#define* directive Most C programs define constant values using the *#define* preprocessor directive, as shown here:

```
#define MAX_SIZE 256
```

That's fine, but it has one potential shortcoming: the *#define* directive does not generate type-safe constants because it is just a preprocessor directive, not a compiler statement.

When you generate a constant using *#define*, your constant has no data type, so your compiler has no way to ensure that operations on the constant are carried out properly—at design time, at run time, or even during debugging. When you work with a constant created with the *#define* directive, you're strictly on your own; no type-checking is ever done for you.

In contrast, when you define a *const* in a C++ program, you execute a real compiler statement, such as this one:

```
const int MAX_SIZE = 256;
```

This statement declares an integer constant named *MAX_SIZE* and initializes it to a value of 256. Once this operation has taken place, the value of *MAX_SIZE* cannot be changed.

Notice that this statement, unlike the previous *#define* directive, does not begin with a # symbol and does end with a semicolon; those are your clues that it's a real statement executed by your application, not a preprocessor directive.

You can, however, do many things with *const*s that you cannot do with non-*const* variables. You can create *const* arrays, assign pointers to *const*s, create pointers that are *const*s, and create *const* pointers that have the same values as references. You can also write functions that take *const* arguments and return *const* values.

Creating a *const* pointer to a variable   Many of these operations can be mixed and matched. For example, the following statement creates a *const* pointer to an integer variable and assigns to the pointer the value of a reference, all in one step:

```
int *const pAnIntVar = &anIntVar;   // constant pointer,
                                    // ordinary variable
```

It's important to understand that in the preceding statement, the pointer named *pAnIntVar* is a *const*, but the variable that it points to is an ordinary variable. Consequently, the address that is stored in the *pAnIntVar* pointer cannot be changed later, but the value of the variable that *pAnIntVar* points to can be changed.

Creating a pointer to a *const* variable   When the variable that is pointed to is a *const* but the pointer is not a *const*, just the reverse happens. In this case, the value of the variable that is pointed to cannot be changed later, but the address stored in the pointer that accesses the variable can be changed, making it point to a different location, as shown here:

```
const int *pAnIntVar;    // constant variable,
                         // ordinary pointer
```

Creating a *const* pointer to a *const* variable   Finally, you can use the *const* qualifier to create a *const* pointer to a *const* integer. Then the pointer you have created can't be changed later, and neither can the variable that it points to, as shown here:

```
const int const *pAnIntVar;    // constant variable,
                               // constant pointer
```

Using the *const* qualifier in function definitions   The *const* type qualifier is often used in function definitions. For example, the following statement defines a function that returns a *const*:

```
const int TestConstFunc(int x, int y);
```

Here's the definition of another function that returns a *const* pointer to an ordinary variable:

```
int *const TestConstFunc(int x, int y);
```

And here's a function that returns an ordinary pointer to a *const* variable:

```
const int *TestConstFunc(int x, int y);
```

Last we have a function that returns a *const* pointer to a *const* variable:

```
const int const *TestConstFunc(int x, int y);
```

Passing *const* arguments to functions   You can also use *const*s as arguments in function calls. In fact, you can pass *const* arguments to functions in a number of different ways, such as in the following statement:

```
void *TestConstFunc(const int a, int *const b,
                const int *c, const int const *d);
```

C++ Classes

Once you know how a *struct* works in a C++ program, you've come a long way toward learning how classes work in C++. In essence, a C++ class is a C-style *struct* with a few simple but far-reaching enhancements. In the following paragraphs, you'll see how *struct*s have evolved into classes in C++.

Declaring Classes

In a C++ program, you declare a class in the same way that you declare a *struct*. To declare a simple class, all you do is write a *struct* definition and substitute the keyword *class* for the keyword *struct*. For example, the following code fragment is a declaration of a *struct*:

```
struct EmpInfo {
    char* m_name;
    char* m_dept;
    char* m_position;
    long m_salary;
    void PrintInfo(EmpInfo empData);
};
```

> **NOTE**   In the preceding code fragment, notice that the *EmpInfo struct* has a member function named *PrintInfo*. In C++, a *struct*—like a class—can contain member functions. But this feature of a C++ *struct* is rarely used. The general feeling among C++ programmers seems to be that if you're going to create a *struct* with member functions, you might as well go ahead and create a class because classes are more powerful than *struct*s and can make use of inheritance and other useful features that *struct*s do not have. You'll learn much more about the many features of classes in the remainder of this chapter and in Chapter 4.

By changing the keyword *struct* to the keyword *class, EmpInfo* becomes a class instead of a *struct*, as shown here:

```
class EmpInfo {
    char* m_name;
    char* m_dept;
    char* m_position;
    long m_salary;
    void PrintInfo(EmpInfo empData);
};
```

> **NOTE** The *EmpInfo* class created in the preceding example has four member variables: *m_name, m_dept, m_position,* and *m_salary.* In Visual C++, the recommended convention for writing the name of a member variable is to precede it with the letter *m* followed by an underscore. This convention helps to distinguish member variables from ordinary variables.

Declaring a class in a C++ program has the same effect as declaring a *struct*. When you declare a C++ class, no memory for the class is allocated until you create an object from a class. Creating an object from a class is called *instantiating* an object. An object created from a class is known as an *instance* of that class.

Access Specifiers

C++ uses *access specifiers* to allow a class to control access to the class's data members. Access specifiers can be used to permit access to specific members of a class while restricting access to other class members. This capability can prevent private data members from being changed inadvertently by functions that access them—a problem that is often caused by the sloppy use of global variables in C programs.

There are three access specifiers in C++: *public, protected,* and *private.* When you declare a class member to be public, it can be freely accessed inside and outside its class. Data members that are declared as protected are accessible from the class's member functions but cannot be accessed by other classes or other parts of the program. When a member of a class is declared as private, it is inaccessible not only from other classes and other parts of the program but also from derived classes. (Derived classes are described in Chapter 4, "Objects and Member Functions.")

Inline Member Functions

Some C++ functions contain only a few lines of code, and some consist of a single line of code only. For example, the following member function sets a member variable named *m_age* to the value passed to the function:

```
void Person::SetAge(int age)
{
    m_age = age;
}
```

The overhead cost of a function call must be paid each time you want to set the *m_age* member variable—quite a price for a single line of code.

To help avoid the overhead of a function call, C++ provides *inline functions,* which are similar to C macros. An inline function is like a normal function, but it is expanded in line. This decreases the execution time of a program but increases its size (due to multiple inline copies of the function). Shorter member functions can be (and often should be) declared as inline functions.

There are two methods for declaring an inline function in a C++ program. The first is to declare and define the function using an all-in-a-row syntax in the function's definition. Using this method, the previous example would look like the following:

```
void SetAge(int age) { m_age = age; }
```

Notice that an inline function definition has all the ingredients of an ordinary "out-of-line" function definition—namely, a function heading followed by a function body that is enclosed in braces, or curly brackets. The only significant difference is that in an inline function definition, all these ingredients appear on the same line.

The second method for declaring an inline function is to use the *inline* function modifier when you create the function. You'll see an example of using the *inline* function modifier in Chapter 4, "Objects and Member Functions."

Example: The EMPINFO Program

Listing 3-4 on the following page—a sample program named EMPINFO—demonstrates the three concepts we've seen in this section: classes, access specifiers, and inline functions.

EMPINFO.CPP

```cpp
#include <iostream.h>

class EmpInfo {
private:
    char* m_name;
    char* m_dept;
    char* m_position;
    long m_salary;
public:
    void PrintInfo();
    void SetName(char* name) { m_name = name; }
    void SetDept(char* dept) { m_dept = dept; }
    void SetPosition(char* psn) { m_position = psn; }
    void SetSalary(long sal) { m_salary = sal; }
    const char* GetName() { return m_name; }
    const char* GetDept() { return m_dept; }
    const char* GetPosition() { return m_position; }
    const long GetSalary() { return m_salary; }
};

void EmpInfo::PrintInfo()
{
    cout << "Name: " << m_name << '\n';
    cout << "Department: " << m_dept << '\n';
    cout << "Position: " << m_position << '\n';
    cout << "Salary: " << m_salary << '\n';
}

void main()
{
    // instantiate an object
    EmpInfo empInfo;

    // assign values to member variables
    empInfo.SetName("Zippy");
    empInfo.SetDept("Entertainment");
    empInfo.SetPosition("Actor");
    empInfo.SetSalary(35000);

    // print data
    empInfo.PrintInfo();
}
```

Listing 3-4. *Using a class in a C++ program.*

How the EMPINFO program works

The EMPINFO program shown in Listing 3-4 is divided into the following three parts:

- The first part of the program is a declaration of a class named *EmpInfo,* shown here:

```
class EmpInfo {
private:
    char* m_name;
    char* m_dept;
    char* m_position;
    long m_salary;
public:
    void PrintInfo();
    void SetName(char* name) { m_name = name; }
    void SetDept(char* dept) { m_dept = dept; }
    void SetPosition(char* psn) { m_position = psn; }
    void SetSalary(long sal) { m_salary = sal; }
    const char* GetName() { return m_name; }
    const char* GetDept() { return m_dept; }
    const char* GetPosition() { return m_position; }
    const long GetSalary() { return m_salary; }
};
```

Notice that there are eight inline functions (*SetName, SetDept, SetPosition, SetSalary, GetName, GetDept, GetPosition,* and *GetSalary*) and one normal function (*PrintInfo*).

The member variables of the *EmpInfo* class are declared as private, so member functions from another class cannot access them. The *EmpInfo* class's member functions, however, are declared as public, which means that member functions from other classes can access them.

- The second part of the program is the definition of the *PrintInfo* function, shown here:

```
void EmpInfo::PrintInfo()
{
    cout << "Name: " << m_name << '\n';
    cout << "Department: " << m_dept << '\n';
    cout << "Position: " << m_position << '\n';
    cout << "Salary: " << m_salary << '\n';
}
```

> **NOTE** Notice that the name of the *EmpInfo* class—followed by a pair of colons (::)—precedes the name of the *PrintInfo* function. In C++, a pair of colons used in this way is called a *scope resolution operator*. The scope resolution operator is a standard mechanism for defining a member function of a class. For more details, see the section "The Scope Resolution Operator" on page 79.

■ The third part of the program is the *main* function. In the *main* function, the following line of code instantiates an object of the *EmpInfo* class:

```
EmpInfo empInfo;
```

The object instantiated is named *empInfo*.

After the *empInfo* object has been instantiated, its member variables are *initialized,* or assigned their initial values, as shown below. Notice that initialization operations, not assignment operations, are used to carry out this step.

```
// assign values to member variables
empInfo.SetName("Zippy");
empInfo.SetDept("Entertainment");
empInfo.SetPosition("Actor");
empInfo.SetSalary(35000);
```

Finally, *PrintInfo* is called to print the contents of the *empInfo* object's member variables, as shown here:

```
// print data
empInfo.PrintInfo();
```

Data Encapsulation

In C++, access specifiers are the key to data encapsulation. By using access specifiers, a class can control access to member variables and member functions. When data is protected by encapsulation, functions that call other functions can access data in the functions being called—and request actions involving the data—without knowing specific details about how the data is manipulated or how the actions are performed.

When you execute the EMPINFO program, it produces the output shown in Figure 3-3.

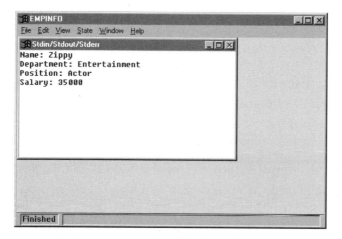

Figure 3-3. *Output of the EMPINFO program.*

Constructors and Destructors

In C++, special functions exist for instantiating and destroying objects. A function that performs any necessary initialization—for example, allocating memory for an array—when an object is instantiated is known as a *constructor*. A function that performs any housekeeping that must be done after the object is destroyed is called a *destructor*. For example, a destructor can ensure that any memory allocated to an object is deallocated. Constructors provide an easy—and safe—way to instantiate objects. Destructors provide an easy and safe way to destroy objects when they are no longer needed.

Along with their primary job of constructing objects, constructors can also perform special kinds of operations, such as converting data from one type to another and making copies of objects. Constructors are often used, for example, to make copies of strings that are implemented as objects of the Visual C++ *CString* class. (For more information about the *CString* class, see Chapter 6, "The MFC Library.")

Creating Objects Without Constructors

When you instantiate an object in C++, the compiler always calls a constructor. If you don't provide a constructor for a particular class, the compiler creates a simple constructor when you declare the object and uses the constructor to instantiate your object.

Because the compiler automatically creates a constructor when an object is declared, you can define and use a class without explicitly writing a constructor for the class.

But constructors that are created by the compiler are often too primitive to be very useful, and good C++ programmers rarely, if ever, trust the compiler to provide a constructor by default. The safest way to instantiate an object is to write an explicit constructor. That doesn't cost anything, so most experienced C++ programmers write explicit constructors for the classes they use in their programs.

A constructor is easy to recognize because it always has the same name as the class in which it is declared. In a class definition, a constructor can be declared using this format:

```
class HighClass {
public
    HighClass();
    ⋮
```

The *HighClass* constructor takes no arguments. A constructor that takes no arguments is called a *default constructor,* or a *null constructor.*

A destructor, like a constructor, has the same name as the object with which it is associated. The name of a destructor, however, is always preceded by the tilde symbol (~), as in this example:

```
~HighClass() {}
```

A destructor takes no arguments and never returns a value.

When an object that has a destructor goes out of scope or is otherwise about to be destroyed, the object's destructor is automatically invoked. You never have to make an explicit call to an object's destructor when the object is no longer needed.

NOTE You can see that no return values are specified for the *HighClass* constructor and destructor. In C++, constructors and destructors never return a value, so you are not allowed to specify a return type—not even *void*—when you define a constructor or destructor. If you try to specify a return type, the Visual C++ compiler reports an error.

Defining a constructor

Once a constructor has been declared, it must be implemented. Constructors, just as other kinds of functions, are often declared in header (.H) files and are then defined in corresponding implementation (.CPP) files. The *HighClass* constructor declared in the preceding example could be defined in the corresponding implementation file in this way:

```
HighClass::HighClass()
{
    // body of function definition
}
```

When you write a constructor that takes arguments, the constructor can use the values of those arguments for any legal purpose—for example, to perform any special kinds of assignment operations that the object being constructed might require, such as specifying the initial values of member functions of the object. Of course, code must be provided inside the constructor to make use of any arguments it requires.

Default Function Arguments

Sometimes you'll write a function that almost always uses the same value for one of its arguments. For example, a drawing program might include a tool that draws a square at specified *xy*-coordinates using a specified color. You might write a function whose declaration looks similar to this:

```
void DrawSquare(int x, int y, int color);
```

This function takes three arguments: an *x* value, a *y* value, and a color value. If you know that the color will usually be black, you might be tempted to write a second function that takes only *x* and *y* values; the function would draw a black square at the specified location. C++ provides a way to write a single function that will draw the square using black but still allow you to specify a different color as needed, as shown here:

```
void DrawSquare(int x, int y, int color = BLACK);
```

In this function, the color argument is a *default argument*. Default arguments always appear at the end of the argument list.

When a class has a member function that provides default values for its arguments, you can call the function without passing arguments to it. If you don't pass any arguments to the function, the function uses the default values provided in its argument list.

Alternatively, you can choose to pass arguments to a function that is equipped with default values for its argument list. When you pass arguments to such a function, they override the default values that are provided in the function's declaration.

Listing 3-5 demonstrates a class named *HighClass* whose constructor uses default values.

DEFAULT.CPP

```
#include <iostream.h>

class HighClass {
public:
    HighClass(char* nm = "Sharon", int x = 33)
        { m_name = nm; m_x = x; }
```

Listing 3-5. *Using constructors with default arguments.*

```
    ~HighClass() {}
    char* m_name;
    int m_x;
};

int main()
{
    HighClass myObject;
    cout << myObject.m_name << '\n';
    cout << myObject.m_x << '\n';
    return 0;
}
```

Copy Constructors

A *copy constructor*, as you might guess from its name, is a constructor specifically designed to copy objects. In C++, copy constructors provide a means of copying a complex structure such as an object in a single step.

N **OTE**   Copy constructors are not the only mechanisms for copying objects in C++. You can also copy an object by overloading the assignment operator (=). Operator overloading is described in Chapter 4, "Objects and Member Functions."

Custom copy constructors are often used in C++ because the C++ language does not provide a robust generic copy constructor that can automatically make a copy of any object. The Visual C++ compiler does have the capability of copying simple objects without requiring copy constructors, but if you need a copy constructor that will make a copy of a more complex object, you must provide your own copy constructor (or use one that has been provided in a class library).

Because the default copy constructor mechanism in C++ is so limited, it is almost never used in real-world programming. Learning to write copy constructors is really a part of learning to program in C++.

Declaring a copy constructor

A copy constructor always takes one argument—a reference to a class—and, being a constructor, never returns a value.

After you have declared a copy constructor, you can define it in the same way that you define any constructor, as in the following example:

```
YourClass::YourClass(YourClass& anObject);
{
    // body of copy constructor
}
```

After you have declared and defined a copy constructor, you can invoke it by executing statements such as the following:

```
YourClass objectA;              // define an object
YourClass objectB = objectA;    // copy objectA
```

When these two statements are executed, an object named *objectA* already exists. The first statement instantiates an object of the same class named *objectB*, and the second statement copies *objectA* to *objectB*.

Techniques for writing copy constructors

In rare situations, when you have a very simple object to copy, you can let the compiler write a *shallow* copy constructor for you. At other times, you'll need to write a *deep* copy constructor. Here are the differences:

- A shallow copy, sometimes called a *memberwise copy,* copies every data member of an object but does not copy strings or pointer data. If the object being copied contains a pointer, the pointer is copied verbatim to the destination object, but the information pointed to by the pointer is not copied. Shallow copying is not appropriate if the object being copied is any more complex than a pointerless *struct*. In most situations, you should forget about shallow copying.

- A deep copy copies the source object and all the data that is pointed to by the source object's pointers and then resets the pointers in the destination object to point to the data that has been copied. In other words, a deep copy copies everything. A deep copy is the only safe kind of copy, so in virtually every situation it is the kind of copy constructor you should use.

Example: The CPYCONST Program

The CPYCONST program shown in Listing 3-6 demonstrates how a copy constructor can be used in a C++ program. The program's *main* function instantiates an object named *myMoney* and then uses a copy constructor to make a copy of *myMoney*. The copy of *myMoney* is named *moMoney*.

CPYCONST.CPP

```cpp
#include <iostream.h>

class Money {
    int m_dinero, m_centavo;
public:
    Money() {}          // null constructor
    Money(Money&);      // copy constructor
    Money(int dol, int pen) : m_dinero(dol), m_centavo(pen) {}
    int GetDollars() { return m_dinero; }
    int GetCents() { return m_centavo; }
};

Money::Money(Money& cash)
{
    m_dinero = cash.m_dinero;
    m_centavo = cash.m_centavo;
};

int main()
{
    Money myMoney(29, 95);
    Money moMoney = myMoney;
    int d = moMoney.GetDollars();
    int c = moMoney.GetCents();
    cout << "The price is $" << d << '.' << c << ".\n";
    return 0;
}
```

Listing 3-6. *Demonstrating a copy constructor.*

Because the CPYCONST program copies an object that contains no pointers, the copy constructor the program uses is quite straightforward, as shown on the following page.

```
Money::Money(Money& cash)
{
    m_dinero = cash.m_dinero;
    m_centavo = cash.m_centavo;
};
```

When you call the preceding copy constructor, it copies the *m_dinero* and *m_centavo* member variables from the source object to the destination object. The *Money* class has only two member variables, so that completes the copying operation.

Initializer Lists

In the course of demonstrating the use of copy constructors, Listing 3-6 introduces another useful feature of C++: *initializer lists* in calls to constructors. In Listing 3-6, an initializer list appears in the following constructor definition:

```
Money(int dol, int pen) : m_dinero(dol), m_centavo(pen) {}
```

Notice that the argument list of the *Money* class's constructor is followed by a colon and then by a pair of constructs that look like calls to C functions. In this case, those constructs are not functions but serve as an initializer list for the *Money* class's constructor.

The initializer list that is supplied for the *Money* class initializes a pair of member variables named *m_dinero* and *m_centavo*. The operation of the initializer list is quite straightforward: when the constructor is called, the *m_dinero* member variable is initialized to the value of the *dol* argument that is passed to the constructor, and the *m_centavo* member variable is initialized to the value of the constructor's *pen* argument. Thus, the constructor works exactly as if it were defined this way:

```
Money::Money(int dol, int pen) {
    m_dinero = dol;
    m_centavo = pen;
}
```

As you can see, initializer lists are optional. Many C++ programmers like them because they take up a little less space than conventional member-variable initializations and because they keep the initialization of member functions separate from the rest of the code in a constructor.

The Scope Resolution Operator

C++ provides the scope resolution operator (::) as another way to access member functions and member variables of a class. When a scope resolution operator appears between the name of a class and the name of a function in a C++ program, as in the following example, it means that the specified function is a member of the specified class:

```
EmpInfo::PrintInfo();
```

In C++, the scope resolution operator is always used in the headings of member functions that are not declared in line. (Inline member functions are described in the section "Inline Member Functions" on page 67.) The scope resolution operator is also often used to call functions that are outside the scope of the calling function. For example, to call a member function named *CStructView::OnDraw* from a function that is defined outside the definition of the *CStructView* class, you could execute this kind of statement:

```
CStructView::OnDraw();
```

There are some important differences between the way the scope resolution operator works and the way the arrow and dot operators work in C++ programs. The main difference is that the scope resolution operator is used to access members of classes, and the dot operator and the arrow operator are used to access members of specific objects.

Using the scope resolution operator inside functions

You can also use the scope resolution operator inside function definitions in C++ programs. In the following example, the scope resolution operator is used in two different ways inside a function definition (as well as being used in the function definition's heading):

```
void CMyView::ShowInfo()
{
    ::MessageBox("We are inside the ShowInfo function.");
    EmpInfo::PrintInfo();
}
```

The scope resolution operator appears by itself in front of a call to a function named *MessageBox* and also appears in a call to the *EmpInfo::PrintInfo* member function.

In the first statement, shown here, there is no class name in front of the scope resolution operator:

```
::MessageBox("We are inside the ShowInfo function.");
```

That means that the function being called—*MessageBox*—is not a member of any class. (In this case, *MessageBox* is a function provided by the Windows API. When you call the function, it displays a modal dialog box containing the message you have specified. When the user clicks the OK button, the message box closes.)

There are two reasons for using a scope resolution operator. One reason is to distinguish the function that is being called from some other function that has the same name but is in a different scope. To illustrate a case such as this, look again at the call to the *MessageBox* function, shown here:

```
void CMyView::ShowInfo()
{
    ::MessageBox("We are inside the ShowInfo function.");
    EmpInfo::PrintInfo();
}
```

Suppose that when you execute the *MessageBox* call, you know that the *CMyView* class has a member function named *ShowInfo::MessageBox*. In C++, when a function that is in scope and a function that is out of scope have the same name and the same argument list, the version of the function that is in scope is usually called. In this kind of situation, you can use the *::MessageBox* construct to override this default scoping behavior and call the Windows API version of the *MessageBox* function. If you don't use the *::MessageBox* construct, the *ShowInfo::MessageBox* function is the function that is called.

The second reason for using the scope resolution operator is to let readers of your code know that the function you are calling is not a member function of the class from which the call is made. Using the scope resolution operator in this kind of situation is not mandatory, but it can help other readers of your code understand what's going on when you're using a class that has a lot of member functions.

The *this* Pointer

One word you often see in C++ programs is "this." That's because every object in a C++ program is equipped with a pointer to itself named *this*. Whenever a program calls a nonstatic member function (most member functions are nonstatic; static member functions are described in Chapter 4, "Objects and Member Functions"), the *this* pointer is passed to the member function that is called. The member function can then use the *this* pointer to access other members of the object's class.

In C++ programs, member functions often use the *this* pointer as an argument when they call other functions. The called function can then use the *this* pointer to access the calling function's object.

The sample program in Listing 3-7 shows how the *this* pointer works.

```
THIS.CPP

#include <iostream.h>

class YourClass {
public:
    YourClass() {}          // default constructor
    ~YourClass() {}         // destructor
    void* IAm() { return this; }
};

int main()
{
    void* pClass;
    YourClass anObject;
    pClass = anObject.IAm();
    cout << "pClass's pointer is "
         << pClass << '\n.';
    return 0;
}
```

Listing 3-7. *Using the* this *pointer.*

In this example, the class named *YourClass* has a member function named *IAm* that returns the *this* pointer of a *YourClass* object, as shown here:

```
void* IAm { return this; }
```

When you execute the program, its *main* function instantiates a *YourClass* object and then calls the *IAm* member function. The program then stores the *this* pointer returned by *IAm* in a pointer variable named *pClass*, as shown here:

```
pClass = anObject.IAm();
```

When the *YourClass* object's *this* pointer has been stowed away for safe-keeping, the *main* function prints out the pointer it has stored in the *pClass* variable. The output of the program looks something like the following. (Of course, the actual address printed out varies.)

```
pClass's pointer is 0x603f223011786
```

What's Next?

This chapter is the first of two chapters that focus on C++ classes, objects, and member functions. The chapter introduces C++-style *struct*s and C++ classes and objects.

Other topics covered in this chapter included various type specifiers and qualifiers, the *this* pointer, access specifiers, and constructors and destructors.

In Chapter 4, "Objects and Member Functions," you'll explore the topics introduced in this chapter in more detail, and you'll also be introduced to other features of C++ and principles of C++ object-oriented programming. By the time you finish Chapter 3 and 4, you'll have all the background in C++ that you need to start writing object-oriented programs using the Visual C++ development environment.

Objects and Member Functions

You are now halfway through a crash course on the fundamental features of generic C++ and the basic principles of object-oriented programming. In Chapter 3, "C++ Basics," you learned how the C++ class evolved from the humble C-language *struct* and how you can use classes and other kinds of C++ constructs in your Visual C++ programs. In this chapter, you'll see in more detail how objects are instantiated from C++ classes and how objects and member functions are used in Visual C++ applications. This chapter takes you deeper into the territory of object-oriented programming by fleshing out some of the topics introduced in Chapter 3 and by providing the rest of the background you'll need to start using classes, objects, and member functions in your Visual C++ programs.

This chapter covers the following major topics:

- Derived classes, class hierarchies, and inheritance—the corner-stones of C++ object-oriented programming

- Polymorphism and virtual member functions, which let you specify the version of a member function that is executed by a derived class

- Function overloading and operator overloading—mechanisms that make C++ more versatile

- Static member variables—a C++ feature similar to global variables

- Mechanisms known as friend classes and friend functions, which are used for sharing protected data

- The *new* and *delete* operators—the C++ operators for allocating memory

Class Hierarchies and Inheritance

In Chapter 3, "C++ Basics," you saw how member functions and member variables can be declared inside C++ classes. You also saw how the *private*, *protected*, and *public* access specifiers can control access to member variables and member functions.

In this chapter, you'll learn how classes can be derived from other classes and how base classes and derived classes can be organized into architectures known as *class hierarchies*. When you derive a class from another class in a C++ program, the derived class inherits member variables and member functions from its *base class*—also referred to as its *parent class*—and can add member variables and member functions of its own.

By arranging base classes and derived classes into class hierarchies, you can simplify software development by developing code that can be transported easily from application to application. This capability is the key to code reusability in C++ programs.

Understanding Class Hierarchies

When a class is derived from a base class, the derived class inherits all the member variables and member functions of its base class. Member variables and member functions declared as private in the base class are not accessible to derived classes, however.

When a class is derived from a base class, more classes can be derived from the derived class. In this way, a derived class can also become a base class. Multiple levels of classes that are derived from each other form a class hierarchy. Each class in the hierarchy inherits the member variables and member functions of its respective base class.

How Derived Classes Work

Figure 4-1 illustrates the way a derived class works in a C++ program. The diagram shows how a derived class inherits the member functions and member variables of its base class. The derived class also adds member variables and member functions of its own.

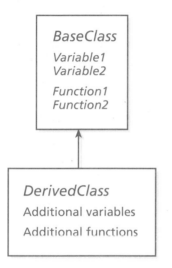

Figure 4-1. *How derived classes and base classes are related in a C++ program.*

Why Use Derived Classes?

In C++, class derivation and class hierarchies are used for a number of reasons, including the following:

- **A base class can inherit some behaviors and originate others—** When you use a base class to derive a new class, the new class is a new data type that inherits all the qualities of the base class without disturbing the relationships the base class might have with other parts of the program. If you are already using the base class in your program, its behavior remains intact for objects that use it, but for objects that require different behaviors, the member functions of the derived class can be used to modify the behavior of the base class without altering the base class's code.

- **Hold the source code—**You don't need access to the source code for the base class when you want to derive a class from a base class. If you have access to a header (.H) file that defines a base class, you have all you need to derive classes from that base class. That means you don't have to share your source code with developers who use it; just supply them with your header files, and they can derive their own classes.

■ **You can manage hierarchy behavior by using abstract classes**— Abstract classes are general-purpose classes that do nothing by themselves but are specifically designed to be used as base classes. The only purpose of an abstract class is to serve as a base for derived classes. Derived classes can then add the implementation details. For example, you could define an abstract class to manage objects in a list. Then you could provide it with member functions that insert, change, delete, reorder, and search for entries in the list without having to know any details about objects in the list.

■ **You can get the benefits of polymorphism**—When you set up a class hierarchy on a foundation of base classes and derived classes, you can make use of other properties of the object-oriented languages, such as *polymorphism*. Polymorphism lets descendants of a class override a member function of that class with member functions that have the same name but different effects.

As you move through the material in this chapter, you'll learn more about all these reasons for using derived classes.

Example: Deriving a Class

Listing 4-1, a program named HIERARCH, shows how a class can be derived from a base class in a C++ program and demonstrates a simple class hierarchy. The HIERARCH program is adapted from the EMPINFO program presented in Listing 3-4 on page 68 in Chapter 3. It shows how the EMPINFO program could be redesigned if the company using the program opened branch offices abroad and hired employees in more than one country.

To meet the needs of an international company, the designers of the HIERARCH program have derived a new class, named *OffshoreEmpInfo*, from the *EmpInfo* class that was used in the EMPINFO program.

HIERARCH.CPP

```cpp
#include <iostream.h>

// base class
class EmpInfo {
public:
    // constructor and destructor
    EmpInfo() {}
    ~EmpInfo() {}
private:
    char* m_name;
    char* m_dept;
    char* m_position;
    long m_salary;
public:
    void SetName(char* name) { m_name = name; }
    void SetDept(char* dept) { m_dept = dept; }
    void SetPosition(char* position)
        { m_position = position; }
    void SetSalary(long salary)
        { m_salary = salary; }
    void PrintInfo();
};

// derived class
class OffshoreEmpInfo : public EmpInfo {
public:
    // constructor and destructor
    OffshoreEmpInfo() {}
    ~OffshoreEmpInfo() {}
private:
    char* m_country;
public:
    void SetCountry(char* country)
        { m_country = country; }
    void PrintInfo();
};

void EmpInfo::PrintInfo()
{
    cout << "Name: " << m_name << "\n";
    cout << "Department: " << m_dept << "\n";
    cout << "Position: " << m_position << "\n";
    cout << "Salary: " << m_salary << "\n";
}
```

Listing 4-1. *Demonstrating a derived class.*   *(continued)*

Listing 4-1. *continued*

```
void OffshoreEmpInfo::PrintInfo()
{
    EmpInfo::PrintInfo();
    cout << "Country: " << m_country << "\n";
}

int main()
{
    // class object instance declaration
    OffshoreEmpInfo empInfo;

    // populate the EmpInfo class with data
    empInfo.SetName("Daisyduck Feliciano");
    empInfo.SetDept("Entertainment");
    empInfo.SetPosition("Vocalist");
    empInfo.SetSalary(24000);
    empInfo.SetCountry("Bulgaria");
    empInfo.PrintInfo();
    return 0;
}
```

When you execute the HIERARCH program, it displays the output shown in Figure 4-2.

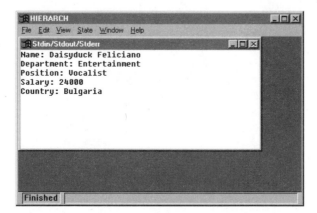

Figure 4-2. *The output of the HIERARCH program.*

Rules of Inheritance in C++

Because the *OffshoreEmpInfo* class is derived from the *EmpInfo* class, it inherits all the public member functions that are declared inside the definition of the *EmpInfo* class. The *OffshoreEmpInfo* class adds one new member function and two new member variables that are not members of its base class, as shown here:

```
private:
    char* m_country;
public:
    void SetCountry(char* country)
        { m_country = country; }
    void PrintInfo();
```

Along with these new members, the *OffshoreEmpInfo* class can use all of its inherited member functions in the same way that its base class uses them.

In Figure 4-1 on page 85, notice that the arrow connecting the derived class to the base class points upward—not downward as you might expect. This convention is used in C++ class diagrams because members of base classes are visible to derived classes, but members of derived classes are not visible to their base classes.

Declaring a Derived Class

Here is the declaration of the *OffshoreEmpInfo* class:

```
// Derived class
class OffshoreEmpInfo : public EmpInfo {
public:
    // constructor and destructor
    OffshoreEmpInfo() {}
    ~OffshoreEmpInfo() {}
private:
    char* m_country;
public:
    void SetCountry(char* country)
        { m_country = country; }
    void PrintInfo();
};
```

Notice that the heading of a derived-class declaration contains the names of both the derived class and the derived class's base class. The name of the derived class is separated from the name of the base class by two elements: a colon and an access specifier.

Only two access specifiers—*public* and *private*—can be used in the header of a derived-class declaration. The *private* access specifier is used rarely because derived classes are almost always publicly derived from their base classes in C++ programs. You can hide a derived class from the rest of a program by declaring it as private, but there is usually no reason to do this.

Constructing Derived Classes

When you instantiate an object of a derived class, the compiler executes the constructor of the object's base class before it executes the constructor of the derived class. This is not important in the HIERARCH program because both the *EmpInfo* base class and the *OffshoreEmpInfo* derived class have default null constructors. But if a base class has a constructor that requires arguments, they can be provided by a constructor of a derived class.

To illustrate, suppose that a base class has a constructor such as this:

```
BaseClass(char* nm, int x);
```

Then suppose that a class derived from *BaseClass* has a constructor something like this:

```
DerivedClass(char* nm, int x) : BaseClass(nm, x)
    { m_name = nm; m_x = x; }
```

In this kind of situation, you can provide the arguments for *BaseClass* at the same time that you create an object of *DerivedClass*. To do that, invoke the *DerivedClass* constructor using the following statement:

```
DerivedClass myObject("Mikey", 6);
```

When you invoke the *DerivedClass* constructor using this sort of statement, the *DerivedClass* constructor automatically calls the *BaseClass* constructor. The result is that the *m_name* and *m_x* member functions of the object you have instantiated are initialized to the values "Mikey" and 6.

Listing 4-2 shows how this kind of operation can work in a C++ program.

```
CONSTRCT.CPP

#include <iostream.h>

class BaseClass {
public:
    BaseClass(char* nm, int x)
        { m_name = nm; m_x = x; }
    ~BaseClass() {}
```

Listing 4-2. *Constructing a derived class.*

```
    char* m_name;
    int m_x;
};

class DerivedClass : public BaseClass {
public:
    DerivedClass(char* nm, int x) : BaseClass(nm, x)
        { m_name = nm; m_x = x; }
    ~DerivedClass() {}
    char* m_name;
    int m_x;
};

int main()
{
    DerivedClass myObject("Jackie", 24);
    cout << myObject.m_name << "\n";
    cout << myObject.m_x << "\n";
    return 0;
}
```

Overriding Member Functions

Derived classes can replace, or *override,* member functions they inherit from their base classes. Listing 4-3, a sample program named OVERRIDE, shows how base-class member functions can be overridden.

OVERRIDE.CPP

```
#include <iostream.h>

// base class
class EmpInfo {
public:
    // constructor and destructor
    EmpInfo() {}
    ~EmpInfo() {}
private:
    char* m_name;
    char* m_dept;
    char* m_position;
    long m_salary;
```

Listing 4-3. *Overriding base-class member functions.*   *(continued)*

Listing 4-3. *continued*

```
public:
    void SetName(char* name) { m_name = name; }
    void SetDept(char* dept) { m_dept = dept; }
    void SetPosition(char* position)
        { m_position = position; }
    void SetSalary(long salary)
        { m_salary = salary; }
    virtual void PrintInfo();
};

// Derived class
class OffshoreEmpInfo : public EmpInfo
{
public:
    // constructor and destructor
    OffshoreEmpInfo() {}
    ~OffshoreEmpInfo() {}
private:
    char* m_country;
public:
    void SetCountry(char* country)
        { m_country = country; }
    void PrintInfo();
};

void EmpInfo::PrintInfo()
{
    cout << "\nName: " << m_name << "\n";
    cout << "Department: " << m_dept << "\n";
    cout << "Position: " << m_position << "\n";
    cout << "Salary: " << m_salary << "\n";
}

void OffshoreEmpInfo::PrintInfo()
{
    EmpInfo::PrintInfo();
    cout << "Country: " << m_country << "\n";
}

int main()
{
    // Class object declarations
    EmpInfo* empInfo1 = new EmpInfo;
    OffshoreEmpInfo* empInfo2 = new OffshoreEmpInfo;
    OffshoreEmpInfo* empInfo3 = new OffshoreEmpInfo;
```

```
        // populate the EmpInfo classes with data
        empInfo1->SetName("Zippy");
        empInfo1->SctDcpt("Entertainment");
        empInfo1->SetPosition("Actor");
        empInfo1->SetSalary(34000);
        empInfo1->PrintInfo();

        empInfo2->SetName("Daisyduck Feliciano");
        empInfo2->SetDept("Entertainment");
        empInfo2->SetPosition("Vocalist");
        empInfo2->SetSalary(24000);
        empInfo2->SetCountry("Bulgaria");
        empInfo2->PrintInfo();

        empInfo3->SetName("Wolfgang Amadeus Mozart");
        empInfo3->SetDept("Transportation");
        empInfo3->SetPosition("Piano Mover");
        empInfo3->SetSalary(17000);
        empInfo3->SetCountry("Austria");
        empInfo3->PrintInfo();

        return 0;
}
```

Figure 4-3 shows the output of the OVERRIDE program.

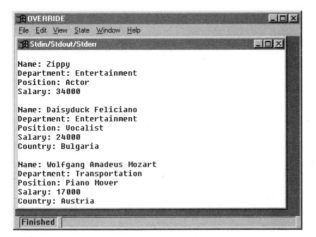

Figure 4-3. *Output of the OVERRIDE program.*

The OVERRIDE program implements a base class named *EmpInfo* and a derived class named *OffshoreEmpInfo*. The program's *main* function instantiates one object of the *EmpInfo* class and two objects of the *OffshoreEmpInfo* class. Then the program assigns data to the objects that have been instantiated.

After each of the three objects has been created, a function named *PrintInfo* is called to print the data stored in the object. It's important to note, however, that the program defines two different *PrintInfo* member functions. One version is used to print the data stored in the base-class object, and a different version is used to print data stored in objects of the derived class.

Here is the definition of the *EmpInfo::PrintInfo* member function that is used to print data stored in the *EmpInfo* class:

```
void EmpInfo::PrintInfo()
{
    cout << "\nName: " << m_name << "\n";
    cout << "Department: " << m_dept << "\n";
    cout << "Position: " << m_position << "\n";
    cout << "Salary: " << m_salary << "\n";
}
```

The other version of the *PrintInfo* member function is named *OffshoreEmpInfo::PrintInfo*. It overrides the base-class version of the *PrintInfo* member function and prints data stored in the derived *OffshoreEmpInfo* class. Here is its definition:

```
void OffshoreEmpInfo::PrintInfo()
{
    EmpInfo::PrintInfo();
    cout << "Country: " << m_country << "\n";
}
```

In the *OffshoreEmpInfo::PrintInfo* function, the *OffshoreEmpInfo* class uses the scope resolution operator (::) to call its base class's *PrintInfo* member function. The *EmpInfo::PrintInfo* member function prints four lines of text—the name, the department, the position, and the salary—and then the *OffshoreEmpInfo::PrintInfo* member function prints one more line, the country.

> ### Switch Statements and Overridden Member Functions
>
> One way to determine whether you are making enough use of overridden member functions is to consider how often you find yourself writing switch statements—and how long and complex they are. If you find that you're writing a lot of long switch statements, you might find that you can implement the same functionality by replacing your switch statements with sets of derived classes that have overridden member functions.
>
> This technique might require an overhaul in some of your programming techniques, but it will be worth it in the long run. You'll quickly see how much sense it makes to use overridden member functions instead of monster switch statements in your C++ programs.

Polymorphism and Virtual Member Functions

A key concept in the world of object-oriented programming is *polymorphism*. Polymorphism is a way to give a name to an action that is performed by similar objects, with each object implementing the action in a manner appropriate to the object.

The key to polymorphism in C++ is a type of function known as a *virtual function*. A virtual function is the mechanism by which derived classes override member functions of base classes. To create a virtual function in a C++ program—and thereby implement polymorphism—you declare the function using the keyword *virtual*, as in the following statement:

```
virtual void Display();
```

Example: Using a Virtual Function

Listing 4-4 on the following page, the VIRTUAL program, demonstrates the use of a virtual member function. The VIRTUAL program declares a base class named *BaseClass* and a derived class named *DerivedClass*, each of which defines a separate version of a member function named *Display*. The *BaseClass::Display* function is a virtual member function, and *DerivedClass::Display* is a function that overrides *BaseClass::Display*.

VIRTUAL.CPP

```cpp
#include <iostream.h>

class BaseClass
{
// base-class members
public:
    virtual void Display() { cout << 100 << "\n"; }
};

class DerivedClass : public BaseClass
{
// derived-class members
public:
    void Display() { cout << 200 << "\n"; }
};

void Print(BaseClass* bc)
{
    bc->Display();
}

int main()
{
    BaseClass* pMyBaseClass = new BaseClass;
    DerivedClass* pMyDerivedClass = new DerivedClass;

    Print(pMyBaseClass);
    Print(pMyDerivedClass);

    return 0;
}
```

Listing 4-4. *Using virtual functions.*

The VIRTUAL program displays the output shown in Figure 4-4.

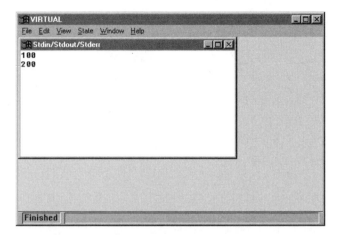

Figure 4-4. *Executing a virtual member function.*

How the VIRTUAL Program Works

In the VIRTUAL program, the virtual member function *Display* is defined as follows in the declaration of *BaseClass*:

```
virtual void Display() { cout << 100 << "\n"; }
```

This function is overridden inside the declaration of *DerivedClass*, as follows:

```
void Display() { cout << 200 << "\n"; }
```

As you can see, the virtual version of the *Display* member function displays the value 100. The version of the function that is overridden in the *DerivedClass* declaration displays the value 200.

Calling the *Print* function

In the VIRTUAL program's *main* function, one base-class object and one derived-class object are instantiated. The *main* function then calls the *Print* function, as shown on the following page.

```
int main()
{
    BaseClass* pMyBaseClass = new BaseClass;
    DerivedClass* pMyDerivedClass = new DerivedClass;

    Print(pMyBaseClass);
    Print(pMyDerivedClass);

    return 0;
}
```

In turn, the *Print* function calls the *BaseClass::Display* member function and the *DerivedClass::Display* member function. Be sure to notice, however, that the *Print* function does not call these two functions using two different pointers. Instead, it uses the same pointer—specifically, the pointer named *bc*—which, as you can see by examining the *Print* function's heading below, is a pointer to a *BaseClass*!

```
void Print(BaseClass* bc)
{
    bc->Display();
}
```

Virtual Functions and Nonvirtual Functions

When a derived class overrides a base-class member function that is not declared as virtual and then calls the function using a pointer to the base class, the results are quite different. If *Display* were not declared as virtual in the previous example, the program would execute the base-class version of the function twice.

What happens when a derived-class object calls a base-class virtual member function and the derived class calling the function does not have a customized version of the function? Nothing much, really. The compiler simply executes the base class's version of the function, behaving the same way it would if the function were not virtual.

Benefits of Using Virtual Functions

If a member function of a base class is declared as virtual, you can derive other classes from that class that include a member function with the same name. When the function is called at run time, the derived class's version of the function is the one that is executed.

The benefit of virtual functions is that objects that share a common base class can be used in a uniform manner. For example, you might define a base class named *Shape* with a virtual *Draw* member function and then derive a *Circle* class and a *Square* class from *Shape* that contain their own *Draw* member functions. Every object instantiated from these classes can call the *Draw* member function; the compiler ensures that the correct *Draw* function is called.

V-Tables

Until object-oriented languages came along, programs called functions in a straightforward way. When a procedural program called a function, the compiler knew exactly which function was being called and exactly where in memory the function resided. Therefore, when an application called a function, the call to the function was simply built into the program when the program was compiled. This technique is known as *early binding*, or *static binding*.

When a C++ program calls a nonvirtual function, the function is called using static binding, in the same way that it would be called in a C program. However, when a C++ program calls a virtual function through a pointer to a class, the compiler calls the function using a technique known as *late binding*, or *dynamic binding*.

C++ implements dynamic binding using *virtual function tables*, or *v-tables*. A v-table is an array of function pointers that the compiler constructs for every class that uses virtual functions. For example, in the VIRTUAL program that appears in Listing 4-4 on page 96, the *Display* function is defined as a virtual function, so the compiler creates separate v-tables for two different versions of the *Display* function: one for *BaseClass* and one for *DerivedClass*.

Here's how v-tables work: When a C++ program is compiled, the compiler creates all the v-tables that the program uses and stores them in a memory location that is accessible to all the objects in the program. When the program creates a class that accesses a virtual function in a base class, the code for each instance of the class contains a hidden pointer to the v-table used by the base class.

When an object instantiated from a derived class calls a virtual function declared in a base class through a pointer to a v-table used by the base class—that is, when the object calls a base-class virtual function using dynamic binding—the compiler doesn't know at link time which object will be calling the virtual function. That means that the compiler doesn't know at link time which version of the virtual function will be called when the program is executed because the program doesn't call the function through a pointer to a specific derived class, but rather through a pointer to a base class that can (and usually does) have multiple derived classes.

In C++, v-tables are the mechanisms that resolve this ambiguity. The reason v-tables work is that they are not built at link time by the compiler. Instead, they are built at run time by the application in which they appear. That means that an application using v-tables can resolve references that make use of each v-table on the spot, when the program is executed.

Because the compiler doesn't know which version of the function will be accessed when the program is linked, the program itself must evaluate each calling statement at run time, when it can determine which version of the function to call. So, when a program uses dynamic binding to call a function through a pointer supplied by a v-table, the calling statement is evaluated at run time, and the correct version of the virtual function is called.

Figure 4-5 shows how a v-table works in C++. Suppose that while a program is running, it encounters a reference to a virtual function. When the reference is encountered, the object on the left is in scope, and the object's v-table pointer contains the address of an entry in the object's v-table.

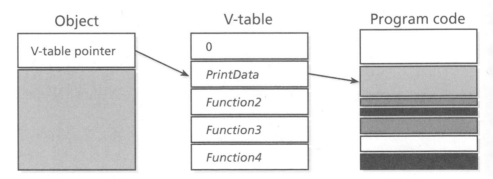

Figure 4-5. *How a v-table works.*

Now assume that when a reference to a virtual function is encountered, the object's v-table pointer points to the second entry in the object's v-table. In Figure 4-5, the second entry in the object's v-table is the *PrintData* function. The *PrintData* function, which resides in the code segment of the program, is the function that's called. Because the call to a virtual function is indirect—through a pointer to an object—the code for the implementation of a virtual function does not have to be in the same code segment as the caller of the virtual function.

A v-table that is set up for a class contains one function pointer for each virtual function in the class. Listing 4-5 demonstrates how v-tables are used in applications that make use of virtual functions.

EMPDATA.CPP

```
#include <stdio.h>
#include <iostream.h>

// base class
class Employee {
public:
    // constructors and destructors
    Employee() {}
    ~Employee() {}
    virtual void PrintData() = 0;
    void SetName(char* name) { m_name = name; }
    void SetDept(char* dept) { m_dept = dept; }
    void SetPosition(char* position)
        { m_position = position; }
    void SetSalary(long salary)
        { m_salary = salary; }

protected:
    char* m_name;
    char* m_dept;
    char* m_position;
    long m_salary;
};
```

Listing 4-5. *Using virtual functions.* *(continued)*

Listing 4-5. *continued*

```cpp
class ExemptEmp : public Employee {
// class description
public:
    // constructor and destructor
    ExemptEmp(char* name, char* dept, char* position,
        long salary);
    ~ExemptEmp() {}
    void PrintData();
};

class SalesEmp : public Employee {
// class description
public:
    // constructor and destructor
    SalesEmp(char* name, char* dept, char* position,
        long salary, long sales, float commissionPercent);
    ~SalesEmp() {}
    void PrintData();

private:
    char* m_country;
    long m_sales;
    long m_commission;
    float m_commissionPercent;
    long m_totalPay;
};

class OffshoreEmp : public Employee {
// class description
private:
    char* m_country;
public:
    // constructor and destructor
    OffshoreEmp(char* m_name, char* m_country, char* m_dept,
        char* m_postion, long m_salary);
    ~OffshoreEmp() {}
    void PrintData();
};

ExemptEmp::ExemptEmp(char* name, char* dept, char* position,
    long salary)
{
    m_name = name;
    m_dept = dept;
    m_position = position;
    m_salary = salary;
}
```

```
OffshoreEmp::OffshoreEmp(char* name, char* country, char* dept,
    char* position, long salary)
{
    m_name = name;
    m_country = country;
    m_dept = dept;
    m_position = position;
    m_salary = salary;
}

SalesEmp::SalesEmp(char* name, char* dept, char* position,
    long salary, long sales, float commissionPercent)
{
    m_name = name;
    m_dept = dept;
    m_position = position;
    m_salary = salary;
    m_sales = sales;
    m_commissionPercent = commissionPercent;
    m_commission = (long)(m_sales* commissionPercent);
    m_totalPay = m_salary + m_commission;
}

void ExemptEmp::PrintData()
{
        cout << "\nName:  " << m_name;
        cout << "\nDepartment: " << m_dept;
        cout << "\nPosition: " << m_position;
        cout << "\nSalary: " << m_salary << "\n";
}

void OffshoreEmp::PrintData()
{
        cout << "\nName:  " << m_name;
        cout << "\nDepartment: " << m_dept;
        cout << "\nPosition: " << m_position;
        cout << "\nSalary: " << m_salary;
        cout << "\nCountry:  " << m_country << "\n";
}

void SalesEmp::PrintData()
{
        cout << "\nName:  " << m_name;
        cout << "\nDepartment: " << m_dept;
        cout << "\nPosition: " << m_position;
        cout << "\nSalary: " << m_salary;
```

(continued)

Listing 4-5. *continued*

```
            cout << "\nSales:   " << m_sales;
            cout << "\nCommission Level: " << m_commissionPercent;
            cout << "\nCommission:  " << m_commission;
            cout << "\nTotal Pay:  " << m_totalPay;
}


int main()
{
    Employee* emp[3];

    emp[0] = new ExemptEmp("Abraham Abernathy", "Coffee Shop",
        "CEO", 22000);
    emp[1] = new OffshoreEmp("Wolfgang Amadeus Mozart",
        "Transportation", "Piano Mover", 24000, "Austria");
    emp[2] = new SalesEmp("Babette Baker", "Sales",
        "Salesperson", 17000, 2200, .15);
    for (int c = 0; c < 3; c++)
        emp[c]->PrintData();
    for (c = 0; c < 3; c++)
        delete emp[c];

    return 0;
}
```

In Listing 4-5, the *ExemptEmp* class, the *SalesEmp* class, and the *Offshore-Emp* class have separate v-tables for the *PrintData* function. When the program calls the *PrintData* function, the pointer to the function points to the version of the function appropriate for the class that is currently in scope. Thus, the correct function is called.

Pure Virtual Functions and Abstract Classes

A member function that not only *can* be overridden but *must* be overridden is called a *pure virtual function*. When a class contains at least one pure virtual function, the class is known as an *abstract class*. An abstract class is a class from which objects cannot be created.

To turn a virtual member function into a pure virtual member function, all you have to do is assign the function a value of 0 (effectively, a NULL pointer). For example, in the EMPDATA program shown in Listing 4-5, the *Employee::PrintData* function is a pure virtual function, as you can see in this statement from the definition of the *Employee* class:

```
virtual void PrintData() = 0;
```

In C++, a statement such as this is all it takes to create an abstract class. You can declare an entire class as an abstract class simply by placing one pure virtual member function declaration inside the class's definition.

How Abstract Classes Are Used in the EMPDATA Program

In the EMPDATA program, the *Employee* class is an abstract class in which the pure virtual function *PrintData* is declared.

Notice that there are no *Employee* objects in the program; you couldn't create any if you wanted to because, as mentioned previously, you can't create objects from an abstract class. But *ExemptEmp*, *OffshoreEmp*, and *SalesEmp* are all derived from the *Employee* class. That's allowed—in fact, that's what abstract classes are there for. The only purpose of an abstract class is to serve as a base class for derived classes.

Similarly, the only purpose of a pure virtual function is to serve as a root function for other functions. You cannot instantiate an object that belongs to an abstract class, and you cannot directly call a pure virtual function; you can, however, call an overridden version of a pure virtual function.

The main characteristic of a pure virtual member function is that it must be overridden by classes derived from the class to which the function belongs. In the EMPDATA program, the *PrintData* function is overridden by three derived classes: *ExemptEmp*, *OffshoreEmp*, and *SalesEmp*.

Virtual Functions: Pros and Cons

Although dynamic binding is a powerful feature of C++, not all functions in a program should be virtual functions. Because virtual functions are called indirectly, they do add some overhead (although not much) to an application and, therefore, slow down the program's execution speed slightly. So, when you design a class, you really should use the *virtual* keyword only for functions that you expect to be overridden.

If you make a function virtual and discover later that there is little chance of it being overridden, you can remove the *virtual* keyword from the declaration of the function and save a little overhead. But nothing terrible will happen if you fail to notice that the function isn't overridden and forget to remove its *virtual* designation.

Function Overloading and Operator Overloading

If you've ever worked as a mechanic or an electrical engineer, "overload" is probably not a happy-sounding word. In C++, however, overloading is the name of a very useful mechanism. C++ uses two kinds of overloading: *function overloading* and *operator overloading*. Both of these are major—and beneficial—features of the C++ language.

Function Overloading

When you develop applications in C++, using function overloading can add great flexibility to your applications. To implement function overloading, you write two or more functions that share the same name but have different argument lists. When a function is overloaded, the compiler decides which version to call by using *argument matching*—that is, by comparing the numbers and types of the arguments that are passed to the function with the numbers and types of the arguments in the argument list of the functions.

When you implement function overloading, you can execute whichever version of the function you want by calling the function using the appropriate set of arguments. If the class you are using has two member functions with the same name but with different argument lists, you can rest assured that the function you want will be called.

By using function overloading, you can give the same name to member functions that perform different, but similar, operations. You can even give the same name to entire groups of functions. For example, suppose you want to write two different functions to display a window—one function requiring a size provided as an argument, and another requiring no argument but using a default size. You could write a pair of overloaded member functions in this fashion:

```
void DisplayWindow();
void DisplayWindow(CRect winRect);
```

After you create these overloaded member functions, you could call either one. This statement would call the first *DisplayWindow* function:

```
DisplayWindow();
```

The following statements would call the second *DisplayWindow* function:

```
CRECT winRect(10, 10, 50, 200);
DisplayWindow(winRect);
```

Function overloading is often used in C++ because it imposes almost no run-time penalty and requires practically no overhead.

Listing 4-6 demonstrates how you can use function overloading in a C++ program.

MEMOVER.CPP

```
#include <iostream.h>

void PrintMsg(char* name, char* weapon, int ability)
{
    cout << name << "\n";
    cout << weapon << "\n";
    cout << ability << "\n\n";
}

void PrintMsg(int n)
{
    cout << n << "\n\n";
}

void PrintMsg(char* message)
{
    cout << message << "\n\n";
}

int main()
{
    // calling overloaded functions
    PrintMsg("ghosts", "goblins", 6);
    PrintMsg(5000);
    PrintMsg("How are you today?\n");

    return 0;
}
```

Listing 4-6. *Using member function overloading.*

Listing 4-6 contains three overloaded versions of a member function named *PrintMsg*. The first version takes three arguments of varying types, the second takes one integer argument, and the third takes one string argument.

Each of these member functions performs a similar task; each displays a message on the screen. But in C++, because of function overloading, each *PrintMsg* member function is recognized as a different function. When you run the MEMOVER program, it displays the output shown in Figure 4-6.

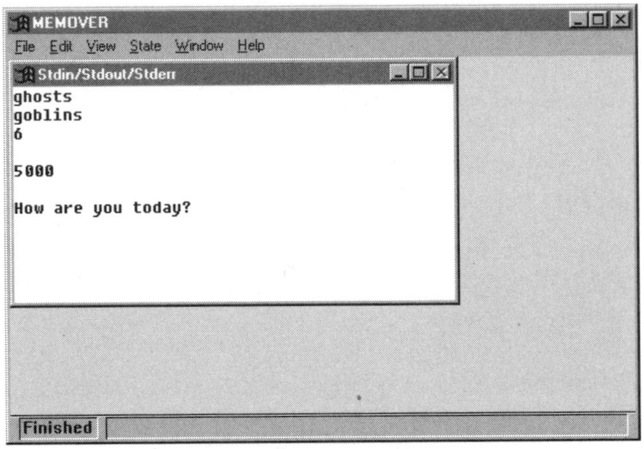

Figure 4-6. *Output of the MEMOVER program.*

Constructor overloading

In C++, you can overload constructors as well as ordinary member functions. In fact, constructor overloading is used extensively in C++. It's very common to see a class that has two constructors, one with arguments and one without. Many constructors have even more overloaded versions. Here's an example of what a pair of overloaded constructors might look like in the definition of a class:

```
HighClass {
    HighClass();
    HighClass(int paramA, int paramB);
}
```

Operator Overloading

Operators, as well as member functions, can be overloaded in C++. And operator overloading, like function overloading, is a common feature of C++ programs.

With operator overloading, you can customize operators such as the addition operator (+), the subtraction operator (−), the assignment operator (=)

and the increment and decrement operators (++ and ––) to make the operators behave differently when they are used with objects of different classes.

As an illustration of how operator overloading works, consider the addition operator. Ordinarily, you use the addition operator simply to add numbers together. At times, however, you might want to use the addition operator to concatenate a pair of strings, such as the following:

```
StringClass myString, string1, string2;
myString = string1 + string2;
```

In fact, the addition operator is often overloaded to work as a concatenation operator when used with string objects in C++.

Writing Operator-Overloading Functions

To overload an operator in C++, you must declare and define an operator-overloading function (usually a member function). A function that overloads an operator always contains the keyword *operator*. For example, here is a declaration of a member function that overloads the addition operator:

```
Money operator+(int);
```

In the declaration, you follow the *operator* keyword with the operator you want to overload. Then, inside parentheses, you place the name of the data type that you want your overloaded operator to affect.

After you have declared an operator-overloading member function inside a class definition, you can implement your overloaded operator. Then you can use your overloaded operator with the data type you have specified.

> **NOTE** When you overload an operator, normal scope rules apply; if you overload the operator inside a class definition—which is usually the case—the operator is overloaded only within the scope of its class.

An example of operator overloading

Listing 4-7 on the following page shows how you can overload the addition operator to add two floating-point numbers (which represent monetary values) and store the result in two member variables of a class. One member variable is used to store the dollar value of the result, and the other is used to store the cent value of the result.

OPEROVER.CPP

```cpp
#include <iostream.h>
#include <math.h>
#include <stdlib.h>

class Money {
public:
    double dollars;
    double cents;
public:
    Money() {}                      // default constructor
    ~Money() {}                     // destructor
    Money(double);                  // conversion from double
    Money operator+(Money m);       // operator overloading
};

Money Money::operator+(Money m)
{
    ldiv_t result;

    cents += m.cents;
    dollars += m.dollars;

    if (cents > 99) {
        result = ldiv((long)cents, 100);
        dollars = dollars + result.quot;
        cents = (double)result.rem;
    }

    return *this;
}

Money::Money(double cash)       // conversion constructor--
{                               // converts fp to Money
    double frac, n;
    frac = modf(cash, &n);      // a math.h function
    cents = frac * 100;
    dollars = n;
}

int main()
{
    double c, d;
    float deposit1 = 3.50;
    float deposit2 = 4.63;
```

Listing 4-7. *Operator overloading.*

```
        Money totalCash = deposit1 + deposit2;

        d = totalCash.dollars;
        c = totalCash.cents;

        cout << "You now have " << d << " dollars.\n";
        cout << "You also have " << c << " cents.\n";

        return 0;
}
```

When you execute the OPEROVER program, it tells you what value is stored in each member variable of a *Money* object named *totalCash*. The output of the program is shown in Figure 4-7.

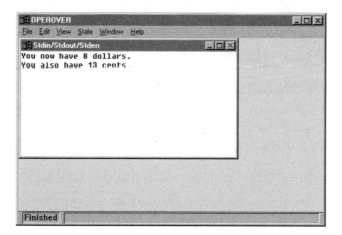

Figure 4-7. *Output of the OPEROVER program.*

Static Member Variables

Everyone who uses global variables knows how dangerous they can be. The problem is that global variables are simply too vulnerable. Any function can change the value of a global variable; all too often, a global variable is inadvertently modified from somewhere way out in left field by a function that you might not even remember writing. Unexpected changes in global variables can wreak havoc on programs and can be enormously difficult to track down.

You can use global variables in C++, but you are strongly encouraged not to. The recommended alternative is to use a different kind of variable that C++ provides: a *static member variable*. Static member variables have built-in safety features that make them less likely than ordinary global variables to be changed inadvertently.

When a class has a static member variable, only one copy of the variable exists, and that single copy is shared by all objects instantiated from the class. Thus, a static member variable can provide a class with all the benefits of a global variable, but without many of the risks.

One typical use of a static member variable in a C++ program is to keep track of the number of objects in a list. Each time a program creates an object in the list, you can increment the value of the static member variable, and each time an object is destroyed, you can decrement the variable. In this way, the static member variable can always provide the number of currently active objects in the list.

Creating Static Member Variables

When you define a class, you can create a static member variable for the class by preceding the variable's declaration with the *static* keyword. For example, this statement declares a static member variable named *count*:

```
static int count;
```

If you do not declare a member variable as static, it is nonstatic by default.

When you declare a static member variable, a fixed memory location is allocated for the variable at link time; that location remains the same for the life of the program. In this sense, a static member variable works the same as a global variable.

However, access to a static member variable is more limited than access to a global variable. After you have initialized a static member variable, functions outside its class can access it only by using the scope resolution operator (::), preceded by the name of the class in which the variable is declared. To make this technique work, of course, you must make the static variable a public member of the class. And that act removes much of the protection against misuse that is enjoyed by a static member variable. If you want to make a static member variable accessible outside a class, you should take other precautions, such as keeping the static member variable private and allowing it to be changed from outside the class only through a public static member function. (Static member functions are described later in this chapter.)

Declaring and Defining Static Member Variables

Listing 4-8 shows how a static member variable can be used in a C++ program.

```
STATIC.CPP

#include <iostream.h>

class SampleClass {
public:
    static int staticVar;        // declare static member variable
    SampleClass() {}
    void SetStaticVar(int a) { staticVar = a; }
};

int SampleClass::staticVar;      // define static member variable

int main()
{
    SampleClass myObject;          // define local object
    myObject.SetStaticVar(100); // initialize static data member
    cout << SampleClass::staticVar << "\n";
    SampleClass::staticVar = 200;
    cout << SampleClass::staticVar << "\n";
    myObject.staticVar = 300;
    cout << SampleClass::staticVar << "\n";
    return 0;
}
```

Listing 4-8. *Using a static member variable.*

In Listing 4-8, a static member variable named *staticVar* is defined inside the definition of a class named *SampleClass*. Then, between the *Sample-Class* definition and the program's *main* function, *staticVar* is defined as shown on the following page.

```
int SampleClass::staticVar;
```

Because static member variables can be shared by multiple functions, they must be defined and declared in this peculiar way. You must *declare* a static member variable inside a class definition, but you must *define* it outside the definition of its class.

When a static member variable has been declared and defined, it is accessible from any member function of its class. If it is a public or a protected member variable, you can also access it from other classes—or from outside any class—in accordance with normal rules of accessibility.

Accessing Static Member Variables

In Listing 4-8, *SampleClass* has a member function named *SetStaticVar* that can be called to set the value of the static member variable *staticVar*, as shown here:

```
void SetStaticVar(int a) { staticVar = a; }
```

In the *main* function, the following statement sets the value of *staticVar* by calling the member function *SetStaticVar*:

```
myObject.SetStaticVar(100);
```

Because access to *staticVar* is public, the *main* function can also set the value of *staticVar* by accessing the variable directly, as shown here:

```
SampleClass::staticVar = 200;
```

Notice that in this statement, the scope resolution operator—preceded by the name of *SampleClass*—is used to access *staticVar*.

Another statement in the *main* function of Listing 4-8 accesses *staticVar* with the dot operator (.), preceded by the name of the object *myObject*, as shown below. This construct is possible because a public static member variable can be called from anywhere in its module.

```
myObject.staticVar = 300;
```

It's important to remember that because *staticVar* is a static member variable, only one copy of the variable exists. That means that each assignment statement in the *main* function assigns a value to the same memory location, overwriting the previous value of *staticVar*.

Private Static Member Variables

A static member variable, like any other member variable, can be public, protected, or private. If a static member variable is private, it cannot be accessed from a function outside its class unless access to it is specifically granted—for example, through friendship status (described in the section "Friendly Classes and Friendly Functions," on page 117) or through a public member function.

Listing 4-9 shows how a program can use a private static member variable to keep track of objects that belong to a class.

PRIVATE.CPP

```
#include <iostream.h>

class LittleList {
private:
    static int ct;        // declare static member variable
public:
    LittleList() { ct++; }
    ~LittleList() { ct--; }
    static int GetCount() { return ct; }   // static member
                                           // function
};

int LittleList::ct = 0;    // initialize static member variable

int main()
{
    LittleList obj1, obj2, obj3;     // define local objects
    cout << "Number of objects: " << LittleList::GetCount()
        <<    "\n";
    return 0;
}
```

Listing 4-9. *Using a private static member variable.*

Listing 4-9 includes a static member variable named *ct*. Although access to *ct* is private, the variable is initialized by using the same technique that would be used to define any other static member variable—from outside the variable's class in a statement that accesses the variable using the scope resolution operator, as shown on the following page.

```
int LittleList::ct = 0;
```

The static member variable *ct* is used to keep a running count of three objects—named *obj1*, *obj2*, and *obj3*—in a class named *LittleList*. Each time an object of the *LittleList* class is instantiated, the object's constructor increments the *ct* variable, as shown here:

```
LittleList() { ct++; }
```

Similarly, each time an object's destructor is called, *ct* is decremented, as shown here:

```
~LittleList() { ct--; }
```

Because *ct* is a private variable, the only way to access *ct* from outside its class is through a member function. In Listing 4-9, *ct* is accessed through a public member function named *GetCount,* as follows:

```
cout << "Number of objects: " << LittleList::GetCount() << '\n';
```

Static Member Functions

Now that you know about static member variables, you will probably not be surprised to find out that C++ programs also have static member functions. As you learned in Chapter 3, "C++ Basics," an ordinary, nonstatic member function can access any member of the class in which the function is declared. A static member function, by contrast, can access only the static member variables defined for a class.

You declare a static member function by preceding its definition with the *static* keyword. If you do not declare a member function as static, it is nonstatic by default. For example, inside the definition of a class named *Object-Count*, you can declare a static member function named *Count* this way:

```
class ObjectCount;
{
private:
    int x;
```

```
protected:
    static int ct;
public:
    static int Count(); // declare static member function
}
```

In this class definition, the static member function *Count* can access the static member variable *ct*, but it cannot access the nonstatic member variable *x*. That's because a static member function can access only static member variables and other static member functions, not nonstatic member variables or nonstatic member functions.

Another feature of a static member function is that it has no *this* pointer. As discussed in the section "The *this* Pointer," on page 81 in Chapter 3, the *this* pointer is a hidden pointer to the current object and is secretly passed to a member function. The member function can then use that unseen pointer to access any other member of its class. Because a static member function is not associated with any particular object of a class, a static member function has no *this* pointer.

Friendly Classes and Friendly Functions

In at least one respect, C++ is a friendly language. In a C++ program, you can declare classes and functions to be friends of each other—and in C++, as in life, there are special bonds between friends.

To declare friend classes and friend functions, you use the *friend* keyword, usually inside a class definition. You can use *friend* in three ways:

- When a class declares a friend class, the class that is granted friendship status has access to all members of the class that contains the *friend* declaration.

- A class can also grant friendship status to a member function of another class. By preceding the declaration of the member function with the keyword *friend*, you can declare that the specified nonmember function is a friend of the class being defined.

- Finally, a class can grant friendship status to a function that is not a member of another class—that is, to a stand-alone function that appears anywhere in a program.

Here's an example of using the *friend* keyword in a class declaration to indicate that a member function of another class is a friend:

```
class HighClass {
private:
    void MyFriend();
protected:
    friend int OtherClass::FriendMembFunc();
};
```

Here the member function *OtherClass::FriendMembFunc* is declared as a friend of *HighClass*.

One-Way Friendships

One important fact about *friend* declarations is that they are effective in only one direction. In the preceding definition of *HighClass*, *OtherClass-::FriendMembFunc* is declared to be a friend of *HighClass*, so that function has access to all the members of *HighClass*. But *HighClass* does not have access to members of *OtherClass*. If such access were granted, it would have to be granted inside the class definition of *OtherClass*.

Friend functions and friend classes can be useful when you want to relax the access rules that ordinarily apply to member variables. For example, suppose you write a function that has to execute a public member function of a class repeatedly because the function needs access to a private member variable of a class. In such a situation—which arises often in C++ programming—each read or write of the desired member variable requires the overhead that normally results from a call to a function. To eliminate this overhead, you can specify that the function requiring access is a friend of the class that owns the desired member variable.

You can also use friend classes to prevent class descriptions from growing to unwieldy lengths. If there is a particular set of variables and functions that a class refers to only rarely, you can place them in a class by themselves and then make that class a friend of the class that refers to them from time to time. That way, the variables and functions that are accessed infrequently can be kept separate from the class that sometimes accesses them.

> **NOTE**   If you find that in your applications you're using friends all over the place to circumvent the mechanisms for data protection and code protection built into C++, you should take a close look at your programming habits. The truth is that friends, while useful at times, should not appear very often in your C++ programs.

Listing 4-10 shows how friend classes and friend functions can be used in a C++ program. In this program, a class named *FriendClass* grants friendship access to a class named *FriendlyClass2* and to the *main* function. *FriendlyClass2* then exercises its friendship rights by initializing a member variable named *privateVar2* to the value stored in *privateVar*, which is a private member variable of *FriendClass*.

FRIENDS.CPP

```cpp
#include <iostream.h>

class FriendClass {
private:
    friend class FriendlyClass2;
    friend main();
    int privateVar;
    FriendClass() : privateVar(500) {} // private constructor
public:
    int GetPrivateVar() { return privateVar; }
};

class FriendlyClass2 {
private:
    int privateVar2;
public:
    FriendlyClass2(FriendClass* x) :
        privateVar2(x->privateVar) {} // constructor
    int GetPrivateVar2() { return privateVar2; }
};

int main()
{
    int x, y;
    FriendClass* myFriendlyClass = new FriendClass;
    FriendlyClass2 myFriendlyClass2(myFriendlyClass);
```

Listing 4-10. *Using friends.*   *(continued)*

Listing 4-10. *continued*

```
    x = myFriendlyClass->GetPrivateVar();
    cout << x << "\n";

    y = myFriendlyClass2.GetPrivateVar2();
    cout << y << "\n";

    return 0;
}
```

Because *FriendlyClass2* is declared as a friend, it has direct access to the private member variable of *FriendClass* named *privateVar*. The *privateVar* variable is declared in the definition of *FriendClass*.

Listing 4-10 contains an interesting precaution that helps prevent misuse of the friend mechanisms. The safeguard is that the constructor of *Friend-Class* is designated as private. That means that only friends of *FriendClass* can instantiate *FriendClass* objects. Another special feature of the program is that its *main* function is declared as a friend of *FriendClass*. This permits the *main* function to instantiate *FriendClass* objects, as shown in the following:

```
int x, y;
FriendClass* myFriendlyClass = new FriendClass;
FriendlyClass2 myFriendlyClass2(myFriendlyClass);

x = myFriendlyClass->privateVar;
cout << x << "\n";

y = myFriendlyClass2.GetPrivateVar2();
cout << y << "\n";
```

When you execute the program in Listing 4-10, the *main* function instantiates two objects: one named *myFriendlyClass* and one named *myFriendlyClass2*. *myFriendlyClass* is constructed on the heap, and *myFriendlyClass2* is constructed on the stack.

The *FriendClass* constructor uses an initializer list (see the section "Initializer Lists" on page 78 in Chapter 3) to set the value of a private variable named *privateVar* to 500. When an object of *FriendlyClass2* is instantiated, it obtains the value of *FriendClass*'s *privateVar* and stores that value in a private variable of its own, named *privateVar2*. This is permitted because *FriendlyClass2* is a friend of *FriendClass*.

When the *main* function has instantiated a *FriendClass* object and a *FriendlyClass2* object, *main* obtains the values of the variables *Friend-Class::privateVar* and *FriendlyClass2::privateVar2* and displays them. The *main* function is able to obtain the value of *FriendClass::privateVar* directly because *main* is a friend of *FriendClass*. However, *main* is not a friend of *FriendlyClass2*. Therefore, *main* has to obtain the value of *FriendlyClass2::privateVar2* in a more conventional way: by calling a member function that retrieves the value of the variable.

The *new* and *delete* Operators

In many ways, C++ is a higher-level language than C. One area in which this truth is evident is the area of memory management. In C, you're generally on your own when it comes to allocating and deallocating memory. Because C does not allocate memory space for data when you declare a pointer, you must allocate the memory yourself by calling the *malloc* function or by performing some other action to allocate memory manually.

C++ is a little kinder than that. In C++, instead of calling a function to allocate or deallocate memory, you invoke an operator. C++ provides two memory management operators—*new* and *delete*—that allocate and deallocate memory from the heap (also called the *free store*).

The *new* and *delete* operators are more reliable than the *malloc* and *free* functions because the Visual C++ compiler performs type checking each time a program allocates memory with *new*. Another advantage stems from the fact that C++ implements *new* and *delete* as operators, not as functions. That means that *new* and *delete* are built into the C++ language itself, so programs can use *new* and *delete* without including any header files.

Still another important feature of the *new* and *delete* operators is that they don't require typecasting—and that makes *new* and *delete* easier to use than *malloc* and *free*.

The *new* Operator

When you call the *malloc* function in a C program, you pass a size to *malloc*, and the function returns a *void* pointer, which you must cast to whatever data type you want. Using the *new* operator is similar but simpler. The *new* operator also returns a pointer, but it isn't a *void* pointer, so you don't have to cast the pointer to the data type for which you are obtaining memory. Instead, *new* returns the kind of pointer you have requested. To illustrate, you can obtain memory for an object named *memBlock* by writing the following pair of statements:

```
MemStruct* memblock;
memblock = new Memory;
```

If you want to be more concise, you can write this code:

```
MemStruct* memBlock = new Memory;
```

The *new* operator can also allocate memory for data structures that are not objects of classes. For example, this code fragment allocates memory for an array of integers:

```
int* intArray;
intArray = new int[1000];
```

This more concise statement has the same effect:

```
int* intArray = new int[1000];
```

Both of the preceding examples declare a pointer named *intArray* and initialize it to the address returned by *new*. If a pointer of the requested size is available, *new* returns a pointer to the beginning of a block of memory of the specified size. If there is not enough dynamic storage available to satisfy a request, *new* returns 0.

Each time you compile an expression that invokes the *new* operator, the compiler performs a type check to verify that the type of the specified pointer is the correct type for the memory being allocated. If the types don't match, the compiler issues an error message.

The *delete* Operator

When you allocate memory with the *new* operator, you can delete it with the *delete* operator. The *delete* operator is easy to use, but, like the C *free* function, it can be dangerous if you don't use it wisely. But by exercising some commonsense precautions, you can prevent mishaps.

The *delete* operator is safe if the pointer to the object being deleted is NULL or if the pointer correctly addresses allocated memory. Problems arise, however, if a nonzero pointer does not actually have memory allocated for an object at its address and a program attempts to delete at that pointer's address.

What's Next?

You have now completed a two-chapter crash course in classes, objects, and the fundamentals of object-oriented programming. This chapter covered many important topics, including class hierarchies, virtual member functions, inheritance and polymorphism, and function and operator overloading. Other topics covered included static member variables, the *friend* function modifier, and the *new* and *delete* operators. Now we're ready to shift our focus back to Visual C++ and start creating some really challenging Visual C++ programs. You'll start doing that next, in Chapter 5, "Visual C++ Tools."

Visual C++ Tools

Microsoft Visual C++ version 1.0 is two products in one: a C++-based software-development system and a graphics based, user interactive delivery system for the classes and member functions provided in the Microsoft Foundation Class (MFC) Library version 2.0.

The first four chapters of this book introduced you to the Visual C++ development environment, the basics of programming in Windows, and the fundamentals of the C++ language. In this chapter, you'll learn more about the Visual C++ programming environment. You'll also take an in-depth look at the Visual C++ compiler, the Visual C++ linker, and all the other program-development tools built into Visual Workbench: App Studio, ClassWizard, the Visual C++ debugger, and the Visual C++ Source Browser. By the end of this chapter, you'll be familiar with all the tools you need to create full-featured Visual C++ applications, and you'll get a chance to write a customized Windows-based Visual C++ application yourself.

The main topics of this chapter include:

- Visual C++ projects and the files and classes that AppWizard creates
- Using App Studio to manage resources, including bitmaps and menus
- Building a Visual C++ application
- Creating message handlers using ClassWizard

■ Using the Visual C++ debugger to help you develop error-free applications

To demonstrate the use of Visual Workbench, this chapter presents a sample application named SCRAMBLE. You can build the SCRAMBLE application from scratch, or you can copy the program from the CHAP05 directory on the companion CD-ROM and simply read along. SCRAMBLE is an MDI (multiple-document interface) application that displays a bitmap resource. SCRAMBLE starts out simple: it displays a single bitmap image in a child window. You can display as many child windows as you want, but they each display the same bitmap image. Later code is added so that each child window can be controlled separately, turning the display of the bitmap on or off.

TIP If you want to build the SCRAMBLE program from scratch instead of opening the program's files and reading along, be sure to copy the ARCHES.BMP file from the SCRAMBLE project on the companion CD-ROM to your own SCRAMBLE application's directory.

The SCRAMBLE program isn't very complicated, but it's useful for learning about the Visual C++ tools, and it serves as a good framework for creating a graphics-based application. You'll add more features to the SCRAMBLE program in Chapter 6, "The MFC Library."

If you've ever written a graphics-based program for MS-DOS, you might think that creating the SCRAMBLE program will be a heavy burden. Fortunately for us, the Visual C++ tools, in combination with the MFC library, help lighten the load. Let's get started by reacquainting ourselves with AppWizard, the Visual C++ project-generating tool we encountered in Chapter 1, "Introducing Visual C++."

Visual C++ Projects

The first step in writing a Visual C++ application is to create a *project*. A project is a collection of files that are needed to build an application using the Visual C++ development environment. When you create a Visual C++ application using AppWizard, AppWizard automatically generates a project for your application. AppWizard then places all the files that it creates for your program in the project it has created.

Every Visual C++ version 1.0 project is built around a special kind of file known as a *makefile*. AppWizard automatically creates a makefile and places it in your project. A makefile is a text file that always has the file-name extension .MAK. It contains the names of all the files that make up a Visual C++ project, and it describes the relationship that those files have with each other in a language that the Visual C++ compiler and linker can understand. A makefile also contains commands and switches for compil-ing and linking those files. When you build a Visual C++ application by choosing the Build or the Rebuild All item from the Project menu, Visual C++ builds your application by executing the commands in the makefile.

A Visual C++ project can contain both source code files and precompiled object code files known as *libraries.* When the Visual C++ compiler has converted an application's source code into object code, Visual C++ links the application's compiled object code with any precompiled object code libraries that are included in the project.

Table 1-2 on page 13 in Chapter 1 lists the kinds of files that are generated when you create and build a Visual C++ application. When you build this chapter's sample program, you will create a project named SCRAMBLE. The files that make up the SCRAMBLE project are listed in the section "Files in the SCRAMBLE Project," on page 132.

Creating the Basic SCRAMBLE Project

The SCRAMBLE application that you'll create in this chapter is a custom-ized AppWizard program. (SCRAMBLE is similar to SCRIBBLE, a sample tutorial program that's also provided on the companion CD-ROM. The main difference between the two programs is that SCRAMBLE lets you display a bitmap and SCRIBBLE lets you draw freehand lines.)

When AppWizard creates an application framework, the framework is de-signed using a *document-and-view architecture.* To support this architec-ture, AppWizard always creates a *document object* that is derived from the MFC library's *CDocument* class and a *view object* that is derived from the MFC library's *CView* class. The *CDocument* class provides every document object with special features that support the automatic loading and saving of information stored on disk. The *CView* class provides every view object with special features that support the creation and handling of images that can be displayed in windows or printed on a printer. When you customize an application framework created by AppWizard, most of the changes you make are in the program's document and view files. (We'll learn more about document and view classes later in this chapter and in Chapter 6, "The MFC Library.")

To create a project for the SCRAMBLE application, follow these steps:

1. Open Visual Workbench.

2. Choose the AppWizard item from the Project menu to open the MFC AppWizard dialog box, shown here:

3. In the Directory list box, select the directory in which you want to place your new project.

4. Type a name for your project in the Project Name edit box. (To create a project for this exercise, type the name *scramble*.) When you type the name of a project in the Project Name edit box, AppWizard displays the same name in the New Subdirectory edit box and then places the project files in a new directory with that name.

5. AppWizard can equip a new project with a number of features. To see these features, click the Options button. Visual Workbench displays the Options dialog box, shown here:

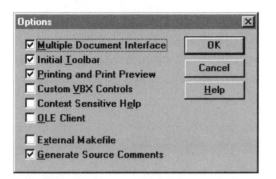

This dialog box is very straightforward: select an option to include that feature; deselect an option to skip that feature. One option does not work as an on/off toggle: AppWizard generates an SDI (single-document interface) application if you deselect the Multiple Document Interface check box. The options that are selected by default—Multiple Document Interface, Initial Toolbar, Printing And Print Preview, and Generate Source Comments—suit our needs quite well for now, so click Cancel to close the Options dialog box.

> **NOTE** MDI was the preferred architecture for Microsoft Windows 3.1–based applications, but SDI is gaining new stature with Windows 95. There are two reasons for this: Microsoft has determined that SDI applications are easier for users to understand, and the Windows 95 task bar makes it easy to switch from one window to another. (Switching between windows was the main feature that made MDI programs useful in Windows 3.1.) So legions of Windows programmers are now brushing up on writing SDI programs.

6. Click the Classes button to preview the file and class names that AppWizard is about to assign to your project. AppWizard displays the Classes dialog box, shown on the following page.

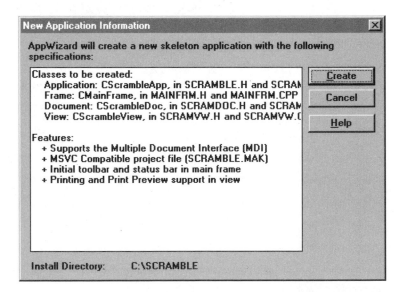

AppWizard tries to assign suitable names to the files that make up
the project and to the MFC library classes that are created for the
project, but sometimes these names are not very intuitive, and you
might want to change them. To do so, select the appropriate class
name in the New Application Classes list box, and then edit the
text in the appropriate edit box. The default names for the
SCRAMBLE files and classes are fine, so click Cancel to close the
Classes dialog box.

7. Click OK in the MFC AppWizard dialog box. AppWizard displays
the New Application Information dialog box, shown here:

The New Application Information dialog box contains a concise summary of the class names, filenames, and options to be generated.

8. Click the Create button, and AppWizard creates the files for the SCRAMBLE project.

Files and Classes in AppWizard Projects

AppWizard creates four MFC library classes in each project it generates. Chapter 6, "The MFC Library," describes the four classes, but for now, here is a brief overview of each of these classes so that you'll have an idea of how each one is used in a Visual C++ project:

- Every framework-based Visual C++ program has an *application class* that is derived from the MFC library's *CWinApp* class. When AppWizard generates a Visual C++ application, the application is implemented as an object derived from the *CWinApp* class. This application object provides member functions for initializing each instance of an application that the user starts.

- Every Visual C++ program that AppWizard creates has a *main window class* named *CMainFrame*. When AppWizard creates an SDI application, *CMainFrame* is derived from the MFC library's *CFrameWnd* class; when AppWizard creates an MDI application, *CMainFrame* is derived from the MFC library's *CMDIFrameWnd* class.

- Every project created by AppWizard has a *document class* that is derived from the MFC library's *CDocument* class. A document class contains member functions for storing, saving, and retrieving data. All data in an MFC application should be managed by the application's document class.

- Every project that AppWizard creates has a *view class* that is derived from the MFC library's *CView* class. Every *CView*-derived object is "attached" to a *CDocument*-derived object and contains functions to help it display data from that document.

Files in the SCRAMBLE Project

If you open the directory that contains the SCRAMBLE project—from the Windows 95 desktop or from the Windows 3.1 File Manager—you'll see that AppWizard has created the following files for the SCRAMBLE project:

- **SCRAMBLE.H**—The header file for the SCRAMBLE application's *CScrambleApp* class.

- **SCRAMBLE.CPP**—The implementation file for the SCRAMBLE application's *CScrambleApp* class.

- **MAINFRM.H**—The header file for the SCRAMBLE application's *CMainFrame* class. (AppWizard always names this file MAINFRM.H, no matter what you name your project.)

- **MAINFRM.CPP**—The implementation file for the SCRAMBLE application's *CMainFrame* class. (AppWizard always names this file MAINFRM.CPP, no matter what you name your project.)

- **SCRAMVW.H**—The header file for the SCRAMBLE application's *CScrambleView* class.

- **SCRAMVW.CPP**—The implementation file for the SCRAMBLE application's *CScrambleView* class. Of particular interest is the *OnDraw* member function. *OnDraw* draws the client area of a *CView*-derived window whenever the window needs to be updated. You'll learn more about view classes in Chapter 6, "The MFC Library." The SCRAMVW.CPP file is presented in Listing 5-1 on page 159.

- **SCRAMDOC.H**—The header file for the SCRAMBLE application's *CScrambleDoc* class. The SCRAMDOC.H file is shown in Listing 5-1.

- **SCRAMDOC.CPP**—The implementation file for the SCRAMBLE application's *CScrambleDoc* class. You'll learn more about document classes in Chapter 6, "The MFC Library." The SCRAMDOC.CPP file is presented in Listing 5-1.

- **SCRAMBLE.DEF**—The SCRAMBLE application's *module-definition file*. In Visual C++, a module-definition file contains important information about an application. This information includes the name and description of the application and the initial size of the application's local heap. The Visual C++ version 1.0 compiler requires a module-definition file for every application it builds, so AppWizard creates one automatically.

- **SCRAMBLE.MAK**—The SCRAMBLE application's makefile. As mentioned previously, a makefile is a text script that the Visual C++ compiler uses to compile and link a project. It specifies the relationships between all the project's source files and library files, and it provides other important information such as compiler and linker switches.

- **SCRAMBLE.RC**—A text file that defines all resources (such as menus, dialog boxes, and bitmaps) used by the SCRAMBLE application. When AppWizard generates a project, it automatically creates a *resource script* (.RC) file that defines an initial set of resources, including an About dialog box, a bitmap used by the application's toolbar, an application icon, an accelerator key resource, a string-table resource, and either one or two menus (one for an SDI application; two for an MDI application).

- **SCRAMBLE.RES**—The compiled version of a resource script file.

- **Resource files**—When AppWizard generates a project, it creates a directory named RES and stores several resource files in it. These files include icon (.ICO) files for your application and a bitmap (.BMP) file for your application's toolbar. You can edit these resources using App Studio.

- **RESOURCE.H**—A text file that defines the ID (identifier) numbers assigned to your application's resources. App Studio assigns these ID numbers to new resources automatically.

- **STDAFX.H**—A header file in which you can place *#include* directives for other header files used by your application. All the files in your application include the STDAFX.H file, so including a header file in the STDAFX.H file makes the header file accessible to all the files in your project. When you create an AppWizard project, its STDAFX.H file initially includes the AFXWIN.H file and the AFXEXT.H file.

- **STDAFX.CPP**—The implementation file that accompanies the STDAFX.H header file. When you compile your Visual C++ project, the STDAFX.CPP and STDAFX.H files are used to build a precompiled header (.PCH) file named STDAFX.PCH. A precompiled header file contains compiled code for an unchanging part of your project, such as the Windows and MFC header files. Precompiled header files speed up the build process considerably.

Adding a Bitmap:
Managing Resources with App Studio

When you use AppWizard to develop a Visual C++ application, AppWizard creates a resource script file (.RC) and places it in your application's project. A resource script file is a text file that contains information about resources such as menus, bitmaps, icons, toolbars, and dialog boxes. AppWizard also places information about default resources, such as an About box and a default menu bar, in the resource script file.

When you have built a Visual C++ project with AppWizard, you can edit the resources that AppWizard has created—and add more resources of your own—by using a Visual C++ tool named *App Studio*. In Visual C++ version 1.0, App Studio is a stand-alone application that you open by choosing the App Studio item from the Tools menu. When you execute App Studio, it provides several graphically based resource editors that you can use to create various kinds of resources. For example, App Studio provides a bitmap editor for creating and editing bitmaps, a dialog editor for creating and editing dialog boxes, and a menu editor for creating and editing menus.

When you start App Studio from Visual Workbench, App Studio opens the resource script file that AppWizard has created for your project. You can then navigate to the various editors that App Studio provides and use them to edit your project's resources.

To demonstrate how App Studio can minimize the work involved in adding resources to your project, we'll use it to add a bitmap image to the SCRAMBLE project. Open the SCRAMBLE project (if it is not already open) and choose App Studio from the Tools menu. You'll see the App Studio window, shown in Figure 5-1.

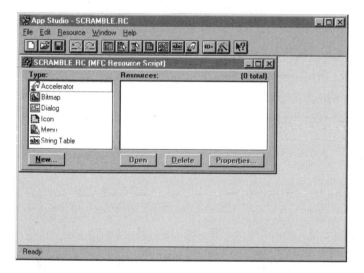

Figure 5-1. *The App Studio window.*

The Type list box displays a list of resource types; the Resources list box displays a list of the resources of the selected type. We'll add a single bitmap image—the ARCHES.BMP file—to the project. Follow these steps to add the bitmap:

1. Select Bitmap in the Type list box. App Studio displays IDR_MAIN-FRAME in the Resources list box. (This is the bitmap image used by the project's toolbar.)

2. Choose Import from the Resource menu. The Import Resource dialog box appears, as shown on the following page.

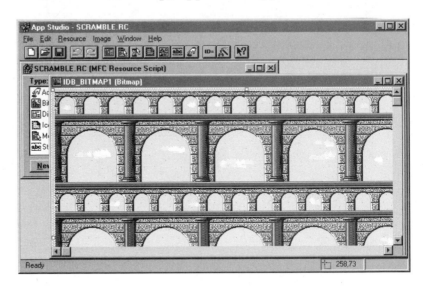

3. Select the ARCHES.BMP file, and click OK. (If the ARCHES.BMP file does not appear, you must copy the file from the SCRAMBLE project on the companion CD-ROM to your project's directory.) The Import Resource dialog box closes, and a new window, named IDB_BITMAP1 (Bitmap), appears in App Studio, as shown here:

You'll also see the graphics palette, the untitled window shown here:

The graphics palette contains tools for manipulating images and a color palette you can use to select foreground and background colors. (You'll find complete information about the graphics palette in the online help.)

4. Choose Properties from the Resource menu. The Properties window, another untitled window, appears as shown here:

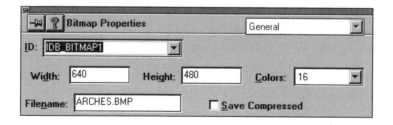

The Properties window is used to control the appearance and behavior of the resources you create. For now, simply note the default ID that App Studio assigned to this resource: IDB_BITMAP1. (In Visual C++, all resources—bitmaps, menus, and so on—have ID numbers that are assigned automatically by App Studio and are defined in the header file RESOURCE.H.)

5. Choose Exit from the App Studio File menu, and save your changes.

Writing Code to Display the Bitmap

In Chapter 2, "Introduction to Windows Programming," you learned how to draw in windows using DCs (device contexts) and GDI (graphical device interface) objects such as brushes and pens. In Chapter 4, "Objects and Member Functions," you were introduced to the Visual C++ equivalents of DCs and GDI objects: the *CDC* class, which encapsulates device contexts, and the *CGdiObject* family of classes, which include *CGdiObject*-derived classes such as *CBrush* and *CPen*.

In Visual C++, a bitmap is an object of the *CBitmap* class. The *CBitmap* class, like *CBrush*, *CPen*, and other graphics classes, is derived from the MFC library's *CGdiObject* class. Bitmaps are used in much the same way that other kinds of *CGdiObject*-derived objects are used. Using bitmaps requires a few more steps, however, because they are usually loaded from files or as a resource, whereas *CGdiObject*-derived objects such as brush and pen objects are generally created on the fly.

Working with Bitmaps

To load a bitmap resource and use it in a Visual C++ program, you follow these general steps:

1. Construct an object of the *CBitmap* class.

2. Load the bitmap into memory using the *CBitmap::LoadBitmap* member function.

3. Use the *CDC::CreateCompatibleDC* member function to create a device-context object that is compatible with the output device being used.

4. Select the *CBitmap* object you have constructed in memory into the device-compatible *CDC* object.

5. Use a *CDC* member function such as *CDC::BitBlt* or *CDC::StretchBlt* to copy your *CBitmap* object from memory into the *CDC* object.

These steps are described in more detail in the sections that follow.

IP It is better to create a bitmap in memory and then to copy it to the screen than to paint the bitmap directly to the screen. Your computer's screen refreshes itself many times each second, and if you try to paint directly to the screen during a screen refresh, you often see unsightly flashes and other undesirable side effects. If you copy a bitmap into memory and then transfer it to the screen using *CDC::BitBlt* or *CDC::StretchBlt*, these types of problems are minimized.

Loading the bitmap

In Visual C++, the first step in creating and displaying a bitmap is to construct an object of the *CBitmap* class. We need a member variable to store the bitmap, a member function that provides access to the bitmap, and member functions to load and unload the bitmap. All data in an MFC-based application is stored in the application's document class, so open the SCRAMDOC.H file and add the following lines to the *CScrambleDoc* class declaration:

```
private:
    CBitmap* m_pArches;
    CBitmap* m_pBackground;
public:
    CBitmap* GetBackground() { return m_pBackground; }
    void LoadBackground(CBitmap*);
    void UnloadBackground();
```

GetBackground is an inline function that simply returns a pointer to the background bitmap. (The *m_pBackground* member variable and the *Load-Background* and *UnloadBackground* member functions aren't necessary for this version of the SCRAMBLE application, but they'll make life easier later in this chapter, when we add menu commands to turn the background bitmap on or off.)

Now open the SCRAMDOC.CPP file, and edit the *CScrambleDoc* class con̶structor and destructor as shown here:

```
CScrambleDoc::CScrambleDoc()
{
    m_pArches = new CBitmap;
    if (m_pArches)
    {
        m_pArches->LoadBitmap(IDB_BITMAP1);
    }
    m_pBackground = m_pArches;
}

CScrambleDoc::~CScrambleDoc()
{
    if (m_pArches)
    {
        delete m_pArches;
        m_pArches = NULL;
    }
}
```

The *LoadBitmap* function instantiates a *CBitmap* object on the heap, stores the object's address in the *m_pArches* member variable, and loads the bitmap resource. (*LoadBitmap*, a member function of the *CBitmap* class, has two overloaded versions: one that takes a resource ID as a parameter, and one that takes a pointer to a resource name as a parameter.)

While you're working in SCRAMDOC.CPP, add the *LoadBackground* and *UnloadBackground* functions, as shown here:

```
void CScrambleDoc::LoadBackground(CBitmap* pBackground)
{
    m_pBackground = pBackground;
}

void CScrambleDoc::UnloadBackground()
{
    m_pBackground = NULL;
}
```

Drawing the bitmap

Now we need to draw the bitmap. *OnDraw*, a member function of the *CView* class, is called whenever part of a window is *invalidated* (needs to be redrawn). AppWizard automatically creates an *OnDraw* function in every view-class implementation file it creates, but it's up to you to provide the drawing code. Open the SCRAMVW.CPP file, and edit the *CScramble-View::OnDraw* member function so that it looks like this:

```
void CScrambleView::OnDraw(CDC* pDC)
{
    CScrambleDoc* pDoc = GetDocument();
    CBitmap* pBitmap;
    BITMAP Bitmap;
    CDC dc;

    pBitmap = pDoc->GetBackground();
    if (pBitmap)
    {
        dc.CreateCompatibleDC(pDC);
        CBitmap* pOldBitmap = dc.SelectObject(pBitmap);

        pBitmap->GetObject(sizeof(Bitmap), &Bitmap);
        pDC->BitBlt(0, 0,
                    Bitmap.bmWidth,
                    Bitmap.bmHeight,
                    &dc,
                    0, 0,
                    SRCCOPY);
        dc.SelectObject(pOldBitmap);
    }
}
```

This code is slightly more involved, but it's not too hard to understand if you take it one step at a time. For example, the following statement returns a pointer to the document class and stores it in the *pDoc* variable:

```
CScrambleDoc* pDoc = GetDocument();
```

GetDocument is a member function of the *CDocument* class.

After we have the pointer, we can call the *CScrambleDoc::GetBackground* function with the following statement:

```
pBitmap = pDoc->GetBackground();
```

We then create a compatible device context and select the bitmap into it with these statements:

```
dc.CreateCompatibleDC(pDC);
CBitmap* pOldBitmap = dc.SelectObject(pBitmap);
```

We're almost ready to draw the device context using the *CDC::BitBlt* function, which copies a rectangular area from a bitmap to a corresponding rectangle in the current device context. If you look up the *CDC::BitBlt* function in the online help, you'll see that it is prototyped as follows:

```
BOOL BitBlt(int x, int y, int nWidth, int nHeight,
    CDC* pSrcDC, int xSrc, int ySrc, DWORD dwRop);
```

The *x* and *y* arguments specify the upper left corner of the rectangle to which the bitmap will be copied, *nWidth* and *nHeight* are the width and height of the bitmap, *pSrcDC* is the device context into which the bitmap has been selected, *xSrc* and *ySrc* specify the upper left corner of the rectangle in the bitmap, and *dwRop* is the raster operation to be performed. (A complete list of raster operations and a description of each can be found in the online help. We will also cover bitmap operations in more detail in Chapter 10, "Visual C++ Graphics.") For this version of SCRAMBLE, we need the *SRCCOPY* operation, which simply copies the bitmap verbatim.

We now have all the information we need except the height and width of the bitmap. Fortunately, the *GetObject* function can fill in the holes. The following statement stores information about the bitmap in a structure named *Bitmap*:

```
pBitmap->GetObject(sizeof(Bitmap), &Bitmap);
```

Armed with this information, we're ready to call *BitBlt*, as follows:

```
pDC->BitBlt(0, 0,
            Bitmap.bmWidth,
            Bitmap.bmHeight,
            &dc,
            0, 0,
            SRCCOPY);
```

That's it. Now we're ready to build the SCRAMBLE application.

Deleting GDI Objects

Under Win16, it's very important to delete GDI objects after you've finished using them because GDI memory is owned by the system. If you fail to delete a GDI object, the memory it is using is not freed until the user restarts Windows. Freeing GDI objects is less important under Win32 because GDI memory is allocated to a process and is freed when the process terminates. However, it's still good programming practice to delete GDI objects after you've finished using them.

Building a Visual C++ Application

After you have created an application framework—with or without AppWizard—you can either build it (compile and link it) or simply compile it without linking.

To build a program, choose Build or Rebuild All from the Project menu. (Alternatively, you can click the Build or the Rebuild All button on the Visual Workbench toolbar.) The Build command builds a program by recompiling only files that have changed since the last build. To build a program by compiling all files, choose the Rebuild All command. To compile a file without linking it, open the file and choose the Compile File command from the Project menu.

Compiling an Application

The Visual C++ compiler is actually two compilers in one: a C compiler and a C++ compiler. The Visual C++ compiler determines a file's language by checking its filename extension. The job of the Visual C++ compiler is to translate source code files (text files with the extension .C or .CPP) into machine-readable files called *object files* (files with the extension .OBJ).

The compiler is integrated with the rest of the Visual C++ development system, so you can run it without leaving the Visual C++ editor. In fact, the compiler runs in the background, so you can do other work on your computer—even leave the Visual C++ environment, if you want—while your application is being compiled. When compilation is complete, Visual C++ beeps, notifying you that you can return to the editor to verify that your program has compiled successfully.

While the compiler is working, it displays a running summary of its progress in an output window. Error and warning messages are displayed as problems, and potential trouble spots are detected. The compiler stops and displays an error message if it encounters a fatal error.

Changing the build mode

By default, AppWizard-generated projects are built in *Debug mode*. (The other option is *Release mode*.) A project built in Debug mode is much larger than when it's built in Release mode because it contains information such as debugging symbols used by the Visual C++ debugger. It's a good idea to build a project in Debug mode until you're sure it is fully debugged. Then you can switch to Release mode and rebuild the project.

To build a project in Release mode, follow these steps:

1. Choose Project from the Options menu. The Project Options dialog box appears, as shown here:

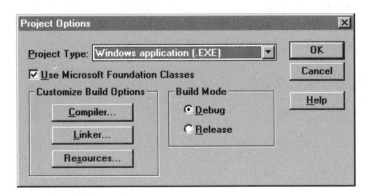

2. Click the Release option button in the Build Mode area of the Project Options dialog box, and then click OK.

3. Click the Rebuild All button on the Visual Workbench toolbar.

The Visual Workbench Source Browser

Another important tool that you'll use when you develop applications in Visual C++ is the Visual Workbench Source Browser, a Windows-based source code browser that uses information generated by the compiler to help you find, examine, and edit related symbols and study the relationships among various symbols. The browser displays a hierarchical view that you can use to examine the symbols you are interested in. For example, you can use the browser to examine the relationships between base classes and derived classes or between calling functions and called functions. You can select any function, variable, type, macro, or class and then see exactly where it's defined and used in your project. You can control all the browser's hierarchy expansions with the mouse.

By default, AppWizard enables browser information in new projects. The Visual C++ compiler creates a browser database file—with the filename extension .BSC—that keeps track of where each symbol in your source code is defined and used. After a .BSC file is created, it becomes part of your project and is updated each time you build your project.

When the Browse dialog box opens, choose the symbol you want to browse for. You control the parameters of your browsing operation by selecting items from the Type, Subset, and Symbol drop-down combo boxes. For example, to display a graph showing the base classes that are used in your application, select the Base Class Graph item from the Type combo box and then click the Display Result button. If your application has any base classes to display, the browser displays them in a tree-like list.

You can also use the browser without opening the Browse window. When you are writing or editing source code using the Visual C++ editor, you can simply use the Browse menu to select a symbol in a source file, jump to its definition or first reference, review all references to the symbol, and return to the original insertion point in your source file.

(continued)

The Visual Workbench Source Browser. *continued*

Although the Source Browser can be a valuable tool when you are developing complex C++ projects, Visual C++ programmers often disable it when they don't need it. That's because when the Source Browser is enabled, it creates a new browser database every time you compile an application, and that can be a time-consuming process. You might want to disable browser information until you start developing projects that are complex enough to make its capabilities useful.

To disable Source Browser information, follow these steps:

1. Choose the Project item from the Options menu.
2. When the Project Options dialog box appears, click the Compiler button.
3. In the C/C++ Compiler Options dialog box, select Listing Files in the Category list box.
4. Deselect the Browser Information option.
5. Close the C/C++ Compiler Options dialog box by clicking OK.
6. Close the Project Options dialog box by clicking OK.

You can learn more about the Source Browser by consulting the online help.

Linking an Application

Although the .OBJ files produced by the Visual C++ compiler are binary (machine-readable) files, they are not executable programs. Executable files (*executables* for short) have header sections containing important run-time information that .OBJ files do not provide. To convert an application's .OBJ files to an executable program, you must use the Visual C++ linker.

The linker has two primary jobs. First it resolves all your application's references to external functions by searching through the library files that the project accesses. Then it links the appropriate library files to your application's object files, producing your project's executable (.EXE) file.

Linking with object code libraries

Linking with object code libraries is an important operation because most Visual C++ applications rely on external libraries that are supplied as part of the Visual C++ development package. You can also create libraries yourself and access them from your Visual C++ applications.

> **NOTE** Functions that are imported from libraries instead of being implemented in an application's source code are sometimes referred to as *external functions*. The process of tracking down functions provided in object code libraries is sometimes referred to as *resolving* external references.

How the Visual C++ linker works

The Visual C++ linker links .OBJ files generated by the Visual C++ compiler to any other object code files that an application might require. When the .OBJ files that make up an application go to the Visual C++ linker, the linker makes a thorough search through the code it is compiling for the names of any functions that are not implemented in the .OBJ files it has received from the compiler. If the linker encounters the names of any functions that are not implemented in the source code of the application being compiled, the linker tries to find the missing functions in any library files that have been incorporated into the application being compiled.

> **TIP** If the Visual C++ linker starts generating vast quantities of errors when you link a program and you know you couldn't possibly have made that many errors in your source code, open the Project Options dialog box and verify that the Use Microsoft Foundation Classes check box is selected. If it isn't selected, and if you are using MFC library classes in your program, select the box and relink. That should solve your problem.

Figure 5-2 on the following page illustrates the Visual C++ build process.

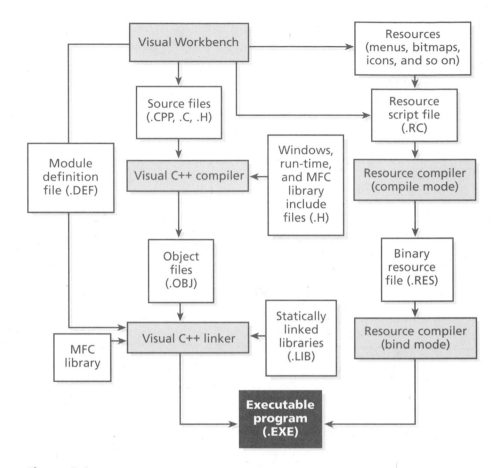

Figure 5-2. *The Visual C++ build process.*

Executing the SCRAMBLE Program

After you have built the SCRAMBLE application, you can execute it by choosing Execute from Visual Workbench's Project menu. When the SCRAMBLE program starts, you can open any number of child windows by choosing the New Window item from the Window menu or by clicking the New Document button on the toolbar.

The SCRAMBLE program might not impress you because each child window displays the same bitmap. Consider, however, that we wrote only about 22 lines of code. In the next few sections, we'll modify the SCRAMBLE program to add menu commands that allow the user to clear and redraw the bitmap in each child window.

Editing Menus with App Studio

One of the most important features of a Windows-based program is its menu bar. AppWizard generates two menu bars for an MDI application: one for its main frame window, and another for its child windows. The application can use more menu bars if necessary.

The SCRAMBLE program has two menu bars: a main frame window menu bar with the resource identifier IDR_MAINFRAME, and a child window menu bar with the resource identifier IDR_SCRAMBTYPE. SCRAMBLE uses the default main frame window menu bar provided by AppWizard, but its child window menu bar has one custom menu, Background. This menu has two items—Arches and Clear—as shown in Figure 5-3.

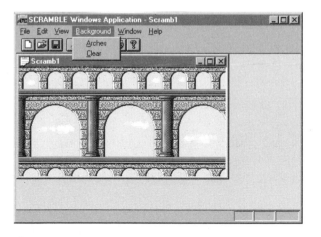

Figure 5-3. *The SCRAMBLE program's Background menu.*

The easiest way to create menus and menu items for Visual C++ programs is to use App Studio. Open App Studio, click on Menu in the Type list box, and you'll see SCRAMBLE's two menu resources, as shown in Figure 5-4 on the following page.

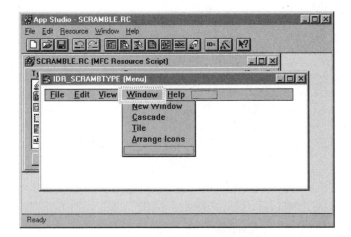

Figure 5-4. *The SCRAMBLE program's menu resources.*

To add the SCRAMBLE application's Background menu and its menu items, follow these steps:

1. Double-click on the IDR_SCRAMBTYPE item in the Resources list box.

2. In the IDR_SCRAMBTYPE window, select the Window menu, as shown here:

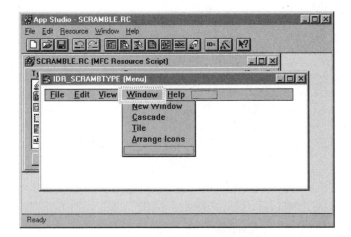

3. Press the Ins key. App Studio inserts a new, untitled menu between the View and Window menus, as shown here:

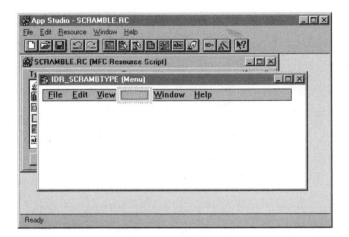

4. Double-click on the new menu. App Studio opens the Properties window, which displays the properties for the new menu.

5. In the Properties window, enter *&Background* in the Caption edit box, as shown here:

6. Double-click on the blank box under the Background menu.

7. Create a new menu item named Arches by entering *&Arches* in the Properties window's Caption edit box.

8. Create a second Background menu item, named Clear, by following the same procedures you used to create the Arches menu item. (Double-click on the blank box at the bottom of the menu to insert a new menu item.) The Background menu, with the Arches and Clear menu items, is shown on the following page.

9. Exit App Studio, and save your changes.

Keyboard Shortcuts

Windows-based programs often include *keyboard shortcuts* for users who prefer to use the keyboard rather than the mouse. A keyboard shortcut lets the user execute a menu command by pressing a key while holding down the Alt key. Keyboard shortcuts are identified by an underlined character in a menu item.

Keyboard shortcuts can be added to menu items by using App Studio; they do not require any special program code. Simply open the Properties window for the appropriate menu resource and add an ampersand (&) in front of the character you'd like to use as the keyboard shortcut.

Creating Message Handlers with ClassWizard

After you have added a menu item, or a set of menu items, to an application, creating message handlers for these menu items is an easy task thanks to ClassWizard, another Visual C++ tool.

To create message handlers for the menu items you have created in the
SCRAMBLE program, follow these steps:

1. Start ClassWizard by choosing the ClassWizard item from Visual
   Workbench's Browse menu. The ClassWizard dialog box appears, as
   shown here:

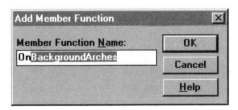

2. Select *CScrambleDoc* in the Class Name list box.

3. Select ID_BACKGROUND_ARCHES in the Object IDs list box.
   (ID_BACKGROUND_ARCHES is the default ID App Studio gave to
   the Arches menu item.)

4. Select the COMMAND item in the Messages list box.

5. Click the Add Function button. The Add Member Function dialog
   box appears, as shown here:

6. Accept the default member function name, *OnBackgroundArches*,
   in the Member Function Name edit box by clicking OK.

Notice that ClassWizard has now added *OnBackgroundArches* to the Member Functions list box, as shown below. (As you'll see later, ClassWizard has actually created a member function named *OnBackgroundArches* and has added it to your SCRAMDOC.CPP source code file. When you finish creating the SCRAMBLE program, this member function will be executed whenever the user chooses the Arches item from the Background menu. Of course, we have not yet written any code for this function. We'll do that in the next section.)

7. Using the same procedure you followed to create the *OnBackgroundArches* member function, create a member function named *OnBackgroundClear* for the ID_BACKGROUND_CLEAR object ID and add it to the Member Functions list box.

8. Click OK to close the ClassWizard dialog box.

Your application now has a Background menu with two menu items: Arches and Clear. You have also created message handlers for these two menu items, but neither of your message handlers contains any executable code, so the menu items don't do anything useful yet. You'll get a chance to fix that now.

Writing Code for Message Handlers

The SCRAMBLE program is almost ready to execute. All we need to do is add a small amount of code to the message handlers for the application's two customized menu items, Arches and Clear. Because we added member functions that load and unload the bitmap to the *CScrambleDoc* class, the message handlers are quite simple. Open SCRAMDOC.CPP, and then edit the *OnBackgroundArches* and *OnBackgroundClear* member functions as follows:

```
void CScrambleDoc::OnBackgroundArches()
{
    LoadBackground(m_pArches);
    UpdateAllViews(NULL);
}

void CScrambleDoc::OnBackgroundClear()
{
    UnloadBackground();
    UpdateAllViews(NULL);
}
```

Rebuild SCRAMBLE, and execute it. Open several child windows, and experiment with the Arches and Clear commands. You should be able to control the image displayed in each child window. Not bad for four extra lines of code!

The Visual C++ Debugger

Unfortunately, even the best programmers occasionally write code that doesn't work properly. To help swat bugs, Visual C++ includes an interactive, graphically based debugging tool built right into the Visual C++ editor. With the Visual C++ debugger, you can track down bugs in programs and correct them.

When you are designing a program, you can examine and correct compiler and linker errors that you encounter during the build process. These errors are usually caused by incorrect language syntax, undeclared variables, or misspelled keywords.

You can also use the Visual C++ debugger during the execution of your program, after all the syntax errors have been corrected and the project has been successfully built. Then you can use the debugger to track down bugs by setting breakpoints and examining variables. When you isolate an error at run time, you can correct it on the spot with the Visual C++ editor and then rebuild your program.

Setting Breakpoints

With the Visual C++ debugger, you can control the execution of your program and examine its state at various points in its execution by setting breakpoints that halt the execution of your program at whatever point in your code you specify. You can also set breakpoints that stop your program conditionally—that is, only when certain specified conditions are met.

Before you try to set a breakpoint, choose the Project item from the Tools menu and check the Build Mode to ensure that the Debug option is selected. You can then set breakpoints by choosing the Breakpoints command from the Debug menu or by clicking the Breakpoint button, shown here, on the Visual Workbench toolbar:

After you have set a breakpoint (or a series of breakpoints), you can start debugging your program by executing it under the control of the debugger. To do that, you choose the Go command from the Debug menu.

Stepping Through a Program

There are other ways to run a program under the control of the debugger. For example, you can step through your program one statement at a time, examining the results of each statement the program executes. As you step through a program, you can select functions that you want to step into or step over. When you step into a function, each line of the function is executed separately. When you step over a function, the entire function is executed. The debugger then stops and positions the insertion point at the end of the function that has been stepped over.

After you have stepped into a function, you can step out of it immediately by choosing the Step Out command, which returns you to the statement from which the function was called. You can step into, step over, and step out of functions by choosing the Step Into, Step Over, and Step Out commands from the Debug menu or by clicking the associated buttons, shown here, on the Visual Workbench toolbar:

You can also place the Visual C++ editor's insertion point on a particular line in a source code file and run your application under the control of the debugger up to the point at which the insertion point appears. This has the effect of turning the insertion point into a breakpoint. To run the debugger and stop execution at the editor's insertion point, simply choose the Step To Cursor command from the Debug menu.

Opening Debugger Windows

The Visual C++ debugger has two windows that you can open by choosing commands from the Debug menu and other windows that you can open by choosing commands from the Window menu. You can open the debugger's Watch window by choosing the Watch item from the Window menu. To open the QuickWatch window, you choose the QuickWatch item from the Debug menu.

The Watch window displays the values of selected variables at each breakpoint. With the QuickWatch window, you can examine the values of variables and change them for subsequent program execution. Figure 5-5 shows the QuickWatch window.

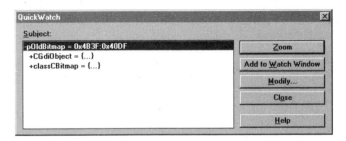

Figure 5-5. *The QuickWatch window.*

Two other windows that can be opened from the Window menu also display aspects of the program's state when it is paused. When execution of a program stops, the Registers window displays the values of your system's microprocessor registers; the Locals window displays the value of variables local to the current function. The Locals window is updated every time there is a change in the scope of variables in the application being debugged.

The Show Call Stack item on the Debug menu displays a list of all nested function calls. To use the debugger's call-stack feature, simply stop execution at a function, and then choose the Show Call Stack command. Visual Workbench opens a dialog box that displays a list of all nested function calls. The current function is the most deeply nested function; it is displayed at the top of the call-stack list. Less deeply nested functions appear farther down in the list. You can double-click on a function in the list to display the source code associated with that function.

When you terminate a debugging operation—either by exiting the program being debugged or by choosing the Stop Debugging command—any breakpoints that you have set remain in place. If you close your project, Visual Workbench stores any breakpoints you have set and restores them when you open the project again. That means that a debugging operation can span editing sessions.

Debugging is an art that you can learn and master with experience. This section has barely touched on the highlights of debugging Visual C++ programs. You can learn more about the Visual C++ debugger and how to use it by choosing the Visual Workbench item from the Help menu and then clicking the button labeled Debugging Your Application.

Listing: The SCRAMBLE Program

This chapter's sample program, SCRAMBLE, is an MDI application that displays a bitmap in child windows. Portions of the program described in this chapter are presented in Listing 5-1. You can find the complete program in this chapter's directory on the companion CD-ROM.

SCRAMDOC.H

```cpp
// scramdoc.h : interface of the CScrambleDoc class
//
//////////////////////////////////////////////////////////////

class CScrambleDoc : public CDocument
{
private:
    CBitmap* m_pArches;
    CBitmap* m_pBackground;
public:
    CBitmap* GetBackground() { return m_pBackground; }
    void LoadBackground(CBitmap*);
    void UnloadBackground();

protected: // create from serialization only
    CScrambleDoc();
    DECLARE_DYNCREATE(CScrambleDoc)

// Attributes
public:

// Operations
public:

// Implementation
public:
    virtual ~CScrambleDoc();
    virtual void Serialize(CArchive& ar);   // overridden for
                                            // document i/o
#ifdef _DEBUG
    virtual void AssertValid() const;
    virtual void Dump(CDumpContext& dc) const;
#endif
protected:
    virtual BOOL    OnNewDocument();

// Generated message map functions
protected:
    //{{AFX_MSG(CScrambleDoc)
    afx_msg void OnBackgroundArches();
    afx_msg void OnBackgroundClear();
    //}}AFX_MSG
    DECLARE_MESSAGE_MAP()
};

//////////////////////////////////////////////////////////////
```

Listing 5-1. *The SCRAMBLE program listing.* *(continued)*

Listing 5-1. *continued*

SCRAMDOC.CPP

```cpp
// scramdoc.cpp : implementation of the CScrambleDoc class
//

#include "stdafx.h"
#include "scramble.h"

#include "scramdoc.h"

#ifdef _DEBUG
#undef THIS_FILE
static char BASED_CODE THIS_FILE[] = __FILE__;
#endif


/////////////////////////////////////////////////////////////////
// CScrambleDoc

IMPLEMENT_DYNCREATE(CScrambleDoc, CDocument)

BEGIN_MESSAGE_MAP(CScrambleDoc, CDocument)
    //{{AFX_MSG_MAP(CScrambleDoc)
    ON_COMMAND(ID_BACKGROUND_ARCHES, OnBackgroundArches)
    ON_COMMAND(ID_BACKGROUND_CLEAR, OnBackgroundClear)
    //}}AFX_MSG_MAP
END_MESSAGE_MAP()

/////////////////////////////////////////////////////////////////
// CScrambleDoc construction/destruction

CScrambleDoc::CScrambleDoc()
{
    m_pArches = new CBitmap;
    if (m_pArches)
    {
        m_pArches->LoadBitmap(IDB_BITMAP1);
    }
    m_pBackground = m_pArches;
}

CScrambleDoc::~CScrambleDoc()
{
    if (m_pArches)
    {
        delete m_pArches;
```

```
        m_pArches = NULL;
    }
}

BOOL CScrambleDoc::OnNewDocument()
{
    if (!CDocument::OnNewDocument())
        return FALSE;
    // TODO: add reinitialization code here
    // (SDI documents will reuse this document)
    return TRUE;
}

/////////////////////////////////////////////////////////////
// CScrambleDoc serialization

void CScrambleDoc::Serialize(CArchive& ar)
{
    if (ar.IsStoring())
    {
        // TODO: add storing code here
    }
    else
    {
        // TODO: add loading code here
    }
}



/////////////////////////////////////////////////////////////
// CScrambleDoc diagnostics

#ifdef _DEBUG
void CScrambleDoc::AssertValid() const
{
    CDocument::AssertValid();
}

void CScrambleDoc::Dump(CDumpContext& dc) const
{
    CDocument::Dump(dc);
}

#endif //_DEBUG
```

(continued)

Listing 5-1. *continued*

```
/////////////////////////////////////////////////////////////
// CScrambleDoc commands

void CScrambleDoc::LoadBackground(CBitmap* pBackground)
{
    m_pBackground = pBackground;
}

void CScrambleDoc::UnloadBackground()
{
    m_pBackground = NULL;
}
void CScrambleDoc::OnBackgroundArches()
{
    LoadBackground(m_pArches);
    UpdateAllViews(NULL);
}

void CScrambleDoc::OnBackgroundClear()
{
    UnloadBackground();
    UpdateAllViews(NULL);
}
```

SCRAMVW.CPP

```
// scramvw.cpp : implementation of the CScrambleView class
//

#include "stdafx.h"
#include "scramble.h"

#include "scramdoc.h"
#include "scramvw.h"

#ifdef _DEBUG
#undef THIS_FILE
static char BASED_CODE THIS_FILE[] = __FILE__;
#endif


/////////////////////////////////////////////////////////////
// CScrambleView

IMPLEMENT_DYNCREATE(CScrambleView, CView)
```

```
BEGIN_MESSAGE_MAP(CScrambleView, CView)
    //{{AFX_MSG_MAP(CScrambleView)
    //}}AFX_MSG_MAP
    // Standard printing commands
    ON_COMMAND(ID_FILE_PRINT, CView::OnFilePrint)
    ON_COMMAND(ID_FILE_PRINT_PREVIEW, CView::OnFilePrintPreview)
END_MESSAGE_MAP()

/////////////////////////////////////////////////////////////
// CScrambleView construction/destruction

CScrambleView::CScrambleView()
{
    // TODO: add construction code here
}

CScrambleView::~CScrambleView()
{
}

/////////////////////////////////////////////////////////////
// CScrambleView drawing

void CScrambleView::OnDraw(CDC* pDC)
{
    CScrambleDoc* pDoc = GetDocument();
    CBitmap* pBitmap;
    BITMAP Bitmap;
    CDC dc;

    pBitmap = pDoc->GetBackground();
    if (pBitmap)
    {
        dc.CreateCompatibleDC(pDC);
        CBitmap* pOldBitmap = dc.SelectObject(pBitmap);

        pBitmap->GetObject(sizeof(Bitmap), &Bitmap);
        pDC->BitBlt(0, 0,
                    Bitmap.bmWidth,
                    Bitmap.bmHeight,
                    &dc,
                    0, 0,
                    SRCCOPY);
        dc.SelectObject(pOldBitmap);
    }
}
```

(continued)

Listing 5-1. *continued*

```
/////////////////////////////////////////////////////////
// CScrambleView printing

BOOL CScrambleView::OnPreparePrinting(CPrintInfo* pInfo)
{
    // default preparation
    return DoPreparePrinting(pInfo);
}

void CScrambleView::OnBeginPrinting(CDC* /*pDC*/,
    CPrintInfo* /*pInfo*/)
{
    // TODO: add extra initialization before printing
}

void CScrambleView::OnEndPrinting(CDC* /*pDC*/,
    CPrintInfo* /*pInfo*/)
{
    // TODO: add cleanup after printing
}



/////////////////////////////////////////////////////////
// CScrambleView diagnostics

#ifdef _DEBUG
void CScrambleView::AssertValid() const
{
    CView::AssertValid();
}

void CScrambleView::Dump(CDumpContext& dc) const
{
    CView::Dump(dc);
}

CScrambleDoc* CScrambleView::GetDocument() // non-debug version
                                           // is inline
{
    ASSERT(m_pDocument->IsKindOf(RUNTIME_CLASS(CScrambleDoc)));
    return (CScrambleDoc*) m_pDocument;
}

#endif //_DEBUG
```

What's Next?

In this chapter, you learned how to use the tools provided by Visual Work-bench to create and build customized Visual C++ applications. You wrote a program using the Visual C++ editor, added a couple of menu items to it with App Studio, and then used ClassWizard to equip your program with message handlers. The result was a Visual C++ application named SCRAMBLE. With the SCRAMBLE program, you can open multiple child windows and you can choose menu items that display or clear a bitmap from the child windows. You can control each child window individually.

In Chapter 6, "The MFC Library," we'll look more closely at the role of the MFC library in creating Visual C++ programs, and you'll have an opportunity to add more features to the SCRAMBLE program. For example, you'll learn how to control the initial size of each child window the program displays, and you'll learn how to add scroll bars and scrolling functionality to the child windows. You'll also learn how to add menu items that let the user display different bitmaps in different child windows.

The MFC Library

In any object-oriented language—including Microsoft Visual C++—one of the most important advantages of using classes is inheritance. As you learned in Chapters 4 and 5, inheritance allows objects to be derived from other objects. In C++, derived classes can inherit data members and functions from base classes, so designers of software development systems can create large libraries of C++ classes with specific relationships between classes built in.

One such library is the Microsoft Foundation Class (MFC) Library version 2.0 included with Visual C++ version 1.0. The MFC library is designed to help programmers use the power of C++ to build Windows-based applications. This is an important development in the evolution of Windows programming because code reusability is a goal that has long eluded users of the Windows API (application programming interface). Because the Windows API is not an object-oriented development tool and does not support inheritance, every application written under the Windows API has to be created essentially from scratch.

To solve that problem, the MFC library provides a set of C++ classes that are not only reusable but also transportable to a growing variety of computer platforms. Programs written using Visual C++ and the MFC library are compatible with computers based on the Intel 386/486/Pentium family of microprocessors and with other systems, including DEC, MIPS, and even Apple Macintosh computer systems. In addition to its portability to variety of platforms, the MFC library is also compiler-independent; it is used not only by Microsoft but also by other compiler and tool vendors (including Symantec, Watcom, MetaWare, and others). Visual C++ is not the only software development platform that supports the MFC library.

When you create an application using AppWizard, AppWizard generates skeleton program using classes and member functions provided in the MFC library. Your main job as a Visual C++ programmer is to add functionalities specific to your application. In this chapter, you'll see how AppWizard uses classes and member functions provided by the MFC library to create Visual C++ applications and how you can build on AppWizard's application frameworks to create specialized MFC applications. The following topics are covered:

- How the MFC library can be used with Visual C++ to create well-behaved programs

- How the classes and member functions implemented in the MFC library work together in Visual C++

- How AppWizard constructs application frameworks using MFC library classes

- How MFC applications handle events, messages, and other features of Windows-based programs

The chapter includes a new version of the SCRAMBLE program that demonstrates many of the topics introduced in the text. Using the SCRAMBLE program, we'll also look at how you can easily add some new features to an application by using Visual C++ tools. Here are some of the features of the SCRAMBLE program:

- It can display multiple background bitmaps in individual document windows simultaneously.

- It can create and display backgrounds in solid colors—even custom-designed colors—using a predefined Color dialog box provided by the MFC library.

- It lets you execute menu commands using custom-designed toolbar buttons.

- It places check marks next to currently active menu items.

- It lets you specify the initial size and many other characteristics of its main frame window and its child windows.

- Its child windows contain scroll bars and support scrolling.

Figure 6-1 shows the output of this chapter's SCRAMBLE program.

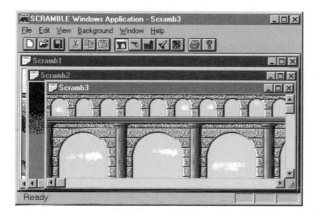

Figure 6-1. *Output of the SCRAMBLE application.*

About the MFC Library

As you learned in Chapter 5, "Visual C++ Tools," Visual C++ is a graphics-based, user-interactive delivery system designed to support MFC applications. AppWizard and the other tools included with Visual C++ help you build MFC applications as quickly and easily as possible, using graphics-based interfaces that take advantage of dialog boxes, drop-down menus, and mouse-generated commands.

The MFC library encapsulates most of the Windows API to take advantage of the object-oriented features of C++ programs. The MFC library calls functions implemented in the Windows API to create windows, dialog boxes, device contexts, controls, common GDI objects such as brushes and pens, and other standard Windows items. The classes that are used to create these kinds of objects provide MFC users with a convenient C++ interface to the structures in Windows that the classes encapsulate.

The single characteristic that sets the MFC library apart from other class libraries that are available for Windows is its very close mapping to the Windows API. When you need more direct access to the Windows API than the MFC library provides—for example, when you want to make an API call—you can call the API function directly. In fact, you can generally mix calls to the MFC library quite freely with direct calls to the Windows API.

The MFC library is designed to be used as a tool for developing with the Windows API, not as a substitute for the Windows API. It encapsulates Windows functions only when there is a clear advantage in doing so. Because the MFC library makes as much use as possible of functionalities that are already built into the Windows API, MFC programs are relatively small and fast—an accomplishment that many critics of C++ claimed was impossible in the early days, when the C++ language was struggling to get off the ground.

> **NOTE** During the early days of C++, some detractors leveled charges that C++ applications had to be big and slow. That never was true, and the MFC library is one of many well-designed C++ class libraries that have become showpieces of small, fast C++ code packages.

A Brief History of the MFC Library

Although the original designers of the MFC library might not have known it, from the beginning the MFC library was destined to become what Microsoft spokespeople now call the C++ API for Windows, or the "new Windows API." The MFC library was designed from the ground up to use only a subset of C++, which means that the MFC library does not attempt to exploit every feature available in C++. For example, it does not support multiple inheritance because this feature does not seem to fit in well with the overall architecture of the MFC library.

Version 1.0 of the MFC library shipped with Microsoft C/C++ version 7.0—the last version of C++ that Microsoft made available before the introduction of Visual C++. MFC version 1.0 contained just over 50 classes that provided a basic encapsulation of the Windows API.

MFC version 1.0 wasn't nearly as large or complex as its successors, but it was designed with expandability in mind, so it was a good foundation for future versions of the MFC library. MFC version 1.0 got C++ programmers started with the MFC library by providing the following:

- Diagnostic classes

- Support for collections and strings

- A proprietary method of exception handling that could be modified to accommodate future growth

- Basic Windows API classes for windowing and building simple applications

MFC Version 2.0

MFC version 2.0, which was introduced along with Visual C++ version 1.0, is provided on the companion CD-ROM. MFC version 2.0, like MFC version 1.0, is designed to be easily expandable and is a good foundation for the future growth of the MFC library.

MFC version 2.0 added a great deal of new support for Windows-based programming, including the following features:

- Support for a new document-and-view architecture. When you use AppWizard to generate a Windows-based program, the application framework created by AppWizard supports documents that can be displayed in multiple views. For more information, see the section "Using Documents and Views in MFC Programs" on page 192.

- A new set of architecture classes, including command classes, document and view classes, dialog box classes, and form-view classes. All these varieties of classes are described later in this chapter and in subsequent chapters.

- Seamless integration with a new set of GUI (graphical user interface) programming tools supported by Visual C++. These new tools include AppWizard, ClassWizard, and the other graphics-based utilities described in this chapter and in other chapters in this book.

MFC: The New Windows API

From the outset, the MFC library was designed in a more orderly way than the traditional Windows API (which has been criticized—quite justly—for being designed in some awkward and peculiar ways), and it has a more orderly architecture. It neatly encapsulates functions provided by the Windows API, arranges them in a structured and much more comprehensible order, and provides support for almost all Windows API procedures, including the following:

- Message management using message maps (which are covered in Chapter 7, "Of Mice and Messages")

- Memory management, including both memory allocation and cleanup operations after objects are destroyed

- Graphics, screen, and device I/O using simple encapsulation mechanisms

- Management of windows and controls using C++ classes

- Tasking operations

The MFC library's role in Windows-based applications

When you write an MFC application, you can let the MFC library handle all your window management, messaging, and resource management. The MFC library is equipped with C++ classes that encapsulate both MDI (multiple-document interface) and SDI (single-document interface) applications.

The MFC library also supports message management. MFC is equipped with a powerful message-handling mechanism that can automatically map messages to member functions in C++ classes that you use in your application. MFC also provides default responses for many commonly used messages. This means that you don't have to write a handler for every message your application uses. However, if you want a particular message handled in a way that differs from the way that the MFC library handles it, you can always override MFC's default behavior and write your own message handler.

In an MFC program, these are some of the tasks that MFC library classes and member functions can perform:

- Track memory allocation.

- Report memory leaks.

- Track and report unfreed resources.

- Handle common types of I/O. The MFC library has a mechanism for routing screen I/O to a particular part of an AppWizard-generated application framework, where the application can implement its own behavior.

- Provide built-in support for common types of file I/O operations, such as the New, Open, and Save commands on the File menu.

The MFC library carries out these operations using member functions, many of which encapsulate Windows API calls. These MFC member functions can make your applications simpler and safer, at a cost of almost no additional overhead.

The MFC library also simplifies the handling of Windows objects by taking on many data management chores. For example, many MFC library classes use the *this* pointer provided by the C++ language to perform tasks that rely on Windows handles in Windows API programs.

Handles, pointers, and the MFC library

In Windows API applications, handles are used to access various kinds of Windows objects—windows, menus, icons, controls—and even items that don't represent visible objects, such as instances of applications. In MFC programs, these objects are not usually accessed with handles. More often, they are accessed using pointers to C++ objects.

Suppose that an MFC application calls an MFC member function to create a new Windows object. In turn, the MFC library calls a Windows API function, which creates the object and returns a handle to the object. When the MFC function that called the Windows API function obtains a handle to the object created, the handle is automatically stored in a public member variable of the newly created object. Later, if the application that created the object needs the new object's handle for some reason, the program can retrieve the handle by accessing the public member variable in which the handle has been stored.

In the sample code presented in this book, you'll see many examples of how C++ pointers are used instead of handles in MFC programs. After you become familiar with MFC programming, you'll rarely need to access the handles of the objects that you use in your Visual C++ programs. But in rare situations when you need access, it will be there.

Other parameters that are used in calls to Windows API functions are not used in calls to MFC functions. Often the MFC library doesn't need the extra arguments because it already has the information that those arguments would provide.

Although MFC applications and Windows API–style applications are equipped with different sets of functions, the functions provided in the MFC library have a familiar look if you're used to working with the Windows API. The parameters that Visual C++ programs pass to MFC member functions are similar to the parameters that are expected by corresponding Windows API functions, with certain fairly consistent exceptions—such as the fact that handle parameters are usually not required in calls to MFC functions.

Secrets of the MFC Gurus

The designers of the MFC library used many clever tricks to make MFC small and fast. Here are a few:

- **Using Windows data handling**—The MFC library never duplicates any data that's already used by Windows. Instead, MFC simply uses the data from Windows.

- **Calling Windows code**—The MFC library never duplicates operations that Windows already provides. Therefore, MFC doesn't reinvent the wheel by re-creating operations that Windows already has code to handle.

■ **Using inline functions to call the Windows API**—As noted in Chapter 3, "C++ Basics," C++ inline functions are short functions that are embedded in your application at design time instead of being called in the traditional way each time they are accessed. In the MFC library, many calls to Windows API functions are implemented as inline functions. This means that when your MFC application is compiled and executed, it calls Windows API functions directly whenever possible, instead of calling an MFC function that calls a Windows API function. Using inline code in this way increases the speed and efficiency of MFC applications.

■ **Using macros when it makes sense to use them**—C-language macros are often handy and efficient substitutes for short functions, but macros have received a lot of bad press because they don't perform type checking. In C++, inline functions offer the same advantages as C macros, with the added benefit of type checking, so C++ programmers have even less reason to use macros. However, there are times when it makes sense to use them. For example, as you'll see in Chapter 7, "Of Mice and Messages," the MFC library uses macros to map messages to message handlers by embedding direct calls to message handlers in your source code at design time. In this kind of message mapping, the lack of type checking that macros have been criticized for poses no danger because all the macros used in the MFC message-mapping system are thoroughly debugged and are placed in your code automatically. Used in this way, macros are probably the speediest message-handling mechanism that could be incorporated into a Windows-based program.

The MFC Library Class Hierarchy

The MFC library is a set of more than 100 classes that are implemented in more than 60,000 lines of code. Most of this code is encapsulated in C++ classes, and all of it is optimized, pretested, and ready to use in your Visual C++ programs.

MFC's *Afx* Functions

The only functions in the MFC library that aren't encapsulated in C++ classes are the Visual C++ *application framework functions*—a special group of global functions. *Afx* functions, which begin with the letters *Afx,* are global functions that are provided to interface as seamlessly as possible between the MFC library and the C-language Windows API.

There are many *Afx* functions in the MFC library. For example, *Afx-MessageBox* is a global function that displays a message dialog box. Another *Afx* function is *AfxWinMain*, the MFC equivalent of the *WinMain* function used in traditional Windows API–style programs. You'll learn more about the *WinMain* function in the section "The *WinMain* Function" on page 186.

Most classes in the MFC library are descended from a root class named *CObject*, which some pundits have referred to as "the mother of all classes." All classes descended from *CObject* inherit important capabilities, such as built-in diagnostic capabilities and the ability to *serialize* files—that is, to store them on disk and read them from disk automatically.

Some MFC library classes, such as *CString* and *CTime*, are not derived from the *CObject* class because they do not require serialization capabilities or the other features that derivation from *CObject* provides. (Both *CString* and *CTime* are described in more detail in Chapter 7, "Of Mice and Messages.")

> **IP** By convention, the names of all classes provided in the MFC library begin with a capital C. So if you create classes of your own that are not derived from MFC library classes, it might be a good idea to start their names with some other letter.

The classes in the MFC library can be divided into the categories listed in Table 6-1. Many of the classes listed in the table are described in more detail in later sections of this chapter and in Chapter 7.

Class Category	Description
MFC framework classes	The MFC framework classes contribute to the architecture of an application framework. They are diagrammed in Figure 6-2 on page 181.
CObject (the MFC library root class)	*CObject* is the root class of almost all other classes in the MFC library.
Windows application class (*CWinApp*)	Every Visual C++ application built with the MFC framework has a single application object. This object is always an instance of the *CWinApp* class.
File classes	The MFC library provides file classes that you can use to write functions for I/O processing. You won't have to use these classes much if you let MFC handle file I/O for you. The four file classes provided by the MFC library are *CFile*, *CMemFile*, *CStdioFile*, and *CArchive*. They encapsulate functions that handle disk-file storage, files stored in memory, file I/O operations, and file archiving.
Collection classes	Visual C++ supplies a large set of collection classes for handling aggregates of data such as arrays, lists, string lists, and collections of mapped data. These classes, all derived from *CObject*, include *CObArray* and *CObList* (for C++ objects), *CStringList* (for strings), and various mapping objects such as *CMapPtrToWord*, *CMapWordToOb*, and *CMapStringToPtr*.

Table 6-1. *Categories of MFC library classes.*   *(continued)*

Table 6-1. *continued*

Class Category	Description
Diagnostic classes	The MFC library's diagnostic classes can help you debug your application. The diagnostic classes are *CDumpContext* and *CMemoryState*.
Exception classes	The MFC library exception classes provide a set of exception-handling mechanisms that are described in the *Visual C++ Class Library Reference*. The base class in this group is *CException*. Other exception classes include *CArchiveException*, *CFileException*, and *CMemoryException*.
Miscellaneous support classes	The miscellaneous group of classes encapsulates strings, graphics coordinates, and time and date information. It includes the classes *CPoint*, *CRect*, *CSize*, *CString*, *CTime*, and *CTimeSpan*.
Command-related classes	These classes, and their descendants, provide objects that encapsulate messages to windows. There are two command-related classes. One is *CCmdTarget*, which serves as the base class for all classes of objects that can receive and respond to messages. The other class in this category, *CCmdUI*, provides objects that can be used to update user-interface objects such as menu items and toolbar buttons.
Document classes	Document classes are related to documents and, indirectly, to views. (View classes are described later in this table.) *CDocTemplate* is the base class for document templates, which are described in the section "Using Documents and Views in MFC Programs" on page 192. Other

Class Category	Description
	classes in the document group include *CDocument*, the base class for user-defined document classes; *CSingleDocTemplate*, used to create SDI applications; and *CMultiDocTemplate*, used to create MDI applications.
Visual object classes	The visual object classes in the MFC library provide user-interface objects such as windows, dialog boxes, controls, and menus.
Window classes	All window classes are derived from *CWnd*, the largest class in the MFC library. Classes derived from *CWnd* include *CFrameWnd*, the base class for the main frame window of SDI applications; *CMDIFrameWnd*, the base class for the main frame window of MDI applications; and *CMDIChildWnd*, the base class for document windows in MDI applications.
Dialog classes	The base class *CDialog* and its descendants encapsulate the implementations of dialog boxes. Descendants of *CDialog* include several classes that provide standard dialog boxes for common operations. Common-dialog classes include *CFileDialog*, *CPrintDialog*, *CFontDialog*, *CColorDialog*, and *CFindReplaceDialog*.
View classes	Objects created from the MFC library view classes draw the client areas of frame windows and provide input and output for information stored in documents. View classes include *CView*, *CScrollView*, *CEditView*, and *CFormView*.

(continued)

Table 6-1. *continued*

Class Category	Description
Control classes	The MFC library control classes encapsulate the functionality of common dialog box controls. Control classes include *CStatic* (for static controls), *CEdit* (for edit controls), and *CButton* (for dialog box button controls).
Device-context classes	The MFC library device-context classes encapsulate device-context objects provided in the Windows API. The base class in the DC group is the *CDC* class, which encapsulates the graphical objects known as *HDC* objects in C-language programs. Other classes in the device-context group include *CClientDC*, *CPaintDC*, *CWindowDC*, and *CMetaFileDC*. Chapter 10, "Visual C++ Graphics," explains and illustrates the use of the *CDC* class.
Drawing object classes	The MFC library drawing object classes encapsulate handle-based GDI objects. They are designed to be used with *CDC* objects. The MFC library's drawing object classes are described in Chapter 10, "Visual C++ Graphics."
Menu class	*CMenu* encapsulates the functionality of both drop-down and popup menus.

The MFC Framework Classes

The MFC framework classes include a set of 10 classes that AppWizard uses to instantiate objects every time it creates an application framework. These classes are diagrammed in Figure 6-2.

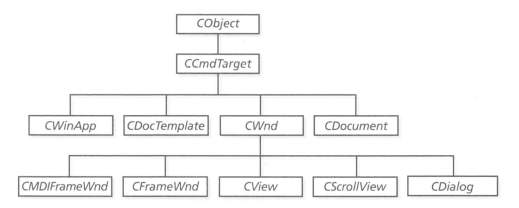

Figure 6-2. *The MFC framework class hierarchy.*

The *CObject* Class

As mentioned, most of the classes in the MFC library—and all the classes that AppWizard uses when it generates an application framework—are derived from the *CObject* class. You can also derive your own objects from the *CObject* class—and that is often a very good idea. Deriving your own classes from the *CObject* class (or from MFC library classes derived from *CObject*) can provide your classes with many useful features, such as support for serialization, availability of C++ class information at run time, and retrieval of diagnostic information while you're debugging your programs.

These advantages don't cost much; the only overhead added by a *CObject*-derived class is a few virtual functions and a single *CRuntimeClass* structure. (The *CRuntimeClass* structure makes it possible to create objects of specified classes at run time and lets you retrieve information about objects and classes at run time.)

The *CCmdTarget* Class

CCmdTarget is a class with special capabilities for handling messages and commands that are triggered by the user or originated by the system. When Windows detects such an event, it dispatches an appropriate message or command that is then passed to an object derived from the *CCmdTarget* class.

Objects derived from *CCmdTarget* are the only kinds of objects that can handle messages. If a message is dispatched and no *CCmdTarget* object can be found to handle it, the system eventually handles the message by executing a *CWnd* member function named *DefWindowProc*, which

181

handles the default processing of messages. The *DefWindowProc* procedure is explained in more detail in Chapter 7, "Of Mice and Messages."

MFC library classes derived from *CCmdTarget* include *CWinApp*, *CWnd*, *CFrameWnd*, *CView*, and *CDocument*. Because all these classes are derived from *CCmdTarget*, they all have built-in capabilities for handling messages and commands. So whenever you create an application object, a window object, a view object, or a document object in an MFC application, your object has message-handling capabilities.

When you want to create a new class that needs to handle messages, you can derive your class from one of the MFC library classes derived from *CCmdTarget*. MFC applications don't often derive classes directly from the *CCmdTarget* class, but they often instantiate objects from *CCmdTarget*'s child classes.

The *CWinApp* Class

In an MFC application, the *CWinApp* class encapsulates all functions that make the application run and terminate. When an MFC framework application starts up, one of the first things it must do is construct a *CWinApp*-derived object. Before an MFC program creates any windows or other objects, it must instantiate a *CWinApp* object. Only then can the program perform any other kinds of actions.

In an MFC application, the most noteworthy feature of the program's *CWinApp*-derived class is that it always overrides a *CWinApp* member function named *InitInstance*. The *CWinApp::InitInstance* member function initializes an MFC program by performing the following tasks:

- Loading standard file options from an .INI file, including the names of the most recently used (MRU) files

- For an MDI application, creating a main frame window

- Processing the command line to open a document specified on the command line or to open a new, empty document

- Creating *document templates,* which manage documents, views, and frame windows

- Registering document templates that you have created

Every MFC framework application overrides *InitInstance* to provide its own particular set of functionalities. Typically, an MFC program overrides *InitInstance* to construct its main window object and to set a *CWinApp* member variable named *m_pMainWnd* to point to that window. When the window that is pointed to by an application's *m_pMainWnd* member variable is closed, the Visual C++ framework automatically terminates the application.

The *CWnd* Class

When you create an MFC application, its main frame window and all its child windows are instantiated either from the *CWnd* class or from its subclasses, such as *CFrameWnd*, *CMDIFrameWnd*, and *CView*. The dialog boxes and controls used in an MFC program are also instantiated from classes derived from *CWnd,* such as *CDialog*, *CButton*, *CControlBar*, and *CToolbar*. (Dialog box and control classes are covered in detail in Chapter 8, "Dialog Boxes," and Chapter 9, "Managing Data.")

Because the *CWnd* class is itself derived from the *CCmdTarget* class, objects derived from the *CWnd* class have message-handling capabilities built in. That means that *CWnd*-derived objects can implement message-handler functions that are activated through message maps. In fact, most messages in your MFC applications will generally be handled by objects derived either directly or indirectly from the *CWnd* class.

When AppWizard creates an MFC framework, two *CWnd*-derived classes are created: a class named *CMainFrame* that serves as the program's main frame window, and a *CView* class from which the program's *CView* object is created.

The *CFrameWnd* and *CMDIFrameWnd* Classes

CFrameWnd, a child class of *CWnd*, is the base class of the main frame window object used in every MFC application. When AppWizard creates an SDI application, the program's only window is a main frame window instantiated from the *CWnd* class. When you use AppWizard to create an MDI application, the program's main frame window is an instance of the *CMDIFrameWnd* class, which is derived from *CFrameWnd*. When AppWizard generates the framework for an MDI application, a class named *CMainFrame* is automatically derived from the *CMDIFrameWnd* class.

The *CView, CScrollView,* and *CDocument* Classes

Every framework-based MFC application contains at least one object derived from the poetic-sounding *CView* class. Objects derived from the *CView* class have a special kind of relationship with objects derived from the *CDocument* class. This relationship is based on the fact that *CDocument*-derived classes are specially designed to help applications store and manage data, whereas *CView*-derived classes are specially designed to display that data in windows.

Because *CView*-derived objects and *CDocument*-derived objects work together, every framework-based MFC application has at least one *CDocument*-derived class as well as at least one *CView*-derived class. Objects instantiated from *CDocument*-derived classes are often called *document objects,* and objects instantiated from *CView*-derived classes are often referred to as *view objects.*

In an MFC program, a single document class object can be associated with multiple view objects. For example, a document used in a spreadsheet program might have two kinds of view objects: one view object for displaying spreadsheet data in cells on a grid, and another view object for storing the same information in a graph.

The reverse is not true, however: an MFC program cannot associate multiple document objects with the same view object. When a view object in an MFC program displays information, that information must always come from the same document object; if information from a different document object is to be displayed, it must be displayed using a different view object.

Because information stored in *CDocument* objects is often displayed in windows, the *CDocument* class has a function named *GetDocument,* which *CView* objects can use to access data stored in *CDocument* objects. To help applications print information stored in *CDocument* objects, the *CDocument* class also has member functions that can automatically interface applications with printers.

When AppWizard creates an MFC application, a view class derived from *CView* and a document class derived from *CDocument* are always created, and files defining and implementing both classes are automatically created and added to the project. The SCRAMBLE program introduced in

Chapter 5 has a *CView*-derived class named *CScrambleView* and a *CDocument*-derived class named *CScrambleDoc*. The *CScrambleView* class is defined and implemented in a pair of files named SCRAMVW.H and SCRAMVW.CPP, and the files that define and implement the *CScrambleDoc* class are named SCRAMDOC.H and SCRAMDOC.CPP.

In the Chapter 5 version of the SCRAMBLE program, the *CScrambleView* class was derived from the *CView* class. In this chapter's version of the program, *CScrambleView* is derived from *CScrollView*, which is in turn derived from the *CView* class. *CScrollView* is a class that includes scrolling capabilities and all the capabilities of the *CView* class. We'll examine the scrolling capabilities of the *CScrollView* class in the section "Adding Scrolling to the SCRAMBLE Program's Views" on page 212.

The *CDocTemplate* Class

To associate document objects with their corresponding view objects and with the main frame window of your application, the MFC library provides an object called a *document template*. Document templates provide information that describes all the relationships that an MFC application has with its main frame window, its documents, and its views. Document templates are derived from the *CDocTemplate* class.

In an MFC application, each document that is created is associated with a different document template. To keep track of the document template with which a document is associated, the MFC framework uses a constant called a *document type*.

When AppWizard generates an application framework, AppWizard assigns a type identifier to the one document type it creates. For example, this chapter's SCRAMBLE program contains one type of document, which has the type identifier *IDR_SCRAMBTYPE*. If an application creates additional document types, it must create a new document template for each new document type.

A document template identifies the resources (such as menu, icon, and accelerator-table resources) that are used by the framework with that document type. A document template also stores strings containing additional information about the document, including those listed on the following page.

- The name of the document type (for example, "Worksheet")

- The filename extension used to identify documents of the type being created (for example, ".TXT")

- Other strings that might be needed to provide information about the document type being created

How an MFC Program Works

One of the most puzzling problems that can confront an MFC novice is figuring out exactly what happens when an MFC program starts. No matter how many times you search through the code that AppWizard creates for an MFC framework, you'll never find a *WinMain* function, a *WndProc* function, or any of the other kinds of functions that traditional Windows-based programs have. In the framework code that AppWizard generates, you also won't find a function that calls the program's *InitInstance* member function. But we know that *InitInstance* has to be called in order for an MFC program to execute. So how does *InitInstance* get called, anyway?

As you'll soon see, the answer is quite simple. Although AppWizard doesn't generate any source code for a *WinMain* function or a window procedure function when it generates an application framework, the object code that's generated when you build a framework application does contain a *WinMain*-style function and a *WndProc*-style function—and both those functions work in exactly the same way that they work in traditional Windows-based applications. You never see *WinMain* or *WndProc* in the source code that AppWizard creates because those functions are not created by AppWizard; instead, they're provided in object code libraries that are linked with your application, and they're pulled into your application from those libraries at link time.

The *WinMain* Function

In an MFC application, just as in a Windows API-style program, the *WinMain* function is the first function that executes. All other functions are called, either directly or indirectly, from *WinMain*. When the *WinMain* function ends, the application terminates.

Where's My *WinMain* Function?

Although every MFC application function contains a *WinMain* function, you don't have to write it, and neither does AppWizard. That's because the *WinMain* function is prewritten and precompiled and is provided in a statically linked library that's shipped with Visual C++. When you build a framework-based MFC application, the Visual C++ compiler binds the *WinMain* function's object code to the executable code of the application it is building. So no one has to write (or generate) any source code to implement the MFC library's *WinMain* function.

Because the *WinMain* function is provided in an object code library and is bound to your application's code at link time, you can't find it by searching through the files that AppWizard has created for your application—it simply isn't there. Fortunately, though, the MFC library does provide a way for you to examine an application's *WinMain* function so that you can see how it works. In fact, Microsoft provides the complete source code for all MFC library classes and member functions in every copy of Visual C++ it distributes. That's a big benefit to developers of MFC programs. In fact, it's vital; neither the Visual C++ debugger nor the Visual C++ Source Browser would work properly if Microsoft did not provide the source code for all the classes and global functions that are implemented in the MFC library.

You can track down the MFC source code by opening the MSVC folder on the companion CD-ROM and then opening the MFC subfolder. Inside the MFC folder, you'll find the SRC folder, which contains all the MFC implementation files. The source code for the MFC library's *WinMain* member function is in a file named WINMAIN.CPP. Other important functions are defined in the APPCORE.CPP file, including *CWinApp::Run* and *CWinApp::PumpMessage*, which are discussed later in this section.

(continued)

Where's My *WinMain* Function? *continued*

The header files that define the MFC classes are also provided in the MSVC\MFC folder. To find them, look inside the INCLUDE folder. The object code libraries that your application links with to access the MFC library are there too; to locate the object code libraries, look in the MSVC\MFC\LIB folder.

The MFC source code that is provided in the MSVC\MFC\SRC and MSVC\MFC\INCLUDE folders can be very useful in many different kinds of situations. For example, when you're debugging an MFC program and an error halts your debugger at a line of code in a source file, you'll often find that the function in which the debugger has halted is one that you didn't write and that you know absolutely nothing about. When that happens, Visual C++ novices are often puzzled (or panic-stricken!) because they don't realize that this function is an MFC function that is defined in MSVC\MFC\INCLUDE and implemented in MSVC\MFC\SRC. To help prevent this kind of confusion, it's a good idea to learn what kinds of source files are kept in the MSVC\MFC\SRC and MSVC\MFC\INCLUDE folders and what the most common functions in those folders do.

When a framework-based MFC application starts, its *WinMain* function creates a *CWinApp*-derived object for the application that is being executed. *WinMain* creates this object by calling the global function *AfxGetApp* to obtain a pointer to the current instance of the application. Then *WinMain* calls the global function *AfxWinInit* to perform some important initialization procedures such as obtaining an instance handle and setting the *CWinApp::m_nCmdShow* member variable, which specifies some display settings for the application's main frame window. After creating the *CWinApp*-derived object, *WinMain* calls *CWinApp::InitInstance* to initialize the application.

The *InitInstance* Member Function

The *InitInstance* function performs a number of tasks. First it calls a *CWinApp* member function named *SetDialogBkColor* to set the background color of the program's dialog boxes to gray. Then *InitInstance* calls a member function named *LoadStdProfileSettings* to enable and load the program's most recently used file list and the last preview state. After that the *Init-Instance* member function calls the *CWinApp::AddDocTemplate* function to create a document object for the application and to associate that document with the program's main frame window class and view class. (You'll learn more about the *AddDocTemplate* function in the section "Document Templates" on page 197.)

When all that processing is complete, *InitInstance* executes a series of statements to create and open a main frame window and then calls a member function named *OnFileNew* to create a document. When that is done, the *InitInstance* function provides an *if* clause in which you can place any command-line processing statements you need and then returns *TRUE*.

Next *WinMain* calls another *CWinApp* member function, named *Run*, which contains the main message loop of the program being executed. The message loop inside the *Run* member function cycles repeatedly until the user terminates the application. *Run* then returns control to *WinMain*, which terminates the program.

When all that is done, *WinMain* checks to see whether the application has any global initializations to be performed (a rare requirement).

The *Run* Member Function

One of the most important statements in an MFC application's *WinMain* function is the following:

```
nReturnCode = AfxGetApp()->Run();
```

When this statement executes, *WinMain* calls a *CWinApp* member function named *Run*, which is defined in the APPCORE.CPP file. Listing 6-1 shows the source code for the *CWinApp::Run* member function.

```
int CWinApp::Run()
{

    if (m_pMainWnd == NULL)
    {
        TRACE0("Warning: 'm_pMainWnd' is NULL in CWinApp::Run"
            " - quitting application\n");
        ::PostQuitMessage(0);
    }
```

Listing 6-1. *The* CWinApp::Run *member function.*   *(continued)*

Listing 6-1. *continued*

```
#ifdef _DEBUG
    if (!afxData.bWin31 && !afxData.bWin30Compat)
    {
        TRACE0("Warning:running program under Win3.0 but without\n"
            "the 'AfxEnableWin30Compatibility()' API being called\n"
            "Program may not behave correctly under Win3.1\n"
            "Please refer to MFC Technical Note TN034\n");
    }
#endif //_DEBUG

            // acquire and dispatch messages until
            // a WM_QUIT message is received
    for (; ;)
    {
        LONG lIdleCount = 0;
        // check to see if we can do idle work
        while (!::PeekMessage(&m_msgCur, NULL, NULL, NULL,
            PM_NOREMOVE) && OnIdle(lIdleCount++))
        {
            // more work to do
        }

        // either we have a message, or OnIdle returned false

        if (!PumpMessage())
            break;
    }

    return ExitInstance();
}
```

An MFC framework application spends most of its time in its *WinMain* function, and *WinMain* spends most of its time executing the *Run* member function of the *CWinApp* class.

After the *Run* member function does some error checking, it calls a member function named *OnIdle*, which your application can override if it needs to do some processing during idle CPU time. Operations that make use of timers are often carried out inside overrides of the *OnIdle* member function.

The *PumpMessage* Member Function

When *OnIdle* has been called, *Run* calls the *CWinApp* member function named *PumpMessage*. The *PumpMessage* member function, as its name implies, is a *message pump*—a loop that retrieves event messages from the Windows message queue one by one and dispatches them to message handlers.

Message pumps are not unique to MFC programs; they are also used in traditional Windows API–style programs. (API-style message pumps were introduced in Chapter 2, "Introduction to Windows Programming.") The *PumpMessage* member function in a framework-based MFC application is a little longer than a conventional API-style message pump, but it does essentially the same kind of work. Listing 6-2 shows the source code for the *PumpMessage* function in the MFC library's APPCORE.CPP file. *PumpMessage* does more error checking than a conventional API-style message pump, but it too winds up calling *TranslateAccelerator*, *TranslateMessage*, and *DispatchMessage*, the same functions called in an old-fashioned Windows API message pump.

```
BOOL CWinApp::PumpMessage()
{
#ifdef _DEBUG
    if (m_nDisablePumpCount != 0)
    {
        TRACE0("Error: CWinApp::PumpMessage() called when"
            "not permitted\n");
            ASSERT(FALSE);
    }
#endif

    if (!::GetMessage(&m_msgCur, NULL, NULL, NULL))
    {
#ifdef _DEBUG
        if (afxTraceFlags & 2)
            TRACE0("PumpMessage - Received WM_QUIT\n");
        m_nDisablePumpCount++; // application must die
            // NOTE: prevents calling message loop;
            // things in 'ExitInstance'
            // will never be decremented
#endif
        return FALSE;
    }
```

Listing 6-2. *The MFC* PumpMessage *member function.* (continued)

Listing 6-2. *continued*

```
#ifdef _DEBUG
    if (afxTraceFlags & 2)
        _AfxTraceMsg("PumpMessage", &m_msgCur);
#endif

    // process this message
    if (!PreTranslateMessage(&m_msgCur))
    {
        ::TranslateMessage(&m_msgCur);
        ::DispatchMessage(&m_msgCur);
    }
    return TRUE;
}
```

Window Procedures in MFC Programs

As mentioned in Chapter 2, "Introduction to Windows Programming," every Windows API–style program has one *window procedure function*— usually named something like *WndProc*—for each type of window the program uses. These functions typically contain a long switch statement that analyzes each message received from a function named *GetMessage* and routes the message to an appropriate message handler.

In Visual C++, you'll be happy to hear, you'll never have to write another window procedure or another monster switch statement for routing messages to the proper message handlers. In framework-based MFC applications, the framework creates all the window procedures it needs without any help from you. And instead of using long switch statements to route messages, Visual C++ uses a mechanism called a message map, which you'll learn all about in Chapter 7, "Of Mice and Messages."

Using Documents and Views in MFC Programs

At the heart of every framework-based Visual C++ application is a pair of objects called a *document* and a *view*. As mentioned, a document is an object that manages the data used by an application, and a view is an object that manages the display of that data on the screen.

In an MFC program, a document is always an object that is derived from the *CDocument* class, and a view is always an object derived from the *CView* class or from a child class of the *CView* class, such as *CScrollView*, *CFormView*, or *CEditView*. Figure 6-3 shows how a document and a view work together in an MFC application.

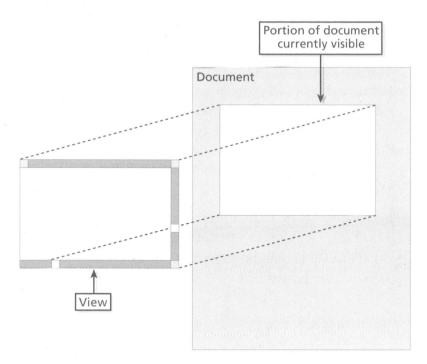

Portion of document currently visible

Document

View

Figure 6-3. *How a document and a view work together in an MFC application.*

Document objects

As Figure 6-3 illustrates, documents and views are very closely linked in Visual C++ applications. The *CDocument* class provides *CDocument*-derived objects with member functions that can automatically read documents from a disk, save documents on a disk, and perform other kinds of document-related operations. To load and save data, *CDocument*-derived objects use *serialization*, which is described in more detail in Chapter 7, "Of Mice and Messages."

View objects

In an MFC application, the view object is the user's window into data stored in a document. When a window contains text or graphics data that can be updated by the user and stored on a disk, a well-behaved Visual C++ program stores that data in a document object and displays it using the view object that the application derives from the *CView* class or from a child class of *CView*. In an MFC program, a view object determines how the data in a document object is displayed and provides GUI tools that let the user interact with that data.

Creating views for SDI and MDI applications

When you generate a Visual C++ framework using AppWizard, the App-Wizard utility displays a dialog box that lets you specify whether you want to create an SDI program or an MDI program. (For details, see Chapter 5, "Visual C++ Tools.") If you tell AppWizard to create an SDI application, AppWizard derives your application's main frame window from MFC's *CFrameWnd* class. If you tell AppWizard to build an MDI application, AppWizard derives your program's main frame window from the *CMDIFrameWnd* class.

This chapter's SCRAMBLE program is an MDI application, so its *CMainFrame* window is derived from the *CMDIFrameWnd* class. The MAINFRM.H file that defines the SCRAMBLE program's *CMainFrame* class is shown in Listing 6-3.

MAINFRM.H
```
// mainfrm.h : interface of the CMainFrame class
//
/////////////////////////////////////////////////////////////////

class CMainFrame : public CMDIFrameWnd
{
    DECLARE_DYNAMIC(CMainFrame)

public:
    CMainFrame();

// Attributes
public:

// Operations
public:

// Implementation
public:
    virtual ~CMainFrame();
#ifdef _DEBUG
    virtual void AssertValid() const;
    virtual void Dump(CDumpContext& dc) const;
#endif
```

Listing 6-3. *The MAINFRM.H file.*

```
protected:     // control bar embedded members
    CStatusBar      m_wndStatusBar;
    CToolBar        m_wndToolBar;

// Generated message map functions
protected:
    //{{AFX_MSG(CMainFrame)
    afx_msg int OnCreate(LPCREATESTRUCT lpCreateStruct);
        // NOTE - the ClassWizard will add and remove member
        // functions here.
        // DO NOT EDIT what you see in these blocks of
        // generated code !
    //}}AFX_MSG
    DECLARE_MESSAGE_MAP()
};

/////////////////////////////////////////////////////////////////
```

If your program uses multiple views, you can derive more document frame window objects from the document class that AppWizard creates for you. To do that, you modify the *CDocTemplate* object that AppWizard creates. For more information about *CDocTemplate* objects, see the section "Document Templates" on page 197.

Creating scrolling views

The *CView* class is derived from the MFC library's *CWnd* class. Because *CScrollView*, *CFormView*, and *CEditView* are derived from *CView*, they also inherit member functions from the *CWnd* class.

In Chapter 5's SCRAMBLE application, the program's view object was derived from the *CView* class. In this chapter's SCRAMBLE program, as you'll see in the section "Adding Scrolling to the SCRAMBLE Program's Views" on page 212, the view object used by the application is derived from the *CScrollView* class.

The *OnInitialUpdate* member function

In an MFC application, the best place to initialize a view is in an override of a virtual member function of the *CView* class, named *OnInitialUpdate*. When you execute a framework-based MFC application, the program's framework calls the *CView::OnInitialUpdate* member function after the application's view has been created and has been attached to its corresponding document object but before any other view-related processing takes place. That makes the *OnInitialUpdate* member function a good place to perform many different kinds of view-object initialization operations.

When a view is derived from *CScrollView* rather than from *CView*—as the view in this chapter's SCRAMBLE program is—it is usually a good idea to specify the size of the view in your application's override of the *OnInitial Update* member function. Why? Because the size of a view is often based on the size of the document object that is associated with the view. Because *OnInitialUpdate* is called after the document associated with a view has been created but before any other view-object initialization takes place, *OnInitialUpdate* is an ideal place to set the size of a view when that size depends on the size of the associated document object.

To override the *CView::OnInitialUpdate* member function, an MFC application must declare its overridden function in the header file associated with its view object. In this chapter's version of the SCRAMBLE program, an overridden *OnInitialUpdate* member function is defined in the SCRAM-VW.H file, the include file that defines the program's *CScrambleView* class. Here is the *OnInitialUpdate* function definition that appears in the SCRAMVW.H file:

```
void OnInitialUpdate();
```

This chapter's SCRAMBLE program implements its *OnInitialUpdate* override in its SCRAMVW.CPP file—the implementation file for the program's *CScrambleView* objects. The following code shows what the implementation of the *OnInitialUpdate* function looks like in the SCRAMVW.CPP file:

```
void CScrambleView::OnInitialUpdate();
{
    CScrollView::OnInitialUpdate()
    SetScrollSizes(MM_TEXT, CSize(500, 500));
}
```

The *OnInitialUpdate* function shown above sets the logical size of MDI child windows to 500 pixels high by 500 pixels wide. If a child window is physically smaller than one of these dimensions, a corresponding scroll bar appears in the window. If a child window is physically larger than these dimensions, it will contain no scroll bars.

NOTE   In the MFC library, a *CSize* object is an object that can be used to define the width and height of any rectangular object. A *CSize* object has two member variables: *cx*, which defines the object's width, and *cy*, which defines the object's height.

Document Templates

As mentioned, a framework-based Visual C++ program manages documents using an MFC object called a *document template*. A document template is an object of the MFC *CDocTemplate* class. In an MFC application, a document template creates and manages all open documents of a particular type. Different types of documents require different document templates. For example, if an application supports both spreadsheets and text documents, a document template for each kind of document must be created. When a document template is created for a particular type of document, that document template handles the creation of all documents of that type and manages the views and frame windows that are associated with those documents.

NOTE   A Visual C++ document template is not the same as a C++ template. A C++ template is a container-class construct that Visual C++ version 1.0 does not support (although later versions do). A Visual C++ document template is quite different—it's an MFC object that manages documents in a Visual C++ program.

To create the document templates that are to be used in an MFC application, you call the *CWinApp* member function *AddDocTemplate*. In the SCRAMBLE program, the following statement in the SCRAMBLE.CPP file calls the *CWinApp:: AddDocTemplate* member function:

```
AddDocTemplate(new CMultiDocTemplate(IDR_SCRAMBTYPE,
    RUNTIME_CLASS(CScrambleDoc),
    RUNTIME_CLASS(CMDIChildWnd),     // standard MDI child frame
    RUNTIME_CLASS(CScrambleView)));
```

In the code above, it looks as if *AddDocTemplate* takes multiple parameters, but that's because the one parameter that the *AddDocTemplate* member function takes is constructed inside the function's argument list. There's only one argument being passed to *AddDocTemplate*: a pointer to an object of a *CDocTemplate*-derived class named *CMultiDocTemplate*.

In an MDI application, the argument passed to *AddDocTemplate* is a pointer to a *CMultiDocTemplate* object. In an SDI program, the pointer that is passed to *AddDocTemplate* is a pointer to an object of the *CSingleDocTemplate* class.

A *CSingleDocTemplate* object can create and store one document of one type at a time. In contrast, a *CMultiDocTemplate* object can maintain a list of many open documents of the same document type. The SCRAMBLE program is an MDI application, so the pointer passed to *AddDocTemplate* in the preceding code is a pointer to a *CMultiDocTemplate* object.

Some applications support multiple document types. For example, an application might support text documents and graphics documents. In such an application, when the user chooses the New command from the File menu, a dialog box is displayed that shows a list of possible new document types to open. For each supported document type, the application uses a distinct document template object.

If your application needs to support two or more document types, you must add an extra call to *AddDocTemplate* for each document type.

Passing arguments to *AddDocTemplate*
Although the *CWinApp::AddDocTemplate* member function takes just one argument, the constructor of the *CMultiDocTemplate* class—which is called inside the argument list in the preceding code—takes four arguments. Those four arguments are a resource identifier and three objects of a class named *CRuntimeClass*. (*CRuntimeClass* is a class in which you can store important information about a dynamically created class.)

The resource ID number passed to the *CMultiDocTemplate* constructor is a constant that identifies a string resource. This string resource is made up of a series of strings that provide various kinds of information about the resources used by the type of document that is associated with the document template's resource. Information stored in a document template's string resource can include information about menus, icons, accelerator tables, and other string resources.

If you're interested in seeing exactly what kinds of substrings are included in a document template's string resource, you can obtain such a list by consulting the *CDocTemplate* entry in the Visual C++ online help. Alternatively, you can call the *CDocTemplate::GetDocString* member function, which returns the string resource of whatever *CDocTemplate* you specify.

How document templates work

Whereas the user of an MFC application creates a new document by choosing the New or Open command from the File menu, the application's document template creates not only a document but also a frame window in which the document can be viewed.

The constructor of a document template specifies what types of documents, windows, and views the template can create. This capability is determined by the arguments you pass to the document-template constructor. Look again at the call to the *AddDocTemplate* function in the SCRAMBLE application, shown here:

```
AddDocTemplate(new CMultiDocTemplate(IDR_SCRAMBTYPE,
    RUNTIME_CLASS(CScrambleDoc),
    RUNTIME_CLASS(CMDIChildWnd)
    RUNTIME_CLASS(CScrambleView)));
```

In this example, a pointer to a new *CMultiDocTemplate* object is passed as an argument to *CWinApp::AddDocTemplate*. Arguments to the *CMultiDocTemplate* constructor include the resource ID associated with the document type's menus and accelerators and three uses of the *RUNTIME-_CLASS* macro. *RUNTIME_CLASS* returns the *CRuntimeClass* object for the C++ class named as its argument. The three *CRuntimeClass* objects passed to the document-template constructor in the preceding code supply the information needed to create new objects of the specified classes during the document creation process—in this case, *CScrambleDoc* objects with *CScrambleView* objects attached. The views are framed by standard MDI child frame windows.

When a Visual C++ application is running, its document templates contain pointers to the *CRuntimeClass* objects used by the application's document, view, and frame window classes. To obtain a pointer to a *CRuntimeClass* object, an application must call the Visual C++ macro *RUNTIME_CLASS*.

Example: The Improved SCRAMBLE Program

Many of the topics we have examined up to now are demonstrated in this chapter's version of the SCRAMBLE program—a sample application that builds on the SCRAMBLE application introduced in Chapter 5.

SCRAMBLE has some pretty fancy features, and they are all described and demonstrated in this section.

Experimenting with the New SCRAMBLE Program

The SCRAMBLE program presented in Chapter 5 displayed only one bitmap, but this chapter's version of the program can open and display many bitmaps, in individual document windows, simultaneously. Amazingly, about all that was needed to add this new capability was to provide some additional bitmaps and create some new menu items and message handlers to display them. Once that was done, the application's MDI framework took over the job of opening and displaying all these bitmaps and managing their individual views and windows.

You can see how well the framework did its part of the work by executing the program and playing around with it a little. In this new version of the SCRAMBLE program, you can open as many windows as you want by choosing the New Window item from the Window menu, and you can close windows in any order by choosing the Close item from the File menu or by clicking the Close box of any window you want to close. You can move windows in front of each other, resize them, and scroll them, and you can clear any bitmaps that are displayed in the program's various windows by choosing the Clear item from the Background menu. You can also change the bitmap shown in any window to another bitmap simply by bringing a window to the front and choosing a different Background menu item.

And you can use a slick-looking Color dialog box to place solid-color bitmaps in windows—even bitmaps displayed in custom colors that you design. But that's a different topic, covered later in this chapter.

How Windows Are Managed in the New SCRAMBLE Program

Although this chapter's SCRAMBLE program can handle multiple windows, it didn't take much work to write the code that creates and manage them. In Chapter 5, "Visual C++ Tools," you learned how to load and display bitmaps in a Visual C++ application. You also learned how to create menu items using App Studio and how to connect menu items to message handlers using ClassWizard. In this chapter's version of the SCRAMBLE program, if you've displayed one bitmap, you've displayed them all. All the other bitmaps used in SCRAMBLE are displayed using the same techniques described in Chapter 5.

Adding Toolbar Buttons to the SCRAMBLE Program

A toolbar is a cool gadget that you can create with little effort when you program in Visual C++. When you generate a Visual C++ program using AppWizard, AppWizard automatically creates a toolbar that contains a standard set of toolbar buttons for file-management operations, editing operations, printing functions, and help files. To learn more about the standard toolbar buttons created by AppWizard, choose the Visual Workbench item from Visual Workbench's Help menu.

The SCRAMBLE program's toolbar

This chapter's SCRAMBLE program's toolbar is shown in Figure 6-4. Along with the standard toolbar buttons created by AppWizard, SCRAMBLE has five additional toolbar buttons, one for each bitmap that you can open when you run the program. The bitmaps are named Arches, Oldwest, Castle, Space, and Color.

Figure 6-4. *The SCRAMBLE program's toolbar.*

When you create a program using AppWizard, you don't have to do anything to create a toolbar; AppWizard does it for you. All you have to do is add whatever buttons you need to the toolbar AppWizard has provided. Follow these steps:

1. Open Visual Workbench if it isn't already open.

2. Open a project that AppWizard has generated.

3. Open App Studio by choosing the App Studio item from the Tools menu.

4. Open the toolbar bitmap for your project's main frame window by clicking on Bitmap in App Studio's Type list box and then double-clicking on *IDR_MAINFRAME*, as shown here:

5. When you edit a toolbar bitmap in App Studio, App Studio's graphics editor uses a splitter window (a window that can be divided into two or more panes) that displays a toolbar in two different sizes. If necessary, move the splitter window's divider to display at least part of the large bitmap in the window's right-hand panel, as shown here:

6. Choose the graphic editor's Grid Settings item from the Image menu, and then check the Tile Grid check box, as shown below, to divide the editor's large toolbar bitmap into a series of tiled grids separated by thin blue lines. By default, each grid measures 16 pixels wide by 15 pixels high—just the right size for a row of toolbar buttons. Click the OK button.

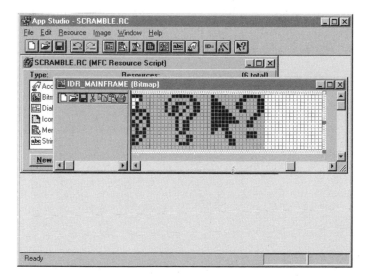

7. Scroll to the end of the toolbar bitmap. Position the cursor over the middle handle on the right edge of the large bitmap, and slide the handle to the right, opening up a new space on the large bitmap displayed in the graphics editor, as shown here:

8. Select the Pick tool (the dotted rectangle) in the graphics palette, as shown on the following page. (If the graphics palette is not displayed, open it by choosing the Show Graphics Palette item from the Window menu.)

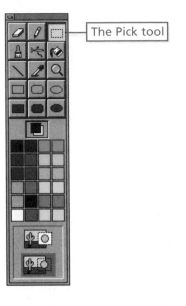

The Pick tool

9. Scroll the bitmap until the printer and help images appear in the window. Using the mouse, select the printer and help images on the toolbar bitmap, and then move both images one tile to the right, opening up a space for a new toolbar button just to the left of the printer image. When you have completed this step, your toolbar should look something like the one shown here:

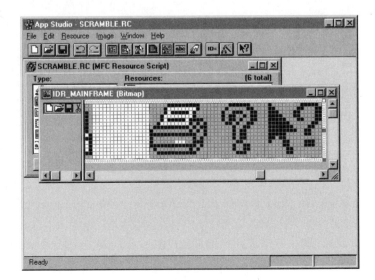

Now you can use the graphics palette to draw a new button inside the space you have opened up on your application's toolbar. Repeat steps 7 through 9 to add one button for each bitmap.

Adding bitmaps to the Background menu

After you have created the new bitmaps, create new menu items that correspond to your new bitmaps on the toolbar by following these steps:

1. Open App Studio from the Tools menu.

2. Select Menu from the Type list box, and then select *IDR_SCRAMB-TYPE* from the Resources list box.

3. Click on the Background menu to add the bitmaps, and then click on the Clear option of the Background menu.

4. Press the Ins key, type the name that you want to give the bitmap (such as *Oldwest*), and then press Enter.

5. Repeat these steps for all your new bitmaps. (For SCRAMBLE, you would also add the Castle, Space, and Color bitmaps.)

6. Use Class Wizard to add functions that respond to the menu item being opened. In this example, you would add *OnBackground-Castle, OnBackgroundOldwest,* and *OnBackgroundSpace* by following the same steps you used to add *OnBackgroundArches* in the section "Creating Message Handlers with ClassWizard" on page 152 in Chapter 5.

Connecting toolbar buttons to menu commands

After you have created the toolbar buttons and added menu items for them, your next job is to associate the buttons with the menu items. That's a much easier job than creating the buttons. To wire your toolbar button to menu commands, follow these steps:

1. Open your project's MAINFRM.CPP file, and find a block of code that looks like that shown on the following page.

```
// toolbar buttons - IDs are command buttons
static UINT BASED_CODE buttons[] =
{
    // same order as in the bitmap 'toolbar.bmp'
    ID_FILE_NEW,
    ID_FILE_OPEN,
    ID_FILE_SAVE,
        ID_SEPARATOR,
    ID_EDIT_CUT,
    ID_EDIT_COPY,
    ID_EDIT_PASTE,
        ID_SEPARATOR,
    ID_FILE_PRINT,
    ID_APP_ABOUT,
};
```

If you think that looks like a set of menu items, you're right. It's a block of code that AppWizard generates when it creates the default menu items and toolbar buttons for an application framework. Its purpose is to associate the menu items that AppWizard has created with their corresponding toolbar buttons. (Notice that spaces between toolbar buttons are indicated by the *ID_SEPARATOR* constant.) When you want to insert a new button in a toolbar that AppWizard has created, you simply add an entry for your new toolbar button in this block of code.

2. Modify the block of code in step 1 to look like the code below. (In this example, taken from this chapter's SCRAMBLE program, one separator and four new buttons have been added to the program's toolbar.)

```
// toolbar buttons - IDs are command buttons
static UINT BASED_CODE buttons[] =
{
    // same order as in the bitmap 'toolbar.bmp'
    ID_FILE_NEW,
    ID_FILE_OPEN,
    ID_FILE_SAVE,
        ID_SEPARATOR,
    ID_EDIT_CUT,
    ID_EDIT_COPY,
    ID_EDIT_PASTE,
        ID_SEPARATOR,
    ID_BACKGROUND_ARCHES,
    ID_BACKGROUND_OLDWEST,
    ID_BACKGROUND_CASTLE
```

```
     ID_BACKGROUND_SPACE,
     ID_BACKGROUND_COLOR,
         ID_SEPARATOR,
     ID_FILE_PRINT,
     ID_APP_ABOUT,
};
```

When you create new toolbar buttons and add them to your application's code, it's important to remember that the entries you make in your code must match the order of the toolbar buttons. Otherwise the toolbar buttons will match the wrong entries in your code, and your toolbar won't work properly. It's also important to remember that before you try to connect a toolbar button to a menu item, you must have a menu item to connect it with. So before you start creating toolbar buttons, be sure you have already created their corresponding menu items and have connected each menu item with a message handler. That way, as soon as you create a toolbar button, it will be ready to use.

3. Recompile your application and run it. That's all there is to it. Your new toolbar buttons should work just fine.

Updating the SCRAMBLE Program's Menu Items

One neat feature of this chapter's SCRAMBLE program is that its menu items update themselves; each time you open a bitmap in a window or bring a window containing a bitmap to the front, a check mark appears next to the menu item bearing the name of the bitmap in the window. It's easy to add this feature to a framework-based MFC program. Here's how:

1. Open a project in Visual Workbench.

2. Open ClassWizard by choosing the ClassWizard command from the Browse menu.

3. Verify that the name of the class associated with your menu item appears in the Class Name list box. (In this case, the *CScrambleDoc* class is selected because it's the class that contains the message handler for the selected menu command.)

4. Click the *Object ID* you want to work on, and then double-click the *UPDATE_COMMAND_UI* message in the Messages list box.

5. Assign a name to your menu-updating command when ClassWizard prompts you for one (the default name is usually sufficient), and then click OK.

6. Open the implementation file associated with your menu item by clicking the Edit Code button. ClassWizard then opens your implementation file at the spot at which it has inserted the menu-update command you requested. For example, to create an updating function for the Arches menu item in the SCRAMBLE program, ClassWizard inserted the following function, which it named *OnUpdateBackgroundArches*:

```
void CScrambleDoc::OnUpdateBackgroundArches(CCmdUI* pCmdUI)
{
// TODO: add your command update UI handler code here
}
```

7. Add *m_uBkgID* to the public section of the SCRAMDOC.H file as follows:

```
UINT     m_uBkgID;
```

8. Write the code that carries out whatever updating operation you want to execute. For example, in the SCRAMBLE program, here is the menu-updating function:

```
void CScrambleDoc::OnUpdateBackgroundArches(CCmdUI* pCmdUI)
{
    if (m_uBkgID == IDB_BITMAP1)
        pCmdUI->SetCheck(TRUE);
    else (pCmdUI->SetCheck(FALSE));
}
```

9. Add the following line at the beginning of the *OnBackgroundArches* function:

```
m_uBkgID = IDB_BITMAP1;
```

10. Repeat steps 8 and 9 for each background type. In SCRAMBLE, you would replace *IDB_BITMAP1* with the following:

   - *IDB_BITMAP2* in functions pertaining to the Oldwest bitmap

   - *IDB_BITMAP3* in functions pertaining to the Castle bitmap

   - *IDB_BITMAP4* in functions pertaining to the Space bitmap

The *OnUpdate* function might look a little cryptic at first, but it is actually quite simple. The most important thing to remember is that every time the user opens a menu, the Visual C++ framework checks to see whether the class associated with the menu item has any menu-updating member functions. If the application has any such member functions, the framework executes them.

For example, when the user of the SCRAMBLE program opens a menu, the application executes the *OnUpdateBackgroundArches* member function, along with any other menu-updating member functions that might exist in the *CScrambleDoc* class. As it turns out, the *CScrambleDoc* class has five menu-updating member functions—one for each of its bitmaps. And the application's framework executes that entire group of menu-updating member functions every time the Background menu is opened.

As mentioned, when the SCRAMBLE program loads and displays the Arches bitmap, it sets an integer member variable named *m_uBkgID* to a value represented by the constant *IDB_BITMAP1*. Subsequently, when the *OnUpdateBackgroundArches* member function is executed, it checks to see whether the value of the *m_uBkgID* member variable is set to the value of the constant *IDB_BITMAP1*. If true, the application places a check mark next to the Arches menu item by calling an MFC member function named *SetCheck* and passing the function a parameter of *TRUE*. If the *m_uBkgID* member variable is not set to the value *IDB_BITMAP1*, *SetCheck* is called with a *FALSE* parameter, and if a check mark already appears beside the Arches menu item, it is removed.

Each time the Background menu item is opened, this process is carried out not only for the Arches menu item, but also for every menu item that is associated with an update UI command message handler. The result of this is that all the appropriate Background menu items are checked and unchecked each time the Background menu opens.

The MFC library contains similar functions for activating and deactivating menu items and for performing other similar kinds of operations. For details, consult the online help.

Creating Solid-Color Bitmaps for the SCRAMBLE Program

If you've experimented with this chapter's version of the SCRAMBLE program, you might have noticed that it has a Color item on the Background menu that creates solid-color bitmaps. When you choose the Color item, the program displays an impressive dialog box called the *common Color dialog box*. In Windows 95, the common Color dialog box is similar to the one shown in Figure 6-5. It might look slightly different in other versions of Windows.

Figure 6-5. *The common Color dialog box.*

The Color dialog box shown in Figure 6-5 is called a common dialog box because the Windows operating system shares it with user-written applications. It is one of several common dialog boxes that the MFC library provides. Other common dialog boxes that are often used in Visual C++ programs are the Open and Save As dialog boxes. You'll learn how to use the common Open and Save As dialog boxes in Chapter 7, "Of Mice and Messages."

The common Color dialog box is another case in which the MFC library does almost all the work and lets your application take the credit. To use the common Color dialog box, all your application has to do is perform the following three actions:

1. Create a *CColorDialog* object.

2. Display the object by calling a *CDialog* member function named *DoModal*.

3. Call a *CColorDialog* member function named *GetColor* to retrieve whatever color value the user has selected.

In this chapter's SCRAMBLE program, the common Color dialog box is displayed when the user chooses the Color item from the Background menu. A message handler named *OnBackgroundColor*—created by ClassWizard in the usual way—is then called, as shown here:

```
void CScrambleDoc::OnBackgroundColor()
{
    CColorDialog dlgColor;

    int iRet = dlgColor.DoModal();
    if (iRet != IDCANCEL)
    {
        m_cBkg = dlgColor.GetColor();
        m_uBkgID = IDB_COLOR
        UnloadBackground();
        UpdateAllViews(NULL);
    }
}
```

To add the Color dialog box to your application, follow these steps:

1. Add the preceding code to the *OnBackgroundColor* function in the SCRAMDOC.CPP file.

2. Add the following line to the public section of the SCRAMDOC.H file:

   ```
   COLORREF m_cBkg;
   ```

3. Add the following line to the RESOURCES.H file:

   ```
   #define IDB_COLOR                    101
   ```

4. Replace the code in the *OnDraw* function that appears in the SCRAMVW.CPP file. The function should appears as follows:

```cpp
void CScrambleView::OnDraw(CDC* pDC)
{
    CScrambleDoc* pDoc = GetDocument();
    CBitmap* pBitmap;
    BITMAP Bitmap;
    CDC dc;

    if (pDoc->m_uBkgID == IDB_COLOR)
    {
        CBrush brushColor(pDoc->m_cBkg);
        CRect rectScreen(0, 0, 0, 0);

        rectScreen.right = ::GetSystemMetrics(SM_CXSCREEN);
        rectScreen.bottom = ::GetSystemMetrics(SM_CYSCREEN);

        pDC->FillRect(&rectScreen, &brushColor);
        return;
    }

    pBitmap = pDoc->GetBackground();
    if (pBitmap)
    {
        dc.CreateCompatibleDC(pDC);
        CBitmap* pOldBitmap = dc.SelectObject(pBitmap);

        pBitmap->GetObject(sizeof(Bitmap), &Bitmap);
        pDC->BitBlt(0, 0,
                    Bitmap.bmWidth,
                    Bitmap.bmHeight,
                    &dc,
                    0, 0,
                    SRCCOPY);
        dc.SelectObject(pOldBitmap);
    }
}
```

Adding Scrolling to the SCRAMBLE Program's Views

You know what a scrolling view is; you've used various kinds of scrolling views in various kinds of programs. In the SCRAMBLE program, a scrolling view is a window-size view that scrolls over a larger bitmap, as shown in Figure 6-6.

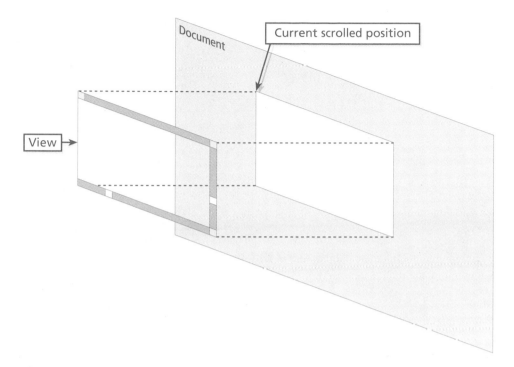

Figure 6-6. *A scrolling view enables you to view different parts of a large document.*

In Chapter 5's SCRAMBLE program, there was no way to view a particular part of a background in a window. In this chapter's version of the program, you can scroll to any part of a bitmap you want because SCRAMBLE now supports scrolling.

For some reason, the Visual C++ version 1.0 AppWizard has no setting for generating programs with scrolling views; if you want your views to scroll, you must set them up for scrolling yourself. This is not a very difficult task—once again, the MFC library does most of the work for you. All you have to do is follow these steps:

1. Open the header file for your application's view class, and change the derivation specified in the heading of your class's definition from *CView* to *CScrollView*. In the SCRAMBLE program, you can

find that change in the SCRAMVW.H file, where the original class-definition header

```
class CScrambleView : public CView
```

has been changed to

```
class CScrambleView : public CScrollView
```

2. Find your view class's *IMPLEMENT_DYNCREATE* and *BEGIN-_MESSAGE_MAP* macros, located in SCRAMVW.CPP, and modify them to refer to your view object as a *CScrollView*-derived object instead of a *CView*-derived object. In the SCRAMBLE application, both these macros appear in the SCRAMVW.CPP file and have been modified to look like this:

```
IMPLEMENT_DYNCREATE(CScrambleView, CScrollView)

BEGIN_MESSAGE_MAP(CScrambleView, CScrollView)
    //{{AFX_MSG_MAP(CScrambleView)
    ⋮
    //}}AFX_MSG_MAP
    // Standard printing commands
    ON_COMMAND(ID_FILE_PRINT, CView::OnFilePrint)
    ON_COMMAND(ID_FILE_PRINT_PREVIEW, CView::OnFilePrintPreview)
END_MESSAGE_MAP()
```

3. In the SCRAMVW.CPP file, add the following code to override the *OnInitialUpdate* function:

```
void CScrambleView::OnInitialUpdate()
{
    CScrollView::OnInitialUpdate();
    SetScrollSizes(MM_TEXT, CSize(
        ::GetSystemMetrics(SM_CXSCREEN),
        ::GetSystemMetrics(SM_CYSCREEN)));
}
```

4. Add the following line to the public section of the SCRAMVW.H file:

```
void OnInitialUpdate();
```

5. Recompile and execute your program. Your program's view window should now have a pair of scroll bars that work just the way you have specified.

> **N**OTE   The first parameter passed to *SetScrollSizes* is a *mapping mode*—that
> is, a definition of the unit of measure that is used to convert logical display
> units to units that match the display specifications of the current display de-
> vice. The *MM_TEXT* mapping mode allows applications to work with device
> pixels by regarding one unit as being equal to one screen pixel. Windows
> uses mapping modes to perform this kind of conversion because the physi-
> cal size of a pixel varies from device to device. Several other mapping
> modes—*MM_HIENGLISH, MM_HIMETRIC, MM_LOENGLISH, MM_LOMETRIC,*
> and *MM_TWIPS*—are useful because they deal with device-independent
> units such as inches or millimeters, which are perfect for dealing with other
> display devices such as printers. For more details, see the *GetDocSize* entry
> in online help.

Customizing a Program's Windows

When AppWizard generates a framework for an application, its default
behavior is to give the program a main frame window that covers about
two-thirds of the screen. This window can appear in various locations,
depending on where it was the last time you closed your application.

When a main frame window has a child window, the Visual C++ framework gives the child window a default size that is somewhat smaller than
the size of its parent window. By default, the upper left corner of this child
window is placed in the upper left corner of the client area of its parent
window.

The MFC library does not provide an easy way to change the default sizes
or the default placements of child or parent windows. However, here are
some tips and tricks that you can use to control the sizes, locations, and
styles of your application's windows.

Changing window characteristics with *SetWindowPlacement*

One way to modify the characteristics of a window is the *CWnd* member
function *GetWindowPlacement*, which returns a structure containing a
specified window's size and location. You can obtain a window's properties (including its size) by calling *CWnd::GetWindowPlacement*, and you
can then call the *CWnd* member function *SetWindowPlacement* to modify
the window's size. When all that is done, call *ShowWindow* to implement
your changes.

This technique can come in handy when you want to specify an exact size for an application's main frame window, and it is especially useful when your main frame window is a special kind of window—for example, a *CFormView*-derived window in which data is displayed.

IP To set up a *CFormView* window, you derive the window from the *CFormView* class instead of from the *CView* class, following the same steps as were used in the preceding exercise to derive a scrolling window from the *CScrollView* class.

To change a window's size by calling *GetWindowPlacement*, open your application's MAINFRM.CPP file, and place a series of statements similar to this in your program's *OnCreate* member function:

```
// adjust main frame window's size and placement
wpl.length = sizeof (WINDOWPLACEMENT)
GetWindowPlacement(&wpl);
wpl.rcNormalPosition.top = 0;
wpl.rcNormalPosition.left = 0;
wpl.rcNormalPosition.right = wpl.rcNormalPosition.right / 2;
wpl.rcNormalPosition.bottom = wpl.rcNormalPosition.bottom / 3;
SetWindowPlacement(&wpl);
ShowWindow(SW_SHOWNORMAL);
```

This code fragment calls *GetWindowPlacement* to set the size of a program's main frame window to one-half its original width and one-third its original height.

For the preceding code to compile without errors, you must add the following line to the public section of your MAINFRM.H file:

```
WINDOWPLACEMENT wpl;
```

In the next section, another technique for setting the position and location of the window is described. If you want to try this technique, remove any code that you added in this section.

Changing the value of the *m_nCmdShow* member variable

When you are creating an MDI application, an alternative way to change the size of its main frame window is to change the value of the application's *m_nCmdShow* variable, a member variable of the *CWinApp* class. The *m_nCmdShow* variable corresponds to the *nCmdShow* variable that

Windows passes to *WinMain* to start an application. When an application starts, the *m_nCmdShow* variable holds a default value that determines the size, location, and style of the main frame window that is being created.

When AppWizard generates a framework for a Visual C++ application, the *InitInstance* function initializes the application's main frame window by calling the *CWnd::ShowWindow* member function. When this call is made, the value of the *m_nCmdShow* variable is passed as an argument to *CWnd::ShowWindow*.

To use this technique in a framework-based MFC program, you modify a block of code that appears in the application's override of the *CWinApp::InitInstance* member function. In a framework application, you can find *CWinApp::InitInstance* in the program's primary implementation file—in SCRAMBLE's SCRAMBLE.CPP file. When AppWizard generates an *InitInstance* member function for a program, it creates a code sequence that looks something like this to display the application's main frame window:

```
// create main MDI frame window
CMainFrame *pMainFrame = new CMainFrame;
if (!pMainFrame->LoadFrame(IDR_MAINFRAME))
    return FALSE;
pMainFrame->ShowWindow(m_CmdShow);
pMainFrame->UpdateWindow();
m_pMainWnd = pMainFrame;
```

When an application executes a code sequence such as this one, the result is a main frame window with a rather odd size, which Microsoft has, for some reason, set up as the standard size for a main frame window. If you want to customize the size of a main frame window, you can do so by making one small modification to the preceding block of code. By adding one line of code, you can expand the size of your application's main frame window to exactly the size of your monitor screen. Here is the code sequence that does this trick:

```
// create main MDI frame window
CMainFrame *pMainFrame = new CMainFrame;
if (!pMainFrame->LoadFrame(IDR_MAINFRAME))
    return FALSE;
m_nCmdShow |= SW_SHOWMAXIMIZED;
pMainFrame->ShowWindow(m_CmdShow);
pMainFrame->UpdateWindow();
m_pMainWnd = pMainFrame;
```

This is the line of code that has been added:

```
m_nCmdShow |= SW_SHOWMAXIMIZED;
```

Calling the *PreCreateWindow* member function

Another way to modify the size of a window in a Visual C++ application is to override the *CWnd* member function *PreCreateWindow*. This technique is a little more complicated, but it is also more versatile. It works in MDI and SDI applications, and it works with child windows as well as with main frame windows. It is the technique that has been used to modify the windows used in this chapter's SCRAMBLE program.

The *CWnd::PreCreateWindow* member function gives applications access to a window-creation process that Windows normally carries out automatically. When AppWizard generates the framework for a Visual C++ application, the framework calls *PreCreateWindow* every time the program is about to create a window, and the program always passes to *PreCreate-Window* a reference to a structure named *CREATESTRUCT*. By changing some of the information stored in *CREATESTRUCT,* your application can change a number of the attributes (including the size) of the window that is about to be created.

Calling *PreCreateWindow* in SDI applications

To change the window attributes in an SDI application, you can override the *PreCreateWindow* function in the source file that creates the program's main frame window. For example, in this chapter's SCRAMBLE program, the following code sequence appears in the MAINFRM.CPP file. It reduces the size of the program's main frame window to 640 by 480 pixels and then centers the window in the monitor display. Then, when the program is executed using a standard-size screen, its main frame window fills the screen. When the application is executed using a larger display, it displays a 640-by-480-pixel main frame window that is placed in the exact center of the screen:

```
BOOL CMainFrame::PreCreateWindow(CREATESTRUCT& cs)
{
    // override of the CWnd::PreCreateWindow function
    cs.cx = 640;
    cs.cy = 480;
```

```
UINT m_screenWidth = GetDC()->GetDeviceCaps(HORZRES);
UINT m_screenHeight = GetDC()->GetDeviceCaps(VERTRES);

// center main frame window
cs.x = (m_screenWidth / 2) - (640 / 2);
cs.y = (m_screenHeight / 2) - (480 / 2);

return CMDIFrameWnd::PreCreateWindow(cs);
}
```

Before you try to compile this program, add the header for the *PreCreate-Window* function to the MAINFRAM.M file. The member function *CDC-::GetDeviceCaps* is called to obtain the size of the monitor currently being used. Then the *CREATESTRUCT* member variables *cs.x* and *cs.y* are set to display the window in the center of the monitor's screen. Because the *PreCreateWindow* member function is called just before the application's main frame window is created, these are the sizes that are used by the *Create* and *ShowWindow* member functions when they are called to create and display the window.

Calling *PreCreateWindow* in MDI applications

With just a little more effort, you can use the *PreCreateWindow* member function to customize child windows in MDI applications. To modify the size of an MDI child window, you must derive a new class from *CMDI-ChildWnd*. Then you must search through your application and replace all references to *CMDIChildWnd* with references to your new class.

That is not usually as difficult as it sounds because a typical application contains only one reference to *CMDIChildWnd*. You can find that reference in the application's *InitInstance* member function.

To customize the attributes of an MDI application's child windows, you must change the class derivation of your application's child windows, and you must then override the *PreCreateWindow* member function to implement your changes.

What's Next?

In this chapter, you saw a brief overview of how an MFC program works, and you got a chance to add an impressive set of features to the SCRAMBLE program. You learned how to create a program that can open and display multiple windows with different background bitmaps simultaneously, and you learned how to create and display bitmaps in customized solid colors using the common Color dialog box provided by the MFC library. You learned how to create a program with toolbar button shortcuts for menu commands and how to update the appearance of menu items automatically. Finally, you learned how to add scroll bars and scrolling capabilities to windows, and how to use some operations that are not very well documented to specify the initial sizes and positions of main frame windows and child windows in Visual C++ programs.

In Chapter 7, "Of Mice and Messages," you'll get a chance to add even more enhancements to the SCRAMBLE application. By the time you finish Chapter 7, your application will be responding to mouse commands, and the user of the application will be able to use the mouse to draw in the windows that the program displays. The program will be able to display screen drawings with and without bitmap backgrounds and bitmap backgrounds with and without screen drawings superimposed over them. And the SCRAMBLE program will use the MFC library's common Open and Save As dialog boxes to open and save files and will support serialization.

Of Mice and Messages

This is the second of two chapters about the Microsoft Foundation Class (MFC) Library version 2.0 and the way it works in framework-based Visual C++ applications. Chapter 6, "The MFC Library," introduced the MFC library and explained some of the fundamental principles of framework-based MFC programming. This chapter sheds some light in some of the murkier corners of MFC operations and introduces several topics that are important to know about in the world of MFC programming.

The following topics are explained and demonstrated in this chapter:

- Message maps—how MFC message maps work and exactly how they are used in Visual C++ programs

- Mouse input—how to use the mouse-handling features provided by Visual C++ and the MFC library

- Collection classes—how collection classes can be used to store MFC objects

- Features of *CObject*-derived classes—how to use member functions provided by the *CObject* class by deriving your own classes from *CObject*

To help you understand the features of the MFC library covered in this chapter, we will use a program named SCRIBBLE. A full copy of the SCRIBBLE program, which is developed in seven steps, appears in the MSVC\MFC\SAMPLES\SCRIBBLE folder of the Visual C++ software provided on your companion CD-ROM. SCRIBBLE is a fairly sophisticated Visual C++ program, so if you want to observe the output of this program at its various stages of development, feel free to open the projects defined in each of the seven subfolders of the MSVC\MFC\SAMPLES\SCRIBBLE folder. In this chapter, we will be using step 5 of the SCRIBBLE program to illustrate how to incorporate mouse-handling capabilities into a Visual C++ program. The Step5 folder is available in the CHAP07 folder on the companion CD-ROM. Figure 7-1 shows the output of the SCRIBBLE program presented in this chapter.

Figure 7-1. *Output of the SCRIBBLE program.*

Understanding Windows Messages

As you know, every time the user of a Windows-based application initiates a Windows event by performing an action such as clicking a mouse button or pressing a key, the Windows operating system generates a message and dispatches it to the program being executed. The application then attempts to handle the message by performing the operation specified in the parameters passed with the message. If the application cannot handle the message, it sends the message back to the Windows operating system, which then disposes of the message by calling a default function named *DefWindowProc*.

The Windows API defines more than 400 kinds of messages, and a well-behaved Windows-based application can handle just about any kind of message that the system might send it. The behavior of a Windows-based application depends on the kinds of messages it responds to and how it responds to each kind of message it receives. This fact of life holds true in framework-based MFC programs as well as in traditional Windows API–style applications.

In the bygone era of Windows API–style programming, Windows developers had to account for many different kinds of messages and had to write all the code that was needed to handle them. They even had to include calls to *DefWindowProc* in their programs to ensure that the system would take care of any messages that their programs weren't equipped to handle.

Today, in the age of Visual C++, it's much easier to handle messages in Windows-based applications. Now when you generate an MFC program using AppWizard, your application has to account for only a handful of the different kinds of messages that traditional Windows API–style applications had to handle. The MFC library performs this bit of magic using a mechanism called a *message map*.

Varieties of Windows Messages

The more than 400 kinds of messages that exist in Windows can be divided into three main categories: standard Windows messages, control notification messages, and command messages. Each is handled in a different way by the Windows operating system.

Standard Windows messages

All Windows messages that begin with the *WM_* prefix—with the exception of the *WM_COMMAND* message—are known generically as *standard Windows messages*, or *Windows messages*. Standard Windows messages are messages that the Windows operating system dispatches in response to events that affect windows and views.

For example, when the user of an application takes an action that creates a new window, the Windows operating system sends a message named *WM_CREATE* to the application that is being executed. Similarly, Windows dispatches a *WM_DESTROY* message when a window is about to be destroyed.

Any MFC library class derived from the *CWnd* class can handle a standard Windows message. This means that standard Windows messages can be handled by *CFrameWnd* objects, *CMDIFrameWnd* objects, *CMDIChildWnd* objects, *CView* objects, *CDialog* objects, and any classes that you might derive from these base classes.

Handling Windows messages in Windows API–style programs   In a traditional Windows API–style application, functions that handle Windows messages are typically called from a monster *switch* statement that usually appears inside a special kind of function called a *window procedure.* (As you saw in Chapter 2, "Introduction to Windows Programming," window procedures are provided by Windows applications but are called by the Windows operating system.) For example, a *WM_DESTROY* Windows message is called at the end of the *switch* statement shown here.

```
long FAR PASCAL _export WndProc(HWND hwnd, UINT message, UINT wParam,
    LONG lParam)
{
static int  wColorID [5] = {WHITE_BRUSH, LTGRAY_BRUSH, GRAY_BRUSH,
    DKGRAY_BRUSH, BLACK_BRUSH};

static WORD wSelection = IDM_WHITE;
HMENU hMenu;

switch (message)
    {
    case WM_COMMAND:
        hMenu = GetMenu(hwnd);
        switch (wParam)
            {
            case IDM_NEW:
            case IDM_OPEN:
            case IDM_SAVE:
            case IDM_SAVE_AS:
                MessageBeep(0);
                return 0;
```

```
            case IDM_EXIT:
                SendMessage(hwnd, WM_CLOSE, 0, 0L);
                return 0;
            }
            break;
    ⋮
    case WM_TIMER:
        MessageBeep (0);
        return 0;

    case WM_DESTROY:
        PostQuitMessage(0);
        return 0;
    }
    return DefWindowProc(hwnd, message, wParam, lParam);
}
```

Handling Windows messages in Visual C++   In a framework-based Visual C++ program, you don't have to write a *switch* statement such as the one shown in the preceding example to handle Windows messages. You can accomplish the same thing interactively, in a much easier way, by using the Visual C++ ClassWizard utility.

When you develop a program using Visual C++, you can create a handler for a Windows message by opening ClassWizard and selecting the name of a view class in the Class Name drop-down list box. Then you select the ID of the view class in the Object IDs list box and the Windows message you want to handle in the Messages list box, as shown in Figure 7-2 on the following page.

After you have selected a Windows message in ClassWizard's Messages list box, click the Add Function button. ClassWizard then creates a skeletal message-handler function for the Windows message you have selected and inserts it into your application's source code. It's then up to you to equip your new message-handler function with the code you want to execute whenever your application receives the kind of message you have selected. To do that, you simply click ClassWizard's Edit Code button, and ClassWizard takes you to the spot in your source code at which it has inserted your new message-handler function.

You've already seen what MFC message handlers look like. You'll learn more about how they are called and how they work in the section "Message Maps" on page 230.

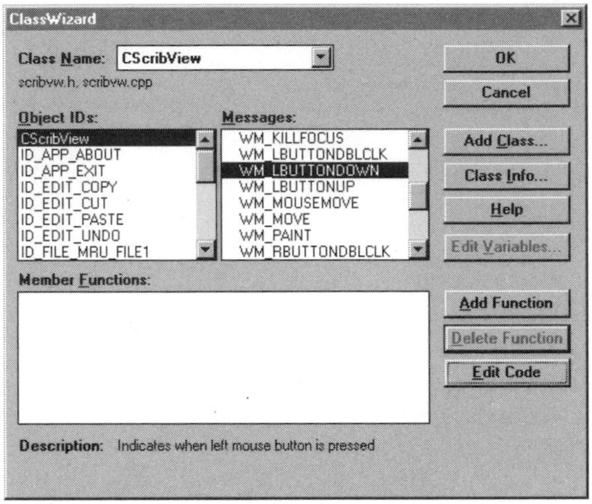

Figure 7-2. *Windows messages displayed in ClassWizard's Messages list box.*

Control-notification messages

As mentioned, the only *WM_* message that is not a standard Windows message is the *WM_COMMAND* message. Actually, *WM_COMMAND* is used to identify two different kinds of messages: control-notification messages and command messages.

Control-notification messages, or control notifications, are messages that controls and other kinds of child windows send to their parent windows. For example, when the user of an application changes the text displayed in an edit control, the edit control that is being modified sends its parent window a special kind of control-notification message, which is called an *EN_CHANGE* message. It is then up to the control's parent window to handle the message.

A control-notification message, like a standard Windows message, can be handled by any MFC class derived from the *CWnd* class. There is one important difference, however, between a control-notification message and a standard Windows message. Because control-notification messages are automatically generated by controls, they don't appear in message maps, and you don't use ClassWizard to add them to applications. So you won't find any control-notification messages in the ClassWizard dialog box.

Command messages

A command message is a message that is triggered by a user-interface event such as selecting a menu item, clicking a toolbar button, or pressing an accelerator key. To create a command message using ClassWizard, you select the ID of a menu item in ClassWizard's Object IDs list box, and then you select the *COMMAND* item in ClassWizard's Messages list box. If you click the Add Function button, ClassWizard then creates a message-handler function for the command you have specified and places it in the source code of the class whose name appears in the Class Name list box.

How Windows API–Style Programs Handle Command Messages

Command messages are different from standard Windows messages and control-notification messages in two main ways: they are handled differently by the Windows operating system, and they can be handled by a wider variety of objects. Handlers for command messages can be defined not only by windows and view objects but also by documents, document templates, and even Windows applications themselves (that is, by objects derived from the *CWinApp* class). You'll learn more about how command messages work in MFC programs in the section "Message Maps" on page 230. First let's take a closer look at how they work in traditional Windows API–style programs.

The *switch* statement on page 224 began like this:

```
switch (message)
    {
    case WM_COMMAND:
        hMenu = GetMenu(hwnd);
        switch (wParam)
            {
            case IDM_NEW:
            case IDM_OPEN:
            case IDM_SAVE:
            case IDM_SAVE_AS:
                MessageBeep(0);
                return 0;
```

(continued)

```
        case IDM_EXIT:
            SendMessage(hwnd, WM_CLOSE, 0, 0L);
            return 0;
    }
    ⋮
}
```

In this part of the *switch* statement, a variable named *message* is checked
to see whether it is equal to the constant *WM_COMMAND*. If it is, another
variable, named *wParam*, is checked to see whether it contains a menu
item ID such as *IDM_NEW*, *IDM_ OPEN*, *IDM_SAVE*, *IDM_SAVE_AS*, or
IDM_EXIT. If the *wParam* variable does contain the ID of a menu item, an
appropriate menu-item message-handler function is called.

Because the *switch* statement appears in a window procedure (*WndProc*),
the *message* and *wParam* arguments that it checks are parameters that
have been triggered by events and have been passed directly to it from the
Windows operating system.

How MFC Programs Handle Command Messages

Now that you know how a Windows API–style program handles command
messages, it's time to take a look at how command messages are handled
in framework-based MFC programs.

As mentioned in Chapter 6, "The MFC Library," every Visual C++ version
1.0 program has a *WinMain* function that is defined in an MFC source file
named APPCORE.CPP. Near the end of this *WinMain* function is a call
to an MFC member function named *CWinApp::Run.* The heart of this *Run*
member function is a *while* loop (nested inside a *for* loop) that repeatedly
checks for CPU idle time (to give background processes a chance to execute). The *for* loop then calls another *CWinApp* member function named
PumpMessage. The following code shows the *for* loop that appears in the
MFC framework's *CWinApp::Run* member function:

```
// acquire and dispatch messages until a WM_QUIT message is received
for (; ;)
{
    LONG lIdleCount = 0;
    // check to see whether we can do idle work
    while (!::PeekMessage(&m_msgCur, NULL, NULL, NULL, PM_NOREMOVE)
        && OnIdle(lIdleCount++))
```

```
    {
        // more work to do
    }
    // either we have a message, or OnIdle returned false
    if (!PumpMessage())
        break;
}
```

PumpMessage is a *CWinApp* member function that is implemented in the
APPCORE.CPP source file. The heart of the *CWinApp::PumpMessage*
member function is shown here:

```
// process this message
if (!PreTranslateMessage(&m_msgCur))
{
    ::TranslateMessage(&m_msgCur);
    ::DispatchMessage(&m_msgCur);
}
```

How the MFC Framework Dispatches Messages

In the preceding sections, you have seen how Windows API–style programs and framework-based MFC programs handle Windows messages.
Now let's see how the MFC framework detects events, constructs messages
to handle those events, and passes those messages on to MFC applications.

When a *WM_COMMAND* message is dispatched to a framework-based
MFC application, the MFC framework responds to the message by calling
a *CCmdTarget* member function named *OnCmdMsg*. In the MFC library,
the *CCmdTarget::OnCmdMsg* member function is the main message-
implementation routine provided by the framework command architecture. The MFC framework implements a number of *OnCmdMsg* member
functions, each designed for a particular kind of window. When Windows
detects an event and dispatches a message for it, the message is received
and handled by the *OnCmdMsg* member function of the window that receives the message.

Unless you're the sort of person who needs to know how an internal com-
bustion engine works before you get behind the wheel of a car, it's not
very important at this stage of your Visual C++ programming career for
you to remember every detail of how all messages are processed by the
CCmdTarget::OnCmdMsg member function. The *OnCmdMsg* member

functions that the MFC library provides for various kinds of window objects are very complex and intricate functions that you can research for yourself, if you want, by poring through MFC library source files such as WINFRM.CPP, VIEWCORE.CPP, CMDTARG.CPP, and others.

If you aren't interested in doing that, it's sufficient—at least for now—to know that when the MFC framework receives a command message from the operating system, it first determines which *CCmdTarget*-derived object should receive the message and then calls the appropriate *CCmdTarget::OnCmdMsg* member function.

When a *CCmdTarget*-derived class defined in an MFC application receive a *WM_COMMAND* message from the MFC framework, the class's *OnCmdMsg* member function either dispatches the command to an object that is equipped to handle it or handles the command itself by calling its root class's *CCmdTarget::OnCmdMsg* member function.

Message Maps

As you've seen in previous chapters, a message map is a mechanism for mapping messages to member functions of an MFC library class. In an MFC application, message maps can be used by any MFC library class that's derived from the MFC *CCmdTarget* class or from one of the descendants of the *CCmdTarget* class. In a framework-based Visual C++ application, the program's main frame window class, document class, and view class are all derived from the *CCmdTarget* class, so Windows can dispatch messages to all three of these classes, as well as to any of your own classes that are derived from *CCmdTarget* or any of its descendants.

The *CCmdTarget* class (which was introduced in Chapter 6, "The MFC Library") provides the basic support for MFC messaging. In an MFC application, the *CCmdTarget* class ensures that any unhandled messages dispatched to it are passed to the *DefWindowProc* function—the default message-handling function in the Windows API. (In a traditional Windows API–style program, you must call *DefWindowProc* yourself from your program's message-handling *switch* statement, as you saw earlier.)

Benefits of Using Message Maps

In the MFC library, a message map is a macro-based mechanism that works much like a virtual-function override in C++ but requires less processing overhead to implement. The message map calls your application's message handlers in much the same way you would call them yourself in a Windows API–style message-handling *switch* statement. The biggest difference is that you don't have to do all the work of writing a message-handling *switch* statement because AppWizard does it all for you.

A message map—like a virtual function—overrides the message-handling features of the *CCmdTarget* base class. But because message maps are converted to inline code by the Visual C++ preprocessor, they do not use v-tables.

As you saw in Chapter 4, "Objects and Member Functions," *v-tables* are indirect-reference mechanisms that base classes use to override inherited functions in C++ programs. V-tables are ingenious mechanisms that fulfill their tasks admirably for C++ functions, and the designers of the MFC library could have used virtual functions instead of macros to implement message maps. They decided not to because macros are much better dispatchers of messages than virtual functions would have been.

The problem with using virtual functions to dispatch Windows messages is that messages are dispatched at so fast and furious a pace in a Windows-based program that virtual functions—with all the v-table indirection they require—would never be able to do their work fast enough to keep up with the speed of the Windows messaging system. All the indirection that virtual-function v-tables require would be too costly in terms of processing overhead. By implementing message maps as macros that are resolved in line at compile time, the MFC library has kept its application framework lean and mean while freeing Windows programmers from the burdensome task of writing code to account for every message received by every target window.

Binding Message Maps to Your Program

In an MFC program, message maps are called by window procedures that AppWizard imports from object code libraries when it generates your program. The MFC framework supplies a number of different window procedures for various kinds of windows, and AppWizard imports the window procedures it needs from the MFC library when you build your program.

When you link your program, the Visual C++ linker binds the MFC window procedures that AppWizard has selected to your application. You rarely, if ever, have to worry about writing a window procedure of your own when you use AppWizard to generate your Visual C++ programs.

Declaring a Message Map

When you use AppWizard to create a source file for a *CCmdTarget*-derived class, the ClassWizard utility declares a message map for your class in your class's header file and creates the message map in the source code file that implements the class's member functions. This means that for every message map that appears in a class's implementation file, there is a message-map declaration in a corresponding header file.

This message-map declaration is easy to spot because it is bracketed by a set of special symbols: //{{ and //}}. An additional clue is that the //{{ and //}} symbols in the class's header file enclose one or more message-handler declarations preceded by the keyword *afx_msg*. For example, the following class definition contains a message-map declaration that in turn contains definitions for the message handlers *OnLButtonDown*, *OnLButtonUp*, *OnFilePrint*, and *OnFilePrintPreview*:

```
class CNewprojView: public CView {
{
 :
protected:
    //{{AFX_MSG(CNewprojView)
    afx_msg void OnLButtonDown(UINT nFlags, CPoint point);
    afx_msg void OnLButtonUp(UINT nFlags, CPoint point);
    afx_msg void OnFilePrint();
    afx_msg void OnFilePrintPreview();
    //}}AFX_MSG
DECLARE_MESSAGE_MAP()
};
```

As the preceding example shows, the *DECLARE_MESSAGE_MAP* macro is always declared inside the definition of a class that is equipped with a message. By convention, this macro declaration appears at the end of the class's definition.

All four of the message-handler declarations that appear in this message-map declaration work the same way—for example, *OnLButtonDown* defines a message handler that is executed whenever Windows sends a *WM_LBUTTONDOWN* message to the *CCmdTarget*-derived class in which the message map is defined.

The last two message-handler declarations in the message map call printing-related message handlers when the user chooses their corresponding menu commands.

The Off-Limits Zone in a Message-Map Declaration

In the declaration of a class that contains a message map, the code nested inside the symbols //{{ and //}} is code that is generated automatically by ClassWizard. Although you are sometimes permitted to make minor editing changes inside this block of code, you should never manually delete any functions that are delimited by the //{{ and //}} symbols, and you should never manually insert any code into that portion of a message-map declaration. ClassWizard provides all the mechanisms you need to make substantive changes in that block of code.

You can, however, write message-handler functions manually in framework-based MFC programs. There are many Windows messages that ClassWizard does not recognize, and when your application needs a handler for such a message, you must write it yourself. In this situation, all you have to do to make your message-handler declaration legal is to place it outside the //{{ and //}} delimiters in the declaration of your message map.

Implementing a Message Map

When you create a source file for a class by using AppWizard, the App-Wizard utility places the class's message map in the .CPP source code file that implements the class's member functions.

When a message map appears in a .CPP file, it is always bracketed by the macros *BEGIN_MESSAGE_MAP* and *END_MESSAGE_MAP*, as shown here:

```
BEGIN_MESSAGE_MAP(CNewprojView, CView)
    //{{AFX_MSG_MAP(CNewprojView)
    ON_WM_LBUTTONDOWN()
    ON_WM_LBUTTONUP()
    ON_COMMAND(ID_FILE_PRINT, CView::OnFilePrint)
    ON_COMMAND(ID_FILE_PRINT_PREVIEW, CView::OnFilePrintPreview)
    //}}AFX_MSG_MAP
END_MESSAGE_MAP()
```

> **NOTE** When you define a macro that implements a message-handler function, don't place a semicolon at the end of each line. That's because a message map implements calls to message handlers as preprocessor macros, not as C++ statements.

This message-map implementation corresponds to the message-map declaration shown in the previous example. It contains four macros that respond to Windows messages. The first two macros in the message map—*ON_WM_LBUTTONDOWN* and *ON_WM_LBUTTONUP*—correspond to a pair of standard Windows messages that Windows dispatches in response to mouse clicks.

The last two entries in the message map that begin with *ON_COMMAND* are called in response to command messages. The *ID_FILE_PRINT* macro is called when the user chooses the Print item from the File menu, and the *ID_FILE_PRINT_PREVIEW* macro is called when the user chooses the Print Preview item from the File menu.

If you look closely, you'll notice that the syntax of the two printing-related macros that appear in the message map is a little different from that of the mouse-related macros. That's because the two printing-related macros are activated by command messages, whereas the two mouse-related macros are activated by standard Windows messages.

Messages That ClassWizard Recognizes

ClassWizard is not equipped to handle all the varieties of messages that a Windows application can encounter, but it can create message handlers for quite a few of them. Table 7-1 lists some of the most important standard Windows messages for which ClassWizard can create handlers.

To see a complete list, open ClassWizard and select the class name displayed in the Object ID list box. The messages that ClassWizard can manage for the class that you have selected appear in the Messages list box. If your application needs to handle a message that isn't on the list, you can simply write a message handler yourself, using the information you have learned in this chapter and referring to the online help as required.

Windows Message and Corresponding MFC Member Function	Description
WM_CANCELMODE OnCancelMode	Notifies a window to cancel internal modes
WM_CHAR OnChar	Passes keyboard events to the currently active window
WM_CLOSE OnClose	Cleans up the window and closes it
WM_CREATE OnCreate	Indicates that a window is being created
WM_DESTROY OnDestroy	Indicates that a window is about to be destroyed
WM_DROPFILES OnDropFiles	Indicates that a file has been dropped
WM_ERASEBKGND OnEraseBkgnd	Indicates that a window's background needs erasing
WM_HSCROLL OnHScroll	Indicates a click in a horizontal scroll bar
WM_KEYDOWN OnKeyDown	Indicates that a nonsystem key has been pressed
WM_KEYUP OnKeyUp	Indicates that a nonsystem key has been released

Table 7-1. *MFC message-handler member functions.*

(continued)

Table 7-1. *continued*

Windows Message and Corresponding MFC Member Function	Description
WM_KILLFOCUS *OnKillFocus*	Indicates that a window is about to lose the input focus
WM_LBUTTONDBLCLK *OnLButtonDblClk*	Indicates a double click of the left mouse button
WM_LBUTTONDOWN *OnLButtonDown*	Indicates that the left mouse button has been pressed
WM_LBUTTONUP *OnLButtonUp*	Indicates that the left mouse button has been released
WM_MOUSEMOVE *OnMouseMove*	Indicates movement of the mouse cursor
WM_MOVE *OnMove*	Indicates that the position of a window has changed
WM_PAINT *OnPaint*	Indicates that a window needs repainting (but use *OnDraw* for views)
WM_RBUTTONDBLCLK *OnRButtonDblClk*	Indicates a double click of the right mouse button
WM_RBUTTONDOWN *OnRButtonDown*	Indicates that the right mouse button has been pressed
WM_RBUTTONUP *OnRButtonUp*	Indicates that the right mouse button has been released
WM_SETCURSOR *OnSetCursor*	Displays the appropriate mouse cursor shape
WM_SETFOCUS *OnSetFocus*	Indicates that a window has gained the input focus
WM_SHOWWINDOW *OnShowWindow*	Indicates that a window is about to be hidden or shown
WM_SIZE *OnSize*	Indicates a change in window size
WM_TIMER *OnTimer*	Indicates that an interval set on a timer has elapsed
WM_VSCROLL *OnVScroll*	Indicates a click in a vertical scroll bar

"Must-handle" windows messages

Of the Windows messages in Table 7-1, a few must be handled by all Windows-based applications. Table 7-2 lists that subset of "must-handle" Windows messages.

Message	Event
WM_CREATE	Initialization immediately after a window is created
WM_DESTROY	Cleanup when a window object is being destroyed
WM_PAINT	Painting or updating a window's client area
WM_CLOSE	Cleanup when a window is being closed

Table 7-2. *Messages that every Windows-based application must handle.*

Some of the Windows messages listed above are sent to your application when an event takes place, some are sent from a control in a dialog box or window to that dialog box or window, and some are sent from a dialog box or window back to the button or control.

Creating Message Handlers with ClassWizard

Sometimes you have to create a handler yourself for a message that Class-Wizard doesn't recognize. In most cases, however, you can let ClassWizard do all that work for you.

To create a message handler using ClassWizard, follow these steps:

1. From Visual Workbench, open a project.

2. Choose ClassWizard from the Browse menu.

3. In the Object IDs list box, select the same class name as appears in the Class Name drop-down list box (in this example, *CScribView*). ClassWizard displays a list of Windows messages that your view can receive in the Messages list box, shown on the following page.

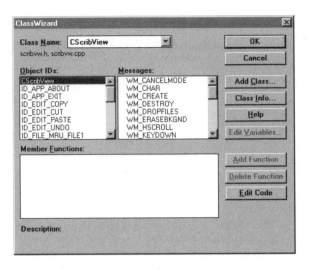

4. In the Messages list box, select the name of a Windows message for which you want to define a message-handler function (in this example, *WM_LBUTTONDOWN*).

5. To define a message-handler function for the message you have selected, click the Add Function button. ClassWizard then creates a message-handler function and places the name of that function, along with the name of a message-map macro, in the Member Functions list box. (In this example, the name of the message-handler member function that ClassWizard has created is *OnLButtonDown*, and the name of the corresponding message-map macro is *ON-_WM_LBUTTONDOWN*.) When a new message-handler function has been created, ClassWizard displays a small hand icon in the Messages list box next to the name of the message that corresponds to the new message-handler function.

6. Close ClassWizard by clicking the OK button.

> **MPORTANT** If you use ClassWizard to delete a message-handler function, ClassWizard removes the handler's message-map entry but does not remove the message-handler function associated with the message or any other references that you have made to the message-handler function in your other code. If such items exist, you must delete them by hand. ClassWizard warns you about this every time you attempt to delete a message-handler function. Heed the warning—if you don't, ClassWizard can lose track of what it's doing and break your application.

The Story So Far

At this point, if you examine the definitions and implementation files for the class you're working on, you'll see that ClassWizard has taken the liberty of writing some code for you. For example, if you worked through the preceding exercise to create an *OnLButtonDown* message handler for the SCRIBBLE program's *CScribView* class, you'll find that ClassWizard has updated the SCRIBVW.H and SCRIBVW.CPP files as follows:

■ When ClassWizard creates a message-handler function for a Windows message, it declares the function in the appropriate class's header file. In this example, ClassWizard has placed the following declaration of an *OnLButtonDown* member function in the SCRIBBLE application's SCRIBVW.H file:

```
//{{AFX_MSG(CScribView)
afx_msg void OnLButtonDown(UINT nFlags, CPoint point);
//}}AFX_MSG
```

Notice that ClassWizard has placed the declaration inside the //{{ and //}} delimiters that always enclose message-map definitions created by ClassWizard. Also notice that ClassWizard has provided your new *OnLButtonDown* member function with a set of parameters that the system will automatically pass to *OnLButtonDown* whenever a *WM_LBUTTONDOWN* message is dispatched.

You won't ever have to worry about passing these parameters to the *OnLButtonDown* member function. In fact, in most situations, you won't ever have to be concerned with exactly how *OnLButton-Down* gets called or exactly how it is connected to the dispatching of the *WM_LBUTTONDOWN* message. The MFC framework takes care of all those details automatically in the *WinMain* function, the message pump, and all the window procedures that it creates for you and embeds in your application. All you have to do is write the code that is executed when the user presses the left mouse button and place it in the body of the message-handler member function.

■ ClassWizard places a corresponding definition of the member function in the class's implementation file. In the SCRIBBLE program, ClassWizard places the declaration shown on the following page in the SCRIBVW.CPP file.

```
void CScribView::OnLButtonDown(UINT nFlags, CPoint point)
{
    // TODO: add your message handler code here
    // and/or call default
    CView::OnLButtonDown(nFlags, point);
}
```

ClassWizard places a member function such as this in your source code each time you call on it to create a message-handler function, but it is up to you to write the code inside the brackets that will provide your new handler with its functionality. When you write a program that uses an *OnLButtonDown* message-handler function, for example, you have to supply the code that will make your application do what you want it to in response to a click of the left mouse button.

ClassWizard does take care of a couple of other details for you, however. For instance, notice that ClassWizard has again provided the *OnLButtonDown* message-handler function with a pair of parameters (*nFlags* and *point*) that will be passed to it automatically whenever a *WM_LBUTTONDOWN* message is dispatched. Although your application does not have to be concerned with how these parameters are passed, the code that you write for your message handler is free to make use of them in any way you want.

The *nFlags* argument tells *OnLButtonDown* whether a special key, such as the Ctrl key or the Shift key, was held down when the user pressed the left mouse button. The *point* argument is a *CPoint* structure that specifies the window coordinates at which the mouse button was pressed. You can use the coordinate information passed to *OnLButtonDown* when you write your application's custom *OnLButtonDown* message handler.

■ ClassWizard connects the message handler it has created with the appropriate Windows message by writing a message-map entry that corresponds to the new message handler. It places this message-map entry in the implementation file of the class for which it has created a message handler. In this example, ClassWizard added an *ON_WM-_LBUTTONDOWN* entry to the message map in the SCRIBVW.CPP file, as shown on the following page.

```
BEGIN_MESSAGE_MAP(CScribView, CScrollView)
    //{{AFX_MSG_MAP(CScribView)
    ON_WM_LBUTTONDOWN()
    //}}AFX_MSG_MAP
END_MESSAGE_MAP()
```

Writing Code for Message Handlers

This section uses the SCRIBBLE program to show how you can write code for messages in framework-based MFC applications. The SCRIBBLE application is a simple drawing program that contains member functions that let the user draw on the screen by moving the mouse. It also has a document class in which it can store the lines, or strokes, that make up a drawing. Because a drawing is typically made up of many strokes, the SCRIBBLE document uses an object instantiated from the *CObList* collection class to store a list of all the strokes the user has drawn. In the MFC library, a collection class is a class that can store and manipulate objects stored in lists or arrays. To learn how collection classes can be used to store MFC objects, see "Storing Strokes in a Document" on page 249.

Different Strokes

In the SCRIBBLE program, a stroke is made up of a list of points. As the user draws in a window by dragging the mouse, the program keeps track of points in the window as the mouse passes over them and stores those points in an array. The array in which the points are stored is an object of an MFC library class named *CDWordArray*. The *CDWordArray* class is a collection class in which *DWORD* variables can be stored.

The SCRIBBLE program begins constructing a stroke as soon as the left mouse button is pressed. The program adds points to the stroke's *CDWordArray* object until the mouse button is released. Then it stores the stroke it has collected and adds the stroke to the list of strokes that it maintains. Each time the left mouse button is pressed, SCRIBBLE begins constructing a new stroke; this process continues until the user terminates the program. When the program ends, the user is given an opportunity to save the drawing that has been created.

Figure 7-3 on the following page shows a SCRIBBLE window in which the user has used the mouse to draw some strokes.

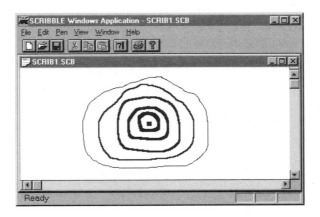

Figure 7-3. *Strokes drawn in a SCRIBBLE window.*

Storing Strokes in an Array

As the user draws a stroke in a window, SCRIBBLE's document object stores the stroke in a member variable named *m_pointArray*. In the SCRIBBLE program, the *m_pointArray* variable is an object of the *CD-WordArray* class.

When the user finishes drawing a stroke and releases the left mouse button, SCRIBBLE stores the stroke in a member variable named *m_strokeList* In SCRIBBLE, *m_strokeList* is a member variable of type *CObList*. *CObList* is an MFC collection class that can create and maintain a list of any collection of *CObject*-derived objects.

Writing a Message Handler Step by Step

Earlier in this chapter, you learned how to use ClassWizard to create a message-handler member function named *OnLButtonDown* for the SCRIBBLE program. You also saw how the *OnLButtonDown* message handler is called through the *CScribView*'s message map when Windows dispatches a *WM_LBUTTONDOWN* message to the view object.

Here are the steps taken to add the *OnLButtonDown* message handler to the SCRIBBLE program. (This code was added before step 5.)

1. Add an empty *OnLButtonDown* member function to the SCRIBBLE program by following the step-by-step exercise presented on page 237 in the section "Creating Message Handlers with ClassWizard."

2. Add the code shown below to *OnLButtonDown*. (You can find this code in the CSCRIBVW.CPP file in this chapter's sample-code folder on the companion CD-ROM.)

```
void CScribView::OnLButtonDown(UINT nFlags, CPoint point)
{
    // When the user presses the left mouse button, he or
    // she might be starting a new stroke or selecting or
    // deselecting a stroke.
    // CScrollView changes the viewport origin and the
    // mapping mode. It's necessary to convert the point
    // from device coordinates to logical coordinates,
    // such as those stored in the document.
    CClientDC dc(this);
    OnPrepareDC(&dc);
    dc.DPtoLP(&point);

    m_pStrokeCur = GetDocument()->NewStroke();
    m_pStrokeCur->AddPoint(point); // add first point to
                                   // the new stroke

    SetCapture();          // capture the mouse coordinates
                           // until button is released
    m_ptPrev = point;      // serves as the MoveTo anchor point
                           // for the LineTo as the user drags
                           // the mouse
    return;
}
```

3. Remove the first parameter name (*nFlags*) from the implementation of the *OnLButtonDown* member function. The SCRIBBLE program doesn't use the information passed to *OnLButtonDown* in this argument, and removing the name of the parameter from the *OnLButtonDown* function's argument list avoids a compiler warning that the parameter is not referenced. The revised *OnLButtonDown* declaration looks like this:

```
void CScribView::OnLButtonDown(UINT, CPoint point)
```

When the SCRIBBLE program's *OnLButtonDown* message handler is complete, the user can start drawing a stroke on the screen by pressing the left mouse button. As the user draws this new stroke, the SCRIBBLE program stores it in a document that can later be transferred to a storage medium such as a disk. For details on how the SCRIBBLE program stores strokes in a document, see the section "Storing Strokes in a Document" on page 249.

Converting Device Coordinates to Logical Coordinates

As shown in the previous example, when the left mouse button is pressed, the *OnLButtonDown* member function calls a *CScribDoc* member function named *NewStroke* to start the actual drawing. Also notice that the *OnLButtonDown* member function calls two other MFC member functions, *OnPrepareDC* and *DPtoLP*. Here are the statements in which *OnPrepareDC* and *CDC::DPtoLP* are called:

```
OnPrepareDC(&dc);
dc.DPtoLP(&point);
```

Why does *OnLButtonDown* call *OnPrepareDC* and *DPtoLP*? Because the Windows operating system and the SCRIBBLE program use different kinds of coordinates to track the movements of the mouse as a stroke is being drawn. Windows uses window coordinates (sometimes called *device coordinates*) to inform the *OnLButtonDown* member function of the current position of the mouse. But when the SCRIBBLE program stores the coordinates of the user's strokes in an array, it expresses them in *logical coordinates*—that is, coordinates that describe points on the document that is being drawn on, not coordinates that describe points in the window that is being displayed.

This difference is important in the SCRIBBLE program because the window in which SCRIBBLE displays strokes is a scrolling window. Because SCRIBBLE windows can be scrolled, a stroke drawn in a SCRIBBLE window can appear in various places within the view, depending on where the view is positioned on the document. So, before a dot drawn on the screen with the mouse is stored in the document being displayed, the device coordinates that are used to track mouse movements must be converted to the logical coordinates that the SCRIBBLE program uses to store strokes in documents.

Fortunately, Windows can perform that calculation for you. First you call *OnPrepareDC* to notify the current device context that some coordinates are being changed. Then you call the *CDC::DPtoLP* member function to change the *OnLButtonDown* function's device coordinates (expressed as a *device point*, or *DP*) to a pair of logical coordinates (expressed as a *logical point*, or *LP*) that can be stored in the SCRIBBLE program's document.

You call another MFC member function, named *LPtoDP*, to convert logical coordinates to device coordinates. SCRIBBLE calls *LPtoDP* in its *OnDraw* and *OnUpdate* member functions before it transfers strokes that have been stored in a document to a window to be displayed on the screen.

Writing an *OnMouseMove* Message Handler

In the SCRIBBLE application, from the time the left mouse button is pressed to the time it is released, a message handler named *OnMouseMove* tracks the path of the mouse and provides the SCRIBBLE program with the information it needs to draw that path in the program's view window. Once the *OnLButtonDown* message handler has received a message from the mouse indicating that the left mouse has been pressed, the *OnMouse-Move* message handler is called repeatedly (every time the user moves the mouse) until the left mouse button is released. Each time *OnMouseMove* is called, it connects the previous mouse location with the current mouse location and saves the new location. That location is then used as the previous location the next time *OnMouseMove* is called.

As the *OnMouseMove* message handler is called repeatedly, the SCRIBBLE program uses a local *CClientDC* object (an object derived from the MFC library's *CDC* class) to draw the path of the mouse in the client area of the currently active window.

Writing an *OnMouseMove* message handler step by step

Here are the steps taken to add the *OnMouseMove* member function to the SCRIBBLE program.

1. Add an *OnLButtonDown* message handler to the SCRIBBLE program, as outlined earlier, and add the SCRIBBLE program's functionality to the *OnLButtonDown* member function.

2. Following the steps outlined in the section "Creating Message Handlers with ClassWizard," on page 237, replace the default implementation of the *OnMouseMove* member function with the code shown on the following page. (This code has already been added to the version of the SCRIBBLE program presented in this chapter.)

```
void CScribView::OnMouseMove(UINT nFlags, CPoint point)
{
    // mouse movement is interesting in the SCRIBBLE
    // application only if the user is currently drawing a
    // new stroke by dragging the captured mouse

    if (GetCapture() != this)
        return;     // if this window (view) didn't capture
                    // the mouse, the user isn't drawing in
                    // this window

    CClientDC dc(this);
    // CScrollView changes the viewport origin and mapping
    // mode. It's necessary to convert the point from
    // device coordinates to logical coordinates, such as
    // are stored in the document.
    OnPrepareDC(&dc);
    dc.DPtoLP(&point);

    m_pStrokeCur->AddPoint(point);

    // draw a line from the previous detected point
    // in the mouse drag to the current point
    CPen* pOldPen = dc.SelectObject(
        GetDocument()->GetCurrentPen());
    dc.MoveTo(m_ptPrev);
    dc.LineTo(point);
    dc.SelectObject(pOldPen);
    m_ptPrev = point;
    return;
}
```

3. Remove the first parameter name (*nFlags*) from the declaration of *OnMouseMove* to avoid a compiler warning that this parameter is not referenced. The *OnMouseMove* declaration should then look like this:

```
void CScribView::OnMouseMove(UINT, CPoint point)
```

When SCRIBBLE calls the *OnMouseMove* message handler, *OnMouseMove* checks to see whether the left mouse button is being held down. If it is, *OnMouseMove* calls the *CDC::MoveTo* and *CDC::LineTo* member functions to draw a new line in the currently active window.

OnMouseMove also calls the *CView::OnPrepareDC* and *CDC::DPtoLP* member functions to convert the current mouse location to a set of logical coordinates and then calls the *CStroke::AddPoint* member function to add the newest point to the stroke that is being drawn. For more information about how the *CStroke::AddPoint* member function works, see the section "Adding a Point to a Stroke" on page 249.

Writing an *OnLButtonUp* message handler step by step

In the SCRIBBLE application, the *OnLButtonUp* message handler ends any stroke that is currently in progress when the user releases the left mouse button. The *OnLButtonUp* member function draws a line to connect the current stroke to its last point—that is, the point where the user has released the mouse. Then the *OnLButtonUp* member function relinquishes control of the mouse, freeing it for more drawing or for other uses by your application.

To add an *OnLButtonUp* member function to the SCRIBBLE program, follow these steps:

1. Add an *OnLButtonUp* member function and an *OnMouseMove* member function to the SCRIBBLE program by following the step-by-step procedures presented earlier.

2. Remove the first parameter name, *nFlags*, from the declaration of *OnLButtonUp* in order to avoid a compiler warning that this parameter is not referenced. The *OnLButtonUp* declaration then looks like the following:

   ```
   void CScribView::OnLButtonUp(UINT, CPoint point)
   ```

3. Following the same procedures you used to fill in the code for your *OnLButtonDown* message handler and your *OnMouseMove* message handler, add the code below to the *CScribView* class's SCRIBVW.H and SCRIBVW.CPP files. (This code has already been added in the version of the SCRIBBLE program presented in this chapter.)

   ```
   void CScribView::OnLButtonUp(UINT, CPoint point)
   {
       // mouse button up is interesting in the SCRIBBLE
       // application only if the user is currently drawing
       // a new stroke by dragging the captured mouse
   ```

(continued)

```
        if (GetCapture() != this)
            return;  // if this window (view) didn't capture
                     // the mouse, the user isn't drawing
                     // in this window

        CScribDoc* pDoc = GetDocument();
        CClientDC dc(this);

        // CScrollView changes the viewport origin and mapping
        // mode. It's necessary to convert the point from device
        // coordinates to logical coordinates, such as are
        // stored in the document.
        OnPrepareDC(&dc);  // set up mapping mode and
                           // viewport origin
        dc.DPtoLP(&point);

        CPen* pOldPen = dc.SelectObject(pDoc->GetCurrentPen());
        dc.MoveTo(m_ptPrev);
        dc.LineTo(point);
        dc.SelectObject(pOldPen);
        m_pStrokeCur->AddPoint(point);

        // Tell the stroke item that we've finished adding points
        // to it. This is so that it can finish computing its
        // bounding rectangle.
        m_pStrokeCur->FinishStroke();

        // tell the other views that this stroke has been added
        // so that they can invalidate this stroke's area in
        // their client area
        pDoc->UpdateAllViews(this, 0L, m_pStrokeCur);

        ReleaseCapture();   // release the mouse capture
                            // established at the beginning
                            // of the mouse drag
        return;
    }
```

OnLButtonUp calls the *CDC::MoveTo* and *CDC::LineTo* member functions to draw a new point in the currently active window.

The *OnLButtonUp* member function also calls the *CView::OnPrepareDC* and *CDC::DPtoLP* member functions to convert the current mouse location to a set of logical coordinates and then calls the *CStroke::AddPoint* member function to add the newest point to the current stroke. Finally, *OnLButtonUp* calls the *CStroke::FinishStroke* member function to complete the current stroke.

Storing Strokes in a Document

As the user of the SCRIBBLE application uses the mouse to draw on the screen, the program's document object (named *CScribDoc*) stores all the coordinates that make up each completed stroke in an array and creates and maintains a list of all the strokes the user has drawn. The program's document object also keeps track of the properties of the pen that is being used to create the drawing.

Starting a new stroke

As you saw earlier, the *CScribDoc::OnLButtonDown* member function begins each new stroke by calling a member function named *CScribDoc::NewStroke*. The *NewStroke* member function is defined as follows in the SCRIBDOC.CPP source file:

```
CStroke* CScribDoc::NewStroke()
{
    CStroke* pStrokeItem = new CStroke(m_nPenWidth);
    m_strokeList.AddTail(pStrokeItem);
    SetModifiedFlag();    // mark the document as having been
                          // modified, for purposes of
                          // confirming File Close
    return pStrokeItem;
}
```

The *NewStroke* member function uses the C++ *new* operator to construct a new *CStroke* object dynamically, initializing it with the current pen width (which is stored in a member variable named *m_nPenWidth*). *NewStroke* calls a *CObList* member function named *AddTail* to add the new stroke to the list. Then *NewStroke* calls a *CDocument* member function named *SetModifiedFlag* to notify the SCRIBBLE program that a change has been made in the document. Finally, *NewStroke* returns a pointer to the new stroke that has been added to the list of strokes.

Adding a point to a stroke

When the user holds down the left mouse button and moves the mouse, the *CScribView::OnMouseMove* member function calls *AddPoint*, a member function of the *CStroke* class. The *CStroke* class, a class derived from *CObject,* is defined in the SCRIBDOC.H source file and is implemented in SCRIBDOC.CPP. The *CStroke::AddPoint* member function is defined in the SCRIBDOC.CPP file as shown on the following page.

```
void CStroke::AddPoint(CPoint pt)
{
    m_pointArray.Add(MAKELONG(pt.x, pt.y));
}
```

The *CStroke::AddPoint* member function calls a *CDWordArray* member function named *Add* to add a new point to the current stroke. This new point is added to the stroke currently stored in the member variable named *m_pointArray*, which is an object of the *CDWordArray* class.

Finishing a stroke

When the user finishes drawing a stroke by releasing the left mouse button, the *CScribView::OnLButtonUp* message handler is called. The *OnLButtonUp* member function completes the stroke and then calls the *CStroke::AddPoint* member function to add the new point to the current point array. Then *OnLButtonUp* calls a *CStroke* member function named *FinishStroke*. The following code shows how the *CStroke::FinishStroke* member function is defined in the SCRIBDOC.CPP file:

```
void CStroke::FinishStroke()
{
    // Calculate the bounding rectangle. It's needed for smart
    // repainting.

    if (m_pointArray.GetSize()==0)
    {
        m_rectBounding.SetRectEmpty();
        return;
    }
    CPoint pt = GetPoint(0);
    m_rectBounding = CRect(pt.x, pt.y, pt.x, pt.y);

    for (int i=1; i < m_pointArray.GetSize(); i++)
    {
        // if the point lies outside the accumulated bounding
        // rectangle, inflate the bounding rectangle to include it
        pt = GetPoint(i);
        m_rectBounding.left   = min(m_rectBounding.left, pt.x);
        m_rectBounding.right  = max(m_rectBounding.right, pt.x);
        m_rectBounding.top    = max(m_rectBounding.top, pt.y);
        m_rectBounding.bottom = min(m_rectBounding.bottom, pt.y);
    }

    // Add the pen width to the bounding rectangle. This is necessary
    // to account for the width of the stroke when invalidating
    // the screen.
```

```
    m_rectBounding.InflateRect(CSize(m_nPenWidth,-(int)m_nPenWidth));
    return;
}
```

The *FinishStroke* member function calculates the bounding rectangle of the stroke that has just been finished so that the stroke can later be drawn to the screen or in a document as efficiently as possible. That's all *Finish-Stroke* has to do because the *CStroke::AddStroke* function has taken care of all necessary stroke-drawing and stroke-storing details.

Redrawing Strokes in the SCRIBBLE Window

When the SCRIBBLE program needs to redraw all the strokes in a window— for example, when a window is created or resized, or when it becomes active after being partly or completely obscured by another window— the MFC framework calls the *CScribView::OnDraw* member function. The following code shows how the *OnDraw* member function is defined in the SCRIBVW.CPP file:

```
void CScribView::OnDraw(CDC* pDC)
{
    CScribDoc* pDoc = GetDocument();

    // get the invalidated rectangle of the view or, in the case
    // of printing, the clipping region of the printer dc
    CRect rectClip;
    CRect rectStroke;
    pDC->GetClipBox(&rectClip);
    pDC->LPtoDP(&rectClip);

    // Note: CScrollView::OnPaint will have already adjusted the
    // viewport origin before calling OnDraw, to reflect the
    // currently scrolled position.
    // The view delegates the drawing of individual strokes to
    // CStroke::DrawStroke.
    for (POSITION pos = pDoc->GetFirstStrokePos(); pos != NULL;)
    {
        CStroke* pStroke = pDoc->GetNextStroke(pos);
        rectStroke = pStroke->GetBoundingRect();
        pDC->LPtoDP(&rectStroke);
        if (!rectStroke.IntersectRect(&rectStroke, &rectClip))
            continue;
        pStroke->DrawStroke(pDC);
    }
}
```

How the *OnDraw* member function works

The first thing the *CScribView::OnDraw* member function does is calculate the bounding rectangle of the current window by calling the MFC library's *CDC::GetClipBox* member function. *GetClipBox* retrieves the dimensions of the current boundaries of the current window and places these dimensions in the *CRect* object whose pointer is passed to it in the *rectClip* parameter.

When this work is complete, the *OnDraw* member function uses a *for* loop to draw the current stroke array in the active window. This *for* loop repeatedly calls the *CScribDoc::GetNextStroke* function to get the next stroke. It then calls *CStroke::GetBoundingRect* to ensure that only the areas of the window that need redrawing are redrawn, and then calls *CStroke::Draw-Stroke* to do the drawing. Also, the *CDC::LPtoDP* member function is called to convert the logical coordinates stored in SCRIBBLE's document object to the device coordinates that are needed to draw inside the currently active window.

Drawing the first stroke

As you've seen, the *OnDraw* member function draws strokes by calling a pair of *CStroke* member functions named *GetFirstStrokePos* and *Get-NextStroke*. The *GetFirstStrokePos* member function is defined this way in the SCRIBDOC.CPP file:

```
POSITION CScribDoc::GetFirstStrokePos()
{
    return m_strokeList.GetHeadPosition();
}
```

The *CStroke::GetFirstStrokePos* member function obtains the position of the first stroke stored in a *CObList* object by calling a *CObList* member function named *GetHeadPosition*. *GetFirstStrokePos* returns a pointer to the first stroke object in the list. (The positions of objects stored in a *CObList* object are expressed using a data type named *POSITION*, which is defined in the MFC library.

Drawing the next stroke

The *CStroke::GetNextStroke* function returns the *CStroke* object that is stored at a specified position in a stroke list. It is defined this way in the SCRIBDOC.CPP file:

```
CStroke* CScribDoc::GetNextStroke(POSITION& pos)
{
    return (CStroke*)m_strokeList.GetNext(pos);
}
```

The *GetNextStroke* member function calls the *GetNext* member function of the *CObList* class, which returns a pointer to a *CObject*-derived object stored in the list.

Creating and Managing a *CPen* Object

In the *OnLButtonUp* member function shown on page 247, a *CScribDoc* member function named *GetCurrentPen* is used to retrieve a pointer to the *CPen* object that is currently being used to draw strokes on the screen. *GetCurrentPen* is an application-defined helper function that provides restricted, type-safe public access to the protected data member *m_penCur*. In a similar way, the *NewStroke*, *GetFirstStrokePos*, and *GetNextStroke* member functions provide public access to the protected data structure stored in the *m_strokeList* member variable.

CDocument::GetCurrentPen is an inline member function that is defined as follows in the SCRIBDOC.H file:

```
public:
    CPen*   GetCurrentPen( ) { return &m_penCur; }
```

GetCurrentPen simply returns a pointer to the current *CPen* object, which is defined as a protected member variable of the *CScribDoc* class.

Understanding MFC Library Classes

As noted at the beginning of this chapter, most MFC library classes are derived from a root class named *CObject*. It's important for you to learn as much about the *CObject* class as you can because it contains many useful member functions that can add an enormous amount of power to the classes and objects that you create in your MFC programs.

To use the member functions provided by the *CObject* class, you have to derive your own classes from *CObject* or from a class derived from *CObject*. Because most of the classes in the MFC library are derived from *CObject,* deriving a class from almost any class in the MFC library gives you access to all member functions that can be inherited from *CObject.*

The only MFC library classes that aren't derived from *CObject*, and therefore don't inherit from it, are special-purpose classes such as *CString, CTime, CRect, CPoint,* and *CSize.* Other classes that are not derived from *CObject* include *CArchive, CDumpContext, CFileStatus, CMemoryState, CRect, CRuntimeClass,* and *CTimeSpan.* For a complete list of classes that aren't derived from *CObject,* as well as those that are, see the Microsoft Foundation Class Library Reference topic in the online help.

All the topics discussed in this chapter relate in one way or another to features that classes and objects in MFC applications can inherit from the *CObject* class. Objects derived from *CObject* or its descendants are the only kinds of objects that can implement message maps and handle mouse events using ClassWizard message handlers. In this section, we'll take a look at some of the most important features of the *CObject* class.

Features of the *CObject* Class

Objects instantiated from the *CObject* class or its descendants inherit *CObject* features such as the following:

■ **Support for serialization**—An object from the *CObject* class or any one of its descendants can automatically load and save information by using a *CObject* mechanism called serialization. To take advantage of this feature, all you have to do is override the *CObject* member function *Serialize* by writing a small amount of code. You'll learn how to add serialization to *CObject*-derived classes in the section "Files and Serialization" on page 255.

■ **Diagnostic support**—When you create a program using AppWizard, you can build two versions of your application: a debug version and a release version. The debug version of an AppWizard application contains debugging information that the Visual C++ debugger requires. The release version of a program—the version you build when your application is ready to ship—contains no debugging information and takes up considerably less disk space.

When your Visual C++ application is in the development and debugging stage, the MFC library provides a number of features that can help. For example, when you use the C++ *new* operator to instantiate a *CObject*-derived object on the heap, the MFC library provides a macro named *ASSERT_VALID* that you can call to determine whether your object has been successfully created. There is also a slightly less powerful macro, *ASSERT*, that you can call to test the value of an expression. One common use of the *ASSERT* macro is to test a value returned by a function to see whether the function has returned an error.

■ **Support for MFC collection classes**—The MFC library contains several collection classes—that is, classes in which arrays or lists of objects (or pointers to objects) can be stored. MFC collection classes have many special features that make them easy to create, traverse, and manage. MFC collection classes include *CObList* (for storing lists of objects), *CStringList* (for storing lists of strings), *CPtrList* (for storing lists of pointers), and more. The MFC library also provides collection classes for storing arrays. Array-style collection classes include *CObArray, CStringArray, CByteArray, CPtrArray,* and others. To take full advantage of the MFC collection classes, the objects you store in them must be objects that are derived from the *CObject* class or one of its descendant classes. For information about how collection classes can be used to store MFC objects, see the section "Storing Strokes in a Document" on page 249.

Files and Serialization

As a user of Windows, you have at least a general understanding of how Windows-based applications typically handle files. Usually, a Windows-based application creates a document object when the user of the program selects the New command from the File menu. In a framework-based Visual C++ program, as soon as a document is created, a view that is associated with the document is displayed on the screen.

To open an existing document, a Windows user typically chooses the Open command from the File menu. The application then displays a common Open dialog box that allows the user to navigate to an existing file and open it.

The MFC library provides several mechanisms to help you create and manage files in your Visual C++ applications in response to user commands. Three of these mechanisms are listed here:

■ User-interface objects, such as menu items, that can help the user of your application perform file-related operations

■ A *CFile* class and two *CFile*-derived classes (*CStdioFile* and *CMemFile*) that are equipped with member functions for creating, deleting, and managing files

■ A higher-level file-related mechanism called serialization, which lets you equip your programs with automatic file-loading and file-saving capabilities by writing just a few lines of code

These three MFC mechanisms for dealing with file I/O are covered in more detail in the sections that follow.

Opening Files in an MFC Program

To open an existing document in a Windows-based application, the user customarily chooses the Open command from the File menu. AppWizard does not automatically provide a message-handler function for opening files in response to this command, but you can easily create one—and if your application uses the MFC serialization mechanism described later in this chapter, you can supply a small amount of code that will open files automatically.

If your application doesn't use serialization, you can support the Open command by using ClassWizard to create a message-handler function for the *ID_FILE_OPEN* message. In an MFC application, choosing the Open command causes Windows to issue an *ID_FILE_OPEN* message, which is one of the menu commands that ClassWizard can automatically create message handlers for.

To create an item on the File menu by using ClassWizard, you follow the general steps for creating message handlers that were outlined earlier, in the section "Creating Message Handlers with ClassWizard" on page 237. ClassWizard automatically equips your application's document class with an *ID_FILE_OPEN* message handler.

When AppWizard generates a Visual C++ framework, Save and Save As commands on the File menu are also provided automatically. You can also create message-handler functions for these commands using ClassWizard.

Performing File I/O with the *CFile* Class

The *CFile* class is a convenient interface for general-purpose binary file operations. It is equipped with a number of member functions that you can use to open and close files and to read and write file data.

To supply more specialized file services, the MFC library provides two other classes—the *CStdioFile* and *CMemFile*. Both *CStdioFile* and *CMemFile* are derived from the *CFile* class.

Opening a file using a *CFile* object

To open a file using a *CFile* object, follow these general steps:

1. Instantiate the file object from the *CFile* class, without specifying a path or permission flags. File objects are usually created on the stack rather than on the heap.

2. Open the file object you have created by calling the *CFile::Open* member function, supplying a path and permission flags as arguments with your *Open* call. *CFile::Open* returns a nonzero value if the file is opened successfully. If the specified file cannot be opened, a zero value is returned.

The following code shows how to create a new file with read/write permission (replacing any previous file with the same path):

```
char* pszFileName = "\\test\\myfile.dat";
CFile myFile;

if (!myFile.Open(pszFileName,
        CFile::modeCreate | CFile::modeReadWrite)) {
        TRACE("Can't open file %s\n",pszFileName);
}
```

Reading from a file using a *CFile* object

To read data from files and write data to files, you can call the *CFile::Read* and *CFile::Write* member functions. The MFC library also provides a *CFile::Seek* member function for moving to a specific location within a file.

The prototype of the *CFile::Read* member function is shown here:

```
virtual UINT Read(void FAR *lpBuf, UINT nCount)
    throw(CFileException);
```

The first argument to *CFile::Read* is a pointer to a text buffer. The second argument is an unsigned integer (*UINT*) variable specifying the number of bytes to read. The *Read* member function returns a *UINT* variable specifying the number of bytes that were actually read. If the requested number of bytes cannot be read because an *end-of-file* (*EOF*) *marker* is reached, *Read* returns the actual number of bytes read. If a read error occurs, an *exception* is thrown. (In the MFC library, an exception is an error that can be handled using a special kind of mechanism called an exception handler.)

Writing to a file using a *CFile* object

You can write to a file using a *CFile* object by calling the *CFile::Write* member function. The prototype of the *Write* member function is shown in this code fragment:

```
virtual void Write(void FAR *lpBuf, UINT nCount)
    throw(CFileException);
```

As you can see, the prototype of the *CFile::Write* member function is identical to the prototype of *CFile::Read*, with one exception: *Write* does not return an integer specifying a number of bytes. If a *CFile::Write* call results in an error, the function simply throws an exception. The following code fragment shows how an MFC program can write to and read from a file using a *CFile* object:

```
char        szBuffer[256];
UINT        nActual = 0;

myFile.Write(szBuffer, sizeof(szBuffer));
myFile.Seek(0, CFile::begin);
nActual = myFile.Read(szBuffer, sizeof(szBuffer));
```

Closing a file using a *CFile* object

To close a file using a *CFile* object, call the *CFile::Close* member function. *CFile::Close* closes the file and flushes buffers if necessary.

If you have created a *CFile* object on the stack, the object is automatically closed and then destroyed when it goes out of scope. It is important to note that calling the *CFile::Close* member function does not delete the physical file associated with the *CFile* object. To remove a file associated with a *CFile* object from the system, call *CFile::Remove*. For details on how to call *CFile::Remove*, see the online help.

Retrieving a file's status using a *CFile* object

To get and set information about a file associated with a *CFile* object, you can call the *CFile::GetStatus* member function. You can also call *CFile::GetStatus* to determine whether a file exists. If the specified file does not exist, *GetStatus* returns 0.

For more information about *GetStatus* and an example showing how it is used, see the online help for Visual C++.

The Serialization Mechanism

When you derive an object from the *CObject* class, the Visual C++ framework automatically gives your object the ability to read and write file information. As mentioned, the process of automatically writing an object to or reading an object from a storage medium such as a disk file is called serialization. By taking advantage of the serialization capabilities of the *CObject* class, you can serialize all your application's data by writing a few lines of code.

The serialization mechanism is based on an I/O technique called *streaming*. In the MFC library, streaming lets applications use the same kinds of procedures to perform many different kinds of I/O operations. MFC applications can use streaming to transfer information to and from files, printers, standard I/O devices such as the monitor and the keyboard, and even different computer systems connected across a network.

The MFC serialization mechanism uses data streaming in a specialized way that is a little different from most other kinds of streaming operations The main difference is that the serialization mechanism reads and writes binary data, whereas other kinds of streaming operations read and write character data. But in other respects, serialization and ordinary data streaming use exactly the same kinds of operations. So once you understand the general principles of how data streaming works in C++, it's easy to understand MFC serialization.

Objects and Operators Used in Stream I/O

In conventional C++ stream-based I/O, both output and input are handled as streams of bytes. Most C++ programs send output to files, disk drives, and other devices using a C++ I/O connection named *cout* and receive input from files, disk drives, and other devices using a C++ I/O connection named *cin*.

The *cin* and *cout* I/O connections are generally used with a pair of overloaded operators called the *insertion operator* (<<) and the *extraction operator* (>>) in order to perform the same kinds of operations that the *printf* and *scanf* functions perform in C. The extraction operator, an overloaded version of the bitwise >> operator, is used with the *cin* I/O connection to retrieve input from the user and also to retrieve input from files. The insertion operator, an overloaded version of the bitwise << operator, is used with the *cout* I/O connection to send output to devices such as monitors and printers as well as to files.

In a text-based C++ program, for example, the following statement prints the text "Hello, world!" to standard output (ordinarily the screen):

```
cout << "Hello, world!";
```

Executing this statement has the same effect as executing the following *printf* statement in C:

```
printf("Hello, world!");
```

C++ programs can use the *cin* I/O connection and the extraction operator to retrieve information from the keyboard. For example, a text-based C++ program could use the following statements to create an integer variable named *x*, prompt the user to type in a value, and set *x* to the value typed i by the user.

```
int x;
cout << "Input a value for x:";
cin >> x;
```

C++ programs can also use *cin* >> statements with *CString* objects and other kinds of variables.

NOTE The insertion and extraction operators are not extensively used for keyboard and screen I/O in Visual C++ applications because most Visual C++ programs are graphics-based and generally use graphics-based objects, such as dialog box controls, to manage screen and keyboard I/O. (You'll learn much more about how MFC programs use dialog box controls as user-interface devices in Chapter 8, "Dialog Boxes," and Chapter 9, "Managing Data.") But it's still important for Visual C++ programmers to learn about the *cin* and *cout* I/O connections and the insertion and extraction operators because specialized versions of all those devices are often used for other purposes—such as serialization—in Visual C++ programs.

Using the << and >> Operators

The insertion operator (<<) and the extraction operator (>>) are not technically part of the C++ language, but Visual C++ defines them in a file named ISTREAM.H, in the same way that all major implementations of C provide a STDIO.H library that defines the *printf* and *scanf* family of functions.

Many C++ programmers like the stream-based I/O mechanisms provided by C++ better than the *printf* and *scanf* family of C-language functions because the stream-based I/O mechanisms used in C++ have syntax rules that are much easier to master. For example, in C++, the << and >> operators can be used with either strings or numeric variables, without the need for any formatting characters. Consider the following short (but complete) text-based C++ application:

```
#include <iostream.h>
int main()
{
    int price = 5;
    cout << "The price is $" << price << ".\n";
    return 0;
}
```

The output of this short and sweet program is shown here:

```
The price is $5.
```

Once you get accustomed to using the << and >> operators, you might find that they are easier to use than the *printf* and *scanf* functions because they do not require the use of formatting characters or the contorted syntax that formatting characters often require.

Implementing Serialization in MFC Programs

As noted earlier in this chapter, the MFC library's *CObject* class provides built-in support for the serialization mechanism. Any class derived from *CObject* has the *CObject* class's serialization capabilities built in.

The *CObject* class supports serialization by overriding the insertion operator (<<) and the extraction operator (>>) in order to write and read object data to and from storage media. Because the *CObject* class overrides the insertion and extraction operators in this way, any object derived from *CObject* or one of its descendant classes can perform serialization operations by making use of *CObject*'s overridden << and >> operators.

Before an MFC application can use the serialization mechanism, however it must instantiate two other kinds of objects: a *CFile*-derived object and an *archive object*. An archive object is an object that is instantiated from an MFC class named *CArchive*. It is essential to create a *CObject*-derived object before you can use the serialization mechanism because serialization is handled by a *CObject* member function named *Serialize*. It is also essential to create a *CArchive*-derived object because the *CObject::Serialize* member function takes a reference to a *CArchive*-derived object as a parameter. In the SCRIBBLE application presented in this chapter, for example, the following member function declaration appears in the definition of the *CScribDoc* class:

```
virtual void Serialize(CArchive& ar);
```

After you have constructed a *CFile*-derived object and a *CArchive* object, you can open a file object for reading and writing and attach it to your archive object. Because the serialization mechanism can handle both input and output, you must specify whether you want to use the archive for loading or for storing information. Then you can use the *CArchive* member function *Serialize* to read data from or write data to your file, depending on whether you have opened it for reading or for writing.

Implementing Serialization in AppWizard Programs

As mentioned, in a framework-based MFC application, you don't have to write the code that creates the classes and member functions required to support serialization because AppWizard does all that for you. In an application generated by AppWizard, the *CObject*-derived class that is used to support serialization is the program's *CDocument* object.

As you know, AppWizard creates a *CDocument* object for every application framework it generates. When AppWizard creates a *CDocument* object for an application it is generating, it also creates a *CFile*-derived object and a *CArchive* object and performs all the work that is needed to make sure that all three of these objects work together to support serialization. AppWizard even creates a *CArchive::Serialize* member function and places it in the source file that implements the program's *CDocument* object. The application can then implement serialization by adding some code to the *Serialize* member function that AppWizard has created.

When AppWizard creates a *Serialize* member function for a *CDocument*-derived class, the function looks like the one shown here:

```
void CScribDoc::Serialize(CArchive& ar)
{
    if (ar.IsStoring())
    {
        // TODO: add storing code here
    }
    else
    {
        // TODO: add loading code here
    }
}
```

As you can see, a *Serialize* member function created by AppWizard is capable of both saving and loading information. You must decide what kinds of data and objects you want your program to retrieve when it restarts and store when it terminates. It's up to you to write the code that does the job, but you don't have to make an explicit call to the *Serialize* member function that AppWizard has created. Once AppWizard has equipped an application with a *Serialize* member function, the program's framework calls *Serialize* at the appropriate times.

Implementing Serialization in the SCRIBBLE Program

In the SCRIBBLE application presented in this chapter, three lines of code have been added to the *CScribDoc::Serialize* member function that appears in the SCRIBDOC.CPP file, as shown here:

```
void CScribDoc::Serialize(CArchive& ar)
{
    if (ar.IsStoring())
    {
        ar << m_sizeDoc;
    }
    else
    {
        ar >> m_sizeDoc;
    }
    m_strokeList.Serialize(ar);
}
```

Once you have a general idea of how the << and >> operators work, it isn' hard to figure out what's going on here. The *CObject::Serialize* member function always takes one parameter: a reference to a *CArchive* object. In this example, the name of the *CArchive* object is *ar*. When the SCRIBBLE application's framework calls *Serialize*, the application's framework automatically passes a reference to the *ar* object to the *Serialize* member function.

The *IsStoring* function is used to determine whether the function is saving or loading data. If *IsStoring* returns *TRUE*, the *Serialize* function is being used to store information, so the << operator is used to store whatever information is being saved in an archive. If *IsStoring* returns *FALSE*, the *Serialize* member function is being used to retrieve information, so the >> operator is used to load data into memory.

In the preceding example, two things are serialized: a piece of data and an MFC object. The piece of data is a member variable named *m_sizeDoc*, which contains the size of a SCRIBBLE document. The *Serialize* function is used to save this value when a SCRIBBLE document is closed and to retrieve the same value whenever the same document is reopened.

The MFC object that the SCRIBBLE application serializes is an instantiation of a class named *CStroke*. In the preceding example, the following statement serializes a *CStroke* object:

```
m_strokeList.Serialize(ar);
```

This statement demonstrates one of the most powerful features of the MFC serialization mechanism: the ease with which you can serialize a complete MFC object in a Visual C++ program. An MFC object derived from the *CObject* class is serialized by calling its *Serialize* member function. In this case, a *Serialize* member function that AppWizard has created for a *CDocument*-derived object calls the *Serialize* member function of the *m_strokeList* object.

In the SCRIBBLE application, the *m_strokeList* member variable is an instantiation of an MFC library class named *CObList*. It is declared as follows in the SCRIBDOC.H file:

```
protected:
    CObList m_strokeList;    // each member of the list is a CStroke
```

As mentioned, the *CObList* class is an MFC collection class that provides a mechanism for storing lists of other MFC objects. In the SCRIBBLE application, a stroke that the user draws is stored in an object instantiated from the *CStroke* class. *CStroke* objects are stored in the *m_strokeList* object, which is instantiated from the *CObList* collection class.

Because the *CObList* class is derived from the *CObject* class, the SCRIBBLE program doesn't have to do anything to serialize its *m_strokeList* object except execute the following statement:

```
m_strokeList.Serialize(ar);
```

Things get a little tricky here, however, because the *m_strokeList* object in the SCRIBBLE program is derived from the *CObject* collection class that is used to store other objects—in this case, strokes that are drawn in a window by the user.

What makes this tricky is that the *CObList* object in the SCRIBBLE program stores *CStroke* objects. Because a *CStroke* object is an application-defined object, not an MFC-defined object, the MFC library has no way of knowing exactly how to store it in an archive.

For this reason, the SCRIBBLE program has to override the *Serialize* member function that the MFC library provides to all objects derived directly or indirectly from the *CObject* class. In the SCRIBBLE application, the *CStroke* class's *Serialize* member function is overridden as shown here:

```
void CStroke::Serialize(CArchive& ar)
{
    if (ar.IsStoring())
    {
        ar << m_rectBounding;
        ar << (WORD)m_nPenWidth;
        m_pointArray.Serialize(ar);
    }
    else
    {
        ar >> m_rectBounding;
        WORD w;
        ar >> w;
        m_nPenWidth = w;
        m_pointArray.Serialize(ar);
    }
}
```

The SCRIBBLE program's *CStroke* class serializes three kinds of objects, listed below. You can probably guess what these objects do and why they have to be serialized when a SCRIBBLE document is to be saved or retrieved.

- A *CRect* object named *m_rectBounding*, which describes the bounding rectangle that surrounds the stroke.

- A *UINT* object named *m_nPenWidth* (cast here to a *WORD* data type, for reasons that will be explained in the next section). The *m_nPenWidth* object defines the width of the pen that is used to draw the stroke.

- A *CDWordArray* object named *m_pointArray*, which can be serialized with an unadorned call to its own *Serialize* member function because it is a direct instantiation of an MFC library class. The *m_pointArray* object contains the coordinates of all the points that are needed to draw the stroke in a SCRIBBLE window.

Because each stroke drawn in a SCRIBBLE window has all three of these properties, all three properties have to be serialized to provide a complete description of each stroke used in the SCRIBBLE program.

Serializable Data Types

Although the MFC library defines an enormous number of data types, Microsoft has kept the implementation of the MFC serialization mechanism simple by equipping it to recognize only a small number of data types. The six data types that you can use in a *Serialize* member function are listed in Table 7-3.

Data Type	Description
BYTE	8 bits unsigned
WORD	16 bits unsigned
LONG	32 bits unsigned
DWORD	32 bits unsigned
float	32 bits
double	64 bits, IEEE standard

Table 7-3. *Serializable data types.*

Although the number of data types recognized by the serialization mechanism seems limited, you can actually serialize data of any data type by casting unrecognized data types to one of the types shown in Table 7-3. For example, the following statement in the *CStroke* class's *Serialize* definition casts a *UINT* data type, which *Serialize* does not recognize, to a *WORD* data type, which is recognized by the MFC serialization mechanism:

```
ar << (WORD)m_nPenWidth;
```

MFC's Serialization Macros

When you derive an object from the *CObject* class or one of its descendant classes, you must invoke a pair of MFC macros: the *DECLARE_SERIAL* macro and the *IMPLEMENT_SERIAL* macro. The *DECLARE_SERIAL* macro is always placed in the definition of a class, and the *IMPLEMENT_SERIAL* macro is placed in the class's implementation file. Subsequently, when the Visual C++ macro preprocessor encounters these two macros, it replaces them with MFC-generated source code that defines and implements various functions that are needed to implement serialization in the class for which they are defined.

OTE You don't have to place the *DECLARE_SERIAL* and *IMPLEMENT_SERIAL* macros in the header and implementation files of your application's document class. The document class that is generated for a framework application is created using serialization, so it already has all the serialization support it requires, and it doesn't need any more. When you derive a class of your own from *CObject* or one of its descendants, however, you must use the *DECLARE_SERIAL* and *IMPLEMENT_SERIAL* macros to implement your class's built-in serialization capabilities.

The *DECLARE_SERIAL* macro is straightforward. It takes just one parameter: the name of the class that will be calling the *Serialize* member function. In the SCRIBBLE program, the *CStroke* class's *DECLARE_SERIAL* macro is declared as follows in the SCRIBDOC.H file:

```
DECLARE_SERIAL(CStroke)
```

In the SCRIBBLE application, the *IMPLEMENT_SERIAL* macro for the *CStroke* class is defined this way in the SCRIBDOC.H file:

```
IMPLEMENT_SERIAL(CStroke, CObject, 2)
```

As shown, the *IMPLEMENT_SERIAL* macro takes three parameters. The first two arguments to the *IMPLEMENT_SERIAL* macro are the name of the class and the name of its base class. The third argument—the schema number—is essentially a version number for objects of the class being equipped with serialization. A schema number is always an integer greater than or equal to 0. When the MFC library's serialization code reads an object into memory, it checks the schema number of the object's class. If the schema number of the object that is stored on disk does not match the schema number of the class, MFC throws a *CArchiveException*, preventing your application from reading an incorrect version of the object.

Opening and Closing Documents in an MFC Program

The MFC framework automatically calls a member function named *CDocument::OnNewDocument* when a new document is created. It calls a member function named *CDocument::OnOpenDocument* when a document is opened. When AppWizard generates an application framework, it automatically creates a skeletal *OnNewDocument* member function for you. But if you want to use an *OnOpenDocument* member function, you must supply it yourself.

Because a document can be created with either the New command or the Open command on the File menu, the SCRIBBLE program's *CScribDoc* class overrides both the *OnNewDocument* and the *OnOpenDocument* member functions of *CDocument* to perform necessary document initialization. Both these initializations are the same in SCRIBBLE, however, so both overrides call an application-specific member function named *InitDocument*.

The following code shows the override of the *OnNewDocument* member function that appears in the SCRIBDOC.CPP file:

```
BOOL CScribDoc::OnNewDocument()
{
    if (!CDocument::OnNewDocument())
        return FALSE;
    InitDocument();
    return TRUE;
}
```

The override of the *OnOpenDocument* member function is shown here:

```
BOOL CScribDoc::OnOpenDocument(const char* pszPathName)
{
    if (!CDocument::OnOpenDocument(pszPathName))
        return FALSE;
    InitDocument();
    return TRUE;
}
```

And the *InitDocument* member function is defined in the SCRIBDOC.CPP file as shown here:

```
void CScribDoc::InitDocument()
{
    m_bThickPen = FALSE;
    m_nThinWidth = 2;      // default thin pen is 2 pixels wide
    m_nThickWidth = 5;     // default thick pen is 5 pixels wide
    ReplacePen();          // initialize pen according to current width
    // default document size is 8 by 9 inches, with one logical unit
    // mapped to 0.01 inch (MM_LOENGLISH mapping mode)
    m_sizeDoc = CSize(800,900);
}
```

OTE   The *InitDocument* member function also sets the initial size of documents created by the SCRIBBLE program to 800 units by 900 units, measured in a *mapping mode* called *MM_LOENGLISH*. MFC document objects can be measured in several different mapping modes, some of which are suitable for screen displays and others of which are more suitable for printing. The *MM_LOENGLISH* mapping mode specified in the SCRIBBLE program's *InitDocument* member function is a mode that works best with screen displays. For more details about MFC mapping modes, see the companion CD-ROM online help files.

The SCRIBBLE program's *InitDocument* member function initializes a set of default properties for a pen object and then calls a member function named *ReplacePen*. The *ReplacePen* member function calls an MFC member function named *DeleteObject* to free any system storage that SCRIBBLE might be using for the pen object being created. Then *ReplacePen* creates a new pen by calling a member function named *CPen::CreatePen*.

In the SCRIBDOC.CPP file, the *ReplacePen* member function is defined as shown here:

```
void CScribDoc::ReplacePen()
{
    m_nPenWidth = m_bThickPen? m_nThickWidth : m_nThinWidth;
    // change the current pen to reflect the new user-specified width
    m_penCur.DeleteObject();
    m_penCur.CreatePen(PS_SOLID, m_nPenWidth, RGB(0,0,0));
    // solid black
}
```

Clearing the SCRIBBLE Program's Window

When you execute the SCRIBBLE program, you can clear all strokes from a window by choosing the Clear All command from the Edit menu. SCRIBBLE then executes the message-handler function shown here:

```
void CScribDoc::OnEditClearAll()
{
    DeleteContents();
    SetModifiedFlag();  // mark the document as having been modified,
                        // for purposes of confirming File Close
    UpdateAllViews(NULL);
}
```

The *OnEditClearAll* member function calls a *CDocument* member function named *DeleteContents* to delete all the *CScribDoc* class's data and then calls another *CDocument* member function, named *SetModifiedFlag,* to notify the SCRIBBLE program that the contents of its document object have been changed. After that, *OnEditClearAll* calls a third *CDocument* member function, named *UpdateAllViews,* to update all the views of the program's *CScribDoc* object.

Overriding the *DeleteContents* member function

CDocument::DeleteContents is an MFC member function that provides a convenient way to destroy a document's data. The MFC framework automatically calls the *DeleteContents* member function whenever it is necessary to delete a document's contents without destroying the document itself. For example, the framework automatically calls an SDI application's *DeleteContents* function when the user chooses the New command from the File menu.

The SCRIBBLE program overrides the *DeleteContents* member function by iterating through the *CObList* object in which strokes are stored. The following code shows how SCRIBBLE overrides *DeleteContents*:

```
void CScribDoc::DeleteContents()
{
    while (!m_strokeList.IsEmpty())
    {
        delete m_strokeList.RemoveHead();
    }
}
```

For each stroke object in the SCRIBBLE program's list of strokes, the *DeleteContents* function calls *RemoveHead*, a member function of the MFC library's *CObList* class, and then invokes the C++ *delete* operator. This action destroys all strokes stored in the list.

Changing Pen Widths

When you execute the SCRIBBLE program, you can change the width of the pen used for stroke drawing by choosing the Pen Widths item from the Pen menu. SCRIBBLE then displays a Pen Widths dialog box similar to the one shown in Figure 7-4 on the following page.

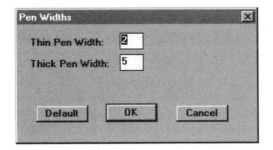

Figure 7-4. *The Pen Widths dialog box.*

The Pen Widths dialog box lets you set two pen widths: a thick pen width, which is used when the user selects the Thick Line item from the Pen menu, and a thin pen width, which is used when the user deselects the Thick Line item. When you program with Visual C++, you can use App Studio to create dialog boxes such as the one shown in Figure 7-4, and you can use ClassWizard to connect dialog box controls to message handlers and to pass information back and forth between dialog box controls and class member functions.

 OTE Chapter 8, "Dialog Boxes," shows how to design dialog boxes. Chapter 9, "Managing Data," shows how to pass data back and forth between dialog box controls and class member functions by using an MFC mechanism called DDX/DDV (dialog data exchange and dialog data verification).

When you select the Thick Line menu item, SCRIBBLE executes the *OnPenThickOrThin* member function shown here:

```
void CScribDoc::OnPenThickOrThin()
{
    // toggle the state of the pen between thin and thick
    m_bThickPen = !m_bThickPen;

    // change the current pen to reflect the new user-specified
    // width
    ReplacePen();
}
```

The *OnPenThickOrThin* member function sets the current pen width by toggling a Boolean member variable named *m_bThickPen*, which keeps track of whether a thin pen or a thick pen is being used, and then calls a member function named *ReplacePen*.

SCRIBBLE then executes the following *OnUpdatePenThickOrThin* member function, which places or removes a check mark next to the Thick Line menu item to show whether the pen currently being used is a thick pen:

```
void CScribDoc::OnUpdatePenThickOrThin(CCmdUI* pCmdUI)
{
    // add check mark to Thick Line menu item if the current
    // pen width is "thick"
    pCmdUI->SetCheck(m_bThickPen);
}
```

The *ReplacePen* member function calls the *CPen::DeleteObject* member function. The *DeleteObject* function destroys the current pen and then calls the *CPen::CreatePen* member to create a new pen with the width that the user has specified.

What's Next?

In this chapter, you learned how message maps work in Visual C++ programs, and you learned how Visual C++ programs recognize and respond to mouse events. In Chapter 8, "Dialog Boxes," you'll learn how to use App Studio and ClassWizard to create dialog boxes and many different dialog box controls. In Chapter 9, "Managing Data," you'll learn how to transfer information back and forth between dialog box controls and the member functions used in Visual C++ programs. Then in Chapter 10, "Visual C++ Graphics," you'll learn how to develop a program that creates screen displays using device-independent bitmaps. You'll also learn how to create lightning-fast animation using small DIB objects called sprites.

Dialog Boxes

Dialog boxes are one of the most important features of Windows-based applications. No matter what kind of Windows-based program you decide to create, chances are better than even that you will need to create and manage at least a few dialog boxes. And the more sophisticated your application becomes, the more different kinds of dialog boxes it is likely to require.

This chapter explains how to create and use the three most important varieties of dialog boxes: modal dialog boxes, modeless dialog boxes, and message boxes. Topics covered in this chapter include the following:

- Creating and implementing modal and modeless dialog boxes

- Designing and using dialog box controls

- Using message boxes in your applications

- Creating user drawn dialog box controls

- Creating combo boxes and list boxes and supplying them with text

The sample program presented in this chapter, DLGDEMO, shows you how to create and use several different kinds of controls, including static text controls, edit controls, radio button controls, and owner drawn controls. It also demonstrates how to populate list boxes and combo boxes.

The modal dialog box shown in Figure 8-1 is one of the dialog boxes displayed by the DLGDEMO program.

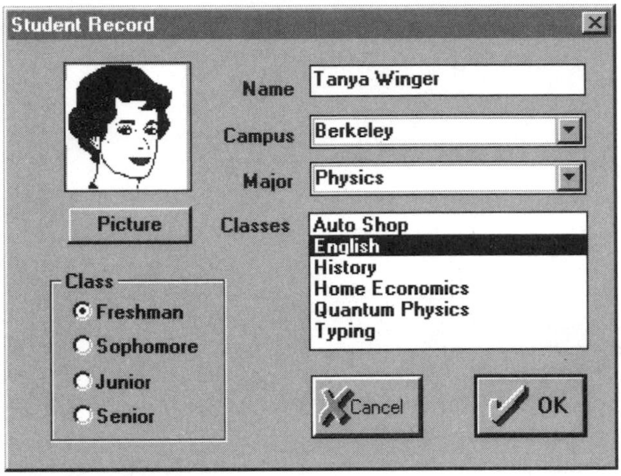

Figure 8-1. *A modal dialog box.*

Creating Dark Gray Backgrounds for Dialog Boxes

In programs written for Windows 95 and Windows NT, "fashionable" dialog boxes have dark gray backgrounds instead of the white backgrounds that date back to the days of Windows 3.0. To create default dark gray backgrounds for your dialog boxes so that they'll look crisp and up-to-date, all you have to do is call the MFC library's *SetDialogBkColor* member function in your program's *InitInstance* function. For example, as shown in the DLGDEMO.CPP file on the companion CD-ROM, the *InitInstance* function of the *CDlgDemoApp* class makes this call to *SetDialogBkColor*:

```
// make dialog backgrounds dark gray
SetDialogBkColor();
```

The *SetDialogBkColor* member function accepts two optional *COLORREF* arguments: one that specifies the background color for the application, and another that specifies the background color for the program's dialog boxes. If you omit both arguments, *SetDialogBkColor* sets the background color of your program's dialog boxes to standard Windows 95 dark gray.

> **N**OTE   The modal dialog box displayed by the DLGDEMO program demon-
> strates the use of dialog controls but doesn't do much else. When you close
> the dialog box, the information entered in its controls is not saved; it simply
> disappears. Chapter 9, "Managing Data," explains how to create dialog
> boxes that write information to a database and read information from a
> database.

Varieties of Dialog Boxes

Dialog boxes fit into two general categories: modal dialog boxes and modeless dialog boxes. A modal dialog box does not allow the user to perform
actions in the application until the dialog box is closed. A modeless dialog
box, on the other hand, lets users perform other actions in the application
while the dialog box is displayed. A third variety of dialog box, the message box, is itself a modal dialog box.

Modal Dialog Boxes

Most dialog boxes used in Windows-based programs are modal dialog
boxes. Typically, a user closes a modal dialog box by clicking the OK or
Cancel button. (Some dialog boxes, including the dialog boxes in this
chapter's sample program, also have Close boxes in their title bars.) In a
well-behaved Windows-based application, clicking the OK button displayed in a modal dialog box confirms any entries the user has made in the
dialog box's controls. Often, clicking the OK button writes data to files or
modifies data being used by the application. The Cancel button (and the
Close box, if there is one) closes a dialog box without taking any other
actions.

Modeless Dialog Boxes

Modeless dialog boxes are somewhat more difficult to implement than
modal dialog boxes, but modeless dialog boxes are more versatile. Modeless
dialog boxes give the user more control over an application and are particu-
larly useful in situations that require a dialog box to remain on the screen
while the user performs other actions in the application. Tool palettes and
find-and-replace dialog boxes, for example, are often implemented as
modeless dialog boxes. In contrast to a modal dialog box, you typically
close a modeless dialog box by clicking its Close box (rather than clicking

the OK or Cancel button) in the same way that you close any document window. Until you close a modeless dialog box, it remains on the screen.

Message Boxes

One popular kind of modal dialog box is the message box. Message boxes are so easy to create and implement that many software designers use them to display error messages during the creation and debugging of programs.

You can implement a message box with one simple command: a call to the Microsoft Foundation Class (MFC) Library version 2.0 member function *MessageBox*. In Visual C++, the *MessageBox* function takes one to three parameters. The three parameters are a message string, a title string, and a flag parameter that controls the appearance, behavior, and other characteristics of the message box being displayed. More information about message boxes is provided later in this chapter.

Components of a Dialog Box

In programs created with the AppWizard framework, every dialog box has two components:

- A resource that identifies the dialog box and specifies the dialog box's controls and their placement in the dialog box window.

- A C++ class derived from the MFC library's *CDialog* class. This class provides an interface for managing the dialog box.

The resource component of a dialog box supplies a template that Windows uses to create and display the dialog box. A dialog box template specifies a dialog box's characteristics, including its size, its location, its style, and the types and positions of its controls. It is possible to create a dialog box without using a template. However, dialog box templates are the usual method for implementing dialog boxes, especially in Visual C++ programs.

From a C++ point of view, a dialog box is implemented as an object of the *CDialog* class. The *CDialog* class is derived from the *CWnd* class and is, therefore, at its core, a window. Ordinarily, a dialog box window has a parent window to which it is attached whenever it is open and visible on the screen.

The controls that appear inside a dialog box are objects of various MFC library classes, such as *CEdit*, *CButton*, and *CScrollBar*. All these classes are also descendants of the *CWnd* class, so it should not be surprising to learn that dialog box controls are implemented as child windows.

Designing a Dialog Box with App Studio and ClassWizard

In a Visual C++ program, the easiest way to design a dialog box and equip it with controls is to use the App Studio dialog box editor. When you design a dialog box with the dialog box editor, App Studio stores your dialog box template resource as a *resource script file*. Then you can use ClassWizard to create a *CDialog*-derived class for your dialog box and to link a message map and a set of variables to its controls.

To create a dialog box, follow these general steps:

1. From Visual Workbench, open App Studio by choosing the App Studio item from the Tools menu.

2. When the main App Studio window opens, double-click the Dialog icon that appears in the Type list box (or double-click the dialog box icon on the App Studio toolbar). App Studio opens a dialog box editor, as shown on the following page, that you can use to create your dialog boxes. (To display the dialog box shown here, double-click the IDD_STUDENT_RECORD item in the Resources list box.) The dialog box editor is equipped with a default modal dialog box that contains an OK button and a Cancel button.

3. When App Studio opens the dialog box editor, you can add other kinds of controls by using the control palette that the dialog editor provides. If you don't see the control palette, shown below, when you open the dialog box editor, you can display it by pressing F2 or by choosing Show Control Palette from the Window menu:

To place a control in a dialog box, simply select the control you want from the control palette, and then click the mouse inside the client area of the dialog box you are creating. App Studio responds by placing a control of the type you have selected into the dialog box's client area in the location you have chosen.

OTE Each dialog box control shown in the control toolbar can be created from a class defined in the MFC library. However, when you create a dialog box control using App Studio, App Studio does not automatically create a C++ class from which objects can be instantiated. The easiest way to create a class for the control is to use ClassWizard; this technique is described in the next section.

---

4. To configure the tab layout of a dialog box using the App Studio dialog box editor, you choose the Set Tab Order item from the Layout menu. App Studio then displays a set of consecutive numbers on the controls inside the dialog box, as shown here:

To change the tab order of the dialog box's controls, you simply click each control in the tab order you want to set, beginning with the control that you want as the default control when your application opens the dialog box. The control that you designate to be first in the dialog box's tabbing order has the focus when your dialog box opens—and if it is an edit control, it contains a cursor.

Integrating Dialog Boxes with Applications

After you have designed a dialog box for a Visual C++ application, you can use the Visual C++ ClassWizard utility to connect, or "bind," your dialog box and its controls to the member functions in your application that give your program's resources their functionality. You can also use ClassWizard to add member variables to dialog box classes and determine how those variables are initialized and displayed.

In Chapter 9, in the section "Creating the TESTAPP Project and Adding DDX Support" on page 315, you'll get an opportunity to create a dialog box with App Studio and then connect its controls to an application using ClassWizard.

When ClassWizard creates a *CDialog*-derived class, it generates both an implementation (.CPP) file and a header (.H) file for the new class. The .H file contains the definition of your dialog class. Be sure to include this header file in any other source files that access your dialog box. The .CPP file contains a message map, a standard constructor, and an override of a *CWnd* member function named *DoDataExchange*. The *DoDataExchange* member function uses a mechanism named DDX (dialog data exchange) to move information back and forth between C++ variables and dialog box controls. DDX is described later in this chapter and in Chapter 9.

Creating and Displaying a Modal Dialog Box

To create and display a modal dialog box, you need to perform two steps. First you must instantiate a dialog box object by calling its constructor. Then you must open the dialog box by calling the *CDialog* function *DoModal*.

Calling a Dialog Box Constructor

In the DLGDEMO program, both these operations take place in a member function named *OnDialogsModal*. The *OnDialogsModal* function is executed when the user chooses the Modal item from the Dialogs menu.

> **N**OTE   In a Visual C++ program, the easiest way to open a dialog box when the user chooses a menu command is to write a message handler using ClassWizard. In the DLGDEMO program, ClassWizard was used to link the *OnDialogsModal* function to a menu item. For more information about using ClassWizard to create message handlers for menu items, see Chapter 5, "Visual C++ Tools," and Chapter 7, "Of Mice and Messages."

The *OnDialogsModal* member function is defined as follows in the MAINFRM.CPP file:

```
void CMainFrame::OnDialogsModal()
{
    CModalDlg modalDlg;
    modalDlg.DoModal();
}
```

The *OnDialogsModal* function calls the constructor *CModalDlg* to instantiate a *CModalDlg* object named *modalDlg* on the stack. *OnDialogsModal* then calls a member function named *modalDlg.DoModal* to display a modal dialog box.

The constructor that is called from the *OnDialogsModal* member function is implemented in the MODAL.CPP file. Here is the definition of the constructor *CModalDlg*:

```
CModalDlg::CModalDlg(CWnd* pParent /*=NULL*/)
    : CDialog(CModalDlg::IDD, pParent),NR_OF_CLASSES(6)
{
    //{{AFX_DATA_INIT(CModalDlg)
    m_classList = ("English");
    m_campus = ("Berkeley");
    m_major = ("Physics");
    m_name = ("Tanya Winger");
    m_freshman = 0;
    //}}AFX_DATA_INIT
}
```

This constructor contains a block of code that initializes a set of member variables associated with dialog box controls. All these variables were created using ClassWizard. As you can see, they appear inside an AFX data block enclosed by the //{{ and //}} delimiters; they are designed to exchange data with dialog box controls using the DDX mechanism.

The DDX Mechanism

The DDX mechanism is examined in detail in Chapter 9, "Managing Data." For now, it's sufficient to know that the DDX system moves data back and forth between controls and variables by calling a *CWnd* member function named *UpdateData*. The *UpdateData* member function takes one parameter: a Boolean variable that specifies the direction in which data is to be moved. If the parameter is set to *TRUE*, data is retrieved from the controls and is stored in variables; if the parameter is set to *FALSE*, the controls of the dialog box are initialized by values stored in the variables associated with the controls. For example, if *CTRL2VAR* is *TRUE*, the following function call moves data from a control to a variable:

```
UpdateData(CTRL2VAR);
```

Conversely, if *VAR2CTRL* is *FALSE*, the following function call moves information from a variable to a control:

```
UpdateData(VAR2CTRL);
```

Calling the *DoModal* Function

When an application calls the *CDialog::DoModal* member function, a dialog resource associated with the specified dialog box object must already exist. The *DoModal* member function loads the appropriate dialog resource and then displays the dialog box associated with the resource.

When the *DoModal* member function opens a dialog box window, the user is not permitted to perform any other action in the application until the dialog box is closed.

While a modal dialog box is open, messages and events related to the controls in the dialog box are typically handled by message maps generated by ClassWizard. The DDX mechanism handles the exchange of data between variables and the dialog box controls.

In the DLGDEMO program, the *DoModal* member function is called in a file named MAINFRM.CPP. When the user clicks the OK button, the application calls the *CDialog* member function *OnOK*. If the user clicks the

Close box, the *OnClose* member function is called, and the dialog box closes. When the user clicks the Cancel button, the *OnCancel* function is called, and the dialog box closes. (The modeless dialog box in DLGDEMO does not have a Cancel button.)

When a Visual C++ application uses the MFC library—as DLGDEMO does—the MFC library's *OnOK* member function calls the *UpdateData* function to copy any data that has been input by the user into any variables that might be associated with the dialog box's controls. *UpdateData* then calls *CDialog::EndDialog*, a function that makes the dialog box invisible. The *DoModal* function then returns. The dialog box is not actually destroyed until the function that called *DoModal* terminates. Then, if the dialog box was instantiated on the stack, its destructor is called, and it is officially destroyed.

Calling the *OnInitDialog* Function

Between the time a dialog box is created and the time it is displayed on the screen, the application framework calls a *CDialog* member function named *OnInitDialog*. The *OnInitDialog* member function is a handy place to put various kinds of initializations used in a dialog box.

To make use of the *OnInitDialog* function, you must override it in your application. The first statement in your override should call its parent function, *CDialog::OnInitDialog*, to ensure that the dialog box's controls are initialized. The *OnInitDialog* member function must return a Boolean value, so be sure your override ends with a *return* statement that is either *TRUE* or *FALSE*. Under ordinary circumstances, it should return a value of *TRUE*.

Listing 8-1 shows how the *OnInitDialog* function is overridden in the DLGDEMO program.

```
BOOL CModalDlg::OnInitDialog()
{
    // first call the parent function
    CDialog::OnInitDialog();

    // initialize array for the Classes list box
    char *m_classes[] = {
```

Listing 8-1. *Overriding the* OnInitDialog *function.*   *(continued)*

Listing 8-1. *continued*

```
        "English",
        "History",
        "Typing",
        "Quantum Physics",
        "Auto Shop",
        "Home Economics"
    };

    // populate the Classes list box
    for (int i = 0;  i < NR_OF_CLASSES; i++)
        ListBox1().AddString(m_classes[i]);

    // load the owner drawn bitmaps
    VERIFY(m_OK.AutoLoad(IDOK, this));
    VERIFY(m_cancel.AutoLoad(IDCANCEL, this));
    VERIFY(m_faceButton.AutoLoad(IDC_FACE, this));

    // highlight the Freshman radio button
    ((CButton *)GetDlgItem(IDC_FRESHMAN))->SetFocus();

    UpdateData(VAR2CTRL);
    return TRUE;
}
```

The *OnInitDialog* function shown in Listing 8-1 performs the following operations:

■ Calls the parent *CDialog::OnInitDialog* member function.

■ Initializes an array of strings named *m_classes*. The strings in this array will appear inside a list box labeled Classes when the dialog box opens.

■ Copies the strings in the *m_classes* array into the Classes list box. This action takes place in a *for* loop that repeatedly calls a member function named *CListBox::AddString* until all the strings in the array are copied.

■ Calls the *CBitmapButton::AutoLoad* member function to load the bitmaps used in the OK and Cancel buttons and in the owner drawn Face button. You'll learn more about the *AutoLoad* function in the section "Calling the *AutoLoad* function" on page 297.

Creating and Displaying a Modeless Dialog Box

Modeless dialog boxes are easier to use—but slightly more difficult to create—than modal dialog boxes. Actually, a modeless dialog box requires only a few more lines of code than a modal dialog box.

The DLGDEMO program contains an example of a modeless dialog box. To display it, simply choose the Modeless item from the Dialogs menu. You can open as many modeless dialog boxes as you want, and you can position them any way you want on the screen. You can also compare the way the modeless and modal dialog boxes work. The difference is obvious—and dramatic.

Figure 8-2 shows the modeless dialog box displayed by the DLGDEMO program.

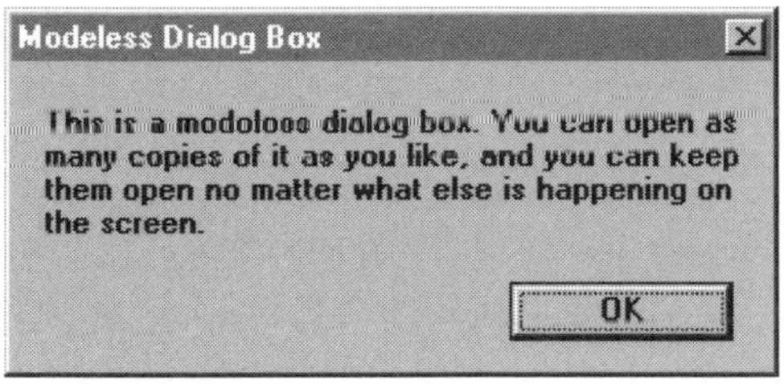

Figure 8-2. *A modeless dialog box.*

To implement its modeless dialog box, the DLGDEMO program instantiates an object of the *CModelessDialog* class. *CModelessDialog* is derived from the MFC library's *CDialog* class, which has all the special requirements of modeless dialog boxes built in.

Constructing a Modeless Dialog Box

Microsoft C/C++ version 7—the immediate predecessor of Visual C++—defined separate classes for modal dialog boxes and modeless dialog boxes. In Visual C++, however, modal and modeless dialog boxes are objects of the same class: the *CDialog* class. That change simplifies the derivation of dialog box objects, but it complicates the creation and handling of modal and modeless dialog boxes because the two kinds of dialog boxes have different characteristics and must be created and managed in different ways. That's why the DLGDEMO program defines a separate class, named *CModelessDialog*, for modeless dialog boxes.

To instantiate a modeless dialog box, you must call an overloaded *CDialog* constructor and then call the member function *CDialog::Create*. (Usually, as you will soon see, the *CDialog::Create* member function is called from inside the constructor of the modeless dialog box.)

In the DLGDEMO program file MAINFRM.CPP, a class named *CModeless-Dialog* is derived from the MFC library's *CDialog* class. Then, when the user chooses the Modeless item from the Dialogs menu, the *OnDialogs-Modeless* function is executed to create a *CModelessDialog* object, as shown here:

```
void CMainFrame::OnDialogsModeless()
{
    GetMenu()->EnableMenuItem (ID_DIALOGS_MODELESS, MF_GRAYED);
    m_pModeless = new CModelessDialog(this);
}
```

The constructor that creates a modeless dialog box in the DLGDEMO program takes one parameter: a *this* pointer. Notice also that the constructor uses the *new* operator to create a dialog box object on the heap. (In contrast, the *CMainFrame::OnDialogsModal* function, which instantiates a modal dialog box, uses a form of the *CDialog* constructor that places a dialog box object on the stack.)

Calling the *Create* Function

After you have constructed a modeless dialog box by calling its constructor, you must create the object by calling the *CDialog::Create* function. In the DLGDEMO program, the *Create* member function is called from inside the *CModelessDialog* constructor, as shown here:

```
CModelessDialog::CModelessDialog(CWnd* pParent)
{
    Create(IDD_MODELESS1, pParent);
}
```

When a Visual C++ program calls the *CDialog::Create* member function, the framework loads the dialog resource for the specified dialog box object. The dialog box then appears when the parent window is created if its *WS_VISIBLE* property is set. Otherwise, your application must call the *CWnd::ShowWindow* member function to make the dialog box visible.

Initializing a Modeless Dialog Box

After a modeless dialog resource is loaded, but before the dialog box appears on the screen, the Visual C++ framework calls the *CDialog::OnInit-Dialog* member function. When an application is creating a modal dialog box, *OnInitDialog* is called from inside the *DoModal* function. However, when a modeless dialog box is being created, *OnInitDialog* is called from inside the *Create* member function.

As mentioned, applications that create modal dialog boxes often override *OnInitDialog* to initialize dialog box controls. You can also override *OnInitDialog* to initialize the controls inside a modeless dialog box.

In the DLGDEMO program, the *OnInitDialog* function is overridden to place modeless dialog boxes on the screen in a cascading pattern, as shown in Listing 8-2.

```
BOOL CModelessDialog::OnInitDialog()
{
    // cascade modeless dialog boxes
    RECT wndRect;
    static int x = 10;
    static int y = 80;

    GetParent()->GetWindowRect(&wndRect);

    SetWindowPos(GetParent(), wndRect.left + x,
        wndRect.top + y, 0, 0, SWP_NOSIZE);

    if (y > 400) {
        x = 10;
        y = 80;
    } else {
        x += 20;
        y += 20;
    }

    return TRUE;
}
```

Listing 8-2. *Overriding* OnInitDialog *to cascade dialog boxes.*

To observe this pattern, simply choose the Modeless command from the Dialogs menu several times. As you open modeless dialog boxes in the DLGDEMO program, the program cascades them, as shown in Figure 8-3 on the following page.

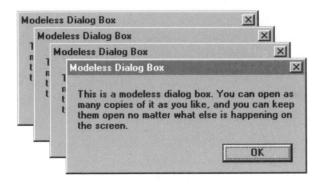

Figure 8-3. *Cascading modeless dialog boxes.*

The *CenterWindow* Member Function

In the DLGDEMO program, the modeless dialog boxes are cascaded. For a completely different look, you can center a dialog box neatly inside a window by calling the *CWnd::CenterWindow* function from inside the *OnInitDialog* function. The *CenterWindow* member function is prototyped as shown here:

```
CenterWindow(CWnd* pAlternateOwner = NULL);
```

If you call the *CenterWindow* function without any parameters, the dialog box you create is centered inside its parent window. To center it inside another window, specify a pointer to the window of your choice in the *pAlternateOwner* parameter.

Overriding *OnOK* and *OnCancel*

One difference between modal and modeless dialog boxes is that code implementing a modeless dialog box must override the *CDialog::OnOK* and *CDialog::OnCancel* member functions. If a modeless dialog box has a Close box, you must also override the *CDialog::OnClose* member function.

Why must these member functions be overridden when a modeless dialog box is closed? The main reason is that in their default *CDialog* versions, al three of these functions close dialog boxes by calling the *CDialog* function *EndDialog*. One important feature of the *CDialog::EndDialog* member function is that it removes a dialog box from the screen but does not free the memory used by the dialog box's resource. As mentioned, that is not important when a modal dialog box is being closed. However, to release the memory used by a modeless dialog resource, an application must call the *CWnd* member function *DestroyWindow*, which frees the memory used by the window (or the dialog box) that is destroyed.

The default versions of the *CDialog* member functions *OnOK*, *OnCancel*, and *OnClose* do not call *CWnd::DestroyWindow*. When you want to destroy a modeless dialog box and free the memory that it uses, you must override these member functions to call *CWnd::DestroyWindow* instead of *CDialog::EndDialog*. Because you don't want *EndDialog* to be called when a modeless dialog box is being closed, your overrides of these three functions should not call their default *EndDialog* member functions.

Unfortunately, when you do not call the default version of *CDialog::OnOK*, you can create another problem. When *CDialog::OnOK* closes a dialog box, it calls the *CDialog::UpdateData* member function to perform any DDX functions that the dialog box might require. If your application contains a modeless dialog box that needs to save any information entered by the user before it closes, you need to call *UpdateData* yourself from your override of the *OnOK* member function.

In the DLGDEMO program, the modeless dialog box has an OK button and a Close box, but it does not have a Cancel button, so the MODELESS.CPP file contains functions that override *OnOK* and *OnClose* but does not contain an override for *OnCancel*. The code that overrides *OnOK* and *OnClose* looks like this:

```
void CModelessDialog::OnOK()
{
    DestroyWindow();
}

void CModelessDialog::OnClose()
{
    DestroyWindow();
}
```

Note that the *UpdateData* function is not called in these functions because the modeless dialog box of the DLGDEMO program does not contain any input fields, and hence, no data needs to be saved.

Calling *PostNcDestroy*

After you have written code that creates a modeless dialog box and have overridden the functions that close it, you must take one more action to ensure that your dialog box operates properly. If you instantiate your *CDialog*-derived object by invoking the *new* operator—which is the usual (and recommended) technique—you should invoke the *delete* operator with the *this* pointer that references your modeless dialog box object to ensure that any objects created by your *CDialog*-derived object are also destroyed.

To invoke the *delete* operator when a modeless dialog box is closed, applications generally override the *CWnd* member function *PostNcDestroy*. *PostNcDestroy* is called by the default *CWnd::OnNcDestroy* member function when a window has been destroyed. To override the *PostNcDestroy* member function to make it invoke *delete*, all you have to do is define *PostNcDestroy* in your dialog box object's .H file and then implement the function in the .CPP file that implements your dialog box object.

In the DLGDEMO program, the following statement in the MODELESS.CPP file overrides *PostNcDestroy* and then invokes the *delete* operator:

```
void CModelessDialog::PostNcDestroy()
{
    delete this;
}
```

Creating and Displaying a Message Box

In a Visual C++ application, you can create and display a message box with just one statement: a call to the *CWnd* member function *MessageBox*. The *CWnd::MessageBox* member function takes one, two, or three parameters: a message string, an optional caption string that is displayed in the message box's title bar, and an optional flag that describes the message box's appearance and behavior. (You don't have to specify a handle to a window, as you did in pre-Visual C++ applications, because the Visual C++ *MessageBox* member function is a member function of the *CWnd*-derived class from which it is called.)

A message box can contain from one to three labeled buttons. To specify how many buttons a message box contains and how they are labeled, you place the flag of your choice in the third parameter of your *MessageBox* call. You can also specify what kind of icon will be displayed in your message—for example, a picture of a stop sign or an exclamation point. For details, see the description of the global *AfxMessageBox* function in the online help.

If you don't specify a caption-string argument, the string "Error" is used by default. If you don't specify a flags argument, the message box you create has only one button—an OK button.

The DLGDEMO program displays a one-button message box when the user chooses the Message item from the Dialogs menu. To display a message box, the MAINFRM.CPP file contains the following function:

```
void CMainFrame::OnDialogsMessage()
{
    MessageBox("Message for you; sign here, please.", "UPS Yes",
        MB_ICONEXCLAMATION);
}
```

Dialog Box Controls

The dialog boxes displayed in this chapter contain various kinds of controls. The following sections describe these controls and explain how each control works. As you read about each control, you can see how it works by running the DLGDEMO program and displaying the appropriate dialog box.

All the controls used here were created with the App Studio dialog box editor. Modal and modeless dialog boxes can be equipped with the same kinds of controls.

Button Controls

The simplest kind of dialog box control is the plain button control, or pushbutton control. When you have placed a button control in a dialog box using App Studio, you can display the Properties window, as shown in Figure 8-4 on the following page, by choosing Show Properties from the

Window menu or by double-clicking the button you have just created. From the Properties window, you can set any, some, or all of the properties listed in Table 8-1.

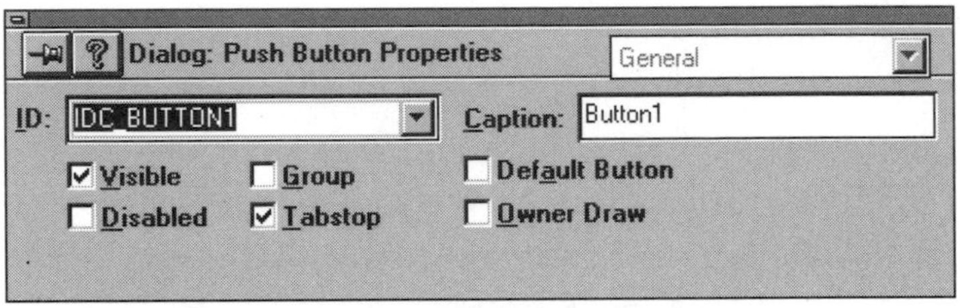

Figure 8-4. *The button control Properties window.*

A button control created in the source code of a program is a member of the MFC library's *CButton* class. However, App Studio does not automatically instantiate a *CButton*-derived object every time it creates a button control. If you want to instantiate a C++ object for a button control created by App Studio, you must do it yourself.

Property	Description	Property Type	Default
ID	Resource's identifier (ID).	Integer or symbol defined by App Studio in the file RESOURCE.H	The string *IDC_BUTTON* followed by a number (for example, *IDC_BUTTON1*, *IDC_BUTTON2*)
Caption	Text that appears inside the control.	*CString*	The string *Button* followed by a number, starting with *1* (for example, *Button1*, *Button2*)
Visible	Determines whether the control is visible when the dialog box opens.	Boolean	*TRUE*

Table 8-1. *Properties of button controls.*

Property	Description	Property Type	Default
Disabled	Determines whether the control is disabled when the dialog box opens.	Boolean	*FALSE*
Group	Specifies whether the control is the first control in a group of controls.	Boolean	*FALSE*
Tabstop	If *TRUE*, the user can move the focus to this control with the Tab key.	Boolean	*TRUE*
Default Button	If *TRUE*, the control is the default button in the dialog box.	Boolean	*FALSE*
Owner Draw	Customizes the appearance of a control.	Boolean	*FALSE*

Most of these properties are self-explanatory, but two deserve special attention: Group and Owner Draw.

The Group property

When you set the Group property of a button control to *TRUE*, your application recognizes the button as the first button in a *group*. In the DLGDEMO program, the four radio buttons labeled Class are members of a group. Notice that when you select one button in the group, the other buttons are automatically deselected.

Each subsequent control in the dialog box's tabbing order belongs to the same group. This grouping procedure continues until the user tabs to another control whose Group property is set to *TRUE*. Then the previous control group ends, and another control group begins.

When you create a dialog box that contains only simple buttons—for example, an OK button and a Cancel button—the setting of the Group property generally has little, if any, effect on the overall operation of the dialog box. However, when you design a dialog box that has other kinds of controls—such as radio buttons and check boxes—the Group properties of your dialog box's controls become more important. (Radio buttons and check boxes are discussed in greater detail later in this chapter.)

When you arrange a cluster of radio buttons in a group, you can link them visually by placing them inside a *group box control*. A group box control is simply a labeled frame. In the DLGDEMO program, the Freshman, Sophomore, Junior, and Senior radio buttons are grouped and placed inside a group box control labeled Class.

The Owner Draw property

In a Windows-based program, an *owner drawn button* is a button that contains a bitmap provided by the developer of an application. Owner drawn buttons are often used in dialog boxes that require customized controls.

An owner drawn button does not have to look like an ordinary Windows-style pushbutton. Instead, the Visual C++ framework lets you display any bitmap you choose inside the button.

If you want to, you can display different bitmaps inside the same button to denote when the button is in different states. An owner drawn button can display up to four application-supplied bitmap states, listed here:

- A bitmap that is displayed when the button is the default button in a dialog box. In this state, the button appears to be in an up position and has a heavy border.

- A bitmap that is displayed when the button is in the up position but is not the default button. In this state, the button appears to be up but does not have a heavy border.

- A bitmap that is displayed when the button is in the down position.

- A bitmap that is displayed when the button is disabled.

Three of the buttons in the DLGDEMO program—the OK button, the Cancel button, and the Face button—are owner drawn buttons. If you click each of these buttons, you'll see that the button's appearance changes while the mouse button is down. That's because when the user clicks an owner drawn button, the *CWnd::OnDrawItem* function automatically switches its bitmap, thus changing its appearance.

Calling the *AutoLoad* function

The MFC library provides two techniques for creating owner drawn buttons: one technique is to call the *CBitmapButton::LoadBitmaps* member function; the other method is to call the *CBitmapButton::AutoLoad* member function. The *LoadBitmaps* function is usually used to load a bitmap when you are creating a bitmap button that is not part of a dialog box; the *AutoLoad* function is used when you create an owner drawn button in a dialog box.

In the DLGDEMO program, the *AutoLoad* member function is called three times to load the bitmaps for the three owner drawn buttons in the Student Record dialog box. The following three function calls appear in the modal dialog box's implementation file, MODAL.CPP:

```
// load the owner drawn bitmaps
VERIFY(m_OK.AutoLoad(IDOK, this));
VERIFY(m_cancel.AutoLoad(IDCANCEL, this));
VERIFY(m_faceButton.AutoLoad(IDC_FACE, this));
```

As the preceding code fragment illustrates, the *AutoLoad* member function takes two parameters: the ID of the bitmap displayed in the control, and a pointer to the parent window of the control—in this case, a pointer to the dialog box in which the control appears.

Although the bitmap's resource ID (identified in the Properties dialog box) is passed as a parameter to the *AutoLoad* function, the reference IDs of the bitmaps themselves are not required. The *AutoLoad* function automatically associates the button with the bitmap. The *AutoLoad* function does this using names based on the caption for the button followed by a one-letter identifier. Four identifiers are possible: *U* (for a button in the up position), *D* (for a button in the down position), *X* (for a disabled button), and *F* (for a focused button). Although you do not need to specify the bitmap names in the call to the *AutoLoad* function, you need to name the bitmaps using the convention described. For example, in the DLGDEMO program, the names of bitmaps used for the Face button are *"FACED"*, *"FACEF"*, *"FACEU"*, and *"FACEX"*, as shown in Figure 8-5.

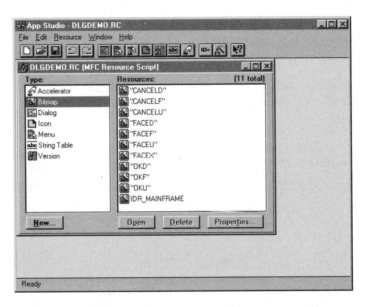

Figure 8-5. *Names of bitmaps used by an owner drawn control.*

When the *AutoLoad* member function finishes loading the bitmaps, it sizes the control to match the size of its bitmaps. (Of course, *AutoLoad* expects all the bitmaps to be the same size.) Then *AutoLoad* subclasses the control (that is, it passes messages that it has received back to its parent window) so that the specified window can display the appropriate bitmaps when it appears on the screen.

Edit Controls

The easiest way to create a *CEdit* class for an edit control is to use Class-Wizard, which was the method used to create the edit controls for the DLGDEMO program.

Every edit control has a standard set of properties and a standard set of
styles that you can set from the App Studio dialog box editor. The standard
properties that you can set using the App Studio dialog box editor are
listed in Table 8-2.

Property	Description	Property Type	Default
ID	Resource's identifier (ID).	Integer or symbol defined by App Studio in the file RESOURCE.H	The string *IDC_EDIT* followed by a number (for example, *IDC_EDIT1*, *IDC-_EDIT2*)
Visible	Determines whether the control is visible when the dialog box opens.	Boolean	*TRUE*
Disabled	Determines whether the control is disabled when the dialog box opens.	Boolean	*FALSE*
Group	Specifies whether the control is the first control in a group of controls.	Boolean	*FALSE*
Tabstop	If *TRUE*, the user can move the focus to this control with the Tab key.	Boolean	*TRUE*

Table 8-2. *Properties of edit controls.*

Edit control styles that you can set from the App Studio Properties window are listed in Table 8-3 on the following page.

Style	Description	Style Type	Default
Align Text	Specifies whether text is aligned left centered, or aligned right. (In a multiline control, text is always aligned left.)	Boolean	Left
Multiline	Creates a multiline edit box control.	Boolean	*FALSE*
Horiz Scroll	Provides a horizontal scroll bar for a multiline control.	Boolean	*FALSE*
Auto HScroll	Automatically scrolls text to the left when the user types a character at the right end of the box.	Boolean	*TRUE*
Vert Scroll	Provides a vertical scroll bar for a multiline control.	Boolean	*FALSE*
Auto VScroll	Automatically scrolls text up one line when the user presses Enter on the last line of a multiline control.	Boolean	*FALSE*
Password	Displays all characters as asterisks (*) as they are typed into the edit box control. This property is not available in multiline controls.	Boolean	*FALSE*
No Hide Sel	Changes the way text is displayed when an edit box control loses and regains focus. If No Hide Sel is set to *TRUE*, selected text in an edit box is displayed as selected at all times.	Boolean	*FALSE*
Border	Creates a border around an edit box control.	Boolean	*TRUE*
Uppercase	Converts all characters to uppercase as they are typed in an edit box.	Boolean	*FALSE*
Lowercase	Converts all characters to lowercase as they are typed in an edit box.	Boolean	*FALSE*

Table 8-3. *Styles of edit controls.*

Style	Description	Style Type	Default
OEM Convert	Converts text typed in an edit box control from the Windows character set to the OEM character set and then back again. This ensures proper character conversion when the application calls the *AnsiToOem* function to convert a Windows string in the edit box control to OEM characters. This style is most useful for edit box controls that contain filenames.	Boolean	*FALSE*
Want Return	Specifies that a carriage return be inserted when the user presses the Enter key while typing text in a multi-line edit box control. If this style is not specified, pressing the Enter key has the same effect as clicking the dialog box's default pushbutton. This style has no effect on a single-line edit box control.	Boolean	*FALSE*
Read-Only	Prevents the user from typing or editing text in an edit box.	Boolean	*FALSE*

Static Text Controls

As you know, static text controls are controls that the user can't edit or otherwise modify. However, the information displayed by a static text control can be dynamically changed at run time. In dialog boxes in Windows, static text controls are used mainly to label other kinds of controls.

In the DLGDEMO program, all the labels in the gray part of the Student Record dialog box are static text controls.

Table 8-4 on the following page lists the main properties of static text controls.

Property	Description	Property Type	Default
ID	Resource's identifier (ID).	Integer or symbol defined by App Studio in the file RESOURCE.H	The string *IDC- _STATIC* without a number appended
Caption	Text displayed by the control.	*CString*	The string *Text* followed by a number, starting with *1* (for example, *Text1*, *Text2*)
Visible	Determines whether the control is visible when the dialog box opens.	Boolean	*TRUE*
Disabled	Determines whether the control is disabled when the dialog box opens.	Boolean	*FALSE*
Group	Specifies whether the control is the first control in a group of controls.	Boolean	*FALSE*
Tabstop	If *TRUE*, the user can move the focus to this control with the Tab key.	Boolean	*TRUE*
No Prefix	Allows an ampersand (&) to be displayed in the control's text string instead of being used as an indication of a keyboard shortcut.	Boolean	*FALSE*

Table 8-4. *Properties of static text controls.*

Property	Description	Property Type	Default
No Wrap	Prevents lines that extend beyond the end of the line from being carried over to the next line by truncating the text.	Boolean	*FALSE*
Text Align	Identifies whether text is aligned left, aligned right, or centered.		LEFT
Simple	Disables No Wrap and Text Align.	Boolean	*FALSE*

Radio Buttons

When you use radio buttons in an application, you should always place them in groups, and you should expect only one radio button to be selected at a time. If you want the user to be able to select more than one button in a group at a time, you should construct your group using a different kind of control. The most likely alternative is a group of check boxes; check boxes are similar to radio buttons, but multiple check boxes in a group can be checked at the same time. Check boxes are discussed later in this chapter.

Creating a group of radio buttons

The easiest way to create a group of radio buttons, as you might guess, is to use App Studio. When you use App Studio to create a group of radio buttons, you should verify that the buttons you create are in sequential order in your dialog box's tab order. (For information about setting the tab order, see "Designing a Dialog Box with App Studio and ClassWizard," on page 279.)

When you set the tab order of a group of radio buttons, be sure that the first radio button in the group has its Group property set. Then check to see that each of the other buttons in the group has its Group property turned off.

Finally, mark the end of your group of radio buttons by turning on the Group property of the first button control that follows your radio button group in your dialog box's tab order.

Table 8-5 lists the properties you can assign to radio button controls using the App Studio Properties window.

Property	Description	Property Type	Default
ID	Resource's identifier (ID).	Integer or symbol defined by App Studio in the file RESOURCE.H	The string *IDC-_RADIO* followed by a number (for example, *IDC-_RADIO1*, *IDC-_RADIO2*)
Caption	Text that labels a radio button.	*CString*	The string *Radio* followed by a number, starting with *1* (for example, *Radio1*, *Radio2*)
Visible	Determines whether the control is visible when the dialog box opens.	Boolean	*TRUE*
Disabled	Determines whether the control is disabled when the dialog box opens.	Boolean	*FALSE*
Group	Specifies whether the control is the first control in a group of controls.	Boolean	*FALSE*
Tabstop	If *TRUE*, the user can move the focus to this control with the Tab key.	Boolean	*FALSE*

Table 8-5. *Properties of radio buttons.*

Property	Description	Property Type	Default
Auto	When a radio button with this property is selected, any other radio buttons in the same group are automatically cleared (deselected). You must set this property to *TRUE* if you are using a group of radio buttons with DDX capabilities.	Boolean	*TRUE*
Left Text	Places the radio button's caption text to the left of the button rather than to the right.	Boolean	*FALSE*

List Boxes

Unfortunately, the Properties window that App Studio supplies for list boxes does not contain a tool for populating a list box with strings. You have to do that in the source code of your application.

A list box stores its strings in a list of *CString* objects, so you can populate a list box by setting up a *CListBox* object and then calling a member function named *CListBox::AddString* to add string objects to the list one by one.

An easier way to populate a list box is to create an array of strings and then copy them into your list box by calling *AddString* repeatedly inside a loop. That is the technique used to populate the list box in the DLGDEMO program. Listing 8-3 on the following page shows how this technique works.

```
// initialize array for the Classes list box
char *m_classes[] = {
    "English",
    "History",
    "Typing",
    "Quantum Physics",
    "Auto Shop",
    "Home Economics"
};

// populate the Classes list box
for (int i = 0; i < NR_OF_CLASSES; i++)
    ListBox1().AddString(m_classes[i]);
```

Listing 8-3. *Populating a list box.*

The code fragment in Listing 8-3 is divided into two sections. The first section defines an array of strings that will be used to populate *ListBox1*. The second section populates *ListBox1* by calling *CListBox::AddString* repeatedly in a *for* loop. To observe the results, run the DLGDEMO program, and choose the Student Record command from the Dialogs menu.

The standard properties of list boxes are listed in Table 8-6.

Property	Description	Property Type	Default
ID	Resource's identifier (ID).	Integer or symbol defined by App Studio in the file RESOURCE.H	The string *IDC_LIST* followed by a number (for example, *IDC_LIST1*, *IDC_LIST2*)
Visible	Determines whether the control is visible when the dialog box opens.	Boolean	*TRUE*
Disabled	Determines whether the control is disabled when the dialog box opens.	Boolean	*FALSE*

Table 8-6. *Properties of list boxes.*

Property	Description	Property Type	Default
Group	Specifies whether the control is the first control in a group of controls.	Boolean	*FALSE*
Tabstop	If *TRUE*, the user can move the focus to this control with the Tab key.	Boolean	*TRUE*

For list box styles that you can set from App Studio, see the online help for Visual C++ on the companion CD-ROM.

Combo Boxes

A combo box is an edit box combined with a drop-down list box that contains *CStrings*. When you create a combo box with App Studio, you can populate it easily by specifying the strings you want in the App Studio Properties window, as shown in Figure 8-6.

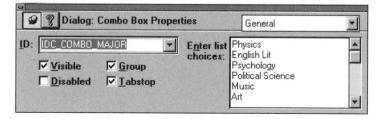

Figure 8-6. *The combo box Properties window.*

In the DLGDEMO program's Student Record dialog box, the Campus and Major boxes are examples of combo boxes.

To create the string that is displayed by a combo box when it opens, you can initialize the string in the combo box's constructor inside the AFX data block that ClassWizard generates in your dialog box object's .CPP file. When the user opens a combo box and selects a different string, the combo box collapses, and the selected string becomes the displayed string.

Table 8-7 on the following page lists the properties of combo boxes.

Property	Description	Property Type	Default
ID	Resource's identifier (ID).	Integer or symbol defined by App Studio in the file RESOURCE.H	The string *IDC-_COMBO* followed by a number (for example, *IDC-_COMBO1*, *IDC-_COMBO2*)
Visible	Determines whether the control is visible when the dialog box opens.	Boolean	*TRUE*
Disabled	Determines whether the control is disabled when the dialog box opens.	Boolean	*FALSE*
Group	Specifies whether the control is the first control in a group of controls.	Boolean	*FALSE*
Tabstop	If *TRUE*, the user can move the focus to this control with the Tab key.	Boolean	*TRUE*
Enter List Choices	Allows the user to enter choices in the combo box.	*CString*	None

Table 8-7. *Properties of combo boxes.*

For combo box styles that you can set from App Studio, see the online help for Visual C++ on the companion CD-ROM.

Check Boxes

Check boxes, like radio buttons, can be arranged in groups. Unlike a radio button, however, a check box can stand alone. The DLGDEMO program doesn't implement any check boxes, but you can find plenty of them in other Windows-based applications.

The standard controls for check boxes are listed in Table 8-8.

Property	Description	Property Type	Default
ID	Resource's identifier (ID).	Integer or symbol defined by App Studio in the file RESOURCE.H	The string *IDC-_CHECK* followed by a number (for example, *IDC_CHECK1*, *IDC_CHECK2*)
Caption	Text that labels a check box.	*CString*	The string *Check* followed by a number, starting with *1* (for example, *Check1*, *Check2*)
Visible	Determines whether the control is visible when the dialog box opens.	Boolean	*TRUE*
Disabled	Determines whether the control is disabled when the dialog box opens.	Boolean	*FALSE*
Group	Specifies whether the control is the first control of a group of controls.	Boolean	*FALSE*

Properties of check boxes.   *(continued)*

Table 8-8. *continued*

Property	Description	Property Type	Default
Tabstop	If *TRUE*, the user can move the focus to this control with the Tab key.	Boolean	*TRUE*
Left Text	Places the caption of the check box to the left of the check box, rather than to the right.	Boolean	*FALSE*
Tri-State	Creates a three-state check box, which can be grayed as well as checked or not checked. A grayed check box indicates that the state represented by the control is undetermined.	Boolean	*FALSE*

What's Next?

You might feel as if you have learned everything there is to know about dialog boxes in this chapter. But wait—there's more. In Chapter 9, "Managing Data," you'll learn how to retrieve information from dialog box controls and use it in your application's member functions. You'll also learn how to move data in the other direction—from your application into a dialog box control.

The mechanisms that make these kinds of data exchanges possible are DDX (dialog data exchange) and DDV (dialog data verification). In Chapter 9, you'll get a chance to experiment with a sample application that shows how you can use the DDX and DDV mechanisms in your own Visual C++ applications.

Managing Data

After you have created and implemented a dialog box, your job is about half done. The next step is usually to find some way to integrate the dialog box with the rest of your application.

When the user of your application opens a dialog box you have created and types some text or selects a list box item, your application needs to be able to detect that a change has been made in the dialog box. If the dialog box controls are not equipped to communicate with the rest of your application, your application has no way of responding to the user's action.

In this chapter, you'll learn how to use a pair of Microsoft Foundation Class (MFC) Library features named DDX (dialog data exchange) and DDV (dialog data verification) to manage data in a Visual C++ application.

With the DDX mechanism, when a user makes a change in a text box, a list box, or a combo box, the application retrieves the information from the control that has been modified and stores it in member variables that belong to an MFC-derived object. Later the information that has been retrieved and stored can be displayed in a different dialog box, stored on a disk, or printed.

You can also move information in the other direction—from an application to controls in the dialog boxes that it displays. Once this link has been set up, you'll be able to initialize the controls in a dialog box by placing data in them before the dialog box opens.

Along with the MFC library's DDX mechanism, this chapter introduces the DDV mechanism, which can perform verification tests on the data that the user enters in a dialog box control. For example, you can use DDV to confirm that a number typed by the user falls within a predetermined range or that a string does not exceed a particular length.

This chapter also expands on the discussion of serialization begun in Chapter 7, "Of Mice and Messages," and shows how you can add printing support to a Visual C++ application. Why are serialization and printing covered in this chapter? Because information that has been retrieved by the DDX mechanism and validated by the DDV mechanism often finds its way to disk storage or to a printer through the MFC library's serialization and printing functions.

The topics we'll cover in this chapter include the following:

- Displaying and manipulating information using edit boxes, combo boxes, and list boxes

- Initializing edit controls with random numbers

- Copying information back and forth between list boxes

- Creating customized DDV functions

- Changing the information displayed in a control when information shown in another control is changed

- Preventing endless loops from hanging up programs that make use of DDV functions

- Verifying user-supplied information automatically

To show you how the DXX and DDV mechanisms work, this chapter presents two sample programs: a simple application named TESTAPP, and a more ambitious sample application named CREATION. The TESTAPP program is designed strictly for instruction; it offers a trivial—but clear—demonstration of how input can be retrieved from a dialog box control. When you execute the program, you can type information in an edit box and then click a button that retrieves what you have typed and displays it in another edit box. That's all the TESTAPP program does.

The CREATION application is more sophisticated. It simulates generating a character for an adventure game. It makes use of a complex collection of controls that can be read from and written to.

The DDX and DDV Mechanisms

The DDX and DDV mechanisms are built into the MFC library and are integrated with ClassWizard and other Visual C++ utilities. To illustrate how the DDX mechanism works, imagine that a dialog box in your application contains an edit control that prompts the user to type a number. If you equip the control with DDX capabilities, your application can move information easily from the control to a C++ member variable.

When you add DDX support to a control, it also gets DDV support. A control with DDV support can verify the information that a user enters in a control. For example, a control with DDV support can verify that a number entered in a control falls within a specified range. If the control is designed to accept character strings, it can verify that the length of a string does not exceed a specified number of characters.

When information entered by a user fails a DDV test, your application can either display a default message box generated by the DDV mechanism or determine for itself what should be done. Typically, when a control with DDV support rejects data input by the user, the application displays a default message box describing the error and requesting valid input. As you will see in the sample programs presented later in this chapter, you can override this default message and substitute your own warning message or take some other action entirely.

The Old Way

Before the advent of DDX/DDV, transferring data from a dialog box control to a variable was a cumbersome process. The usual technique for retrieving data from a control was to call a function such as *GetDlgItemInt* or *GetDlg-ItemText*.

If you want to manage dialog box controls the hard way, you can use this same data-transfer technique in a Visual C++ application. The following code fragment shows how a Visual C++ program can retrieve data from a control by calling *GetDlgItemText* instead of by using the DDX mechanism:

```
void CCreateCharDlg::OnOK()
{

    GetDlgItemText(IDC_EDIT_NAME, m_PlayerName, sizeof(m_PlayerName));
    CDialog::OnOK();
}
```

The *GetDlgItemText* function retrieves a value from a control named *IDC_EDIT_NAME* and stores the value in a member variable named *m_PlayerName*.

All in all, this is a fairly clumsy way to move information back and forth between variables and dialog box controls.

Understanding DDX/DDV: The TESTAPP Program

When you add DDX/DDV support to one or more controls, App Studio and ClassWizard do most of the work for you. First you use App Studio to create a dialog box and place your controls in it. Then you use Class-Wizard to add DDX/DDV capabilities to your controls.

It's as easy to use controls that have DDX/DDV support as it is to create them. To use the DDX/DDV mechanisms, all you need is one function: a *CWnd* member function named *UpdateData*.

The *UpdateData* function takes just one parameter: a Boolean value that specifies whether you want to copy information from a control to a variable or from a variable to a control. As this process takes place, the data being copied can be verified automatically by the Visual C++ DDV mechanism.

You'll learn more about the *UpdateData* function in the section "Understanding the *UpdateData* Command" on page 325.

> **NOTE** If you don't want to work through this exercise but would prefer to read along, open the TESTAPP folder in this chapter's folder on the companion CD-ROM, and then open the TESTAPP project from Visual Workbench.

Creating the TESTAPP Project and Adding DDX Support

To create the TESTAPP project and add DDX capabilities to its controls, follow these steps:

1. From Visual Workbench, create and build a new AppWizard project named TESTAPP. Then launch App Studio by choosing App Studio from Visual Workbench's Tools menu.

2. Select Dialog from the Type list box, and then click the New button. Select Dialog from the Resource Type list box, and then click the OK button. To display the Properties box for the dialog box, double-click on the dialog box. Type *IDD_TESTAPP* in the Resource ID box, and type *Test App* in the Caption box.

3. Use the tool palette to create two static edit boxes. Position one static edit box in the top half of the screen, and position the other below it. Double-click on the top static edit box and enter *Edit Name:* in the Caption box. Double-click on the bottom static edit box, and enter *Show Name:* in the Caption box. Expand both boxes so that the entire text string appears on the screen.

4. Use the tool palette to create two text boxes, and position the boxes to the right of the static edit boxes you created in step 3. Type *IDC_EDIT_NAME* in the Properties box of the top text box, and type *IDC_SHOW_NAME* in the Properties box of the bottom text box.

5. Use the tool palette to create a button, and position the button between the two text boxes that you created in step 4. Double-click on the button to display the Properties box. Type *IDC_COPY* in the ID box, and type *Copy* in the Caption box.

6. Position the controls and expand the boxes as necessary so that your dialog box appears similar to the following:

7. Without leaving App Studio, open ClassWizard by choosing the ClassWizard item from the Resource menu. The Add Class dialog box appears.

8. Enter *CTestDialog* in the Class Name edit box. ClassWizard suggests the default names TESTDIAL.H and TESTDIAL.CPP for the class header and implementation files, as shown here:

9. Click the Create Class button. The ClassWizard dialog box appears, with the new class name, *CTestDialog*, in the Class Name drop-down list box, as shown here:

10. Click the Edit Variables button to open the Edit Member Variables dialog box. Select the IDC_EDIT_NAME item in the Control IDs list box.

11. Click the Add Variable button to open the Add Member Variable dialog box.

12. Specify a name for the variable that will be associated with (or *bound to*) the control. For this example, type *m_editName* in the Member Variable Name edit box, as shown here:

13. Verify that the Value item is selected in the Property drop-down list box and that the CString item is selected in the Variable Type drop-down list box. Then close the Add Member Variable dialog box by clicking OK.

14. When the focus returns to the Edit Member Variables dialog box, you can then enter more information about the variable you are creating. The kind of information you can enter depends on the data type that appeared in the Variable Type edit box in step 13.

    If you were creating a numeric variable, such as an integer, a pair of edit boxes labeled Minimum Value and Maximum Value would appear near the bottom of the Edit Member Variables dialog box. To specify a range for the value of the variable, you would type minimum and maximum values in these two edit boxes.

    Because the variable you are creating is a string, however, the Edit Member Variables dialog box contains an edit box labeled Maximum Characters. In the Maximum Characters edit box, type the number *28*, as shown here:

15. In the Edit Member Variables dialog box, select the IDC_SHOW-
    _NAME item from the Control IDs list box, and repeat steps 10
    through 12 for the *IDC_SHOW_NAME* control. When the Add Mem-
    ber Variable dialog box opens, assign the name *m_showName* to the
    variable associated with the *IDC_SHOW_NAME* control, and click
    OK. Do not type a Maximum Characters value for the *IDC_SHOW-
    _NAME* control.

16. Select the IDC_COPY item in the Control IDs list box, and repeat
    steps 10 through 12 for the *IDC_COPY* control. When the Add Mem-
    ber Variable dialog box opens, assign the name *m_btnCopy* to the
    variable associated with the *IDC_COPY* control. Be sure that the Con-
    trol item is selected in the Property drop-down list box and that the
    CButton item is selected in the Variable Type drop-down list box.

17. Close the Add Member Variable dialog box by clicking OK.

18. Close the Edit Member Variables dialog box by clicking Close.

19. Select the *CTestappView* class in ClassWizard's Class Name drop-
    down list box and Object IDs list box, and then select WM_LBUT-
    TONDOWN in the Messages list box. Click the Add Function button
    to add a message handler for the WM_LBUTTONDOWN message,
    and then exit ClassWizard by clicking the Edit Code button.

20. Edit the *CTestappView::OnLButtonDown* function as shown here:

```
void CTestappView::OnLButtonDown(UINT nFlags, CPoint point)
{
    CTestDialog dlgTest;
    dlgTest.DoModal();
}
```

    And edit the *CTestappView::OnDraw* function as shown here:

```
void CTestappView::OnDraw(CDC* pDC)
{
    pDC->TextOut(0, 0,
        "Click here to open the TestApp dialog box.");
}
```

21. Move to the top of the TESTAVW.CPP file, and add this line near the top, after the other #*include* directives:

```
#include "testdial.h"
```

22. To create a member function that copies the information from the Edit Name text box to the Show Name text box, select the *CTest-Dialog* class from ClassWizard's Class Name drop-down list box. Select the IDC_COPY item from the Object IDs list box, and then select the BN_CLICKED item from the Messages list box.

23. Click the Add Function button to add a message handler for the BN_CLICKED message. Click OK to accept the default member function name *OnCopyClicked*, and then click the Edit Code button and add the following code:

```
void CTestDialog::OnClickedCopy()
{
    UpdateData(CTRL2VAR);
    if((m_editName.GetLength()) < 28)
        m_showName = m_editName;
    UpdateData(VAR2CTRL);
}
```

24. To declare the Boolean values passed to the *UpdateData* function, add the following declarations to the TESTDIAL.H file:

```
#define VAR2CTRL FALSE  // these #defines make DDX clearer
#define CTRL2VAR TRUE
```

25. Build the TESTAPP program by choosing the Build command from the Project menu.

26. Execute your new application by choosing the Execute item from the Project menu. Then open the TestApp dialog box by clicking in the client area of the window. The TestApp dialog box appears, as shown here:

Thanks to the MFC library, you now have a working dialog box equipped with a pair of edit controls with DDX/DDV support named *IDC_EDIT-_NAME* and *IDC_SHOW_NAME*. But at this stage of the TESTAPP program's development, these controls are not yet bound to any particular DDX or DDV functions.

Implementing the DDX/DDV Mechanisms

When you create a class for a dialog box, ClassWizard automatically generates three blocks of code that are used to define and initialize variables that are bound to the controls in the dialog box. Two of these blocks of code, identified in source code by the words *AFX_DATA_INIT* and *AFX-_DATA_MAP*, are created in the dialog box's .CPP file. The third code block, identified by the word *AFX_DATA*, is placed in the dialog box's .H file. (In our example, ClassWizard placed an *AFX_DATA_INIT* block and an *AFX_DATA_MAP* block in the TESTDIAL.CPP file and an *AFX_DATA* block in the TESTDIAL.H file.)

The *AFX_DATA*, *AFX_DATA_INIT*, and *AFX_DATA_MAP* code blocks work in much the same way as the *AFX_MSG* and *AFX_MSG_MAP* code blocks found in every framework-based Visual C++ program. Whenever a DDX or DDV message is dispatched during the execution of an application, the application uses information in the *AFX_DATA*, *AFX_DATA-_INIT*, and *AFX_DATA_MAP* code blocks to locate and then execute the specified code.

The *AFX_DATA* code block

The *AFX_DATA* code block is where ClassWizard declares the variables that are bound to controls. In the TESTDIAL.H file, the *AFX_DATA* block appears in the declaration of the *CTestDialog* class, as shown here:

```
// dialog data
    //{{AFX_DATA(CTestDialog)
    enum { IDD = IDD_TESTAPP };
    CButton     m_btnCopy;
    CString     m_editName;
    CString     m_showName;
    //}}AFX_DATA
```

Notice that this code block begins with the construct

```
//{{AFX_DATA(CTestDialog)
```

and ends with the construct

```
//}}AFX_DATA
```

These two delimiters—similar to those used in the *AFX_MSG* and *AFX-_MSG_MAP* code blocks—identify the *AFX_DATA* code block as a section of code that has been generated by ClassWizard. As such, it should seldom, if ever, be edited. (As you'll see, you can violate this rule sometimes, if you are very careful.)

The *AFX_DATA_INIT* code block

The *AFX_DATA_INIT* code block initializes variables bound to controls. In the TESTDIAL.CPP file, the *AFX_DATA_INIT* code block appears in the constructor of the *CTestDialog* class, as shown here:

```
CTestDialog::CTestDialog(CWnd* pParent /*=NULL*/)
    : CDialog(CTestDialog::IDD, pParent)
{
    //{{AFX_DATA_INIT(CTestDialog)
    m_editName = "";
    m_showName = "";
    //}}AFX_DATA_INIT
}
```

The edit boxes to which the *m_editName* and *m_showName* variables are bound are initialized as empty text strings. You can easily initialize them in some other way, however, by slightly modifying their definitions.

This is one instance in which you can bend ClassWizard's hands-off rule and modify some material inside the //{{ and //}} delimiters. To change the initialization of a dialog box control variable that appears between the //{{*AFX_DATA_INIT* and //}}*AFX_DATA_INIT* delimiters, type something between the quotation marks that initialize one of the variables in the *AFX_DATA_INIT* block.

For example, you can initialize the *IDC_EDIT_NAME* control associated with the *m_editName* variable to the word "Bardot" by simply typing the word between the quotation marks in the *m_editName* definition, as follows:

```
m_editName = "Bardot";
```

Then, when the TestApp dialog box opens, the word "Bardot" will appear in the *IDC_EDIT_NAME* control.

The *AFX_DATA_MAP* code block

The *AFX_DATA_MAP* code block in the TESTAPP application's TESTDIAL .CPP file is shown here:

```
void CTestDialog::DoDataExchange(CDataExchange* pDX)
{
    CDialog::DoDataExchange(pDX);
    //{{AFX_DATA_MAP(CTestDialog)
    DDX_Control(pDX, IDC_COPY, m_btnCopy);
    DDX_Text(pDX, IDC_EDIT_NAME, m_editName);
    DDV_MaxChars(pDX, m_editName, 28);
    DDX_Text(pDX, IDC_SHOW_NAME, m_showName);
    //}}AFX_DATA_MAP
}
```

The AFX data map always appears in a function named *DoDataExchange*. *DoDataExchange* is a *CWnd* member function that is always overridden. In the TESTAPP application, *DoDataExchange* is prototyped as follows in the TESTDIAL.H file:

```
// DDX/DDV support
virtual void DoDataExchange(CDataExchange* pDX);
```

As you will see shortly, in the section "Understanding the *UpdateData* Command" on page 325, the *UpdateData* function mentioned earlier handles data exchanges between controls and variables by calling the *Do-DataExchange* function.

From the *DoDataExchange* function, ClassWizard can call various kinds of DDX-related and DDV-related functions. Many such functions are supplied by the MFC library. If you want to handle data exchanges or data validation in some special way, you can also write customized DDX and DDV functions and call them from inside the *DoDataExchange* function. But you must take care to place them outside the //{{*AFX_DATA_MAP* and //}}*AFX_DATA_MAP* delimiters.

DDX/DDV calls examined

From the *DoDataExchange* function that ClassWizard has placed in your *CTestDialog* implementation file, four calls are made to other functions supplied by the MFC library, as shown here:

```
void CTestDialog::DoDataExchange(CDataExchange* pDX)
{
    CDialog::DoDataExchange(pDX);
    //{{AFX_DATA_MAP(CTestDialog)
    DDX_Control(pDX, IDC_COPY, m_btnCopy);
    DDX_Text(pDX, IDC_EDIT_NAME, m_editName);
    DDV_MaxChars(pDX, m_editName, 28);
    DDX_Text(pDX, IDC_EDIT_SHOW_NAME, m_showName);
    //}}AFX_DATA_MAP
}
```

In the line of code between the two *DDX_Text* calls, the *DoDataExchange* function calls a DDV function named *DDV_MaxChars*. This function sets the maximum length of the *m_editName* variable to 28 characters.

As you can see, each of these calls takes three parameters. The first parameter, *pDX*, is a pointer to a data-exchange object—that is, an MFC object that belongs to the *CDataExchange* class. The other parameters passed to functions that are called from *DoDataExchange* can vary, depending on the function being called.

When *UpdateData* calls the *DoDataExchange* function, the data-exchange object pointed to by the *pDX* parameter supplies important information about the data exchange that is to be executed—for example, whether data is to be transferred from a control to a variable or from a variable to a control.

Understanding the *UpdateData* Command

As mentioned, all DDX and DDV operations depend on a single MFC function: the *CWnd* member function *UpdateData*. The *UpdateData* function can carry out three kinds of operations. It can copy information from a dialog box control to a C++ variable or from a variable to a control. It can also validate information that the user enters in a dialog box control.

DoDataExchange and the *CDataExchange* object

The *UpdateData* member function takes a single parameter: a Boolean value that specifies whether data is to be copied from a variable to a control or from a control to a variable. If you call *UpdateData* with a *FALSE* variable, as shown here, the function copies data from all bound member variables to their associated controls:

```
UpdateData(FALSE);
```

Conversely, if you pass *UpdateData* a *TRUE* value, as shown here, the *UpdateData* function copies data from all controls to their bound variables:

```
UpdateData(TRUE);
```

Although the *UpdateData* function is in charge of handling all DDX and DDV operations associated with a particular dialog box, it does not directly perform all the operations that the DDX/DDV mechanisms require. Instead, it calls another function: *DoDataExchange*. In turn, the *DoData-Exchange* function calls the DDX/DDV functions that actually perform all the DDX and DDV operations that the dialog box requires. Each time *Do-DataExchange* calls a set of DDX/DDV functions, it passes a pointer to a *CDataExchange* object—that is, an object that belongs to the MFC library's *CDataExchange* class.

A *CDataExchange* object is similar to the *CArchive* object used by the *Serialize* member function. (The *Serialize* function was introduced in Chapter 7, "Of Mice and Messages," and is examined more closely in the section "Serialization Revisited" on page 353.) A *CDataExchange* object, like a *CArchive* object, has a member variable named *m_bSaveAnd-Validate*, which is a Boolean variable that is used as a direction flag.

When the *DoDataExchange* function calls a DDX or a DDV function, it passes the *TRUE* or *FALSE* argument that *DoDataExchange* has received from the *UpdateData* function.

Other parameters of the *DoDataExchange* function

When *DoDataExchange* calls a DDX or a DDV function, it passes to the function not only a pointer to a *CDataExchange* object but also any other arguments that the function being called might require. For example, when *DoDataExchange* calls the *DDX_Text* function, the *DoDataExchange* function passes to *DDX_Text* the resource ID of an edit control and the name of the member variable that is bound to the control, as in this example:

```
DDX_Text(pDX, IDC_EDIT_NAME, m_editName);
```

An Easier Way

Although the system described above works well, it is not very intuitive. In fact, passing a *TRUE* or *FALSE* value to *UpdateData* does not seem to make much sense. Even if you pass the *UpdateData* function a *FALSE* value, it still updates data—it just moves the data in a different direction! So it can be difficult to remember which direction is indicated by a *TRUE* value and which direction is indicated by a *FALSE* value.

Fortunately, this bit of potential confusion is easy to clear up. All you have to do is set this pair of *#define*s:

```
#define VAR2CTRL FALSE   // these #defines make DDX clearer
#define CTRL2VAR TRUE
```

> **MPORTANT** Be sure to place the two preceding statements in the TESTAPP program's TESTDIAL.H file. If you don't, you'll get a compiler error because your program won't be aware of the meanings of the *VAR2CTRL* and *CTRL2VAR* constants.

When you have redefined the *TRUE* and *FALSE* variables as shown in the preceding example, you can execute the call

```
UpdateData(VAR2CTRL);
```

when you want to move data from a variable to a control, and you can execute the call

```
UpdateData(CTRL2VAR);
```

when you want to move data from a control to a variable.

In the sample programs presented in this chapter, the *VAR2CTRL* and *CTRL2VAR* constants are used in place of *TRUE* and *FALSE* each time *UpdateData* is called.

Calling the *UpdateData* Function Step by Step

Now that you know how the *UpdateData* function works, you are ready to write a pair of *UpdateData* calls that add DDX and DDV capabilities to the TESTAPP program you started developing earlier in this chapter. To call *UpdateData* from your application, follow these steps:

1. Open the TESTAPP project, and launch ClassWizard by choosing ClassWizard from the Browse menu.

2. In the Class Name drop-down list box, select the *CTestDialog* class.

3. Select the *IDC_COPY* resource ID from the Object IDs list box, and then select the BN_CLICKED message from the Messages list box.

4. Click the Add Function button. ClassWizard displays the Add Member Function dialog box, which prompts you for the name of a function. In the Member Function Name edit box, ClassWizard suggests a name for your new function. Accept this function name, and close the Add Member Function dialog box by clicking the OK button. ClassWizard creates a new function with the default name *On-ClickedCopy* in your application's TESTDIAL.CPP file.

5. When the ClassWizard dialog box regains the focus, click the Edit Code button. ClassWizard then opens the TESTDIAL.CPP file and navigates to the *OnClickedCopy* member function it has generated. At this point, the *OnClickedCopy* function is merely a stub, waiting for you to write a block of code that gives it functionality.

6. Modify the *OnClickedCopy* member function as shown here:

```
void CTestDialog::OnClickedCopy()
{
    UpdateData(CTRL2VAR);
    if ((m_editName.GetLength()) < 28)
        m_showName = m_editName;
    UpdateData(VAR2CTRL);
}
```

You have completed the job of adding DDX and DDV capabilities to the TESTAPP program. Now when the user types an entry in the *IDC_EDIT-_NAME* control and clicks the Copy button, the *if* statement checks to see whether the user's string exceeds the program's limit of 28 characters. If the string is legal, it is copied to the *IDC_SHOW_NAME* edit box.

Running the TESTAPP Program

To see how the TESTAPP program now works, rebuild it and then run it by choosing the Execute item from Visual Workbench's Project menu. When the application starts, click in the window to open the TestApp dia log box, which now has full DDX/DDV capabilities. If you type a string in the Edit Name edit box and then click the Copy button, the application copies the text you have entered to the Show Name edit box, as shown in Figure 9-1.

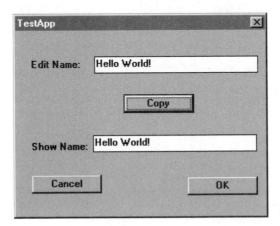

Figure 9-1. *Typing an entry in the TestApp dialog box.*

Here's how it works. When you type a string in the Edit Name edit box and click the Copy button, the *OnClickedCopy* member function carries out the following two operations in quick succession:

1. With the help of the DDX mechanism, *OnClickedCopy* updates all DDX-aware controls in the TestApp dialog box by copying the information that each control contains to the DDX variable that is bound to the control. At the same time, the DDV mechanism verifies that the user has entered no more than 28 characters in the *IDC_EDIT-_NAME* control. If the information that the user has entered in the *IDC_EDIT_NAME* control is less than 28 characters, it is copied from the *m_editName* variable to the *m_showName* variable.

2. All information now stored in DDX-aware variables (including the *m_showName* variable) is copied to the appropriate controls.

Extending DDX/DDV: The CREATION Program

The TESTAPP program is a good elementary example of how the DDX and DDV mechanisms work. In this section, we'll use a program named CRE-ATION to illustrate how these mechanisms can be used in a more sophisticated application. The CREATION program illustrates the kind of coding you might do if you were designing an adventure game. CREATION is an MDI (multiple-document interface) application that can display three related dialog boxes, all of which can be selected from the Character menu, as shown in Figure 9-2.

Figure 9-2. *The CREATION program's Character menu.*

When you choose the Edit item from the Character menu, CREATION displays a modal dialog box named Create A Character, as shown in Figure 9-3 on the following page, in which you can either create a new game character or edit the properties of an existing character.

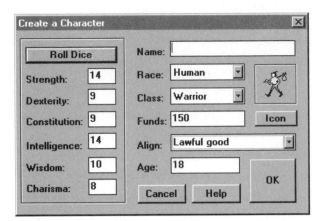

Figure 9-3. *The Create A Character dialog box.*

The Create A Character dialog box contains the following controls:

- **Roll Dice**—When you click this button, the CREATION program executes an algorithm that simulates six rolls of three standard six-sided dice. CREATION uses the sum of a roll of the three dice to set one of six qualities (known in adventure games as *stats*) of a character. In role-playing adventure games, stats are used to determine how well a character is likely to do in combat. They can also affect other kinds of interactions among characters. In the CREATION program, a member function named *CRollDice::RollDice* is used to roll the virtual dice that set a character's stats. The *CRollDice::RollDice* member function is examined in the sidebar "The *RollDice* Member Function" on page 342.

- **Name**—Edit control in which you specify the name of a character. The user can't close the Create A Character dialog box by clicking OK until he or she types an entry in this box. (The user can always close the dialog box by clicking Cancel, however.)

- **Race**—Combo box that the user can use to select the race of a character. Race options are dwarf, elf, gnome, half-elf, halfling, and human; human is the default.

- **Class**—Drop-down list box that the user can use to select a character's class. Class options are cleric, rogue, warrior, and wizard; warrior is the default.

- **Funds**—Edit box that specifies how much cash a character has on hand. When the user changes the setting in the Class combo box, the value displayed in the Funds edit box also changes. As the game progresses, this value will fluctuate as the character spends or acquires money by selling goods or buying equipment.

- **Align**—Combo box that specifies the alignment (moral qualities) of a character.

- **Age**—Edit box that displays the age of a character. The MFC library's DDV mechanism is used to verify that the age typed in this control is a reasonable value.

- **Icon**—Button that does nothing at present but that will display a dialog box in the final version of the game. This dialog box will allow the user to select a bitmap to represent a character.

- **Cancel, Help, and OK**—Standard Cancel, Help, and OK buttons. In the CREATION program, the Help button is not activated.

When you close the Create A Character dialog box by clicking OK, the CREATION application remembers the values you have entered, so you can save your entries on disk, print them out, or display them in another CREATION dialog box named Character Information. The Character Information dialog box is described in the section "The Character Information Dialog Box" on page 352.

In CREATION, choosing the Shop item from the Character menu takes the user's character on a shopping spree in the Mel's Bait Shop And Fashion Boutique dialog box, shown in Figure 9-4 on the following page. At Mel's, the user can equip his or her character for any quest.

At Mel's, the user purchases an item by moving it from the Items Available list box to the Items Being Purchased list box. To do that, he or she clicks on the item in the Items Available list box and then clicks the >> button. If the user changes his or her mind about an item, he or she can return it to the shelf by clicking on the item in the Items Being Purchased list box and then clicking the << button.

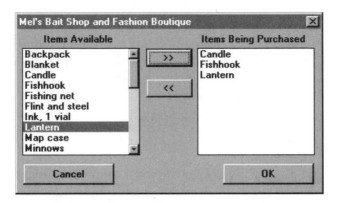

Figure 9-4. *Mel's Bait Shop And Fashion Boutique dialog box.*

When the user closes the Mel's Bait Shop And Fashion Boutique dialog box by clicking OK, the CREATION program records the items he or she has purchased so that they can be printed or displayed in another dialog box.

After the user has created and outfitted a character, he or she can display information about the character and his or her belongings by choosing the Info item from the Character menu. The application then displays a Character Information dialog box similar to the one shown in Figure 9-5.

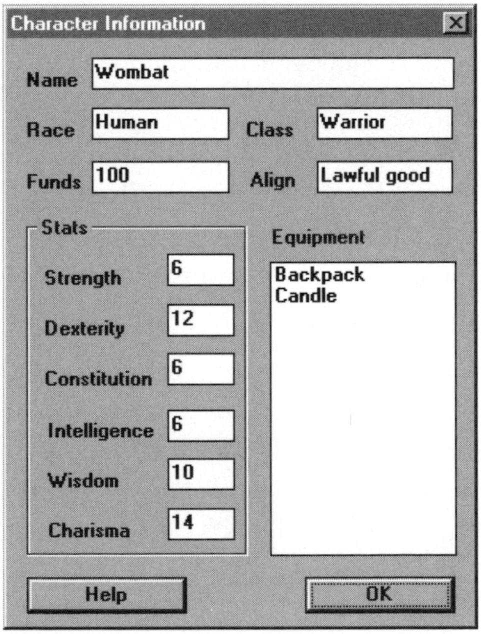

Figure 9-5. *The Character Information dialog box.*

The Character Information dialog box displays all the information the user specified in the Create A Character dialog box, as well as all the purchases made at Mel's. All the controls in the Character Information dialog box are read-only; in order to edit the information, the user must open other dialog boxes.

IP To make a control read-only, create the control in App Studio, and then choose the Properties item from the Resource menu. When the Properties window appears, click on the control, and select the Styles item in the drop-down list box in the upper right corner. Then check the Read Only check box, as shown here:

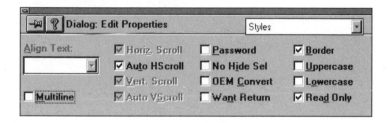

Architecture of the CREATION Program

CREATION is an AppWizard-framework application, so it has AppWizard's standard document-and-view architecture and makes use of all the standard document-and-view files. It also has the following five classes:

- Three classes that encapsulate each of the program's three dialog boxes: *CDlgCreate* (implemented in the DLGCREAT.CPP file), *CDlgEquipment* (implemented in the DLGSUPP.CPP file), and *CDlgInfo* (implemented in the DLGINFO.CPP file).

- A *CRollDice* class, also derived from the MFC library's *CObject* class, which encapsulates an algorithm that can simulate throws of various kinds of dice. (Adventure-style board games often come with various kinds of specially shaped dice that don't have the standard six sides, so the *CRollDice* class can simulate throws of any number of dice that have any number of sides.) The *CRollDice* class is implemented in a source file named DICE.CPP.

- A *CObject*-derived class named *CPlayer*, which encapsulates all the information that the Create A Character dialog box collects. The *CPlayer* class is implemented in a source file named PLAYER.CPP.

Once the CREATION program is initialized and its main window and a child window have been created, most of the action takes place in the application's document and view objects and in the application-generated classes listed above. Figure 9-6 illustrates the architecture of these seven parts of the CREATION program.

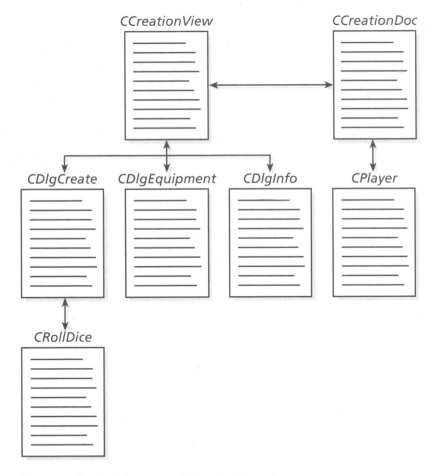

Figure 9-6. *Architecture of the CREATION program.*

Even though the CREATION application's document class (*CCreationDoc*) handles the program's data, the data is actually stored in the application's *CPlayer* object and is accessed by the *CCreationDoc* class only indirectly. To access the data associated with a particular character, the program's document object instantiates a *CPlayer* object each time a character is created. Then the document object uses *Get* and *Set* functions provided by the *CPlayer* class to set and retrieve information about a character.

This arrangement makes sense in the CREATION program because a situation could arise in which several different characters are instantiated and active at the same time. If this happens, the program can easily keep each character's data separate while still maintaining overall control of the data through its document object by using the *Get* and *Set* functions provided by the *CPlayer* class.

The application's view class (*CCreationView*) object must access character data even more indirectly because it is one step further away from the data than the document object is. To illustrate this, suppose that the user has opened the Create A Character dialog box and is creating a character named Zalthar. When the user types *Zalthar* in the Name edit box and then closes the dialog box by clicking OK, the program's *CDlgCreate* object uses the DDX mechanism to retrieve the name from the Name edit box.

The *CDlgCreate* object then executes the following function call to pass the name to the active character object:

```
pDoc->m_pPlayer->SetName(m_editName);
```

As you can see, this statement passes the name to a *CPlayer* member function named *SetName*. The parameter that is passed to the program's *CPlayer* object in this statement is a *CDlgCreate* member variable named *m_editName*. And the *m_editName* member variable is used to store the name that the user has typed in the Create A Character dialog box's Name edit box. Figure 9-7 on the following page illustrates this process.

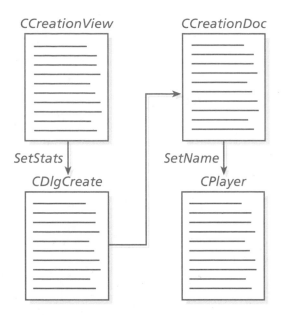

CCreationView   CCreationDoc

SetStats
CDlgCreate

SetName
CPlayer

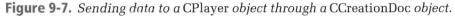

Figure 9-7. *Sending data to a* CPlayer *object through a* CCreationDoc *object.*

Creating a *CPlayer* Object

When the CREATION application opens, code generated by AppWizard creates a view object and a document object in the usual manner. (For a review of how AppWizard creates programs using view and document objects, see the section "Using Documents and Views in MFC Programs" on page 192 in Chapter 6.)

When the CREATION program's document object is created, the document's constructor instantiates a *CPlayer* object. A pointer to this *CPlayer* object is stored in a *CCreationDoc* member variable named *m_pPlayer*. The *CCreationDoc* constructor that initializes the *m_pPlayer* member variable is implemented as follows in the CREATDOC.CPP file:

```
CCreationDoc::CCreationDoc()
{
    m_pPlayer = new CPlayer;
}
```

The definition of the *CPlayer* class, which appears in the PLAYER.H file, is shown in Listing 9-1.

```
class CPlayer : public CObject {

    DECLARE_SERIAL(CPlayer)

// member variables
private:
    WORD m_strength, m_dexterity, m_constitution, m_intelligence, m_wisdom,
        m_charisma;

    CString m_name, m_race, m_class, m_alignment;

    WORD m_funds;

    enum Classes { WARRIOR, WIZARD, PRIEST, ROGUE };

    enum Races { DWARF, ELF, GNOME,
        HALF_ELF, HALFLING, HUMAN };

    enum Abils { STRENGTH, DEXTERITY, CONSTITUTION,
        INTELLIGENCE, WISDOM, CHARISMA };

private:
    CStringList *m_pEquipList;

public:
    void SetEquipList(CStringList* pEquipList);
    const CStringList* GetEquipList()
        { return m_pEquipList; }
    void Serialize(CArchive& ar);

public:
    // constructor and destructor
    CPlayer() { ASSERT_VALID(m_pEquipList =
        new CStringList); }

    ~CPlayer() { delete m_pEquipList; }

    CString GetName() { return m_name; }
    void SetName(CString n) { m_name = n; }

    CString GetRace() { return m_race; }
    void SetRace(CString r) { m_race = r; }

    CString GetClass() { return m_class; }
    void SetClass(CString c) { m_class = c; }
```

Listing 9-1. *Definition of the* CPlayer *class.*   *(continued)*

Listing 9-1. *continued*

```
    CString GetAlignment() { return m_alignment; }
    void SetAlignment(CString a) { m_alignment = a; }

    int GetFunds() { return m_funds; }
    void SetFunds(int f) { m_funds = f; }

    int GetStrength() { return m_strength; }
    int GetDexterity() { return m_dexterity; }
    int GetConstitution() { return m_constitution; }
    int GetIntelligence() { return m_intelligence; }
    int GetWisdom() { return m_wisdom; }
    int GetCharisma() { return m_charisma; }

    void SetStrength(int s) { m_strength = s; }
    void SetDexterity(int d) { m_dexterity = d; }
    void SetConstitution(int c) { m_constitution = c; }
    void SetIntelligence(int i) { m_intelligence = i; }
    void SetWisdom(int w) { m_wisdom = w; }
    void SetCharisma(int c) { m_charisma = c; }

    // copy constructor
    CPlayer& operator=( const CPlayer& b );

    // member functions

    // get information about player
    void SetAbils(WORD strength, WORD dexterity, WORD constitution,
        WORD intelligence, WORD wisdom, WORD charisma);
};
```

Most of the member functions of the *CPlayer* object are *Get* and *Set* functions that the CREATION program uses to retrieve and set character data.

The Create A Character Dialog Box

As you have seen, the CREATION program has the Create A Character dialog box, shown in Figure 9-8, for the creation and editing of game characters. When the user finishes entering character information and clicks the OK button, the *CDlgCreate* object uses the MFC library's DDX mechanism to pass the information along to the program's *CCreationDoc* object. The *CDlgCreate* object then calls some *Set* functions provided by the *CPlayer* object to store the information in the appropriate *CPlayer* member variables.

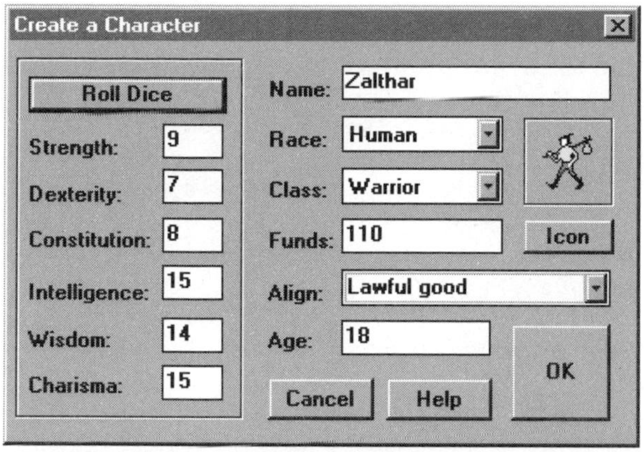

Figure 9-8. *The Create A Character dialog box.*

Opening the Create A Character dialog box

To open the Create A Character dialog box, the user chooses the Edit item from the Character menu. CREATION then executes a message handler named *CCreationView::OnCharacterEdit*. Here's how the *OnCharacterEdit* message handler is implemented in the CREATVW.CPP file:

```
void CCreationView::OnCharacterEdit()
{
    CCreationDoc *pDoc = GetDocument();   // get pointer to
                                          // document object

    CDlgCreate dlgCreate;      // instantiate CDlgCreate dialog box
    dlgCreate.DoModal();       // your basic DoModal function
    dlgCreate.SetStats(pDoc);
}
```

How the Create A Character dialog box works

The *OnCharacterEdit* message handler calls the MFC library's *CDialog::-DoModal* member function to display the Create A Character dialog box. Then, when the dialog box closes, *OnCharacterEdit* calls a member function named *CDlgCreate::SetStats* to copy all the information entered or selected by the user to the *CPlayer* member functions. The *SetStats* member function accomplishes this task with the help of the MFC library's DDX and DDV mechanisms.

The source code for the *CDlgCreate::SetStats* member function that passes the user's data on to the program's *CPlayer* object is shown here:

```
void CDlgCreate::SetStats(CCreationDoc* pDoc)
{
    // move information from dialog controls
    // to pDoc->m_pPlayer object
    ASSERT_VALID(pDoc);
    ASSERT_VALID(pDoc->m_pPlayer);

    // record new player's name
    pDoc->m_pPlayer->SetName(m_editName);
    // record new player's race
    pDoc->m_pPlayer->SetRace(m_comboRace);
    // record new player's class
    pDoc->m_pPlayer->SetClass(m_comboClass);

    // record new player's abilities
    pDoc->m_pPlayer->SetStrength(m_strength);
    pDoc->m_pPlayer->SetDexterity(m_dexterity);
    pDoc->m_pPlayer->SetConstitution(m_constitution);
    pDoc->m_pPlayer->SetIntelligence(m_intelligence);
    pDoc->m_pPlayer->SetWisdom(m_wisdom);
    pDoc->m_pPlayer->SetCharisma(m_charisma);

    // record other stuff
    pDoc->m_pPlayer->SetFunds(m_editFunds);
    pDoc->m_pPlayer->SetAlignment(m_alignment);
}
```

DDX operations in the character creation process

The Create A Character dialog box makes extensive use of the MFC library's DDX mechanism. For example, before the Create A Character dialog box opens, the *CDlgCreate* class uses DDX to initialize the dialog box's controls. This initialization takes place in an override of the *CDialog::OnInitDialog* member function, which the MFC framework calls after a dialog box is created but before it opens.

The *CDlgCreate* class also uses the DDX mechanism to change the contents of the dialog box's stat boxes each time the user clicks the Roll Dice button.

The following code shows how the *CDlgCreate* class uses DDX in the *OnInitDialog* member function:

```
// do the initial dice roll and so on
BOOL CDlgCreate::OnInitDialog()
{
    CRollDice rollDice;          // instantiate a CRollDice object

    // roll dice for ability scores
    rollDice.SetRandomSeed();     // seed random number generator
    for (int c = 0; c < 6; c++)
        // three rolls of 6-sided dice
        m_abils[c] = rollDice.RollDice(3, 6);

    // move rolled scores from variables
    // into the ability controls
    m_strength = m_abils[0];
    m_dexterity = m_abils[1];
    m_constitution = m_abils[2];
    m_intelligence = m_abils[3];
    m_wisdom = m_abils[4];
    m_charisma = m_abils[5];

    // update other controls
    m_editFunds = m_warriorFunds;
    m_comboRace = "Human";
    m_comboClass = "Warrior";

    // move ability variables into dialog controls
    UpdateData(VAR2CTRL);
    return (CDialog::OnInitDialog());
}
```

At the end of this code fragment, the *CDlgCreate::OnInitDialog* member function calls the *UpdateData* member function with a *VAR2CTRL* parameter to initialize the Create A Character dialog box's controls.

The following code shows how DDX is used to change the contents of the Create A Character dialog box's stat boxes:

```
void CDlgCreate::RollTheDice()
{
    CRollDice rollDice;      // instantiate a CRollDice object

    // roll dice for ability scores
    rollDice.SetRandomSeed(); // seed random number generator
    for (int c = 0; c < 6; c++)
        // three rolls of 6-sided dice
        m_abils[c] = rollDice.RollDice(3, 6);
```

(continued)

```
UpdateData(CTRL2VAR);  // copy values into variables

m_editName = m_nameString;

// move rolled scores from variables
// into the ability controls
m_strength = m_abils[0];
m_dexterity = m_abils[1];
m_constitution = m_abils[2];
m_intelligence = m_abils[3];
m_wisdom = m_abils[4];
m_charisma = m_abils[5];

// move ability variables into dialog controls
UpdateData(VAR2CTRL)
}
```

The *RollDice* Member Function

The *CRollDice::RollDice* function, implemented in the DICE.CPP file, can emulate any number of throws of a die with any number of sides. When you call *RollDice*, you can specify how many dice you want to roll, and how many sides each die has, in the arguments you pass to the function. For example, the *RollDice* function in the code above emulates three rolls of a standard six-sided die as shown here:

```
rollDice.RollDice(3, 6);
```

One noteworthy feature of the *RollDice* member function is that it precisely calculates the correct odds for whatever kind of dice roll is specified. For example, when you roll a pair of standard six-sided dice, the numbers least likely to come up are 2 and 12, the next least likely numbers are 3 and 11, and so on. The *RollDice* member function duplicates the real odds precisely.

How does *RollDice* perform these calculations? It's easier than you might expect. To calculate the odds for rolling two standard six-sided dice, the *RollDice* member function simply generates a pair of random numbers from 1 through 6 and then adds them together. The same kind of calculation works for all other combinations you can specify when you call the *RollDice* function.

Here the *CDlgCreate* class makes two calls to the *UpdateData* function. After the *CRollDice::RollDice* function has been called to set the character's stats, a call is issued to *UpdateData* to copy the dice scores into the Create A Character dialog box's variables. At the end of the function, *UpdateData* is called again to move the character's stats to the dialog box's controls.

Using the DDV mechanism

The *CDlgCreate* class uses the DDV mechanism in only one member function—*CDlgCreate::DDV_AgeCheck*, as shown here:

```
void CDlgCreate::DDV_AgeCheck(CDataExchange *pDX, int editAge)
{
    if (editAge < m_minAge)
        MessageBox("You're too young to play this game!",
            "Let's see your ID!", MB_ICONEXCLAMATION);
    if (editAge > m_maxAge)
        MessageBox("You're too old to play!",
            "Sorry, old-timer!", MB_ICONEXCLAMATION);
}
```

The Age edit box   The *DDV_AgeCheck* function is executed when the user enters a value in the Age edit box. Here's how the function works. When the Create A Character dialog box opens, the value displayed in the Age edit box is initialized to 18. In the *DoDataExchange* function that appears in the DLGCREAT.CPP file, two other variables are also linked to the Age edit box: a variable named *m_minAge*, which is initialized to 10, and a variable named *m_maxAge*, which is initialized to 109, as shown below. (Both these initializations take place in the *CDlgCreate::DoDataExchange* member function.)

```
// set min and max ages for the m_editAge variable
m_minAge = 10;
m_maxAge = 109;
```

The Create A Character dialog box's *DoDataExchange* function also contains a customized DDV mapping that affects the Age edit box and its associated *m_editAge* member variable. First the *DDX_Text* function is called to bind the *m_editAge* variable to the Age edit box. Then the *DDV_Age-Check* function is called to validate the text that the user enters in the Age edit box.

Because *DDV_AgeCheck* is a function that ClassWizard knows nothing about, the declaration of the *DDV_AgeCheck* function appears outside the AFX data map in the *DoDataExchange* function.

> **NOTE** Although the call to *DDX_Text* that appears just before the call to *DDV_AgeCheck* in the *DoDataExchange* function was actually generated by ClassWizard, it has been moved out of the AFX data map section of the *Do-DataExchange* function because DDV functions immediately follow any DDX function with which they are associated. Of course, when a DDX or a DDV function is moved out of the AFX data map code block managed by Class-Wizard, you can no longer use ClassWizard to edit or modify the function.

The *CDlgCreate::DDV_AgeCheck* function called by the *DoDataExchange* function is shown on the previous page. As you can see, the function substitutes a pair of custom message boxes for the default message box that is normally displayed when a dialog box control entry fails a DDV test. When the *DDV_AgeCheck* member function is called, it displays one kind of message box when the user enters an age that is too low and another kind of message box when the user enters an age that is too high.

Another kind of data verification The CREATION application provides an additional kind of data validation for the Age edit box. When the user types an entry in the Age edit box and then moves on to another action, the Age control loses the input focus, and a function named *OnKillfocusEditAge* is called.

The implementation of the *CDlgCreate::OnKillfocusEditAge* function used in the CREATION application is shown below. The function appears in the DLGCREAT.CPP file.

```
// this function executes when the Age control
// loses the input focus
void CDlgCreate::OnKillfocusEditAge()
{
    UpdateData(CTRL2VAR); // be sure DDV routine gets called
                          // when this control loses focus

    // check the value of the m_editAge variable
    if (m_editAge < m_minAge || m_editAge > m_maxAge) {
        m_editAge = 18;        // must be m_minAge or older to play
        UpdateData(VAR2CTRL); // correct the situation
```

```
        // as a convenience for the user, be sure
        // that the cursor appears in the Age control
        // when this function returns
        ((CEdit*) (GetDlgItem(IDC_EDIT_AGE)))->SetFocus();
        ((CEdit*) (GetDlgItem(IDC_EDIT_AGE)))->SetSel(0, -1);
    }
}
```

The *UpdateData* function is called with a *CTRL2VAR* parameter to move information from the Age edit box to the *m_editAge* member variable. Then the value of the *m_editAge* variable is checked to see whether it is under the limit specified by the *m_minAge* variable or over the limit specified by the *m_maxAge* variable.

This check is made because the *DoDialogExchange* function never calls just one DDX or DDV function; every time *DoDialogExchange* is executed, it calls *every* DDX/DDV function that it is associated with—and that opens up many possibilities for endless loops. If *DoDialogExchange* calls a DDV function that reports the failure of a validation check, and if *DoDialog-Exchange* does not give the user an opportunity to change the offending entry before *DoDialogExchange* is called again, the result is an endless loop that can hang your application.

To prevent endless loops, the *OnKillfocusEditAge* function first calls *Up-dateData(CTRL2VAR)* and then checks to see whether the entry in the Age edit box is valid. If the value in the Age edit box is not valid, *OnKillfocus-EditAge* immediately changes the value of the *m_editAge* variable to a valid value—18—and then calls *UpdateData(VAR2CTRL)* to place that value in the Age edit box. Because this change is made as soon as an invalid value is detected, it prevents an endless loop.

When *OnKillfocusEditAge* has detected and corrected any invalid information that might have been entered in the Age control, it calls the *Set-Focus* function to restore the input focus to the Age edit box and then calls the member function *SetSel* to select the value (18) that it has just placed in the control. Note that when *GetDlgItem* is called, it must be cast from a *CWnd* member function to a *CEdit* function. This kind of casting was often needed in dialog box routines before the introduction of Visual C++, but it is needed much less often now.

Calculating values displayed in controls

The Funds edit box demonstrates a technique for displaying calculated values in a dialog box control. When the Create A Character dialog box opens, a random number is generated and placed in the Funds edit box. The amount of cash that is allotted to the character depends on the character's class. The allotment specified for each class is calculated in the constructor of the *CDlgCreate* class. To set these allotments, the *RollDice* member function is called four times, as shown here:

```
// calculate character's initial cash allotment and
// initialize the m_editFunds variable
rollDice.SetRandomSeed();      // seed random number generator
m_warriorFunds = rollDice.RollDice(5, 4) * 10;
m_wizardFunds = (rollDice.RollDice(1, 4) + 1) * 10;
m_rogueFunds = rollDice.RollDice(2, 6) * 10;
m_clericFunds = rollDice.RollDice(3, 6) * 10;
```

When the user changes the selection displayed in the Class drop-down list box, the value displayed in the Funds edit box is updated to correspond to the initial allotment that has been calculated for a character of the selected class.

Closing the Create A Character dialog box

The OK button in the Create A Character dialog box also performs some data validation—without any official help from the DDX/DDV mechanisms. When the user clicks OK, the CREATION application calls an overridden *OnOK* member function, defined below, to verify that the user has typed a name for a character in the Name edit box. If no name has been entered when OK is clicked, the program prompts the user for one.

```
// be sure the user has typed a new character's name
if (m_editName == "") {
    MessageBox ("Please give your character a name!",
        "Excuse me ...", MB_ICONEXCLAMATION);
    // put the cursor in the appropriate edit control
    ((CEdit*) (GetDlgItem(IDC_EDIT_NAME)))->SetFocus();
    ((CEdit*) (GetDlgItem(IDC_EDIT_NAME)))->SetSel(0, -1);
    return;
}
```

The Mel's Bait Shop And Fashion Boutique Dialog Box

Applications can use the DDX/DDV mechanisms to manipulate data displayed in list boxes, but the procedure is a little more complicated than most other kinds of DDX/DDV operations. In the CREATION program, the Mel's Bait Shop And Fashion Boutique dialog box shown in Figure 9-9 demonstrates the use of DDX commands in list box operations.

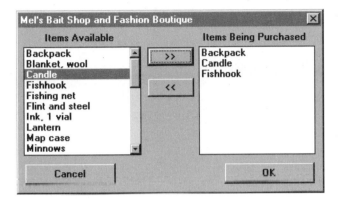

Figure 9-9. *The Mel's Bait Shop dialog box's list boxes.*

The list boxes in the Mel's Bait Shop dialog box

The Mel's Bait Shop dialog box contains a pair of list boxes: Items Available and Items Being Purchased. The user can add or delete items from the Items Being Purchased list box by clicking the << and >> buttons. When the user selects an item in one list box and clicks one of these buttons, the program uses the DDX mechanism to copy the selected string to the other list box.

To display items in the Items Available list box and the Items Being Purchased list box, the *CDlgEquipment* class uses a pair of *CStringList* objects declared in the DLGSUPP.H file. (As you might recall from Chapter 6, "The MFC Library," the *CStringList* class is a serializeable MFC library class that belongs to a group of classes called *collection classes*. In C++, a collection class is a class designed to facilitate the creation and management of collections of objects such as lists and arrays.) The *CStringList* object that stores items listed in the Items Available list box is named *m_pStringList1*. The *CStringList* object that stores items listed in the Items Being Purchased list box is named *m_pStringList2*.

Copying data into list boxes

When the Mel's Bait Shop dialog box opens, the CREATION program fills the Items Available list box with a list of strings obtained from a *struct* named *m_supplyList*. The *m_supplyList struct* is declared in the DLGSUPP.H file, as shown here:

```
struct StructSupplies {
    int quantity;
    char item[NAME_SIZE];
    double price;
    double weight;
};
```

It is implemented in the DLGSUPP.CPP file, as shown here:

```
StructSupplies m_supplyList[] = {
    { 0, "Backpack", 2, 2 },
    { 0, "Candle", .01, .10 },
    { 0, "Fishhook", .60, 0 },
    { 0, "Fishing net", 4, 5 },
    { 0, "Flint and steel", .50, .10 },
    { 0, "Red worms", .01, 0 },
    { 0, "Minnows", .01, 0 },
    { 0, "Pot, iron", .50, 2 },
    { 0, "Pot, copper", 2, .20 },
    { 0, "Lantern", 7, 2 },
    { 0, "Map case", .8, .5 },
    { 0, "Mirror, small metal", 10, .10 },
    { 0, "Oil, 16-oz. flask", .06, 1 },
    { 0, "Quiver", .8, 1 },
    { 0, "Scroll case", .8, .5 },
    { 0, "Parchment, 1 sheet", 2, 0 },
    { 0, "Rope, 50 ft.", 1, 20 },
    { 0, "Rope, 10 ft.", .25, 4 },
    { 0, "Sack, large", .2, .5 },
    { 0, "Sack, small", .05, .10 },
    { 0, "Soap, 1/4 pound", .1, .10 },
    { 0, "Tent, small", 5, 10 },
    { 0, "Torch", .01, 1 },
    { 0, "Pick, thief's", 30, 1 },
    { 0, "Whetstone", .02, 1 },
    { 0, "Wineskin", .8, 1 },
    { 0, "Blanket, wool", .5, 3 },
    { 0, "Quilt", .1, 1.5 },
    { 0, "Ink, 1 vial", 8, .10 }
};
```

Using references to access list box items

To access the strings in the Items Available and Items Being Purchased list boxes, the DLGSUPP.H file defines a pair of member functions named *ListBox1* and *ListBox2*. These two member functions use references and pointers to functions to provide access to the Items Available and Items Being Purchased list boxes, as shown here:

```
// get references to the list boxes
CListBox& ListBox1()
    { return *(CListBox*) GetDlgItem(IDC_LIST1); }
CListBox& ListBox2()
    { return *(CListBox*) GetDlgItem(IDC_LIST2); }
```

When the Mel's Bait Shop dialog box opens, an override of the *CDialog::-OnInitDialog* function is used to copy all the strings in the *m_pStringList1* string list to the Items Available list box. To perform the copying operation, the *OnInitDialog* function calls the *ListBox1* member function. Then *UpdateData* is called to copy the contents of the *m_pStringList1* variable into the Items Available list box, as shown here:

```
// populate the Items Available list box
for (int i = 0;  i < NR_OF_ITEMS; i++)
    ListBox1().AddString(m_supplyList[i].item);

// initialize the Funds edit box
UpdateData(VAR2CTRL);
```

Copying data from one list box to another

To copy the names of items from the Items Available list box to the Items Being Purchased list box, the *CDlgEquipment* class uses a member function named *OnAvail2bought*. The *OnAvail2bought* member function uses a *CStringList* member function named *AddString*—along with the DDX function *UpdateData*—to add the selected string to the Items Being Purchased list box. (*OnAvail2bought* also calls the *CStringList::FindString* function to search the Items Being Purchased list box to confirm that a duplicate string is not being added.)

The *CDlgEquipment::OnAvail2bought* member function, as implemented in the DLGSUPP.CPP file, is shown on the following page.

```
void CDlgEquipment::OnAvail2bought()
{
    // copy selected item from Items Available list box
    // to Items Being Purchased list box
    UpdateData(CTRL2VAR);

    // Duplicate entries not allowed. Search ListBox2
    // for the string being added; if found, don't
    // add it again.
    int retVal = ListBox2().FindString(-1, m_obStr1);
    if (retVal == LB_ERR)  // LB_ERR means no duplicate found
        ListBox2().AddString(m_obStr1);
}
```

Removing items from the Items Being Purchased list box

When the user selects an item in the Items Being Purchased list box and clicks the << button, the CREATION application's *CDlgEquipment* object executes a member function named *OnBought2avail* to remove the selected item. Here is the *OnBought2avail* member function, as implemented in the DLGSUPP.CPP file:

```
void CDlgEquipment::OnBought2avail()
{
    // delete selected item from Items Being Purchased list box
    UpdateData(CTRL2VAR);
    int index = ListBox2().GetCurSel();
    ListBox2().DeleteString(index);
}
```

Closing the Mel's Bait Shop dialog box

When the user closes the Mel's Bait Shop dialog box by clicking the OK button, an *OnOK* message handler is called to record and store the items the user has purchased. Just before the dialog box closes, a *for* loop in the *OnOK* message handler is used to copy all the items in the Items Being Purchased list box into a *CDlgEquipment* member variable named *m_equipList*. The *m_equipList* member variable is an object of the *CStringList* class.

The *OnOK* message handler that copies all the items the character has purchased to the *m_equipList* member variable is shown here:

```
void CDlgEquipment::OnOK()
{
    CString tempStr;

    int nrOfStrings = ListBox2().GetCount();

    for (int c = 0; c < nrOfStrings; c++) {
        ListBox2().GetText(c, tempStr);
        m_equipList.AddTail(tempStr);
    }

    CDialog::OnOK();
}
```

When the Mel's Bait Shop dialog box closes, the *CCreationView*'s *OnCharacterShop* message handler calls a *CCreationDoc* member function named *GetEquipList* to retrieve the information that has been stored in the *CDlgEquipment*'s *m_equipList* member variable. Then *OnCharacterShop* calls a *CCreationDoc* member function named *SetEquipList* to copy the same data into the *CPlayer*'s *m_pEquipList* member variable, as shown here:

```
pEquipList = dialogSupplies.GetEquipList();
pDoc->SetEquipList(pEquipList);
```

Initializing Controls in *OnInitDialog*

When ClassWizard creates a dialog box, it always places the initializations of the dialog box's controls inside the constructor of the dialog box's class. But you should perform most of the initialization functions for your own dialog box controls in an override of the MFC library's *CDialog::OnInitDialog* function. To do that, you must override the *CDialog* class's *OnInitDialog* function.

When you override the *OnInitDialog* member function, you should call the base class *OnInitDialog* member function in your own *OnInitDialog* member function. Then, just before a dialog box is displayed, the DDX mechanism copies the latest values in your dialog box class's member variables to the controls in the dialog box, where they appear when the dialog box opens.

When a dialog box opens, the default implementation of *CDialog::OnInitDialog* calls the *UpdateData* function to initialize the dialog box's controls.

The Character Information Dialog Box

To display information stored in the *CPlayer* object's *m_pEquipList* member variable, the CREATION application provides a simple, read-only dialog box named Character Information, shown in Figure 9-10. To open the Character Information dialog box, the user of the CREATION application selects the Info command from the Character menu.

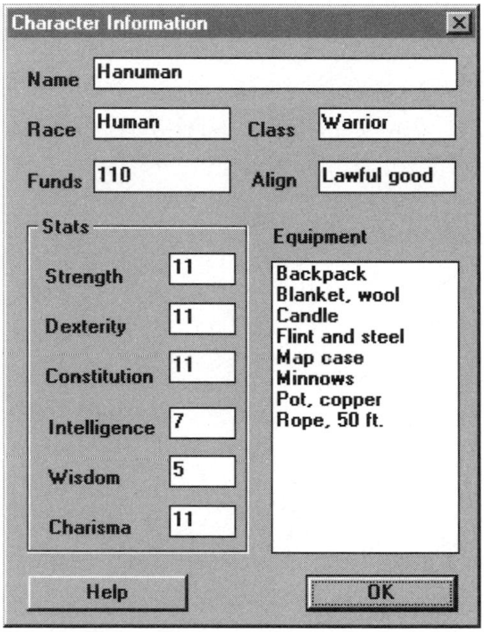

Figure 9-10. *The Character Information dialog box.*

The Character Information dialog box is an object of class *CDlgInfo*. The *CDlgInfo* class is defined in the DLGINFO.H file and is implemented in the DLGINFO.CPP file.

Before the Character Information dialog box opens, the class's *OnCharacterInfo* message handler calls the *CDlgInfo::GetStats* member function to retrieve the current character's stats. The Character Information dialog box object then uses the DDX mechanism to copy character information from member variables into a set of read-only edit boxes.

Here is the definition of the *CCreationView* class's *OnCharacterInfo* message handler:

```
void CCreationView::OnCharacterInfo()
{
    CCreationDoc* pDoc = GetDocument();

    CDlgInfo pDlgInfo;
    pDlgInfo.GetStats(pDoc);

    // ye olde DoModal function
    pDlgInfo.DoModal();
}
```

Serialization Revisited

In Chapter 7, "Of Mice and Messages," you saw how the MFC serialization mechanism can automatically save information on disk and retrieve information from disk. Serialization was used to store graphics objects—specifically, lines drawn in a window. In this section, you'll see how serialization can be used to store and retrieve text data.

Serialization, as you might recall, makes use of an MFC member function named *CObject::Serialize*. When you use AppWizard to generate an MFC application framework, AppWizard automatically implements serialization in the program's *CDocument*-derived class. AppWizard even equips the document class with an empty *Serialize* member function that you can modify any way you want to serialize whatever data you want in your application.

When you implement serialization, the MFC framework automatically saves whatever data your application specifies when the user chooses the Save or Save As item from the File menu and loads whatever data you specify when the user chooses Open from the File menu. Also, if the user modifies a document and then attempts to quit the application, the serialization mechanism displays a prompt asking the user whether the modified data should be saved.

If you want to take advantage of the serialization mechanism in any classes that you define, you must implement serialization yourself. To do so, you must derive the class from the MFC library's *CObject* class, and you must also invoke a pair of macros: a *DECLARE_SERIAL* macro in your class's declaration, and an *IMPLEMENT_SERIAL* macro in the .CPP file that implements your class. (If you need a refresher on how this is done, take another look at the section "Files and Serialization" on page 255 in Chapter 7.)

In the CREATION program, serialization of the *CCreationDoc* class is implemented automatically. However, there is some extra serialization to be taken care of in CREATION, so there is a little extra work to be done.

The CREATION Program's *Serialize* Member Function

The following code shows the *Serialize* member function that AppWizard placed in the CREATDOC.CPP file when the CREATION program was built:

```
// CCreationDoc serialization

void CCreationDoc::Serialize(CArchive& ar)
{
    if (ar.IsStoring())
    {
        // TODO: add storing code here
    }
    else
    {
        // TODO: add loading code here
    }
}
```

If you examine the *Serialize* function in the CREATDOC.CPP file, you'll notice that only one line has been added to the original version of the function created by AppWizard, shown here:

```
m_pPlayer->Serialize(ar);
```

This line has been added to the *CCreationDoc::Serialize* member function because all character data in the CREATION program is stored in member variables of the *CPlayer* class, not in member variables of the *CCreationDoc* class. If the *CCreationDoc* class managed all the program's data directly by storing it in *CCreationDoc* member variables, the *CCreationDoc::Serialize* member function would take care of serializing all the program's data—and would probably be considerably longer.

In the CREATION program, however, the *CCreationDoc* class manages the program's data only indirectly, by calling *GetEquipList* and *SetEquipList* functions provided by the *CPlayer* class.

The line of code added to the *Serialize* member function of the *CCreationDoc* class calls the *Serialize* member function of the *CPlayer* class. That leaves it up to the *CPlayer* class to take care of the actual serialization of the program's data.

The *CPlayer* Class's *Serialize* Member Function

Because the *CPlayer* class is expected to take care of the serialization needs of the CREATION program, the *DECLARE_SERIAL* macro is invoked on behalf of *CPlayer* in the PLAYER.H file and the *IMPLEMENT_SERIAL* macro is invoked for the *CPlayer* class in the PLAYER.CPP file. Because *CPlayer* is derived from *CObject*, those two macros are all the CREATION program requires to make *CPlayer* a serializable class.

To perform the actual work of serializing the CREATION program's character data, an overridden *CObject::Serialize* member function is placed in the PLAYER.CPP file. The following code shows how the *CPlayer* class overrides the *CObject::Serialize* member function:

```
void CPlayer::Serialize(CArchive& ar)
{
    // Only CObject-derived objects and six data-type
    // primitives are serializable. However, you
    // can cast any data type to a serializable data type,
    // and then you can serialize your data. The serializable
    // data types are

    // BYTE:    8 bits unsigned
    // WORD:    16 bits unsigned
    // LONG:    32 bits unsigned
    // DWORD:   32 bits unsigned
    // float    32 bits
    // double   64 bits, IEEE standard

    int nop = 1;

    if (ar.IsStoring())
    {
        ar << m_strength;
        ar << m_dexterity;
        ar << m_constitution;
        ar << m_intelligence;
        ar << m_wisdom;
        ar << m_charisma;
        ar << m_funds;
```

(continued)

```
            ar << m_name << m_race << m_class
                << m_alignment;
    }
    else
    {
        ar >> m_strength;
        ar >> m_dexterity;
        ar >> m_constitution;
        ar >> m_intelligence;
        ar >> m_wisdom;
        ar >> m_charisma;
        ar >> m_funds;
        ar >> m_name >> m_race >> m_class
            >> m_alignment;
    }
    m_pEquipList->Serialize(ar);
}
```

Notice that comments have been inserted to specify the data types that the *Serialize* function recognizes. Those comments are useful because they eliminate the necessity of looking up the *Serialize* function in a reference manual or in online help every time you need to use it.

Fortunately (actually, by design), the character stats in the CREATION program are defined as WORD data types, so they can all be serialized without any need for casting. Four other member variables of the *CPlayer* class—*m_name*, *m_race*, *m_class*, and *m_alignment*—are also serializable without any casting. That's because they are members of the *CString* class, which can be serialized simply by using the *Serialize* function's overridden input operator (>>) and output operator (<<).

The *m_pEquipList* variable can also be serialized without modification because it is an instantiation of the *CStringList* class, which is serializable because it is an MFC library *CObject*-derived class. So the entire *m_pEquipList* member variable—no matter how many *CString* objects it might contain—can be serialized with just this one line:

```
m_pEquipList->Serialize(ar);
```

Adding Printing Support

When AppWizard generates the framework for an MFC application, it provides the program with simple printing capabilities. When the user chooses the Print command from the File menu, the default behavior of an

AppWizard application is to call the program's *OnDraw* function from the *OnPrint* function by using a special device context that sends the output of the *OnDraw* function to a printer. The result is that the application prints a hard copy of whatever is on the screen.

If your application has more complex printing requirements, the MFC library provides solutions. When AppWizard creates a framework application, it inserts three message handlers related to printing in the source file that implements the program's view class. If you want your application to respond to a Print command by doing something other than printing whatever is on the screen, you can implement whatever kind of alternative functionality you want by adding customized code to any or all of these message handlers. If your requirements are still not met, you can add still more printing-related functions.

AppWizard's Printing-Related Functions

Here are the three printing-related message handlers that AppWizard generates:

- *CView::OnPreparePrinting*—Message handler that every framework application calls just before a document is printed or previewed. The default implementation of the *OnPreparePrinting* message handler does nothing; you must override the function to add various kinds of functionalities to your application's printing operations. To implement printing, *OnPreparePrinting* generally calls another member function, named *DoPreparePrinting*, which displays the Print dialog box and then takes care of whatever printing operations the user requests. You'll see exactly how all this works later in this section.

- *CView::OnBeginPrinting*—Message handler that can perform any initialization operations that a print job might require.

- *CView::OnEndPrinting*—Message handler that can perform various kinds of cleanup operations following a print job, such as freeing device contexts.

IP If you know the length of the document you will be printing, you can call a member function named *CPrintInfo::SetMaxPage* from your override of the *OnPreparePrinting* member function to display the maximum page number you specify in the Print dialog box. The CREATION application's *OnPreparePrinting* function calls *SetMaxPage* to set the maximum number of pages that can be printed to 1.

Customized Printing in the CREATION Program

Different kinds of Visual C++ programs require different kinds of printing support. The CREATION application, for example, never displays anything on the screen; it interacts with the user solely through dialog boxes. Consequently, the CREATION application has to take an approach to printing that's entirely different from the approach that AppWizard offers When the user issues a Print command, the program executes an override of a *CView* member function named *OnPrint*. In its overridden version of the *OnPrint* member function, CREATION obtains information about a character from its document object and then calls a member function named *CDC::TextOut* to send that information to a printer.

Calling the *OnPrint* Member Function

The *OnPrint* member function is the function that the MFC library calls when the user of a framework application chooses the Print command. The default implementation of *OnPrint* simply calls *OnDraw*, passing a printe device context, to print whatever is on the screen. But if your application has special printing needs, you can override *OnPrint* to carry out whateve printing operations your program requires.

The CREATION program is equipped with a fairly complex override of th *CView::OnPrint* member function. The CREATION version of the *OnPrint* member function—which you can find in the CREATVW.CPP—is shown in Listing 9-2.

```
void CCreationView::OnPrint(CDC* pDC, CPrintInfo* pInfo)
{
char buffer[20];
CString tempStr;
```

Listing 9-2. *The* CCreationView::OnPrint *member function.*

```
HDC hdc = pInfo->m_pPD->GetPrinterDC();
CDC* pPrDC = pDC->FromHandle(hdc);

// get character's stats
GetStats();

CString name = "Name: " + m_name;
CString race = "Race: " + m_race;
CString klass = "Class: " + m_class;

// stats require int-to-CString conversions
tempStr = itoa(m_strength, buffer, 10);
CString strength = "Strength: " + tempStr;

tempStr = itoa(m_dexterity, buffer, 10);
CString dexterity = "Dexterity: " + tempStr;

tempStr = itoa(m_constitution, buffer, 10);
CString constitution = "Constitution: " + tempStr;

tempStr = itoa(m_intelligence, buffer, 10);
CString intelligence = "Intelligence. " + tempStr;

tempStr = itoa(m_wisdom, buffer, 10);
CString wisdom = "Wisdom: " + tempStr;

tempStr = itoa(m_charisma, buffer, 10);
CString charisma = "Charisma: " + tempStr;

// finally, we print it;
// use current position for text
pPrDC->TextOut(100, 300, "CHARACTER INFORMATION");

pPrDC->TextOut(200, 500, name);
pPrDC->TextOut(200, 600, race);
pPrDC->TextOut(200, 700, klass);

pPrDC->TextOut(100, 900, "STATS");

if (m_strength <= 0)
    pPrDC->TextOut(200, 1100, "No Stats");
else {
    pPrDC->TextOut(200, 1100, strength);
    pPrDC->TextOut(200, 1200, dexterity);
    pPrDC->TextOut(200, 1300, constitution);
    pPrDC->TextOut(200, 1400, intelligence);
    pPrDC->TextOut(200, 1500, wisdom);
    pPrDC->TextOut(200, 1600, charisma);
}
```

(continued)

Listing 9-2. *continued*

```
    pPrDC->TextOut(100, 1800, "EQUIPMENT");

    // print character's equipment
    const CStringList *pEquipList;
    CString strTemp;
    POSITION psn;
    int y = 2000;

    pEquipList = GetDocument()->GetEquipList();

    if (pEquipList->IsEmpty())
        pPrDC->TextOut(200, y, "No Equipment");
    else {
        for (psn = pEquipList->GetHeadPosition();
            psn != NULL; y += 100) {
                strTemp = pEquipList->GetNext(psn);
                pPrDC->TextOut(200, y, strTemp);
        }
    }
}
```

How the *OnPrint* Member Function Works

In the MFC library, a printing operation works, in most respects, like any other graphics operation. To perform a printing operation in an MFC program, you must first obtain a pointer to a device-context object (a *CDC* object). Then you must associate that device context with a particular kind of output device—in this case, a printer. When you have done all that, you can call an MFC member function such as *CDC::TextOut* to write text output to a printer.

In an MFC application, you can obtain a device context for a print job when you override the *CView::OnPrint* member function. But to understand where the device context comes from, you have to trace your way through a rather complex maze of function calls.

Here's how it works. Refer back to Listing 9-2, and you'll see that this is the first executable statement in the *OnPrint* member function:

```
HDC hdc = pInfo->m_pPD->GetPrinterDC();
```

In this statement, the *pInfo* parameter is a pointer to a *CPrintInfo* structure that contains a member variable named *m_pPD*. This *m_pPD* variable is a pointer to a *CPrintDialog* object that has just been used to implement a Print dialog box—in this case, the Print dialog box displayed by the CRE-ATION program's *OnPreparePrinting* member function. Before this Print dialog box closes, it obtains a handle to a device context that can be used for printing. To obtain this handle, an application can call a member function named *CPrintDialog::GetPrinterDC*. And that is exactly what the CRE-ATION program's *OnPrint* function does in the preceding code.

One unusual feature of the *CPrintDialog::GetPrinterDC* member function is that it returns a handle to a device context instead of returning an MFC-style pointer. But that is not a difficult problem to remedy. To convert the handle returned by *GetPrinterDC* to a pointer, *OnPrint* simply calls the *CDC::FromHandle* member function, as shown here:

```
CDC* pPrDC = pDC->FromHandle(hdc);
```

The *GetStats* Member Function

From this point on, understanding the CREATION program's *OnPrint* member function is a snap. First *OnPrint* calls a *CCreationView* member function named *GetStats*, as shown below. The *GetStats* member function obtains player information from the application's document object using the same *Get* and *Set* functions that you encountered earlier. Then the *CDC::TextOut* member function is used to send the information that has just been obtained to a printer.

```
void CCreationView::GetStats()
{
    CCreationDoc* pDoc = GetDocument();

    // get name, race, class, and so on
    m_name = pDoc->m_pPlayer->GetName();
    m_race = pDoc->m_pPlayer->GetRace();
    m_class = pDoc->m_pPlayer->GetClass();

    // get abilities
    m_strength = pDoc->m_pPlayer->GetStrength();
    m_dexterity = pDoc->m_pPlayer->GetDexterity();
    m_constitution = pDoc->m_pPlayer->GetConstitution();
    m_intelligence = pDoc->m_pPlayer->GetIntelligence();
    m_wisdom = pDoc->m_pPlayer->GetWisdom();
    m_charisma = pDoc->m_pPlayer->GetCharisma();
```

(continued)

```
    // get other stuff
    m_cash = pDoc->m_pPlayer->GetFunds();
    m_class = pDoc->m_pPlayer->GetClass();
    m_race = pDoc->m_pPlayer->GetRace();
    m_alignment = pDoc->m_pPlayer->GetAlignment();
}
```

Calling the *GetEquipmentList* Member Function

To obtain information about the equipment that a character has purchased, the *OnPrint* member function calls the *CCreationDoc::GetEquip-
List* member function—the same member function that the Mel's Bait
Shop dialog box uses to obtain lists of supplies. But instead of placing the
list that it obtains in a list box, *OnPrint* calls the *CDC::TextOut* function in
a *for* loop to send the list to a printer, as shown here:

```
pEquipList = GetDocument()->GetEquipList();

if (pEquipList->IsEmpty())
    pPrDC->TextOut(200, y, "No Equipment");
else {
    for (psn = pEquipList->GetHeadPosition();
        psn != NULL; y += 100) {
            strTemp = pEquipList->GetNext(psn);
            pPrDC->TextOut(200, y, strTemp);
    }
}
```

The *CDC::TextOut* member function, which is called several times from
the CREATION program's *OnPrint* member function, is straightforward. It
takes three parameters: a pair of page coordinates and a *CString* object. It
then prints the specified *CString* at the specified location on a page.

This ends our quick discussion of printing text on a page in a Visual C++
program. There are many other things that could be said, of course; there
are various *mapping modes* that determine how text and graphics are written to windows and to printers, and there are many different functions
that can be called to specify what fonts are used for printing, how text is
styled, and what kind of spacing and positioning are to be used when text
is printed and displayed.

Also there are differences between the way text-based printing is handled
in MFC programs and the way things are done when you want to send a

printer exactly what is being displayed in a window—an operation known as *WYSIWYG* (what you see is what you get) printing.

If you'd like to see an example of how WYSIWYG printing can work in an MFC program, you can find one by examining the source code of the SCRIBBLE program presented in Chapter 7, "Of Mice and Messages." The printing procedures that the SCRIBBLE program uses are more complicated than those that are used in the CREATION program, but with the online help, you should be able to figure out how they work.

What's Next?

You've learned a lot in this chapter. You've learned how to use the MFC library's DDX and DDV mechanisms to pass data back and forth between dialog box controls and variables, and you've learned how to use the MFC library's serialization mechanism to save and load data retrieved from dialog box controls. You've also learned how to place strings in list boxes, how to remove strings from list boxes, how to copy strings from one list box to another, and how to move strings back and forth between list boxes and *CStringList* objects.

This chapter also gave you a taste of how MFC collection classes can be used in Visual C++ programs. You saw how *CStringList* objects can be used to create items displayed in list boxes, and you saw how serialization can be used to store collection class objects on disk and retrieve collection class objects from disk.

Last you saw how MFC library classes and member functions can be used to perform printing operations.

The last chapter in this book is the best one. Chapter 10, "Visual C++ Graphics," is all about graphics and computer animation. Read on.

Visual C++ Graphics

You've now seen how you can create an application framework in Visual C++, add to and extend the framework using Visual C++ tools and the Microsoft Foundation Class (MFC) Library version 2.0, and manage the data an application uses. In this chapter, the last in the book, we'll create more sophisticated applications—programs with eye-catching graphics and animation—and build on the knowledge you've gained so far.

The topics covered in this chapter include the following:

- Understanding Windows bitmaps, both device-dependent bitmaps (DDBs) and device-independent bitmaps (DIBs)

- Loading, saving, copying, and displaying device-dependent bitmaps

- Displaying and moving characters over complex backgrounds, a technique known as transparent-background copying

- Creating complex animation sequences using step animation and sprites

- Understanding the architecture of device-independent bitmaps and how to create and use them

To demonstrate graphics and animation in Visual C++ applications, this chapter presents two sample programs: GRAFDEMO and DIBDEMO. The

GRAFDEMO program illustrates the use of DDBs, and the DIBDEMO program introduces DIBs.

Both GRAFDEMO and DIBDEMO demonstrate sprite animation: a flicker-free animation technique that is often used in games and multimedia applications. By using sprite animation, you can move irregularly shaped bitmap images—for example, game characters—over complex backgrounds.

The GRAFDEMO program implements sprite animation using conventional Windows objects, such as GDI (graphics device interface) objects and DC (device-context) objects, and conventional bitmaps. GRAFDEMO also shows how graphics classes implemented in the MFC library can be used to create animation sequences in Visual C++ programs.

Version 2.0 of the MFC library—the version that comes with Visual C++ version 1.0—does not provide a class for creating DIBs, so the DIBDEMO application provides its own DIB class and instantiates objects of that class to create, display, and animate DIBs.

The GRAFDEMO program's screen display is shown in Figure 10-1.

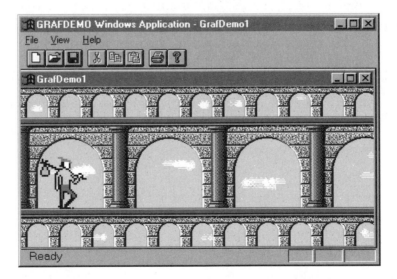

Figure 10-1. *The GRAFDEMO program's screen display.*

Bitmaps

In a bitmap, each dot on the screen, or pixel, corresponds to one or more locations in memory. Figure 10-2 shows a close-up of a bitmap image—specifically, the figure in the GRAFDEMO program.

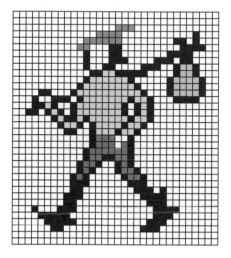

Figure 10-2. *Close-up of a bitmap.*

> **NOTE** Strictly speaking, bitmaps haven't been used in graphics programming for years. The word "bitmap" dates back to the days of monochrome monitors, in which each screen pixel corresponded to a single bit in memory. To a purist, a bitmap is a map of bits, and a bit cannot display colors because it has just two settings: off and on. On a color monitor, it takes more than one bit to represent a screen pixel, but old habits die hard, and even brilliant assembly language programmers continue to use the word "bitmap" to refer to pixel maps. This common usage is followed, reluctantly, throughout this chapter.

How Bitmaps Are Displayed

The first IBM-compatible personal computers had monochrome monitors that could display just one primary color—usually green, white, or amber—on the screen. Screen displays were created by turning individual pixels on and off, so it took only one bit of memory to represent each pixel displayed on the screen.

(continued)

How Bitmaps Are Displayed. *continued*

When you use a scheme that requires a single bit of memory to store the value of a pixel, a 640-by-480-pixel screen requires 307,200 bits of memory, or 38,400 bytes. If you switch to a color monitor, the memory requirements of your screen graphics jump significantly. Many color graphics cards are in use today, and their memory requirements vary—from 1 megabyte (MB) of video memory for a low-end card up to 4 MB (or more) for serious graphics work.

The first color graphics card to come into general use was the color graphics adapter (CGA) card, which could simultaneously produce only 4 colors on a screen with a resolution of 320 by 200 pixels. (A CGA graphics card has three built-in 4-color palettes.) Next came the enhanced graphics adapter (EGA) card, which could produce up to 16 screen colors at a time and offered 64 colors to choose from.

The video graphics adapter (VGA) card, like the EGA card, could produce 16 screen colors simultaneously. Unlike the EGA card, however, the VGA card could select its 16 screen colors from what was at the time a dazzling array of 262,144 colors.

The VGA card—sometimes referred to as the standard VGA card—was succeeded by two newer models, named the 8514 card and the super VGA (SVGA) card. A number of different kinds of SVGA cards have been produced, and several different SVGA resolutions are available. Some SVGA cards can display more than 16 million colors at screen resolutions of up to 1280 by 1024 pixels or more.

The first video card that could produce more than 4 colors simultaneously was the EGA card, which uses 4 bits of memory for each pixel displayed on the screen. Only one of 16 integers (0 through 15) can be stored in 4 bits of memory, and an EGA card assigns each of those 16 integers to a predetermined color. Although some EGA cards might still be in use today, you wouldn't want to write graphics programs using them; they offer dismal color displays.

An SVGA card is not limited to 256 specific colors. In 8-bit color mode, an SVGA card uses a mechanism called a *color lookup table*, or *CLUT,* to select 256 colors from a collection of 262,144 possible colors.

The 8-bit color display produced by early SVGA cards was fairly spectacular in its day, but it's not remarkable by today's standards. Modern SVGA cards have 15-bit, 16-bit, 24-bit, and 32-bit color modes.

A 24-bit graphics card can show 16,777,216 colors on the screen at one time—limited by the number of pixels on screen, of course. This is more colors than the human eye can distinguish and far more colors than any PC monitor now on the market can display. And a 32-bit graphics card can generate more than 4 billion colors at a time.

The 24-bit and 32-bit color modes require a considerable amount of video memory, especially if combined with a high screen resolution. The Microsoft Windows 95 operating system supports screen resolutions of up to 1600 pixels wide by 1200 pixels high. That's 1,920,000 pixels, and if you dedicate 32 bits of memory to displaying each pixel, the display takes 6 MB of memory.

But generally speaking, you probably don't want to restrict yourself to writing applications for such ultra-high-end systems. If you take that route, you won't be able to find enough customers to make the task worthwhile. For now, and in the immediate future, it's probably best to assume that the people who buy your programs have graphics cards that are at least in the SVGA league (256-color displays with a few million colors to choose from) but not to assume anything more.

Varieties of Windows Bitmaps

In Chapter 5, "Visual C++ Tools," and Chapter 6, "The MFC Library," you learned how to use bitmaps, and in Chapter 7, "Of Mice and Messages," you also learned how to draw lines directly to the screen. To create the graphics in these chapters, you used a kind of bitmap called a device-dependent bitmap, or DDB—which was the only kind of bitmap available to Windows programmers until about 1989.

Since then, device-dependent bitmaps have been falling out of favor, and a new kind of bitmap, called a device-independent bitmap, or DIB, has been replacing the DDB in graphics-intensive applications.

OTE   There are actually two kinds of device-independent bitmaps: Windows DIBs, which are used by Windows, and Presentation Manager DIBs, which were designed for use with the Microsoft Presentation Manager. Presentation Manager DIBs are obsolete, and as time passes, there is less need to be concerned with them. All the DIBs used in this chapter's sample programs—and in any other Windows-based programs that you're likely to encounter these days—are Windows DIBs.

Ordinary DDBs are easier to create and use than DIBs, so DDBs are still widely used for situations in which highly precise color rendering is not an issue and lightning-fast animation is not required. But DIBs can produce truer colors on a wider variety of output devices than ordinary DDBs can, and the colors that they produce can be controlled more precisely.

Another advantage that DIBs have over traditional DDBs is that a number of superfast bitmap-copying operations are available for use with DIBs, so applications that use turbocharged DIB-based graphics are starting to leave old-fashioned DDB-based programs in the dust.

DIBs have one feature that can be considered both a blessing and a curse: they have a more complicated architecture than DDBs have. A DIB object is equipped with several kinds of data structures in which it stores important information about itself. When you create a DIB, you can provide it with many kinds of attributes that cannot be set when you create a DDB. Consequently, you have more control over what a DIB looks like when you use it in an application.

Along with the color information needed to display each pixel in a bitmap, a DIB structure has fields for storing other important information about a bitmap—including its size, its color resolution, and a color table that holds values representing each color that the DIB can display.

The size of a DIB's color table can vary, depending on the color resolution of the DIB. For example, a 256-color DIB has a color table that's large enough to hold 256 color codes. DIBs that display more colors can have much larger color tables. You'll learn more about the structures and sizes of different kinds of DIBs in the section "Palettes" on page 407.

To add animation to the sample programs in this chapter, we'll use *sprites—* small bitmaps that can be moved on top of complex backgrounds without destroying the backgrounds. Sprites are the most popular kind of animated figures used in Windows-based programs.

Device-Dependent Bitmaps (DDBs)

The device-dependent bitmap format has been around since the early days of Windows and has many limitations. Besides being highly dependent on the output device for which it was created, a DDB does not have any built-in mechanisms for storing a table of available colors or for storing any information about its color resolution or even its size.

Despite their limitations, DDBs are still used extensively in Windows-based programs. When you need a bitmap that will be used only in the program in which it is created, it is often better to use a DDB. One reason for this is that the MFC library has a class that encapsulates DDBs but does not have a class that encapsulates DIBs.

Creating DDBs

The MFC library encapsulates traditional DDBs in a *CGdiObject*-derived class named *CBitmap*. The *CBitmap* class provides four member functions for creating *CBitmap* objects: *CreateBitmap*, *CreateBitmapIndirect*, *Create-CompatibleBitmap*, and *CreateDiscardableBitmap*. You can forget about the *CreateDiscardableBitmap* function right away; it is rarely seen and is not recommended for use in today's programs. The other three functions are used frequently in Windows-based applications.

The *CreateBitmap* member function

The *CreateBitmap* member function creates a bitmap using a set of attributes specified by five parameters, as shown here:

```
BOOL CreateBitmap(int nWidth, int nHeight, UINT nPlanes,
    UINT nBitcount, const void FAR* lpBits);
```

The *nWidth* and *nHeight* parameters specify the width and height—in pixels—of the bitmap being created. The *nPlanes* parameter specifies the number of color planes to be used in the bitmap; *nBitcount* is the number of color bits per pixel. The *lpBits* parameter points to a short-integer array that contains the initial bitmap bit values. If *lpBits* is *NULL*, the new bitmap is left uninitialized and contains random data.

Because a DDB works best when it is created and displayed using the same output device, it is usually not a good idea to call *CreateBitmap* to create and initialize color bitmaps. A bitmap created by *CreateBitmap* will look different on various display devices because a DDB contains no color information. If you use *CreateBitmap*, there is no guarantee that the correct colors will be displayed.

The *CreateBitmapIndirect* member function

The *CreateBitmapIndirect* member function initializes a bitmap by using values supplied in a *BITMAP* data structure instead of by using a detailed set of parameters. The *CBitmap::CreateBitmapIndirect* member function is shown here:

```
BOOL CreateBitmapIndirect(LPBITMAP lpBitmap);
```

The *lpBitmap* parameter is a pointer to a *BITMAP* structure. The Windows API defines the *BITMAP* structure as follows:

```
typedef struct tagBITMAP {   /* bm */
    int         bmType;
    int         bmWidth;
    int         bmHeight;
    int         bmWidthBytes;
    BYTE        bmPlanes;
    BYTE        bmBitsPixel;
    void FAR*   bmBits;
} BITMAP;
```

CreateBitmapIndirect also has no way of ensuring color accuracy, so you generally shouldn't use it to create and initialize color bitmaps. Instead, you should call *CreateCompatibleBitmap*.

The *CreateCompatibleBitmap* member function

The best way to create a bitmap is to use the *CreateCompatibleBitmap* member function, shown here:

```
BOOL CreateCompatibleBitmap(CDC* pDC, int nWidth,
    int nHeight);
```

When you create a bitmap by calling *CreateCompatibleBitmap,* the bitmap you construct is guaranteed to be compatible with the device context (DC) specified in the function's *pDC* parameter. That means that the bitmap you are creating will use the same number of colors as the specified DC and will be displayed using the same number of bits per pixel. Your application can then select the bitmap you have created as the current bitmap for any memory device that is compatible with the DC specified in the *pDC* parameter.

You can select your new bitmap into the DC specified in the *pDC* parameter by calling the *CBitmap::SelectObject* member function. You'll see how this can be done in the GRAFDEMO sample program presented later in this chapter. If the *pDC* parameter that you pass to *CreateCompatibleBitmap* points to a memory device context, the bitmap that you create has the same format as the bitmap that is currently selected in that device context.

When you call *CreateCompatibleBitmap* to create a bitmap, Windows automatically creates a stock monochrome bitmap as a placeholder and selects it into the device context pointed to by the *pDC* parameter. You can then copy any bitmap image you want into the device context that has been initialized. The image that you copy into the device context replaces the monochrome placeholder bitmap that Windows has created.

Loading and Saving DDBs

Device-dependent bitmaps are not designed to be saved on disk and passed from one application to another. So even though the MFC library supplies a *CBitmap::LoadBitmap* function, it doesn't provide any particular function for saving DDBs on disk.

If you insist on saving a DDB on disk, it is possible to do so by calling the *CBitmap::GetBitmapBits* function and the *CBitmap::GetBitmapDimension* function to cobble together a procedure. But when you need a bitmap that you want to save and reload so that it can be used in more than one application, it is usually a better idea to use a DIB.

OTE   DIBs are not supported by the MFC library, so there aren't any MFC member functions for loading or saving DIBs either. But many people have written routines for loading and saving DIBs, and those routines are widely available.

Copying and Displaying Bitmaps

One reason that device-dependent bitmaps aren't dead yet, despite the obviously superior capabilities of DIBs, is that the MFC library provides a pair of versatile *CDC* member functions for working with DDBs: *CDC::BitBlt* and *CDC::StretchBlt*.

The *CDC::BitBlt* member function copies a bitmap from one block of memory to another; the *CDC::StretchBlt* member function copies a bitmap and resizes it to fit its destination. *StretchBlt* works just like *BitBlt* except that it can increase or reduce the size of the bitmap during the copying process to make the destination bitmap fit in the area into which it is being copied.

NOTE The Windows API also provides a pair of functions for copying DIBs—and these DIB-copying functions are actually faster than the MFC library's DDB-copying functions. But the MFC library functions for copying DDBs offer a large and rich set of copying modes that the DIB-copying functions provided by the Windows API lack. These copying modes support an animation technique called *masking,* which is easier to use than most DIB-based animation techniques, although it is not as fast.

The *BitBlt* and *StretchBlt* member functions

When you use *BitBlt* or *StretchBlt* to copy a bitmap to a location that is already occupied by another bitmap, you can compare each pixel of the source bitmap with the corresponding pixel in the destination bitmap, and you can use the result of this comparison to determine how the pixel being copied should be treated.

By taking advantage of this capability, you can use the *BitBlt* and *StretchBlt* member functions to perform many different kinds of copying operations. You can invert the color of each pixel in either the source bitmap or the destination bitmap, or you can compare each source and destination pixel using a logical *OR, XOR,* or *AND* operation. These operations are controlled by a parameter whose possible values are known as *raster operation codes,* or *ROP codes.*

Transparent-background bitmap-copying operations

By calling *BitBlt* or *StretchBlt* multiple times using different ROP codes, you can perform bitmap-copying operations in which irregularly shaped bitmaps (sprites) are "stamped" onto a complex background without disturbing the surrounding background. This kind of copying operation is sometimes called a *transparent-background copy*—or, more commonly, a *transparent copy*—because it treats the background pixels of the sprite being copied as though they were transparent. When a transparent copy is performed, these transparent background pixels are not copied to the destination bitmap with the sprite that they surround.

Figures 10-3 and 10-4 illustrate the results of nontransparent and transparent bitmap-copying operations.

Figure 10-3. *Result of a nontransparent bitmap-copying operation.*

Figure 10-4. *Result of a transparent bitmap-copying operation.*

To understand how the sprite-copying procedures shown in Figures 10-3 and 10-4 work, it helps to know something more about the syntax of the *BitBlt* and *StretchBlt* member functions. The *BitBlt* member function is shown on the following page.

```
BOOL BitBlt(int x, int y, int nWidth, int nHeight, CDC* pSrcDC,
    int xSrc, int ySrc, DWORD dwROP);
```

The first seven parameters of the *BitBlt* member function are straightforward. The *BitBlt* function can be used to copy a whole bitmap or a rectangular portion of a bitmap from the device context specified by the *pSrcDC* parameter to the device context that is calling the function. The *xSrc* and *ySrc* parameters provide the left and top coordinates of the source rectangle, and the *x* and *y* parameters specify the left and top coordinates of the destination rectangle. The *nWidth* and *nHeight* parameters specify the size of the rectangle being copied.

The *CDC::StretchBlt* member function is similar to *CDC::BitBlt* but has two additional parameters, *nSrcWidth* and *nSrcHeight*, that specify the width and height of the source rectangle. Here is the *StretchBlt* member function:

```
BOOL StretchBlt(int x, int y, int nWidth, int nHeight,
    CDC* pSrcDC, int xSrc, int ySrc, int nSrcWidth,
    int nSrcHeight, DWORD dwROP);
```

The most interesting parameter of the *BitBlt* and *StretchBlt* member functions is the *dwROP* parameter, which is the last parameter passed to both functions. When an application calls *BitBlt* or *StretchBlt*, the *dwROP* parameter is used to specify the raster operation to be performed. Table 10-1 provides a list of ROP codes that you can specify in the *dwROP* parameter when you call the *BitBlt* or *StretchBlt* member function.

ROP Code	Result
BLACKNESS	Turns all output black
DSTINVERT	Inverts the destination bitmap
MERGECOPY	Combines the pattern (brush) and the source bitmap using the logical *AND* operator
MERGEPAINT	Combines the inverted source bitmap with the destination bitmap using the logical *OR* operator

Table 10-1. *ROP codes used by the* BitBlt *and* StretchBlt *member functions.*

ROP Code	Result
NOTSRCCOPY	Inverts the source bitmap and copies it to the destination rectangle
NOTSRCERASE	Inverts the result of combining the destination and source bitmaps using the logical *OR* operator
PATCOPY	Copies the pattern (brush) to the destination bitmap
PATINVERT	Combines the destination bitmap with the pattern (brush) using the logical *XOR* operator
PATPAINT	Combines the inverted source bitmap with the pattern (brush) using the logical *OR* operator; combines the result of this operation with the destination bitmap using the logical *OR* operator
SRCAND	Copies a bitmap to a destination rectangle using the logical *AND* operator
SRCCOPY	Copies the source bitmap to the destination bitmap
SRCERASE	Inverts the destination bitmap, and combines the result with the source bitmap using the logical *AND* operator
SRCINVERT	Combines the pixels of the destination and source bitmaps using the logical *XOR* operator
SRCPAINT	Combines the pixels of the destination and source bitmaps using the logical *OR* operator
WHITENESS	Turns all output white

One common way to perform a transparent copy of a sprite is shown in Figure 10-5 on the following page. First create a black or white mask that has the exact shape of the sprite you are animating (Start), and then copy that mask over a destination background to cut out a sprite-shaped portion of the destination background (Step 1). You can draw the sprite inside the masked area without disturbing the surrounding background in the destination bitmap (Step 2).

Figure 10-5. *Performing a sprite-copying operation.*

There are several methods for using masking operations to transparently copy sprites onto bitmap backgrounds. One easy way is to draw the bitmap on a black background and then stencil it onto the screen through a solid-color mask. That is the technique used to create the sprite-animation action in the GRAFDEMO program. Figure 10-6 shows a sprite bitmap and a mask cutout used in the GRAFDEMO application's bitmap-copying operations.

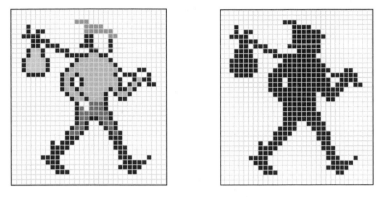

Figure 10-6. *Sprite bitmap and mask used in the GRAFDEMO program.*

Sprite Animation

Once you know how to copy a sprite transparently to a destination background, it isn't difficult to add animation to your sprite-copying operation. You animate the sprite by moving it across its destination background in small incremental steps, in exactly the same way that an object—for example, an automobile—moves across a background in the sequential frames of a movie.

Figure 10-7 shows a sprite animated in this step-by-step fashion in a Visual C++ program.

Figure 10-7. *Animating a sprite.*

It takes a few steps to implement this kind of sprite animation. You must erase the sprite from its original location, make a slight change in its destination coordinates, and copy it transparently to its next location. You must repeat this process as many times as it takes to complete your animation sequence. This is the technique used to implement the animation sequences in GRAFDEMO and DIBDEMO.

Sprite Animation Step by Step

In the *CGrafView::DrawPlayer* function of the GRAFDEMO application, these steps are followed each time a sprite is drawn transparently over the Arches background:

1. A portion of the background is copied to a temporary device context named *m_dcTemp*, using the *NOTSRCCOPY* ROP code to invert the colors being copied, as shown here:

```
// copy portion of background to m_dcTemp, inverting colors
m_dcTemp.BitBlt(0, 0,
    m_zoomRect.right, m_zoomRect.bottom, &m_dcMem,
    m_invalidRect.left, m_invalidRect.top,
    NOTSRCCOPY);
```

2. A mask bitmap is combined with the temporary device context, using the *SRCAND* ROP code to perform a logical *AND* operation, as shown here:

```
// draw mask to m_dcTemp
m_dcTemp.StretchBlt(0, 0,
    m_zoomRect.right, m_zoomRect.bottom, &m_dcMask,
    0, 0, m_bmRect.right, m_bmRect.bottom,
    SRCAND);
```

> **NOTE** When you use the *SRCAND* ROP code, black areas of the source bitmap have no effect on the destination rectangle, so if a source bitmap has a black background (or a white background that has been inverted to black), that area of the destination bitmap is left undisturbed. If a portion of the destination bitmap has been painted white and the corresponding area of the source bitmap is colored, the colors in that area of the source bitmap are copied directly onto the white area of the destination bitmap.

3. A sprite bitmap is combined with the temporary device context, using the *SRCINVERT* ROP code to invert the colors in the temporary device context, as shown here:

```
// draw player to m_dcTemp, and invert destination
m_dcTemp.StretchBlt(0, 0,
    m_zoomRect.right, m_zoomRect.bottom, &m_dcPlayer,
    0, 0, m_bmRect.right, m_bmRect.bottom,
    SRCINVERT);
```

After this operation, the part of the Arches background stored in the temporary device context is restored to its original colors.

NOTE   When you copy a colored image to a destination rectangle using the XOR operator, the colors in the image are reversed, which makes the destination rectangle look like a color negative of the original image.

---

4. The temporary device context is copied to the GRAFDEMO program's main window using a *SRCCOPY* ROP code, as shown here:

```
// copy m_dcTemp to screen
pDC->BitBlt(m_invalidRect.left, m_invalidRect.top,
    m_invalidRect.right, m_invalidRect.bottom, &m_dcTemp,
    0, 0, SRCCOPY);
```

Using Frame Buffers in Animation Programs

The step-by-step operation described above illustrates the use of a *frame buffer*—that is, an area of memory that holds a copy of a screen bitmap so that portions of that bitmap can be copied to the screen whenever they are needed. (Both example programs in this chapter make use of frame buffers.) The appearance of the program's screen display might change constantly during its animation sequence, but the copy of the background bitmap that is stored in a frame buffer is never written to, so its appearance is never altered.

Although sprite bitmaps might obscure various portions of the background bitmap displayed on the screen, and although different portions of that bitmap might be covered by sprites at various times, the copy of the bitmap stored in the program's frame buffer remains unchanged from the time it is loaded until the time it is no longer needed. You can erase a sprite from the screen cleanly, at any time you want, using the copy of the screen background that is stored in your frame buffer. All you have to do is copy a portion of the bitmap stored in your frame buffer into the corresponding area of the screen. If a sprite is in this area of the screen, the image from the frame buffer is copied over the sprite, erasing the sprite from the screen and restoring the part of the background that the sprite previously obscured.

Figure 10-8 illustrates this kind of sprite-removing operation.

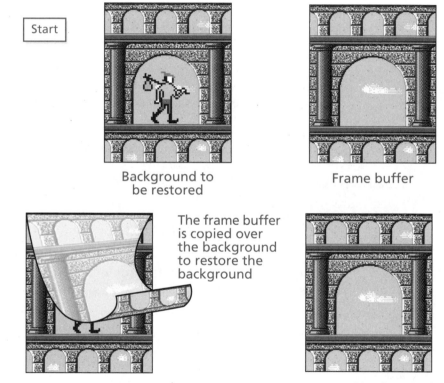

Start

Background to
be restored

Frame buffer

The frame buffer
is copied over
the background
to restore the
background

Restored background

Figure 10-8. *Erasing a sprite but leaving its background intact.*

Avoiding Flickering and Tearing in Bitmap-Copying Operations

To store a background bitmap in a frame buffer, a sprite-animation program typically loads the bitmap into its buffer directly from a disk and then copies the bitmap from its frame buffer to screen memory by calling either the *CBitmap::BitBlt* or the *CBitmap::StretchBlt* member function.

When you use this technique to load a background bitmap from disk, you accomplish two things: you immediately store your background bitmap in a frame buffer that can be used later in animation sequences, and you prevent unsightly flickering and tearing effects as your bitmap is being copied to the screen. That's because the *BitBlt* and *StretchBlt* member functions, like other screen-drawing functions managed by the MFC library and the Windows operating system, take place only during *vertical blank interrupts*—those brief blackout periods between frames during which nothing is being drawn to the screen because the electron beam is moving from the lower right corner back to the upper right corner of the screen.

When you create a Windows-based program, it's very important to draw to the screen only during vertical blank interrupts because that's the only way to ensure that a frame change won't come along midway through a screen-drawing operation and rip through the display you are creating, causing an annoying flicker or even tearing your display into two pieces.

When you load a bitmap from disk and draw it directly to the screen, you never know exactly what your video hardware will be doing when the operation takes place, so you always run the risk of carrying out a sloppy-looking bitmap transfer. But when you load a bitmap into memory and copy it from there to the screen using a *BitBlt* or *StretchBlt* function, the Windows operating system ensures that your bitmap-copying operation is carried out during a vertical blank interrupt, so you can rest assured that your screen-drawing operation will perform smoothly, without any ripping, tearing, or flickering.

Calculating Bounding Rectangles in Animation Sequences

As mentioned, when you animate a sprite by erasing it from one part of a window and repainting it in another, you must be sure to repaint all of the background area that the sprite occupied in its original position. In the GRAFDEMO program, this is accomplished quite easily because the program always knows exactly where the sprite will be situated the next time it moves.

Most sprite-animation programs contain routines to calculate the bounding rectangle around a sprite's new position and its old position so that backgrounds can be repainted efficiently. Consider, for example, the animation sequence shown in Figure 10-9 on the following page.

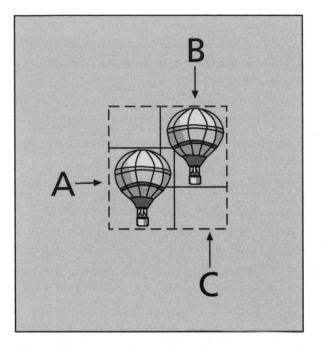

Figure 10-9. *Calculating bounding rectangles of sprites.*

In this animation sequence—demonstrated later in this chapter in the DIB-DEMO program—the routine that handles background repainting must redraw the entire background in rectangle A and the background in rectangle B. Then the sprite that is moved from rectangle A to rectangle B can be drawn over the restored background.

The easiest way to repaint a background in this kind of animation is to calculate a bounding rectangle (rectangle C) that encompasses the sprite's old and new positions and to redraw that section of the window's background. You can construct a bounding rectangle by calling the MFC member function *CRect::UnionRect*. The *UnionRect* member function takes pointers to two *CRect* objects as parameters and constructs a bounding rectangle that encompasses both smaller rectangles.

You'll see how this kind of operation works in the GRAFDEMO program in the section "Drawing a Background" on page 392.

Step Animation

The GRAFDEMO program uses a technique called *step animation* to simulate lifelike motion. The program uses multiple sprite bitmaps and multiple mask bitmaps; each sprite bitmap portrays a different view of a walking character. When the sprites are displayed in sequence, the character appears to be walking.

In the program's source code, the member variables that are used to access the sprites and masks are implemented as arrays. The arrays that hold the sprites and masks are initialized inside the constructor of the program's *CView*-derived class, named *CGrafView*, as shown here:

```
CGrafView::CGrafView()
{
    // TODO: add construction code here
    // create player and mask bitmaps
    for (int n = 0; n < 5; n++) {
        m_bmRtBoy[n] = new CBitmap;
        ASSERT_VALID(m_bmRtBoy[n]);
    }
    for (n = 0; n < 5; n++) {
        m_bmRtBoyM[n] = new CBitmap;
        ASSERT_VALID(m_bmRtBoyM[n]);
    }

    for (n = 0; n < 5; n++) {
        m_bmLfBoy[n] = new CBitmap;
        ASSERT_VALID(m_bmLfBoy[n]);
    }
    for (n = 0; n < 5; n++) {
        m_bmLfBoyM[n] = new CBitmap;
        ASSERT_VALID(m_bmLfBoyM[n]);
    }
```

Along with the sprite and mask bitmaps used for step animation, GRAF-DEMO uses an additional bitmap (associated with a member variable named *m_bmRiseBoy*), shown on the following page, that is a figure of a character holding a balloon. The balloon lifts the character from one floor of a structure to the next higher floor each time the player presses the Up arrow key; when the player presses the other keys, the character moves in the corresponding direction.

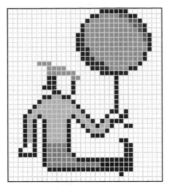

Example: The GRAFDEMO Program

GRAFDEMO is a Visual C++ application that is based on a framework generated by AppWizard and uses AppWizard's conventional document-and-view architecture.

The GRAFDEMO program's view class, *CGrafView*, is implemented in a file named GRAFVIEW.CPP. The program's document class, named *CGrafDoc*, is implemented in a file named GRAFDOC.CPP.

The constructor of the *CGrafView* class initializes two arrays of bitmaps using the C++ *new* operator. One set of bitmaps shows the figure of a player in an adventure game. The other array is set of black masks that outline the player so that the figure can be displayed properly against a complex background without corrupting the background. The bitmaps are stored in arrays so that the program can cycle through the two arrays simultaneously, creating step animation.

GRAFDEMO also uses a third bitmap: a background against which the figure of the character is displayed.

How the GRAFDEMO Program Works

When you start the GRAFDEMO program and select New from the File menu, the program draws a character on the screen. You can then move the character by pressing the arrow keys on your keyboard.

The GRAFDEMO application implements animation by calling the *CDC* member functions *BitBlt* and *StretchBlt*. Although the GRAFDEMO program uses the *BitBlt* member function to copy its background bitmap into a frame buffer and to the screen, the application calls *StretchBlt* in some of its sprite-copying and mask-copying operations. That's because the application stores its sprite bitmap as a 32-by-32-pixel bitmap—the same kind of bitmap that Windows uses to create cursors and icons. But when the sprite is displayed, the *StretchBlt* function is used to enlarge the figure to 64 by 64 pixels—four times larger than when it is loaded into memory.

When you call *StretchBlt* to increase the size of a bitmap, the result is a bitmap with a jagged-edged appearance. To avoid this effect, create a sprite bitmap that is the same size it will be when it is displayed. You can then transfer your sprite to the screen by calling *BitBlt* instead of *StretchBlt*, and the result will be cleaner.

In the GRAFDEMO program, the player sprite was created by enlarging an icon bitmap and using that bitmap as a sprite. That saved a miniscule amount of memory and allowed the same image to be used as the icon for the application and as its sprite.

The GRAFDEMO Program Step by Step

Most of the action in the GRAFDEMO application takes place in the program's *CGrafView* class, which is derived from the MFC library's *CView* class. The following steps trace what happens in the program's *CGrafView* object when you execute the application:

1. The program builds its arrays of sprite and mask bitmaps inside the constructor of the *CGrafView* object. The *CGrafView::OnInitialUpdate* function is then invoked, which calls the *CGrafView::PrepareAnimation* function.

2. For each of the sprite, mask, and background bitmaps that the program uses, it creates a *CDC* object that is compatible with the current device context. The *PrepareAnimation* function creates this *CDC* object by calling *CreateCompatibleDC*, as shown here:

```
// create some device contexts that are
// compatible with the current device context
m_dcPlayer.CreateCompatibleDC(pDC);
m_dcMask.CreateCompatibleDC(pDC);
m_dcMem.CreateCompatibleDC(pDC);
m_dcBackdrop.CreateCompatibleDC(pDC);
m_dcTemp.CreateCompatibleDC(pDC);
```

3. The *PrepareAnimation* function then calls the *CreateCompatible-Bitmap* function to create a background bitmap and a sprite bitmap that are compatible with the output device currently being used. For example, the following code fragment creates a *CBitmap* object named *m_bmBackdrop* that is compatible with the current device context (specified in the *pDC* parameter):

```
// create a screen-size background bitmap
m_bmBackdrop.CreateCompatibleBitmap(pDC,
    pDC->GetDeviceCaps(HORZRES),
    pDC->GetDeviceCaps(VERTRES));
```

4. The *PrepareAnimation* member function then calls *SelectObject* to select the bitmaps into the device contexts. For example, these two statements select bitmaps into current device contexts and store the previous contents of the DCs for safekeeping:

```
// select bitmaps into current device context,
// and save previous bitmaps
m_pOldMapMem = m_dcMem.SelectObject(m_bmMem);
m_dcBackdrop.SelectObject(&m_bmBackdrop);
```

5. Each time the program's main window needs to be redrawn, the MFC framework sends the *OnDraw* member function a pointer to the current view's private device context. In an MFC framework program, the Visual C++ framework supplies a DC pointer named *pDC* and passes it as a parameter to the *CGrafView::OnDraw* member function. You can then use that device-context pointer to draw to your *CGrafView* object's window.

6. During each redrawing operation, the *OnDraw* function calls the *CGrafView::DrawPlayer* function. The *DrawPlayer* function then calls the *BitBlt* function to copy the bitmap associated with *m_dc-Mem* to the bitmap that has been selected into a temporary device context named *m_dcTemp*, as shown here:

```
// copy portion of background to m_dcTemp, inverting colors
m_dcTemp.BitBlt(0, 0,
    m_zoomRect.right, m_zoomRect.bottom, &m_dcMem,
    m_invalidRect.left, m_invalidRect.top,
    NOTSRCCOPY);
```

Notice that when *BitBlt* is called, the bounding rectangle of the source bitmap is named *m_invalidRect*. The bounding rectangle of the destination bitmap is named *m_zoomRect*.

7. The bitmap that has been created in *m_dcTemp* is transferred to the screen, as shown here:

```
// copy the changed portion of m_dcTemp to screen
pDC->BitBlt(m_invalidRect.left, m_invalidRect.top,
    m_invalidRect.right, m_invalidRect.bottom, &m_dcTemp,
    0, 0, SRCCOPY);
```

Constructing Bitmaps in the GRAFDEMO Program

All the bitmaps used in the GRAFDEMO application are created inside the constructor of the program's *CView* class. Listing 10-1 shows the definition of the bitmap constructors used in the GRAFDEMO program.

```
// CView construction/destruction

CGrafView::CGrafView()
{
    // TODO: add construction code here
    // create player and player mask bitmaps
    for (int n = 0; n < 5; n++) {
        m_bmRtBoy[n] = new CBitmap;
        ASSERT_VALID(m_bmRtBoy[n]);
    }
    for (n = 0; n < 5; n++) {
        m_bmRtBoyM[n] = new CBitmap;
        ASSERT_VALID(m_bmRtBoyM[n]);
    }

    for (n = 0; n < 5; n++) {
        m_bmLfBoy[n] = new CBitmap;
        ASSERT_VALID(m_bmLfBoy[n]);
    }
    for (n = 0; n < 5; n++) {
        m_bmLfBoyM[n] = new CBitmap;
        ASSERT_VALID(m_bmLfBoyM[n]);
    }

    m_bmRiseBoy = new CBitmap;
    ASSERT_VALID(m_bmRiseBoy);
```

Listing 10-1. *Bitmap constructors in the GRAFDEMO program.*   *(continued)*

Listing 10-1. *continued*

```
    m_bmRiseBoyM = new CBitmap;
    ASSERT_VALID(m_bmRiseBoyM);

    // create a bitmap for the background
    m_bmMem = new CBitmap;
    ASSERT_VALID(m_bmMem);
}
```

Getting Ready for Animation

After the GRAFDEMO program has created all the bitmaps it uses, a function named *PrepareAnimation* loads the bitmaps into memory and sets their sizes and screen locations. Listing 10-2 gives the source code for the *PrepareAnimation* function.

```
void CGrafView::PrepareAnimation(CDC* pDC)
{
    // this is the floor that the player starts on
    m_currentFloor = m_startY;

    // player starts walking to the right
    m_moveDir = RIGHT;

    // stepCount controls step animation
    m_stepCount = 3;

    m_fFirstKeyPress = TRUE;

    int retVal = m_bmRtBoy[0]->LoadBitmap(IDB_RTBOY1);
    ASSERT (retVal != 0);
    retVal = m_bmRtBoy[1]->LoadBitmap(IDB_RTBOY2);
    ASSERT (retVal != 0);
    retVal = m_bmRtBoy[2]->LoadBitmap(IDB_RTBOY3);
    ASSERT (retVal != 0);
    retVal = m_bmRtBoy[3]->LoadBitmap(IDB_RTBOY4);
    ASSERT (retVal != 0);
    retVal = m_bmRtBoy[4]->LoadBitmap(IDB_RTBOY5);
    ASSERT (retVal != 0);
    retVal = m_bmRtBoyM[0]->LoadBitmap(IDB_RTBOYM1);
    ASSERT (retVal != 0);

        ⋮
```

Listing 10-2. *The* PrepareAnimation *member function.*

```
retVal = m_bmRiseBoyM->LoadBitmap(IDB_RTUPBOYM1);
ASSERT (retVal != 0);

retVal = m_bmMem->LoadBitmap(IDB_ARCHES);
ASSERT (retVal != 0);

// create a rectangle the size of the player bitmap
m_bmRect.SetRect(0, 0, m_bmWidth, m_bmHeight);

// create a rectangle the size of the zoomed bitmap
m_zoomRect.SetRect(0, 0, m_zoomWidth, m_zoomHeight);

// create a background bitmap the size of the player bitmap
m_bmPlayer.CreateCompatibleBitmap(pDC, m_zoomRect.right,
    m_zoomRect.bottom);

// create some device contexts that are
// compatible with the current device context
m_dcPlayer.CreateCompatibleDC(pDC);
m_dcMask.CreateCompatibleDC(pDC);
m_dcMem.CreateCompatibleDC(pDC);
m_dcBackdrop.CreateCompatibleDC(pDC);
m_dcTemp.CreateCompatibleDC(pDC);

// create a screen-size background bitmap
m_bmBackdrop.CreateCompatibleBitmap(pDC,
    pDC->GetDeviceCaps(HORZRES),
    pDC->GetDeviceCaps(VERTRES));

// select bitmaps into current device context,
// and save previous bitmaps
m_pOldMapMem = m_dcMem.SelectObject(m_bmMem);
m_dcBackdrop.SelectObject(&m_bmBackdrop);
}
```

The sprite and the mask are loaded into memory as bitmaps that measure 32 pixels wide by 32 pixels high—the standard size for an icon. Later in the program, the *StretchBlt* function increases the player bitmap size to 64 by 64 pixels when the figure is drawn to the screen.

The GRAFDEMO Program's *OnDraw* Function

Each time the GRAFDEMO program's main window needs to be drawn, the framework calls the *CGrafView::OnDraw* member function to draw the program's background and sprite to the screen. To draw the background,

OnDraw calls a *CGrafView* member function named *DrawBackdrop*. To draw the player, *OnDraw* calls a member function named *DrawPlayer*, as shown in Listing 10-3.

```
void CGrafView::OnDraw(CDC* pDC)
{
    CGrafDoc* pDoc = GetDocument();

    // TODO: add draw code here
    if (m_needsRedraw) {

        // paint background DIB to the screen
        DrawBackdrop(pDC);

        // copy player bitmap from memory to screen
        DrawPlayer(pDC);

        // reset redraw flag
        m_needsRedraw = FALSE;
    }
}
```

Listing 10-3. *The* OnDraw *member function.*

Drawing a Background

The *DrawBackdrop* function uses the *BitBlt* function to draw its view window's background, as shown in Listing 10-4.

```
// paint bitmap to screen
void CGrafView::DrawBackdrop(CDC* pDC)
{
    if (m_needsRedraw) {
        int screenWidth = pDC->GetDeviceCaps(HORZRES);
        int screenHeight = pDC->GetDeviceCaps(VERTRES);

        pDC->BitBlt(0, 0, screenWidth, screenHeight, &m_dcMem,
            0, 0, SRCCOPY);
        m_needsRedraw = FALSE;
    }
}
```

Listing 10-4. *Drawing a background with the* BitBlt *function.*

Drawing a Player

The GRAFDEMO program's *DrawPlayer* member function draws a figure to the screen, as shown in Listing 10-5.

```
void CGrafView::DrawPlayer(CDC* pDC)
{
    CRect rect, winRect, updateRect, tempRect;
    CBitmap* pOldMapMem;

    // m_stepCount controls the step animation
    if (m_stepCount == 4)
        m_stepCount = 0;
    else m_stepCount++;

    // select bitmaps into current device context,
    // and save previous bitmaps

    switch (m_moveDir) {
        case LEFT: {
            m_pOldMapZ =
                m_dcPlayer.SelectObject(m_bmLfBoy[m_stepCount]);
            m_pOldMapMask =
                m_dcMask.SelectObject(m_bmLfBoyM[m_stepCount]);
            break;
        }
        case RIGHT: {
            m_pOldMapZ =
                m_dcPlayer.SelectObject(m_bmRtBoy[m_stepCount]);
            m_pOldMapMask =
                m_dcMask.SelectObject(m_bmRtBoyM[m_stepCount]);
            break;
        }
        case UP: {
            m_pOldMapZ =
                m_dcPlayer.SelectObject(m_bmRiseBoy);
            m_pOldMapMask =
                m_dcMask.SelectObject(m_bmRiseBoyM);
            break;
        }
        case DOWN: {
            m_pOldMapZ =
                m_dcPlayer.SelectObject(m_bmRtBoy[4]);
            m_pOldMapMask =
                m_dcMask.SelectObject(m_bmRtBoyM[4]);
            break;
        }
    }

    // m_bmPlayer is the player-size bitmap defined earlier
    pOldMapMem = m_dcTemp.SelectObject(&m_bmPlayer);
```

Listing 10-5. *Functions for drawing a player.* *(continued)*

Listing 10-5. *continued*

```
// Set smallest clipping rect. (m_invalidRect is
// player's old bounding rectangle + player's
// new bounding rectangle. It was set by the
// functions MoveLeft, MoveRight, MoveUp, and MoveDown.)

pDC->IntersectClipRect(&m_invalidRect);

// copy portion of background to m_dcTemp, inverting colors
m_dcTemp.BitBlt(0, 0,
    m_zoomRect.right, m_zoomRect.bottom, &m_dcMem,
    m_invalidRect.left, m_invalidRect.top,
    NOTSRCCOPY);

// draw mask to m_dcTemp
m_dcTemp.StretchBlt(0, 0,
    m_zoomRect.right, m_zoomRect.bottom, &m_dcMask,
    0, 0, m_bmRect.right, m_bmRect.bottom,
    SRCAND);

// draw player to m_dcTemp, and invert destination
m_dcTemp.StretchBlt(0, 0,
    m_zoomRect.right, m_zoomRect.bottom, &m_dcPlayer,
    0, 0, m_bmRect.right, m_bmRect.bottom,
    SRCINVERT);

// copy the changed portion of m_dcTemp to screen
pDC->BitBlt(m_invalidRect.left, m_invalidRect.top,
    m_invalidRect.right, m_invalidRect.bottom, &m_dcTemp,
    0, 0, SRCCOPY);

if (m_fFirstKeyPress == TRUE) {
    m_needsRedraw = FALSE;
    m_fFirstKeyPress = FALSE;
}

// restore m_dcTemp to its previous use
m_dcTemp.SelectObject(pOldMapMem);
}
```

Moving a Sprite

The GRAFDEMO program executes a member function named *MoveLeft*
when the user presses the Left arrow key and executes a member function
named *MoveRight* when the user presses the Right arrow key. For up and
down movement, functions named *MoveUp* and *MoveDown* are provided

In the GRAFDEMO program, a balloon lifts the character sprite from floor to floor when the user presses the Up arrow key.

Listing 10-6 shows the source code for the *MoveLeft* and *MoveRight* functions used in the GRAFDEMO program.

```
void CGrafView::MoveLeft(CRect clientRect)
{
    // TODO: add your command-handler code here
    CRect oldRect, newRect, tempRect;

    m_moveDir = LEFT;

    // don't allow player to walk off the left edge
    if (m_startX <= 0) {
        m_startX = 0;
        return;
    }

    oldRect.SetRect(m_startX, m_startY, m_startX + m_zoomWidth,
        m_startY + m_zoomHeight);

    // move player 1 pixel to the left
    m_startX--;

    newRect.SetRect(m_startX, m_startY,
        m_startX + m_zoomWidth - 2, m_startY + m_zoomHeight);

    // invalidate changed area
    tempRect.UnionRect(oldRect, newRect);
    m_invalidRect.IntersectRect(tempRect, clientRect);
    InvalidateRect(m_invalidRect, FALSE);

    if (m_fFirstKeyPress == TRUE) {
        m_needsRedraw = FALSE;
        m_fFirstKeyPress = FALSE;
    }

    // now draw the player, and update the window
    DrawPlayer(GetDC());
    UpdateWindow();
}
```

Listing 10-6. *The MoveLeft and MoveRight member functions.*   *(continued)*

Listing 10-6. *continued*

```
void CGrafView::MoveRight(CRect clientRect)
{
    // TODO: add your command-handler code here
    CRect oldRect, newRect, tempRect;
    int rightCoord = m_startX + m_zoomWidth;
    int bottomCoord = m_startY + m_zoomHeight;

    // don't allow the player to walk off the right edge
    if (m_startX >= 576) {
        m_startX = 576;
        return;
    }
    m_moveDir = RIGHT;

    // oldRect is the player's current bounding rectangle
    oldRect.SetRect(m_startX, m_startY, rightCoord, bottomCoord);

    // move player 1 pixel to the right
    m_startX++;
    rightCoord++;

    // newRect is the player's bounding rectangle after moving
    newRect.SetRect(m_startX, m_startY, rightCoord, bottomCoord);

    // invalidate entire changed area (oldRect + newRect)
    tempRect.UnionRect(oldRect, newRect);
    m_invalidRect.IntersectRect(tempRect, clientRect);
    InvalidateRect(m_invalidRect, FALSE);

    // keeps action smooth the first time a key is pressed
    if (m_fFirstKeyPress == TRUE) {
        m_needsRedraw = FALSE;
        m_fFirstKeyPress = FALSE;
    }

    // now draw the player, and update the window
    DrawPlayer(GetDC());
    UpdateWindow();
}
```

Calculating Bounding Rectangles

In the *MoveLeft* and *MoveRight* member functions, rectangles surrounding the old and new locations of the animated character sprite are combined in a single bounding rectangle named *m_invalidRect*. The Windows function *InvalidateRect* is called to invalidate this rectangle. In Windows-based programs, invalidating a rectangle in a window causes that rectangle to be redrawn the next time the window is updated.

When the *InvalidateRect* function returns, a drawing sequence named *DrawPlayer* is called to redraw the portion of the screen that needs to be updated. The *DrawPlayer* function uses the *m_invalidateRect* rectangle to ensure that it redraws only the portion of the screen that contains changes.

To keep the animation flicker-free, *DrawPlayer* performs its drawing operations in memory and then copies the redrawn areas to the screen. That prevents the flickering and flashing that can take place when screen refreshes occur during drawing operations.

Each time the *DrawPlayer* function redraws the animated sprite, *DrawPlayer* calls the *BitBlt* and *StretchBlt* member functions to remove the sprite from its background, advance the sprite to its next position, and redraw the sprite in its new location transparently, using the sprite and mask bitmap-copying operations described earlier.

Device-Independent Bitmaps (DIBs)

The most significant difference between a DIB and an ordinary DDB is that a DIB has a built-in color table that can be used to display the DIB using exactly the same colors that were used to create it, no matter what kind of output device was used in designing the original DIB.

Another useful characteristic of DIBs is that every DIB comes with a built-in set of data structures that contain vital information about the DIB, including its size, the number of colors it can use, and its color resolution. When you load a DIB from a disk or use a DIB in an application, you can easily get your hands on all the important details you might need in order to perform various kinds of bitmap operations.

Still another advantage of using DIBs is that a number of very fast bitmap-copying procedures have become available over the past few years. Some of these operations are provided in the Windows Software Development Kit (SDK), and others have been made available in other SDKs and from other sources. But they all have one thing in common: they can be used only with DIBs, not with traditional DDBs.

How DIBs Speed Copying Operations

One reason that DIB-copying operations can be supercharged to such high speeds is that the DIB construct gives applications direct access to the actual image bits used to display DIBs. In contrast, when you use a DDB in an application, Windows does not give you direct access to the bitmap's image bits. That means that you cannot directly copy the image bits used in a DDB from one memory location to another. Instead, when you want to copy a DDB, you must call *BitBlt* or *StretchBlt* and let the Windows API or the MFC framework do your copying for you.

When you want to copy a DIB from one part of memory to another, you do not face this restriction. Instead of using *BitBlt* and *StretchBlt*, which are versatile but somewhat slow, you can simply call a function that can copy a block of memory from one place to another and use that function to copy your bitmap image.

While you're at it, you can write a bitmap-copying operation that does not copy pixels of a specified color, and you can use that operation to perform transparent sprite-copying operations without using masks. That can cut the time required by your program's sprite-copying operations in half because you won't have to copy a mask every time you want to copy a sprite. And if you need still more speed, you can even get out the old assembler and write your bitmap-copying operation using assembly language.

The fast bitmap-copying operations that are available for DIBs include the *StretchDIBits* function now provided in the Windows API; the *WinGBitBlt* and *WinGStretchBlt* functions, two DIB-copying procedures that Microsoft supplies in a game-oriented software development kit called WinG; and various assembly language copying routines—one of which is available in the WinG package—for performing transparent bitmap-copying operations.

Disadvantages of Using DIBs

Unfortunately, there are also some disadvantages of using DIBs instead of DDBs in your application. One shortcoming of DIBs is that they are not encapsulated in an MFC library class. When you want to use a DIB in an application, you must either implement it with raw Windows API calls or use some kind of homemade, non-MFC DIB class.

This chapter demonstrates the use of DIBs using a homemade *CObject*-derived class named *MDib*. The *MDib* class is not complex because the functionality of the sample application that uses it, DIBDEMO, is limited.

Listing 10-7 shows the definition of the *MDib* class that is used to create the DIB used in the DIBDEMO program. You can find the code shown in Listing 10-7 in the MDIB.H file on the companion CD-ROM.

MDIB.H

```
#ifndef _INC_MDIB
#define _INC_MDIB

// DIB constants
#define PALVERSION  0x300

// DIB Macros
#define IS_WIN30_DIB(lpbi) ((*(LPDWORD)(lpbi)) == sizeof(BITMAPINFOHEADER))
#define RECTWIDTH(lpRect) ((lpRect)->right - (lpRect)->left)
#define RECTHEIGHT(lpRect) ((lpRect)->bottom - (lpRect)->top)
#define DIB_HEADER_MARKER ((WORD) ('M' << 8) | 'B')
#define WIDTHBYTES(bits) (((bits) + 31) / 32 * 4)

// declare handle to a DIB
DECLARE_HANDLE(HDIB);

class MDIB : public CObject
{
public:
    HDIB m_hDIB;
private:
    CPalette *m_pPalette;
    HPALETTE m_hPalette;
    HPALETTE m_hOldPal;
    HPALETTE m_hPal;        // this DIB's palette
    UINT m_cScanLines;
    LPSTR m_lpBits;
    LPBITMAPINFO m_lpBitsInfo;
    DWORD m_DIBWidth;
    DWORD m_DIBHeight;
public:
    MDIB() {}
    ~MDIB() {}

    // inline member functions
    UINT GetNrScanLines() { return m_cScanLines; }
    LPSTR GetPVBits() { return m_lpBits; }
    LPBITMAPINFO GetBitsInfo() { return m_lpBitsInfo; }
```

Listing 10-7. *Definition of the* MDib *class.*   *(continued)*

Listing 10-7. *continued*

```
        DWORD GetDIBWidth() { return m_DIBWidth; }
        DWORD GetDIBHeight() { return m_DIBHeight; }

        // noninline member functions
        BOOL SetDIBInfo();
        BOOL GetDIBInfo(UINT *pScanLines, LPSTR lpBits,
            LPBITMAPINFO lpBitsInfo, DWORD *pWidth,
            DWORD *pHeight);
        BOOL PaintDIB (HDC, LPRECT, HDIB, LPRECT, CPalette* pPal,
            DWORD copyMode);
        BOOL CreateDIBPalette(HDIB hDIB, CPalette* cPal);
        LPSTR FindDIBBits (LPSTR lpbi);
        DWORD DIBWidth (LPSTR lpDIB);
        DWORD DIBHeight (LPSTR lpDIB);
        WORD PaletteSize (LPSTR lpbi);
        WORD DIBNumColors (LPSTR lpbi);
        HDIB ReadDIBFile(CFile& file);
};

#endif // _INC_MDIB
```

DIB Architecture

A DIB can be divided into four parts, and two of those parts (the *BITMAP-INFOHEADER* structure and the color table) can be combined to form a fifth part, the *BITMAPINFO* structure. Figure 10-10 shows the structure of a device-independent bitmap.

The *BITMAPFILEHEADER* structure in a DIB file contains information about the bitmap file itself, and the *BITMAPINFO* structure contains information about the DIB. The color table consists of either an array of *RGBQUAD* structures (containing color combinations composed of varying intensities of red, green, and blue) or an array of colors (each associated with a specific index) called a *color palette*.

The biggest section of memory in a DIB file is usually the image bits section. This section contains a block of pixels stored in memory as an array of bytes. The pixels in a DIB's image bits array are laid out in exactly the same way the DIB's pixels will be laid out when the DIB is displayed in a window. The bigger a bitmap is, the larger its image bits section.

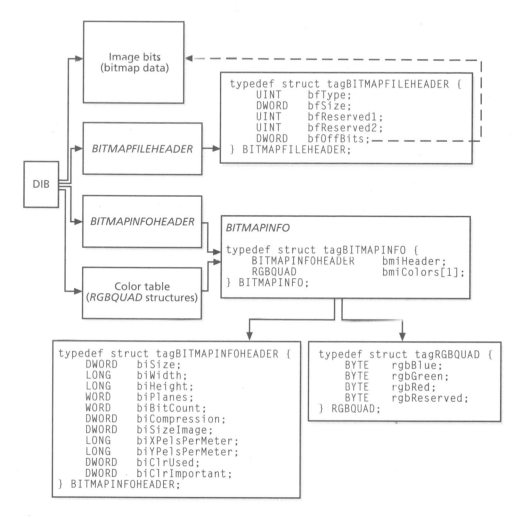

Figure 10-10. *Structure of a DIB.*

Varieties of color tables

DIB files can use two varieties of color tables. After you have created a DIB, you can call a Windows API function named *SetDIBits* to specify what kind of color table you want your DIB to use.

One kind of DIB color table is implemented as an array of 16-bit indexes into a specified color palette. A color palette, often called simply a palette, is a block of memory that provides a DIB's color table with a set of colors.

These colors can come from a palette used by another DIB, or they can come from the system palette—that is, a palette containing colors supported by the computer system that is currently being used. (For more information about how DIBs use palettes, see the section "Palettes" on page 407.)

The other kind of DIB color table contains a set of literal RGB color variables, or *RGBQUAD* structures. When a DIB uses this kind of color table, it doesn't obtain colors from a particular palette but generates its own color set using varying intensities of red, green, and blue.

Splitting a DIB file

One important feature of a DIB file is that its header section can be split from its image bits section. In Figure 10-10 on the preceding page, notice that the image bits block is separate from the three header blocks that make up the rest of the DIB. Also notice that the *bfOffBits* field in the *BITMAPFILEHEADER* structure is connected to the image bits section by a dotted arrow. That's because the *BITMAPFILEHEADER bfOffBits* field is an offset to the image bits section. When you use a DIB in an application, you can always determine where its image bits begin by accessing the *bfOffBits* field.

When you create a DIB, you can physically join its header section to its image bits section if you want, but you don't have to. All you must do is be sure that the offset to the image bits section in your DIB is specified in the *bfOffBits* field of your DIB's *BITMAPFILEHEADER* structure.

The *BITMAPFILEHEADER* structure

As Figure 10-10 illustrates, a DIB file begins with a *BITMAPFILEHEADER* structure that contains information about the DIB file itself, such as the type, size, and layout of the file. Table 10-2 lists the fields contained in a *BITMAPFILEHEADER* structure.

Field	Description
bfType	Specifies the type of file. The entry in this field must be *BM*, or 0x424d in hexadecimal notation. Before you load a DIB file into memory, your application can check this field to see whether the file being loaded is a DIB file.

Table 10-2. *The* BITMAPFILEHEADER *structure.*

Field	Description
bfSize	Specifies the size of the file (not the bitmap) in bytes. The total size of a DIB is the size of the DIB file minus the size of the file header.
bfReserved1	Reserved for future use; must be set to 0.
bfReserved2	Reserved for future use; must be set to 0.
bfOffBits	Specifies the offset, in bytes, from the beginning of the *BITMAPFILEHEADER* structure to the beginning of actual bitmap data in the file. As shown in Figure 10-10, this offset refers to the image bits section.

Finding a DIB's image bits

As mentioned, the *bfOffBits* field contains an offset that you can use to locate the image bits in your DIB. The easiest way to keep track of where a DIB's image bits begin is to ignore the fact that a DIB can be split into two parts and store the DIB's image bits immediately following the color table. Then you can calculate the start of your DIB's bitmap data by calculating the difference between the DIB's starting address and the starting address of the DIB's bitmap data. The DIBDEMO program uses a pair of member functions named *GetDIBInfo* and *SetDIBInfo* to get and set a number of important DIB attributes, including the starting address of a DIB's bitmap data. The *SetDIBInfo* member function is implemented as follows in the MDIB.CPP file:

```
BOOL MDIB::SetDIBInfo()
{
    if (m_hDIB == NULL)
        return FALSE;
    LPSTR lpDIBHdr;        // pointer to BITMAPINFOHEADER
    LPSTR lpDIBBits;       // pointer to DIB bits

    lpDIBHdr = (LPSTR) ::GlobalLock((HGLOBAL) m_hDIB);
    lpDIBBits = FindDIBBits(lpDIBHdr);

    m_cScanLines = (UINT)DIBHeight(lpDIBHdr); // number of scan lines
    m_lpBits = lpDIBBits;                      // bit array address
    m_lpBitsInfo = (LPBITMAPINFO) lpDIBHdr;    // BITMAPINFO address
```

(continued)

```
    m_DIBWidth = DIBWidth(lpDIBHdr);
    m_DIBHeight = DIBHeight(lpDIBHdr);

    ::GlobalUnlock((HGLOBAL) m_hDIB);

    return TRUE;
}
```

Upside-Down DIBs

One odd feature of DIB architecture is that the scan lines in the bit array are arranged upside down with respect to the address of each bit in the DIB file—that is, the bits that make up the last scan line in the file appear first in the bit array, and the bits that make up the first scan line appear last. This curious setup requires some thought and can sometimes lead to surprises when you manipulate bits in your code.

Figure 10-11 shows the upside-down (relative to standard bitmaps) structure of a DIB.

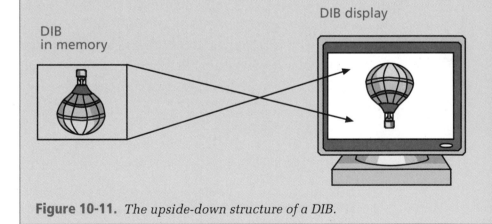

Figure 10-11. *The upside-down structure of a DIB.*

Calculating the size of a DIB's color table

As shown in Figure 10-10 on page 401, a DIB color table is made up of an array of *RGBQUAD* structures. An *RGBQUAD* structure is a simple *struct* made up of 3 bytes plus a 1-byte reserved field. Each of the 3 defined bytes in an *RGBQUAD* structure stores a value ranging from 0 through 255. The first byte holds an intensity value for the color red, the second byte holds an intensity value for green, and the third byte holds an intensity value for blue. Together, these 3 bytes can describe 256^3—or 16,777,216—individual colors. You can get or set the values of all 3 bytes in an *RGBQUAD* structure in a single step by invoking the Windows macro *RGB(rgbBlue, rgbGreen, rgbRed)*.

The length of a DIB's *RGBQUAD* array can vary because DIBs with different color resolutions have color tables of different sizes. The more colors a DIB is capable of displaying, the larger its color table is.

For more information about the *RGBQUAD* array in a DIB's *BITMAPFILEHEADER* structure, see the section "The *RGBQUAD* array" on page 407.

The *BITMAPINFOHEADER* structure

The *BITMAPINFOHEADER* structure in a DIB file contains a wealth of information about the DIB, including the size, width, and height of the DIB; the number of colors used in the DIB; and the size of the DIB's image bits array. Table 10-3 lists the fields that make up the *BITMAPINFOHEADER* structure.

Field	Description
biSize	Specifies the number of bytes required by the *BITMAPINFOHEADER* structure.
biWidth	Specifies the width of the bitmap, in pixels.
biHeight	Specifies the height of the bitmap, in pixels.
biPlanes	Specifies the number of planes for the target device. This value must be set to 1.
biBitCount	Specifies the number of bits per pixel. This value must be 1, 4, 8, or 24.
biCompression	Specifies the type of compression used for a compressed bitmap. For details, see the *BITMAPINFOHEADER* entry in the Windows SDK section of the online help.

Table 10-3. *The* BITMAPINFOHEADER *structure.* *(continued)*

Table 10-3. *continued*

Field	Description
biSizeImage	Specifies the size, in bytes, of the image. You can set this value to 0 if the bitmap is in the *BI_RGB* format.
biXPelsPerMeter	Specifies the horizontal resolution, in pixels per meter, of the target device for the bitmap. An application can use this value to select from a resource group a bitmap that best matches the characteristics of the current device.
biYPelsPerMeter	Specifies the vertical resolution, in pixels per meter, of the target device for the bitmap.
biClrUsed	Specifies the number of color indexes in the color table actually used by the bitmap. If this value is 0, the bitmap uses the maximum number of colors corresponding to the value of the *biBitCount* field. If the *biClrUsed* value is nonzero and the value of the *biBitCount* field is less than 24, *biClrUsed* specifies the actual number of colors that the current graphics device driver will access. If the *biClrUsed* value is nonzero and the value of the *biBitCount* field is 24, *biClrUsed* specifies the size of a color index table that is used to optimize performance of Windows color palettes. (Windows palettes are examined in detail in the section "Palettes" on the facing page.)
biClrImportant	Specifies the number of color indexes that are considered necessary for displaying the bitmap. If this value is 0, all colors are used.

The *BITMAPINFO* structure

A *BITMAPINFO* structure is not a separate entity; it's merely a structure that combines the information in a DIB's *BITMAPINFOHEADER* structure with all the color information that's stored in the DIB's color table.

The purpose of the *BITMAPINFO* structure is to provide a convenient way of handling all the information in a DIB's *BITMAPINFOHEADER* structure and all the color data in its color table without having to calculate the length of the color table every time you need to access it.

N OTE   Because the *BITMAPINFOHEADER* structure used by a DIB has the same starting address as the DIB's *BITMAPINFO* structure, some applications use the same pointer variable to access this address. Some applications use a void pointer for this purpose; others perform whatever kinds of casting operations are necessary to access the desired structure. These kinds of practices result in obscure code and are not recommended.

The *RGBQUAD* array

An *RGBQUAD* array is stored in memory as an array of color indexes. It describes a color in terms of relative intensities of red, green, and blue. Each color index in an *RGBQUAD* array maps to a specific pixel in the bounding rectangle that encloses the bitmap. The size of the array, expressed in bits, is equivalent to the width of this rectangle (expressed in pixels) times its height (also expressed in pixels) times the number of color bits associated with the current display device.

Here is the Windows *typedef* function that defines an *RGBQUAD* structure:

```
typedef struct tagRGBQUAD {
    BYTE rgbBlue;
    BYTE rgbGreen;
    BYTE rgbRed;
    BYTE rgbReserved;
} RGBQUAD;
```

In an *RGBQUAD* structure, the *rgbRed*, *rgbGreen*, and *rgbBlue* bytes specify the intensities of the red, green, and blue colors in each pixel of the DIB being displayed.

Palettes

As mentioned, the colors used by a DIB are determined by an array of color codes called a color palette. The five kinds of palettes that determine the colors used by Windows-based applications are listed on the following page.

- **Hardware palette**—Color lookup table that is built into a video display card. When you use a palette-based display adapter (which is what most video cards are) and specify the *DIB_PAL_COLORS* display mode in your application, the pixels you see on the screen are indexes to the colors that have been placed in your video card's hardware palette.

- **System palette**—Copy of the hardware palette maintained by the Palette Manager, a system utility used by the Windows operating system to set the colors of the system palette and make them available to Windows-based programs. The system palette provides all the colors that can appear on a particular output device at a particular time. Because the number of colors that a video system can display at one time is limited, the system palette is designed to hold a maximum of 256 colors.

NOTE The term "system palette" can be confusing because it is sometimes used instead of the term "hardware palette" to refer to the hardware palette provided by the system's video display hardware.

- **Logical palette**—Palette object created by an application. A logical palette is implemented as an array of colors that an application can use for drawing graphics using a particular device context. When an application has created a logical palette, it can pass those colors to the Palette Manager for use in the system palette.

- **Default logical palette**—*DEFAULT_PALETTE* stock object provided by the GDI (graphics device interface). The default logical palette contains the VGA colors and is used for supporting applications that do not explicitly use palettes.

- **Identity palettes**—Logical palette that contains a set of colors laid out in exactly the same order as the colors in the system palette. By setting up an identity palette, an application can avoid time-consuming index lookups, significantly decreasing processing time.

The System Palette

The system palette is divided into two parts: one for 20 colors that are fixed, or *static,* and one for a collection of colors that applications can modify.

The total number of colors provided by the system palette can vary, depending on the kind of display device being used. However, every system palette has exactly 20 static colors that applications cannot change. Applications can set the remaining colors in the system palette using the Palette Manager.

Sixteen of the 20 static colors in the system palette correspond to the 16 colors used by a standard VGA display. The other 4 static colors were chosen for their visual appeal and are used by the Windows operating system.

> **NOTE** An application can retrieve the size of a device's system palette by calling the *GetDeviceCaps* function and specifying the *NUMCOLORS* constant as the second parameter. To retrieve the horizontal and vertical resolution of a video display or a printer (expressed in pixels per meter), an application can call *GetDeviceCaps* and specify *HORZSIZE* or *VERTSIZE* as the second parameter.

The Default Logical Palette

For applications that need to use only the standard VGA colors, the Windows operating system maintains a default 16-color system palette called the default logical palette. If you want to use the default logical palette in an application, you can access it by selecting the *DEFAULT_PALETTE* stock object into a device context. Then you can use any of the 16 colors provided without being concerned with color tables.

The Window Manager component of the Windows operating system is an example of an application that uses the default logical palette. It uses the default logical palette's 16 static colors to draw window borders and other standard Windows objects.

The Logical Palette

To set up a system palette that can be used to display the colors in a particular DIB, an application must use the colors in the DIB's color table to set up a private palette called a logical palette. The application can then pass these colors to the Palette Manager for incorporation into the system palette.

To create a logical palette, an application must call a Windows API function named *CreatePalette*. Then the application must select the palette into a device context by calling the Windows API *SelectPalette* function. (The *SelectObject* function does not work with palettes.) When all this has been done, the application can call a Windows API function named *RealizePalette* to transfer the colors in its logical palette to the system palette. Only then can the colors specified by the application be used to create screen displays.

Here is the *CreatePalette* function:

```
HPALETTE CreatePalette(const LOGPALETTE FAR* lplgpl);
```

The *lplgpl* argument points to a *LOGPALETTE* structure that contains information about the colors in the logical palette being created.

The *SelectPalette* function is shown here:

```
HPALETTE SelectPalette(HDC hdc, HPALETTE hpal, BOOL fPalBak);
```

In a call to *SelectPalette*, the *hdc* parameter is a handle to the device context into which the logical palette is to be selected, and the *hpal* parameter is a handle to the logical palette. The *fPalBak* parameter specifies whether the palette is a background palette. When a window is associated with a background palette, the setting of the *fPalBak* flag determines whether the window's palette becomes a foreground palette when the window gains the input focus.

The *RealizePalette* function is shown here:

```
UINT RealizePalette(HDC hdc);
```

The *hdc* parameter is the handle of the palette being realized.

The *SelectPalette* and *RealizePalette* functions are usually called in succession, as in the following example:

```
SelectPalette(hDC, hBluePal, FALSE);
RealizePalette(hDC);
```

Figure 10-12 shows the process of obtaining a logical palette for a DIB from the Palette Manager.

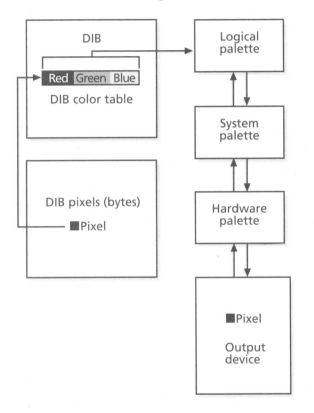

Figure 10-12. *Obtaining a logical palette.*

NOTE Palette objects follow most of the same rules as other graphics objects. They should be deleted when no longer needed by using the *DeleteObject* function, and they must be deselected from all DCs before being deleted (by using *SelectPalette* to select a different palette into the DC). One notable difference is that an application can select a palette object into more than one DC (belonging to a single device) at a time, but the mapping of palette entries from the current logical palette to the system palette remains constant for all of the DCs.

> ### Using Palettes in Multiple Windows
>
> When multiple windows are displayed on the screen, the active, or topmost, window has the highest priority in obtaining the colors it needs for its display from the Palette Manager. If the topmost window does not use all available nonstatic colors to create its display, any colors it does not need can be claimed by the other windows on the screen. Those other windows are sometimes referred to as *background windows.*
>
> If the topmost window has laid claim to all nonstatic colors in the system palette, none of the background windows can set any system palette colors to suit their own requirements. Instead, they must choose the nearest color they can find from the nonstatic colors that the topmost window has placed in its logical palette.
>
> When multiple windows request colors from the Palette Manager, the Palette Manager considers each window's request using a priority based on the order in which the windows were active, with the most recently active window receiving the highest priority. As the requests of various windows are granted, the number of colors available from the system palette decreases. When all nonstatic colors have been used, any remaining windows must settle for using colors that have already been used by higher-priority windows or, in a worst-case scenario, using the 20 static colors.

How the DIBDEMO Program Uses Palettes

In the DIBDEMO application, both *RealizePalette* and *SelectPalette* are called to display the colors in the background DIB's color array. Both these procedures are called from a member function named *CDIBDemoView::OnDoRealize*. The *OnDoRealize* member function is called whenever a window is activated.

Before either *RealizePalette* or *SelectPalette* is called, the *OnDoRealize* member function retrieves a pointer to the background DIB's palette by executing the following statement:

```
m_pBkgPal = pDoc->GetDocPalette();
```

This statement stores a pointer to the background DIB's palette in a variable named *m_pBkgPal*. Then the *OnDoRealize* function executes the following statement:

```
CClientDC appDC(pAppFrame);
```

This statement constructs an object of an MFC library class named *CClientDC*, which is a subclass of *CDC*. A *CClientDC* object is a special kind of *CDC* object that is associated with the client area of a window. It takes care of calling *GetDC* when a window object is constructed and calling *ReleaseDC* when the window is destroyed.

In the preceding statement, a *CClientDC* object named *appDC* is created and associated with a window referred to as *pAppFrame*. This window is defined earlier in the *OnDoRealize* function as the application's main frame window.

When the *CClientDC* object *appDC* has been constructed, the following statement is executed:

```
m_pBkgOldPal = appDC.SelectPalette(m_pBkgPal,
    ((HWND)wParam) != m_hWnd);
```

It selects the *m_pBkgPal* palette—that is, the background DIB's palette—into the application's main frame window. This makes the background DIB's palette the default palette for the DIBDEMO program.

Mapping System Palette Colors to a Logical Palette

When a window displayed by an application is on the desktop, the application can map the colors in the system palette to a logical palette by calling the Windows function *RealizePalette*. Then the colors in the logical palette are displayed.

The *AnimatePalette* member function can be useful when you want an application to display a window and a set of new colors simultaneously. When you want to delay the display of a new set of colors until a particular window opens, you can call *SetPaletteEntries* to set up your new colors and then call *RealizePalette* when the window associated with those colors becomes active.

Creating and Using Logical Palettes

When an application has created and realized a logical palette that matches a DIB's color table, the application can call the *StretchDIBits* function to copy the DIB to the screen using the appropriate colors. When an application calls *StretchDIBits*, Windows performs the requested DIB-copying operation using the process shown in Figure 10-13.

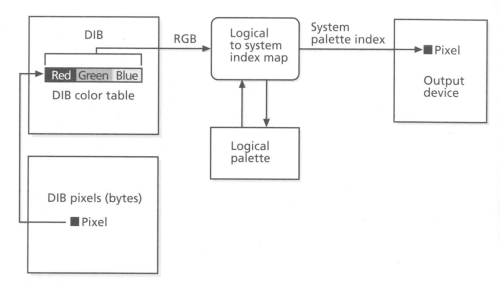

Figure 10-13. *DIB-copying operation resulting from a call* to StretchDIBits.

The DIB-copying operation shown in Figure 10-13 is a roundabout operation that requires a lot of index lookups and consumes a considerable amount of processing time. Every time an application calls *StretchDIBits*, Windows retrieves a color value for each pixel in the DIB and converts that color to an RGB value by looking it up in the DIB's color table. When the system has obtained the RGB value of each pixel from the DIB's color table, it tries to match that color to a color that is defined in the currently selected logical palette. Each logical palette index value the system finds is then translated to an index into the system palette index values. The resulting system palette index value is then passed to the device driver that handles the current output device so that the pixel that has been looked up can be written to the display video memory.

Every time an application calls *StretchDIBits* to copy a DIB to the screen, the system performs this entire operation on every pixel in the DIB.

Streamlining DIB Copying with Identity Palettes

There's got to be a better way. Fortunately, there is: dispensing with the logical-to-system index translation table and letting the system write all the necessary DIB pixel values directly to video memory.

The secret formula for this shortcut is simple: all that is required is that the logical and system palettes being used are identical. In other words, what is needed is an *identity palette.*

An identity palette is a logical palette that contains a set of colors laid out in exactly the same order as the colors in the system palette. By setting up an identity palette, an application can avoid time-consuming index look-ups, significantly decreasing processing time.

Creating an Identity Palette

The best way to create an identity palette is to create a logical palette for the entire color table of the DIB you want to copy and then select that logical palette into the screen DC and realize it. Windows then takes your set of colors and maps them or inserts them into the system palette as it sees fit. This process requires a bit of fancy color-shuffling, but it's worth it because in the long run it speeds up your application's DIB-copying operations considerably.

To perform the color-shuffling that the process depends on, follow these steps:

1. Create a logical palette.

2. Call the Windows API function *GetSystemPaletteEntries* to obtain all system color codes from the system palette.

3. Use these values to define your logical palette by calling the Windows API function *SetPaletteEntries*. If your call to *SetPalette-Entries* is successful, your new logical palette exactly matches the system palette when the call returns. But there is one problem: the

colors in the DIB that you're copying are now all shuffled around because the DIB's pixel values no longer index the correct colors in the logical palette.

4. To repair this damage, for each color in your DIB's color table, call the Windows function *GetNearestPaletteIndex*. This function finds an entry in your new logical palette that matches (or is at least close to) the color in your DIB's color table.

5. Use this information to create a translation table for the DIB pixel values.

6. For each pixel in your DIB, look up the new index value of each pixel in your translation table and write it back to your DIB. If this operation is successful, your DIB's pixels now map correctly to your logical palette. The only possible problem at this point is that some color information might be lost if the original logical palette does not map well to the system palette—but this is unlikely.

7. Reshuffle your DIB's color table in such a way that it contains exactly the same RGB values as your new logical palette, arranged in exactly the same order. This final step is not really essential unless you want to use the new RGB values in your DIB's header later, and this is not often the case in animation programs. If your DIB never gets saved, you probably don't care whether its color table winds up arranged differently from when you started. But be aware that if you ever want to save your DIB back to its original file, the colors in its color table will have a different arrangement from the one that they had when you first loaded the DIB.

Creating and Using DIBs

One way to create a DIB is to call a Windows API function named *CreateDIBitmap*. You can then call the Windows API function named *SetDIBits* to set the image bits of the DIB you have created and to indicate how you want your DIB to produce its colors. If you set the *SetDIBits* parameter *fuColorUse* to a constant named *DIB_PAL_COLORS*, the Windows API creates a color table that consists of an array of 16-bit indexes into a specified palette. If you set the *fuColorUse* parameter to the constant *DIB_RGB_COLORS*, Windows gives you a color table that contains literal RGB color values.

Another way to create a DIB is to allocate memory for it, load it into memory using ordinary file I/O functions (such as the MFC library's *CFile::Read* function), and then copy its color table, its image bits, and its header information into memory in any way you want.

> **NOTE** Creating DIBs from scratch is a complicated and tricky business, and unless you're planning to write a painting or drawing program, you'll probably never need to do so. In the real world of graphics programming, bitmaps are usually created and saved to disk using commercially available applications such as Adobe Illustrator, Macromedia Freehand, or CorelDRAW. They can then be loaded from disk as needed and used in applications such as animation programs and games.

DIB-Copying Operations

After you have copied a DIB into memory and have stored its image bits in a frame buffer, there are two Windows API functions that you can use to transfer your DIB's image bits to the screen. One of these functions is named *StretchDIBits*, and the other is named *SetDIBitsToDevice*.

The *StretchDIBits* function works much like the DDB-copying function *StretchBlt*. It copies the image bits of a DIB from one memory location to another, optionally resizing the bitmap being copied to fit into its destination area. The *SetDIBitsToDevice* function, despite its odd name, is the DIB equivalent of the *BitBlt* function. It copies a bitmap's image from one memory location to another without resizing.

The *StretchDIBits* Controversy

In early versions of Windows NT, *StretchDIBits* was the fastest and most efficient function to use when you wanted to copy a DIB from one block of memory to another—even when you didn't want to resize your DIB—because it was coded more efficiently than the *SetDIBits-ToDevice* function.

(continued)

The *StretchDIBits* **Controversy.**   *continued*

> To copy a bitmap at a 1-to-1 size ratio with *StretchDIBits*, you need to set the source and destination bitmaps to the same size when you call *StretchDIBits*. The function checks the sizes you have specified to see whether they are the same, and then it performs the most efficient bit-copying operation possible, whether or not scaling is required.
>
> In current versions of Windows 95 and Windows NT, Microsoft engineers reportedly have reworked the *SetDIBitsToDevice* function to make it just as fast as *StretchDIBits*. But some Visual C++ programmers have abandoned the *SetDIBitsToDevice* function because it used to be slow and still use *StretchDIBits* exclusively.

Using the *StretchDIBits* Function

As noted earlier, one advantage of using DIBs is that an application can display them directly, without having to create an intermediate memory bitmap. The *StretchDIBits* and *SetDIBitsToDevice* functions can copy all or part of a DIB directly to the specifications of a particular output device, significantly reducing the memory required to display the bitmap.

The *StretchDIBits* function is shown here:

```
int StretchDIBits(HDC hdc, int XDest, int YDest, int cxDest,
    int cyDest, int XSrc, int YSrc, int cxSrc, int cySrc,
    const void FAR* lpvBits, LPBITMAPINFO lpbmi,
    UINT fuColorUse, DWORD fdwRop)
```

StretchDIBits is a Windows API function, not an MFC member function, so you must pass it a handle to a device context in its *hdc* parameter. This DC handle can be associated with either a screen surface or an area of screen memory that's big enough to hold the destination bitmap.

You must also provide *StretchDIBits* with the usual bitmap-copying parameters, such as the size of the source bitmap, the size of the destination bitmap, and the upper left coordinates of the source and destination bitmaps. To copy a complete bitmap from one memory location to another, you simply pass the coordinates (0, 0) in both parameters.

The *StretchDIBits* function also has an *fdwRop* parameter in which you can specify a raster operation (ROP) code. *StretchDIBits* recognizes the same ROP codes as the *BitBlt* and *StretchBlt* functions. (For details, see Table 10-1 on page 376.)

In addition to the standard bitmap-copying parameters, the *StretchDIBits* function expects three parameters that the *BitBlt* and *StretchBlt* functions do not require, as follows:

- The *lpvBits* parameter, which points to the DIB bits. These bits are stored in memory as an array of bytes.

- The *lpbmi* parameter, which points to a *BITMAPINFO* structure that contains information about the DIB.

- The *fuColorUse* parameter, which specifies whether the DIB's color table (the *bmiColors* member of the *lpbmi* parameter) contains explicit RGB values or indexes into the currently realized logical palette. The *fuColorUse* parameter can have one of two values: a pre-defined constant named *DIB_PAL_COLORS*, or a predefined constant named *DIB_RGB_COLORS*. If you specify *DIB_PAL_COLORS* in the *fuColorUse* parameter, the DIB's color table is implemented as an array of 16-bit indexes into the currently realized logical palette. If you specify *DIB_RGB_COLORS*, the DIB's color table contains literal RGB values.

The syntax of the *SetDIBitsToDevice* function is identical to that of the *StretchDIBits* function, except that it does not require a pair of parameters specifying the size of the destination bitmap. Here is the *SetDIBitsTo-Device* function:

```
int SetDIBitsToDevice(HDC hdc, int XDest, int YDest, int cx,
    int cy,int XSrc, int YSrc, UINT uStartScan, UINT cScanLines,
    void FAR* lpvBits, BITMAPINFO FAR* lpbmi, UINT fuColorUse)
```

Using the *SetDIBitsToDevice* Function

The following example shows how an application can call *SetDIBits-ToDevice*:

```
SetDIBitsToDevice(hdc, 0, 0, lpbi->bmciHeader.bcWidth,
    lpbi->bmciHeader.bcHeight, 0, 0, 0,
    lpbi->bmciHeader.bcHeight,
    pBuf, (BITMAPINFO FAR*) lpbi,
    DIB_RGB_COLORS);
```

The *hdc* parameter identifies the device context of the target output device; *SetDIBitsToDevice* uses this information to identify the screen and determine the correct color format for the device bitmap.

The next two parameters specify the point on the display surface at which *SetDIBitsToDevice* will begin drawing the bitmap—in this case, the origin of the device context itself. The fourth and fifth parameters supply the width and height of the bitmap.

The sixth and seventh parameters specify the first pixel in the source bitmap to be set on the display device—in this case, both are 0, so *SetDIBitsToDevice* begins with the first pixel in the bitmap buffer.

The next two parameters are used to define the number of bands in the bitmap. The *uStartScan* parameter is set to 0, indicating that the beginning scan line should be the first in the buffer; the *cScanLines* parameter is set to the height of the bitmap. As a result, the entire source bitmap will be set on the display surface in a single band.

The image bits are contained in the *pBuf* buffer, and the *lpbi* parameter supplies the *BITMAPINFO* data structure that describes the color format of the source bitmap.

The last parameter is a usage flag that indicates whether the bitmap color table contains actual RGB color values or indexes into the currently realized logical palette—in this case, the *DIB_RGB_COLORS* argument specifies that the color table contains explicit color values.

Example: The DIBDEMO Program

This chapter's second sample program, named DIBDEMO, uses device-independent bitmaps to create an animated screen display. Figure 10-14 shows the window that opens when you run the DIBDEMO program.

The DIBDEMO program uses sprite animation to move a balloon image over a complex background. Both the balloon sprite and the background bitmap are implemented as DIBs. You move the balloon sprite by pressing the arrow keys.

Figure 10-14. *The DIBDEMO program's screen display.*

How the DIBDEMO Program Works

The DIBDEMO program, like the GRAFDEMO program presented earlier in this chapter, is built on a framework generated by AppWizard and uses AppWizard's conventional document-and-view architecture. Most of DIBDEMO's drawing operations take place in the DIBVIEW.CPP and DIB-DOC.CPP files. The DIBVIEW.CPP file implements the program's view object, and the DIBDOC.CPP file implements the program's document object.

The DIBDOC.CPP file contains some of the procedures for loading, initializing, and manipulating DIB files. The rest of the program's DIB-related functions are defined and implemented in a pair of files that define and implement a DIB class. These two files are named MDIB.H and MDIB.CPP.

Loading DIBs into Memory

In a Visual C++ program, you can load conventional DDBs into memory by calling the member function *CBitmap::LoadBitmap*. Loading a DIB into memory takes a little more work: first you must initialize a *BITMAPINFO* structure, and then you must create a file in which you can store the DIB.

Next you must open your DIB file, compute the size of the file, and then copy the file into memory. Last you must close your DIB file.

The DIBDEMO program loads DIBs into memory by executing three functions that are implemented in the program's DIBVIEW.CPP file. A function named *LoadBkgDIB* loads the program's background bitmap, a function named *LoadImage* loads a sprite into memory, and a function named *LoadMaskDIB* loads a bitmap mask used for transparent copying.

Listing 10-8 shows how the *LoadBkgDIB*, *LoadImage*, and *LoadMaskDIB* functions work in the DIBDEMO program.

```
void CDIBDemoView::LoadBkgDIB(CDC *pDC)
{
    CDIBDemoDoc* pDoc = GetDocument();

    // copy background DIB from disk
    BOOL bRetVal = pDoc->LoadBkgDIB(m_pDIBBkg, "res\\space.bmp");
    ASSERT(bRetVal);
    ASSERT_VALID(m_pDIBBkg);

    // set background DIB's attributes
    m_pDIBBkg->SetDIBInfo();

    // get some of those attributes
    m_bkgScanLines = m_pDIBBkg->GetNrScanLines();
    m_lpBkgBits = m_pDIBBkg->GetPVBits();
    m_lpBkgBitsInfo = m_pDIBBkg->GetBitsInfo();
    m_bkgDIBWidth = m_pDIBBkg->GetDIBWidth();
    m_bkgDIBHeight = m_pDIBBkg->GetDIBHeight();
}

void CDIBDemoView::LoadImageDIB(CDC *pDC)
{
    CDIBDemoDoc* pDoc = GetDocument();

    // copy background DIB from disk
    BOOL bRetVal = pDoc->LoadImageDIB(m_pDIBImage,
        "res\\balloons.bmp");
    ASSERT(bRetVal);
    ASSERT_VALID(m_pDIBImage);

    // set background DIB's attributes
    m_pDIBImage->SetDIBInfo()
    // get some of those attributes
    m_imageScanLines = m_pDIBImage->GetNrScanLines();
```

Listing 10-8. *The* LoadBkgDIB, LoadImage, *and* LoadMaskDIB *functions.*

```
    m_lpImageBits = m_pDIBImage->GetPVBits();
    m_lpImageBitsInfo = m_pDIBImage->GetBitsInfo();
    m_imageDIBWidth = m_pDIBImage->GetDIBWidth();
    m_imageDIBHeight = m_pDIBImage->GetDIBHeight();

    m_bmWidth = m_imageDIBWidth;
    m_bmHeight = m_imageDIBHeight;
}

void CDIBDemoView::LoadMaskDIB(CDC *pDC)
{
    CDIBDemoDoc* pDoc = GetDocument();

    // copy background DIB from disk
    BOOL bRetVal = pDoc->LoadMaskDIB(m_pDIBMask,
        "res\\balloonm.bmp");
    ASSERT(bRetVal);
    ASSERT_VALID(m_pDIBMask);

    // set background DIB's attributes
    m_pDIBMask->SetDIBInfo();

    // get some of those attributes
    m_maskScanLines = m_pDIBMask->GetNrScanLines();
    m_lpMaskBits = m_pDIBMask->GetPVBits();
    m_lpMaskBitsInfo = m_pDIBMask->GetBitsInfo();
    m_maskDIBWidth = m_pDIBMask->GetDIBWidth();
    m_maskDIBHeight = m_pDIBMask->GetDIBHeight();
}
```

Each of these three functions loads a DIB by calling another function. The three functions called in Listing 10-8 are implemented in the CDIBDEMO-DOC .CPP files. These three functions are named *CDIBDemoDoc::Load-BkgDIB*, *CDIBDemoDoc::LoadImageDIB*, and *CDIBDemoDoc::LoadMaskDIB*.

Copying and Displaying DIBs

The DIBDEMO program displays DIBs by executing a function named *DrawPlayer*. The *DrawPlayer* function is similar in many ways to the function of the same name used in the GRAFDEMO program. The main difference, as you might guess, is that DIBDEMO moves DIBs to and from memory by calling DIB-related member functions, and it displays them by calling DIB-related functions.

The *StretchDIBits* Member Function

Each time the DIBDEMO program opens a window, it draws a background bitmap by calling the Windows API function *StretchDIBits*. Then it uses a mask-copying operation to draw a figure over the background bitmap. It animates the figure using an animation sequence similar to the one used in the GRAFDEMO program.

In the DIBDEMO program's *DrawPlayer* member function, the *StretchDIBits* function is called several times. For example, in the *CDIBDemoView::DrawBackdrop* member function, the *StretchDIBits* function copies a sprite into another bitmap, reversing the sprite's colors, as shown here:

```
// paint bitmap to screen
void CDIBDemoView::DrawBackdrop(CDC* pDC)
{
    CDIBDemoDoc* pDoc = GetDocument();

    if (m_needsRedraw) {
        int retVal = ::StretchDIBits(pDC->m_hDC,
            0, 0, 640, 480,
            0, 0, (int) m_bkgDIBWidth, (int) m_bkgDIBHeight,
            (const void far*) m_lpBkgBits,
            (LPBITMAPINFO) m_lpBkgBitsInfo,
            DIB_RGB_COLORS, SRCCOPY);
        ASSERT(retVal = m_bkgScanLines);
        m_needsRedraw = FALSE;
    }
}
```

The DIBDEMO program's *DrawPlayer* member function also uses the standard bitmap-copying function *BitBlt*. When a sprite has moved, this *BitBlt* function copies the changed portion of a memory bitmap to the screen.

The DIBDEMO program implements the *DrawPlayer* member function in the file DIBVIEW.CPP, as shown in Listing 10-9.

```
void CDIBDemoView::DrawPlayer(CDC *pDC)
{
    CRect rect, winRect, updateRect, tempRect;
    CBitmap *pOldMapMem;

    CDIBDemoDoc* pDoc = GetDocument();
```

Listing 10-9. *The* DrawPlayer *member function.*

```
// select bitmaps into current device context,
// and save previous bitmaps
m_pOldMapZ = m_dcPlayer.SelectObject(m_bmImage);
m_pOldMapMask = m_dcMask.SelectObject(m_bmMask);
m_pOldMapBkg = m_dcBkg.SelectObject(m_bmBackground);

// m_bmBkg is a player-size bitmap defined earlier
pOldMapMem = m_dcBackdrop.SelectObject(&m_bmBkg);

// set smallest clipping rectangle
pDC->IntersectClipRect(m_invalidRect.left, m_invalidRect.top,
    m_invalidRect.right, m_invalidRect.bottom);

// (1) copy portion of background to m_dcBackdrop
SetDIBitsToDevice(m_dcBackdrop.m_hDC,
    0, 0, m_bigRect.right, m_bigRect.bottom, m_invalidRect.left,
    480 - (m_invalidRect.top) - m_zoomHeight, 0, m_bkgScanLines,
    m_lpBkgBits, m_lpBkgBitsInfo, DIB_RGB_COLORS);

// invert colors in bitmap
m_dcBackdrop.BitBlt(0, 0, m_bigRect.right, m_bigRect.bottom,
    NULL, 0, 0, DSTINVERT);

// (2) draw mask to m_dcBackdrop
StretchDIBits(m_dcBackdrop.m_hDC,
    0, 0, (int) m_bigRect.right, (int) m_bigRect.bottom,
    0, 0, (int) m_maskDIBWidth, (int) m_maskDIBHeight,
    (const void far*) m_lpMaskBits, (LPBITMAPINFO) m_lpMaskBitsInfo,
    DIB_RGB_COLORS, SRCAND);

// (3) draw player to m_dcBackdrop and invert destination
StretchDIBits(m_dcBackdrop.m_hDC,
    0, 0, (int) m_bigRect.right, (int) m_bigRect.bottom,
    0, 0, (int) m_imageDIBWidth, (int) m_imageDIBHeight,
    (const void far*) m_lpImageBits,
    (LPBITMAPINFO) m_lpImageBitsInfo, DIB_RGB_COLORS,
    SRCINVERT);

// (4) copy changed portion of m_dcBackdrop to screen
pDC->BitBlt(m_invalidRect.left, m_invalidRect.top,
    m_invalidRect.right, 480 - (m_invalidRect.top) -
        m_zoomHeight,
    &m_dcBackdrop, 0, 0, SRCCOPY);

// restore m_dcBackdrop to its previous use
m_dcBackdrop.SelectObject(pOldMapMem);
```

(continued)

Listing 10-9. *continued*

```
    // return old bitmaps to current device contexts
    m_dcPlayer.SelectObject(m_pOldMapZ);
    m_dcMask.SelectObject(m_pOldMapMask);
    m_dcBkg.SelectObject(m_pOldMapBkg);
}
```

What's Next?

This completes your quest to learn Visual C++. You haven't learned all there is to know, but if you have absorbed even half of what you have encountered in these chapters, you certainly have a good start.

What's next? That's up to you. Visual C++ 1.0 is a 16-bit programming package that has been vastly improved in many areas since it was introduced in 1994. The newest versions of Visual C++ are 32-bit programming packages with an enormous number of new features, including a new Developer Workshop environment that has replaced Visual Workbench; a Component Gallery, which makes Visual C++ code even more reusable by encapsulating classes and objects into portable components; and OLE controls, which leave the old 16-bit VBX controls in the dust.

If you don't want to rush right out and buy a 32-bit version of Visual C++ just yet, that's fine; you can while away many a rainy afternoon with version 1.0 on the companion CD-ROM. But if you like what you've seen so far and want to move on to something even more challenging and even more fun—well, you know what to do.

Happy programming!

Suggestions for Further Reading

To help you continue your study of Visual C++ and object-oriented programming, here is a list of suggestions for further reading. The titles in the list cover a broad range of topics, including the C and C++ programming languages, game programming, and application development.

Andrews, Mark. *C++ Windows NT Programming*. New York: M & T Books, 1995.

———. *Migrating to Windows 95*. Boston: Academic Press, 1996.

———. *Visual C++ Object-Oriented Programming*. Carmel, Ind.: Sams, 1993.

Atkinson, Lee, Mark Atkinson, and Ed Mitchell: *Using Microsoft C/C++ 7*. Carmel, Ind.: Que, 1992.

Barkakati, Nabajyoti. *Microsoft C/C++ 7 Developer's Guide*. Carmel, Ind.: Sams, 1992.

———. *Object-Oriented Programming in C++*. Carmel, Ind.: Sams, 1989.

Booch, Grady. *Object Oriented Design*. Redwood City, Calif.: Benjamin/ Cummings, 1991.

Christian, Kaare. *The Microsoft Guide to C++ Programming*. Redmond, Wash.: Microsoft Press, 1992.

Custer, Helen. *Inside Windows NT*. Redmond, Wash.: Microsoft Press, 1992.

Dewhurst, Stephen C., and Kathy T. Stark. *Programming in C++*. Upper Saddle River, N.J.: Prentice Hall PTR, 1995.

Ellis, Margaret A., and Bjarne Stroustrup. *The Annotated C++ Reference Manual*. Reading, Mass.: Addison-Wesley, 1990.

Finlay, Mark. *Getting Graphic*. New York: M & T Books, 1993.

Hansen, Augie. *C Programming: A Complete Guide to Mastering the C Language*. Reading, Mass.: Addison-Wesley, 1989.

———. *Learn C Now*. Redmond, Wash.: Microsoft Press, 1988.

Hansen, Tony L. *The C++ Answer Book*. Reading, Mass.: Addison-Wesley, 1990.

Hunter, Bruce H. *Understanding C*. Berkeley, Calif.: Sybex, 1984.

Kernighan, Brian W., and Dennis M. Ritchie. *The C Programming Language*, 2d ed. Englewood Cliffs, N.J.: Prentice-Hall, 1985.

King, Adrian. *Inside Windows 95*. Redmond, Wash.: Microsoft Press, 1994.

Klein, Mike. *DLLs and Memory Management*. Carmel, Ind.: Sams, 1992.

Kruglinski, David. *Inside Visual C++,* 3d ed. Redmond, Wash.: Microsoft Press, 1995.

Lafore, Robert. *Object-Oriented Programming in Microsoft C++.* Corte Madera, Calif.: The Waite Group, 1995.

Lampton, Christopher. *Gardens of Imagination.* Corte Madera, Calif.: The Waite Group, 1992.

Lippman, Stanley B. *C++ Primer.* Reading, Mass.: Addison-Wesley, 1990.

Lyons, Eric R. *The Black Art of Windows Game Programming.* Corte Madera, Calif.: The Waite Group, 1995.

Microsoft Corporation. *Microsoft Foundation Class Library Reference.* Redmond, Wash.: Microsoft Press, 1994.

————. *Microsoft Visual C++ Language Reference.* Redmond, Wash.: Microsoft Press, 1994.

————. *Microsoft Visual C++ Programming with MFC and Win32.* Redmond, Wash.: Microsoft Press, 1994.

————. *Microsoft Visual C++ Run-Time Library Reference.* Redmond, Wash.: Microsoft Press, 1994.

————. *Microsoft Visual C++ User's Guide.* Redmond, Wash.: Microsoft Press, 1994.

————. *Microsoft Win32 Programmer's Reference.* Vols. 1–5. Redmond, Wash.: Microsoft Press, 1993.

Murray, William H. III, and Chris H. Pappas. *Microsoft C/C++ 7: The Complete Reference.* Berkeley, Calif.: Osborne McGraw-Hill, 1992.

Perry, Greg. *Absolute Beginner's Guide to C Programming.* Carmel, Ind., 1994.

Rector, Brent E. *Developing Windows 3.1 Applications with Microsoft C/C++,* 2d ed. Carmel, Ind.: Sams, 1992.

Schildt, Herbert. *C++: The Complete Reference.* Berkeley, Calif.: Osborne McGraw-Hill, 1991.

Siegel, Charles. *Teach Yourself C,* 2d ed. Portland, Oreg.: MIS Press, 1993.

Stevens, Al. *Teach Yourself C++,* 3d ed. New York: MIS Press, 1993.

Thompson, Nigel. *Animation Techniques in Win32.* Redmond, Wash.: Microsoft Press, 1995.

Walnum, Clayton. *Dungeons of Discovery.* Indianapolis: Que Corporation, n.d.

Wiener, Richard S., and Lewis J. Pinson. *The C++ Workbook.* Reading, Mass.: Addison-Wesley, 1990.

J–L

M

Q, R

About the Author

Mark Andrews is an author and a game designer who writes documentation for system and graphics software for the 3DO company, a game hardware and software manufacturer located in Redwood City, California. Mark has written more than two dozen books about computers, computer languages, and computer games, including *C++ Windows NT Programming* (M & T Books, 1995) and *Migrating to Windows 95* (Academic Press, 1996). He is currently working on *NetWarriors '96*, a book about Internet games, scheduled for spring publication by Wiley & Sons.

The manuscript for this book was prepared and submitted to Microsoft Press in electronic form. Text files were prepared using Microsoft Word 6.0 for Windows. Pages were composed by Microsoft Press using Adobe PageMaker 6.0 for Windows, with text in Melior and display type in Frutiger Condensed. Composed pages were delivered to the printer as electronic prepress files.

Cover Designer
Robin Hjellen

Interior Graphic Designer
Kim Eggleston

Interior Graphic Artists
Michael Victor, Lori Campbell

Principal Compositor
Barbara Remmele

Indexer
Jan Wright

IMPORTANT—READ CAREFULLY BEFORE OPENING SOFTWARE PACKET(S). By opening the sealed packet(s) containing the software, you indicate your acceptance of the following Microsoft License Agreement.

MICROSOFT LICENSE AGREEMENT
(Book Companion CD)

This is a legal agreement between you (either an individual or an entity) and Microsoft Corporation. By opening the sealed software packet you are agreeing to be bound by the terms of this agreement. If you do not agree to the terms of this agreement, promptly return the unopen software packet(s) and any accompanying written materials to the place you obtained them for a full refund.

MICROSOFT SOFTWARE LICENSE

1. GRANT OF LICENSE. Microsoft grants to you the right to use one copy of the Microsoft software program included with this book (the "SOFTWARE") on a single terminal connected to a single computer. The SOFTWARE is in "use" on a computer when it is loaded into the temporary memory (i.e., RAM) or installed into the permanent memory (e.g., hard disk, CD-ROM, or other storage device) of that computer. You may not network the SOFTWARE or otherwise use it on more than one computer or computer terminal at the same time.

2. COPYRIGHT. The SOFTWARE is owned by Microsoft or its suppliers and is protected by United States copyright laws and international treaty provisions. Therefore, you must treat the SOFTWARE like any other copyrighted material (e.g., a book or musical recording) except that you may either (a) make one copy of the SOFTWARE solely for backup or archival purposes, or (b) transfer the SOFTWARE to a single hard disk provided you keep the original solely for backup or archival purposes. You may not copy the written materials accompanying the SOFTWARE.

3. OTHER RESTRICTIONS. You may not rent or lease the SOFTWARE, but you may transfer the SOFTWARE and accompanying written materials on a permanent basis provided you retain no copies and the recipient agrees to the terms of this Agreement. You may not reverse engineer, decompile, or disassemble the SOFTWARE. If the SOFTWARE is an update or has been updated, any transfer must include the most recent update and all prior versions.

4. DUAL MEDIA SOFTWARE. If the SOFTWARE package contains more than one kind of disk (3.5", 5.25", and CD-ROM), then you may use only the disks appropriate for your single-user computer. You may not use the other disks on another computer or loan, rent, lease, or transfer them to another user except as part of the permanent transfer (as provided above) of all SOFTWARE and written materials.

5. SAMPLE CODE. If the SOFTWARE includes Sample Code, then Microsoft grants you a royalty-free right to reproduce and distribute the sample code of the SOFTWARE provided that you: (a) distribute the sample code only in conjunction with and as a part of your software product (b) do not use Microsoft's or its authors' names, logos, or trademarks to market your software product; (c) include the copyright notice that appears on the SOFTWARE on your product label and as a part of the sign-on message for your software product; and (d) agree to indemnify, hold harmless and defend Microsoft and its authors from and against any claims or lawsuits, including attorneys' fees, that arise or result from the use or distribution of your software product.

DISCLAIMER OF WARRANTY

The SOFTWARE (including instructions for its use) is provided "AS IS" WITHOUT WARRANTY OF ANY KIND. MICROSOFT FURTHER DISCLAIMS ALL IMPLIED WARRANTIES INCLUDING WITHOUT LIMITATION ANY IMPLIED WARRANTIES OF MERCHANTABILITY OR OF FITNESS FOR A PARTICULAR PURPOSE. THE ENTIRE RISK ARISING OUT OF THE USE OR PERFORMANCE OF THE SOFTWARE AND DOCUMENTATION REMAINS WITH YOU.

IN NO EVENT SHALL MICROSOFT, ITS AUTHORS, OR ANYONE ELSE INVOLVED IN THE CREATION, PRODUCTION OR DELIVERY OF THE SOFTWARE BE LIABLE FOR ANY DAMAGES WHATSOEVER (INCLUDING, WITHOUT LIMITATION, DAMAGES FOR LOSS OF BUSINESS PROFITS, BUSINESS INTERRUPTION, LOSS OF BUSINESS INFORMATION OR OTHER PECUNIARY LOSS) ARISING OUT OF THE USE OF OR INABILITY TO USE THE SOFTWARE OR DOCUMENTATION, EVEN IF MICROSOFT HAS BEEN ADVISED OF THE POSSIBILITY OF SUCH DAMAGES. BECAUSE SOME STATES/COUNTRIES DO NOT ALLOW THE EXCLUSION OR LIMITATION OF LIABILITY FOR CONSEQUENTIAL OR INCIDENTAL DAMAGES, THE ABOVE LIMITATION MAY NOT APPLY TO YOU.

U.S. GOVERNMENT RESTRICTED RIGHTS

The SOFTWARE and documentation are provided with RESTRICTED RIGHTS. Use, duplication, or disclosure by the Government is subject to restrictions as set forth in subparagraph (c)(1)(ii) of The Rights in Technical Data and Computer Software clause at DFARS 252.227-7013 or subparagraphs (c)(1) and (2) of the Commercial Computer Software — Restricted Rights 48 CFR 52.227-19, as applicable. Manufacturer is Microsoft Corporation, One Microsoft Way, Redmond, WA 98052-6399.

If you acquired this product in the United States, this Agreement is governed by the laws of the State of Washington.

Should you have any questions concerning this Agreement, or if you desire to contact Microsoft Press for any reason, please write: Microsoft Press, One Microsoft Way, Redmond, WA 98052-6399.

097-000-6